VAIṢṆAVĪ
Women and the Worship of Krishna

VAIṢṆAVĪ

Women and the Worship of Krishna

Edited by
STEVEN J. ROSEN

MOTILAL BANARSIDASS PUBLISHERS
PRIVATE LIMITED ● DELHI

Fisrt Edition: Delhi, 1996
Reprint: Delhi, 1999

ISBN: 81-208-1437-1 (Cloth)
ISBN: 81-208-1438-x (Paper)

Also available at:

MOTILAL BANARSIDASS

41 U.A. Bungalow Road, Jawahar Nagar, Delhi 110 007
8 Mahalaxmi Chamber, Warden Road, Mumbai 400 026
120 Royapettah High Road, Mylapore, Chennai 600 004
Sanas Plaza, 1302, Baji Rao Road, Pune 411 002
16 St. Mark's Road, Bangalore 560 001
8 Camac Street, Calcutta 700 017
Ashok Rajpath, Patna 800 004
Chowk, Varanasi 221 001

PRINTED IN INDIA
BY JAINENDRA PRAKASH JAIN AT SHRI JAINENDRA PRESS,
A-45 NARAINA, PHASE I, NEW DELHI 110 028
AND PUBLISHED BY NARENDRA PRAKASH JAIN FOR
MOTILAL BANARSIDASS PUBLISHERS PRIVATE LIMITED,
BUNGALOW ROAD, DELHI 110 007

VAIṢṆAVĪ: WOMEN AND THE WORSHIP OF KRISHNA

General editor, Steven J. Rosen

INTRODUCTION

If they see
breasts and long hair coming
they call it woman,

If beard and whiskers
they call it man:

but, look, the self that hovers
in between
is neither man
nor woman

O Rāmanātha

—Devara Dasimayya
(tr. by A.K. Ramanujan)

While Hindu society is generally considered patriarchal, it boasts an ancient tradition of Goddess worship as well. This is traceable to the ancient Veda, where goddesses such as Uṣas, Vāc, Rātrī, Aditi, Sarasvatī, Pṛthivī, and other minor female divinities have left their mark. As Hinduism developed, goddesses like Pārvatī, Tārā, Chinnamastā, the Mahāvidyās, and the Mātṛkās began to get more and more popular. This culminated, of course, in the worship of a generic goddess, known as Mahādevī, who is called Durgā, Kālī, Umā, and so on, according to her various manifestations and the regions in which she is worshiped. She is the divine *śakti* of the universe.

From the Vaiṣṇava point of view, the divine feminine energy of the universe implies a divine energetic source; the *śakti*, it is said, comes from the *śaktimān*. The goddess is related to a god. Thus, the goddess as she manifests in the various Vaiṣṇava traditions always has a male counterpart. Sītā relates to Rāma; Lakṣmī belongs to Nārāyaṇa; Rādhā has her Kṛṣṇa. Vaiṣṇavism, when seen from this perspective, may appear like the most patriarchal of the systems of religion found in India.

However, those who study the tradition dceply, delving into the tantric literature and the mystical aspects of early Vaiṣṇava thought, find quite another dynamic at work. Vaiṣṇavism, for such serious students, becomes a type of Śaktism wherein the *pūrṇa-śakti*, or the most complete form of the divine feminine energy, is worshipped as the preeminent aspect of divinity, eclipsing even the male Godhead in certain respects. For example, in Śrī-vaiṣṇavism, Lakṣmī is considered the divine mediatrix, without whom access to Nārāyaṇa is not possible; and in the Gauḍīya tradition Rādhā is seen as the Supreme Goddess, for it is said that She controls Kṛṣṇa with her love. As one prominent *sādhu* has said, "The only reason we have anything to do with Lord Kṛṣṇa is that Śrī Rādhā loves him so much! When she ieaves the Rāsa dance, he cannot go on; when she steals his flute, as in *Gīta-govinda*, he nearly loses his mind."

Although she is, in this sense, Supreme, her predominent position is only a manifestation of *līlā*. Theologically, the male and female aspects of divinity are one—equally whole. Male and female Moiety. As the tradition teaches (*Caitanya-caritāmṛta, Ādi-līlā*, Ch. 4, texts 95-98), *jagat-mohana kṛṣṇa, tāṅhāra mohinī/ataeva samastera parā ṭhākurāṇī// Rādhā—pūrṇa śakti, kṛṣṇa—pūrṇa śaktimān/dui vastu bheda nāi, śāstra paramāṇa//mṛgamada, tāra gandha—yaiche aviccheda/agni, jvālāte—yaiche kabhu nāhi bheda//rādhā-kṛṣṇa aiche sadā eka-i svarūpa/līlā-rasa āsvādite dhare dui-rūpa*: "Lord Kṛṣṇa enchants the world, but Śrī Rādhā enchants even Him. Therefore She is the supreme goddess of all. Śrī Rādhā is the full power, and Lord Kṛṣṇa is the possessor of full power. The two are not different, as evidenced by the revealed scriptures. They are indeed the same, just as musk and its scent are inseparable, or as fire and its heat are nondifferent. Thus Rādhā and Kṛṣṇa are one, yet they have taken two forms to enjoy the relationship of *līlā*." This is the secret position of the goddess in the Vaiṣṇava tradition, and, hopefully, female practitioners of Vaiṣṇavism will eventually benefit from this preeminent position of the feminine Deity.

I do not mean to imply by this that Vaiṣṇava women today have it so bad. In fact, Vaiṣṇavism is, at its heart, a religion of *bhakti*, and in *bhakti* movements women have it quite good, as the essays in this volume should make clear. However, to properly understand the social orientation of Vaiṣṇava women in context, one must study the tradition deeply as well as the expectations and goals of the practitioners themselves. Otherwise, if we study from within our own cultural milieu, with our own preconceived notions of what Vaiṣṇava women should want for themselves and their families, we can only expect a stilted and prejudiced view of women in the Vaisṇava tradition, reflecting perhaps our own Western sense of feminism and human rights.

Contemporary feminists are primarily concerned with secular reality, with achieving social and political equality through education and culture, while Vaiṣṇava women are more concerned with spiritual development. Most feminists relate to religion largely as removed critics, more interested in philosophically decrying God's "manhood" than in attempting practical religious reconstructionism or creating new religious movements founded on feminist premises. "At present," Ursula King notes, "the feminist movement is for the most part still a western, urban, middle-class phenomenon where women have the necessary education and leisure to articulate a powerful protest against the deeply rooted hierarchical and patriarchal structures of oppression embedded in our male-dominated culture."[1] In short, feminism tends to be the intellectual prerogative of a small class of privileged women whose primary concerns do not necessarily focus on the religious pursuit.

And yet, women—feminist or not—do have a genuine concern when it comes to practicing religion. After all, the world's religious traditions have, for the most part, been passed down *by* men (and, arguably, *for* men!). Women, even if they are saints, have often been relegated to the background of religious traditions, their exemplary lives and deeds minimized by a struggling male orthodoxy. At times, spiritually advanced women have been downright neglected or even harassed, making their mark in religious history by a fluke as much as by their own intense devotion. A few examples are well known. As Jane Hirshfield writes,

> Hildegard of Bingen, the famous eleventh-century German mystic and abbess, might easily have been excommunicated as a heretic because of her visions, had they not received the express endorsement of the pope. Teresa of Avila's writing was examined closely by the Inquisition, and she struggled at length with both Church and state authorities in the founding of each new convent of her order. Kassiane, a Greek Orthodox abbess of the ninth century, was flogged in her youth for assisting monks during a time of persecution. Antal, an eighth-century Tamil devotee of Krishna, unwittingly broke a strict taboo of his worship when she was a young child, yet, according to legend, was spared her father's anger by the direct intervention of Krishna on her behalf. Stories with a less happy outcome are those of Sor Juana, the seventeenth-century Mexican nun and woman of letters, whose outspoken defense of a full

> intellectual life for women eventually led to her being stripped of her books and her writing; and of Marguerite Porete, a French visionary, burned at the stake in the fourteenth century.[2]

While it may be argued that conservatism, or a rigid view of how to practice mainstream religion, is more a factor here than is sexism—and that similar atrocities were foisted upon men as well—it cannot be denied that some of the above women, and many others as well, were castigated by their spiritual brethren specifically because of their gender. Serinity Young reminds us that almost every religion, in one way or another, associates women with evil, especially through gender specific dualities: women are often equated with the body and men with the spirit. In fact, Young goes so far as to suggest that women are often associated with evil qualities, such as blood-thirstiness or death (Kālī, Durgā), because of a male fear of sexuality:

> This point is dramatized in the many traditions that link women with sexuality by representing women as sexual temptresses who deflect men from their spiritual goals. This notion receives its fullest development in religions which, while enjoining celibacy on its religious specialists, male or female, particularly empower a male priesthood. Buddhism and Christianity offer dramatic examples of this,. but Hinduism, in its valorization of the powers of celibate male sages, also contains many negative sexual images of women....All of this serves to justify the control of women by men, a justification that is perceived to be divinely given in most sacred law books. Essentially, women are represented as inadequate moral agents who, for their own protection and the protection of their victims (men), must remain under the moral supervision and social constraint of men....Inherent in all of this, of course, is a fear and denigration of sexuality.[3]

There is a difference between a healthy fear and an obsessive one. Since sex is considered one of the most intense material pleasures, it *is* often seen as a distraction from the spiritual path—one can hardly focus on spiritual goals if one is preoccupied with bodily appetites. And so most religious traditions teach that one must be careful when associating with the opposite sex. This should not be based so much on fear as on knowledge. Furthermore, it should be underlined that a close study of the scriptures, especially in the Vaiṣṇava tradition, reveals that it is not just men who have to be careful about sensual indulgence. Women do as well. True, the common conception is that women are the embodiment of *māyā,* or illusion, and this is supported by the *śāstra* (*yopayāti śanair māyā, yoṣid deva-vinirmitā*).[4] So men must be on guard, and religious texts encourage them in this way. Nonetheless, "sexist" remarks found in the scriptures are nearly always counterbalanced by similar statements about men, often in the very next verse.[5] The conclusion, then, is that sexual attraction—for both women *and* men—is dangerous on the spiritual path, for it forges a bond with the body that can easily eclipse a neophyte practitioner's attempt at developing love for God. As stated earlier, although it may be tempting to judge a tradition like Vaiṣṇavism from within our own cultural milieu, and by the standards set by its most novitiate followers, one must become familiar with the *entire* culture, the *complete* scriptural and aesthetic tradition—and one must do fieldwork with advanced followers, appropriate representatives of the tradition—before passing any kind of realistic judgement.

For example, despite apparently sexist remarks found in the scriptures, one will notice that men who become spiritually advanced in the Vaiṣṇava tradition rise beyond materialistic conceptions of women and in fact treat them with the deepest respect, honoring them as representative of the Cosmic Mother and perhaps even a *gopī*, or one who is dear to Kṛṣṇa. Serinity Young (quoted above), who asserts that most religions appear rather sexist on the face of it, admits that there is another side to the way women are perceived by the enlightened traditions of the world. She acknowledges, for example, that femininity is equated with knowledge and even wisdom in most of the major world religions:

> Most religions value wisdom, whether understood to be a practical knowledge of the right way to live or an esoteric knowledge of the secret workings of the universe. From the Sophia of the ancient Greeks and Gnostics to the Prajñā of the Buddhists, wisdom is frequently referred to in feminine terms. That this is more than just a linguistic conceit based on the word wisdom being a feminine noun in several languages (e.g., *prajñā, sophia*) can be seen in the iconographic and literary developments of wisdom in explicitly feminine terms (Proverbs and sometimes Shekhinah). Significantly, more goddesses than gods are associated with wisdom and learning (Athena, Metis, Isis, Sarasvatī, Tārā)...[6]

Bhagavad-gītā, too, associates wisdom with femininity,[7] and perhaps it is this wisdom characteristic of their gender that women must call upon to eke out their place in the religious history of (wo)mankind. Such wisdom is seen, for example, in the life of Bahiṇābāī, who suffered through an abusive marriage and yet was able to taste the bliss of true God consciousness. **Mary McGee** shows us, in this volume, just how Bahiṇābāī did this, and discusses the implications of her devotion. Two essays on Mīrābāī, one by **Andrew Schelling** and the other by **Nancy M. Martin**, show a very different approach to *strīdharma*—while Bahiṇābāī chose to honor her married status, Mīrā did not. Only Kṛṣṇa could she see as her husband. **Dennis Hudson, Nancy Nayar,** and **Katherine Young** bring us to South India, exploring the life of Āṇṭāḷ Āḻvār, "another" Āṇṭāḷ, and then Śrīvaiṣṇavism as a whole, showing that *bhakti* movements are advantageous for women with feminist leanings. **Jan Brzezinski** comes to similar conclusions while looking at women saints in the earlier Gauḍīya tradition, and **Kim Knott** takes this idea further in explicating the Gauḍīya teaching regarding women as it has been interpreted and applied by the modern-day Hare Kṛṣṇa movement. My own essay delves into the esoteric *sādhanā* of both male and female Gauḍīya practitioners, who see themselves as female in the ultimate spiritual analysis.

—Steven J. Rosen

Notes

1. Ursula King, ed., *Women in the World's Religions: Past and Present* (New York: Paragon House, 1987), pp. 201-202.

2. Jane Hirshfield, ed., *Women in Praise of the Sacred* (New York: HarperCollins, 1994), pp. *xxi*.

3. Serinity Young, ed., *An Anthology of Sacred Texts By and About Women* (New York: Crossroad, 1993), pp. *xix*.

4. *Śrīmad Bhāgavatam* 3.31.40.

5. Ibid., 3.31.41.

6. Serinity Young, *op. cit.*, pp. *xxi-xxii*.

7. *Bhagavad-gītā,* 10.34.

MĪRĀBĀI: INSCRIBED IN TEXT, EMBODIED IN LIFE[1]

Nancy M. Martin

Tying bells to her ankles Mīrā danced away.

"I myself became the servant of my Nārāyaṇ." [she said.]
Tying bells to her ankles Mīrā danced away.

People said Mīrābāī was crazy, Mother-in-law said family destroyer.
Tying bells to her ankles Mīrā danced away.

A cup of poison the *rāṇā* sent, drinking it down Mīrā laughed.
Tying bells to her ankles Mīrā danced away.

Mīrā's Lord is the clever Mountain Bearer, so easily the
 Indestructible One was hers!
Tying bells to her ankles Mīrā danced away.[2]

Mīrābāī, the embodiment of absolute devotion to Kṛṣṇa, lived in the sixteenth-century. A member of the Rathor royal family of Merta and Marwar, she married Bhoj Rāj, son of Rāṇā Sāngā of the Sisodiyas of Chittor and Mewar in 1516 C.E.[3] Beyond this, traditional historical sources tell us little of who she was. Instead, the earliest records of her extraordinary life appear among the stories of saints collected and preserved in hagiographic texts called *bhaktamāls* and their commentaries written by members of various religious sects or *sampradāys.* A family of tales emerges of a defiant lover of God who ignored all social expectations for Rajput women of royal households in her day to live out her limitless devotion.

Through the dissemination and expansion of her story and the widespread popularity of songs attributed to her, Mīrā has become more than a sixteenth-century saint to be remembered. Her name is used to define women with particular traits, and other women live out her story as they shape similar lives of religious devotion for themselves, sometimes also composing songs in her tradition, even in her name. To explore the nature of the religious option made available to women in Vaiṣṇava traditions through the example of Mīrābāī, we will turn first to the hagiographic accounts of the life of the sixteenth-century Mīrā Rathor and then to the lives of four twentieth-century women who understand themselves and are understood by others to be living the life of Mīrābāī.

A Rebellious Lover of God

The first account of Mīrābāī appears in the *Bhaktamāl* (ca. 1600) of Nābhādās of the Rāmānandī Sampradāy.[4] In the compact lines of his verse we learn that Mīrā cared nothing for family, honor, or shame and sang and danced fearlessly for her mountain-lifting Lord and Lover, Girdhārī.[5] The author likens her to a *gopī* within this Kali Yug in her unrestrained and shameless love. Her actions met with opposition as evil people plotted her death, but she drank the poison offered as if it were elixir and remained unharmed, continuing to play the drum of devotion in defiance. Mīrā's strength of character emerges clearly in these few lines as does her disregard for all but God.

Other *bhaktamāls* follow the pattern set by Nābhādās. Several decades later Dhruvdās writes of Mīrā as the one who "revealed the quarry of love," who "wandered in the pleasure fields of Vrindavan," and who, "tying bells to her ankles [and] taking up the *kartāls*," danced for her Lord.[6] A few additional descriptive details enter the tradition here, and the attenuated narrative also picks up the coloring of the Rādhāvallabh Sampradāy (of which Dhruvdās is a member) as Mīrā is described entering Vrindavan. The Dādūpanthī Rāghavdās follows Nābhādās very closely in his *bhaktamāl* of 1713 but provides four additional lines.[7] He mentions that Mīrā sat among the saints as well as singing and that these actions led not just some unspecified "evil people" but the rāṇā himself (the ruler of Mewar) to become angry and attempt to kill Mīrā. A member of a *nirguṇa sampradāy* who had converted from a Vaiṣṇava sect, Rāghavdās refers to Mīrā's Lord as Rām, Hari, and Viṣṇu as well as Girdhār and specifically states that it was because of Mīrā's Vaiṣṇava devotion that her life was threatened.[8]

The compact verses of the *bhaktamāls* seem to beg for expansion, and commentaries arose around them. Priyādās, commenting on Nābhādās's text, offers a much more detailed story of Mīrābāī's life in his *Bhaktirasabhodhinī Tīkā* of 1712 that becomes the standard for many later tellings.[9] In the first two stanzas, Mīrā's birth in Merta, her childhood devotion, and her unwilling marriage to a rāṇā are detailed. When she must go to the home of her in-laws, she asks only for her image of the dear Mountain Bearer, Girdhārī Lāl, and her parents cannot refuse. Reaching her new home, she gets into immediate trouble because she will not bow down before the family goddess or her new husband as a proper bride should. Attempts at persuasion are futile, and her mother-in-law becomes angry, reporting to the rāṇā (presumably her husband or an older son) that this new daughter-in-law is useless and arrogant.

The rāṇā builds a separate palace for Mīrā in an attempt to isolate her insolence. She is delighted and proceeds with her devotion, keeping company with holy men and further angering the rāṇā. Her sister-in-law tries to dissuade her from this disgraceful behavior that will shame both her natal and marital families, but she refuses to listen, saying that she has dedicated her life to being with the saints. Poison is sent, but when she drinks it, she is even more beautiful, her face flushed with color and youth. A spy is engaged to inform the rāṇā when she is in the company of sādhus so that the rāṇā may come to kill her. Hearing her speaking words of love to someone within her private chambers, the spy informs the rāṇā who bursts in, sword in hand. He finds Mīrā alone, and she tells him that it is Kṛṣṇa to whom she speaks. He backs out of the room without harming her.

In addition to her relationship with the rāṇā, three other encounters with men are described by Priyādās. A lustful sādhu comes and tells Mīrā that Kṛṣṇa has ordered him to make love to her. She wisely says, "All right, but let's do this right." First she insists he should eat. Having served him, Mīrā sets up a beautifully decorated bed in the midst of the community of devotees and then invites him to have his way with her. Surely there could be no shame in such an act ordained by the Lord himself. The sādhu immediately repents and becomes her disciple. The Moghul emperor Akbar is also said to come with his court poet Tānsen for *darśan* of Mīrā and/or her Lord the Mountain Bearer and to be overwhelmed with delight. Mīrā then goes to Vrindavan and meets Jīv Goswāmī. He has vowed never to look at a woman but breaks that vow in order to meet this great devotee. From there she goes on to Dwaraka, having perceived that the rāṇā is still angry and bent on her destruction. He has a change of heart and sends Brahmins to beg her to return. Going into the temple of Raṇchoḍjī (a form of Kṛṣṇa) to take her leave of him, she merges with the image never to be seen again. The tale ends here.

Mīrā's story as told by Priyādās reflects standard elements in the life stories of other women saints, outlined by A.K. Ramanujan.[10] Mīrā's devotion begins in childhood, and she must find a way to deal with a forced marriage in which she wants no part. She escapes by denying its reality for her—she thinks only of Kṛṣṇa during the ceremony—and eventually by leaving her palace home. As an independent woman she must deal with the lust of some men and testing by male religious authorities. In his account Priyādās speaks directly of the danger of men's lust but not explicitly of a test. A disciple of Nābhādās, he is also said to be a follower of Caitanya and associates Mīrā with a founder of Caitanya's *sampradāy* but does not portray Jīv Goswāmī as involved in any sort of theological debate with her.[11] Other storytellers have other agendas, however, wanting to show that female and/or low-caste saints may be spiritually equal or even superior to male brāhmaṇa religious leaders. In their tellings, Jīv Goswāmī (or sometimes Sanātan Goswāmī or Rūp Goswāmī) is said to refuse to see Mīrā because she is a woman. She responds by sending him the message that as far as she knows there is only one male in Vrindavan and that is Kṛṣṇa. Jīv Goswāmī is chagrined and immediately goes to see her. This is typical of the kinds of stories told of the challenges female saints must face from male religious leaders. Her understanding that she is really married to Kṛṣṇa and her final merger with the image of Raṇchoḍjī in Dwaraka have parallels in the life stories of Āṇṭāḷ and Mahādevīakkā as well.

Within this standard hagiographic form, unique elements of Mīrā's story also emerge. Her high caste and royal status, her total rejection of the expectations placed on a woman of such a family and of the privileges inherent in such a social position, and her intense devotion come through. Steadfastness in the face of every kind of opposition and an independence and strength that meet criticism at every turn mark her life. She suffers for her devotion, but she is defiant. Rather than be the wife of a ruler, she chooses to sing and dance for her Lord and to dedicate her life to the community of devotees who are her true family. No one but Kṛṣṇa can command her allegiance.

Other elements of the narrative tradition of Mīrā emerge in other sources. In the *Pothīpremābodh* (1693), a collection of saints' stories from the Punjab, Mīrā is said to be the disciple of Raidās, the leatherworker *nirguṇī* disciple of Rāmānand.[12] The story of a rāṇī or queen of Chittor being Raidās's disciple is told separately by Priyādās and before him by Anantadās (ca.1588) about the Jhālī Rāṇī, but the claim that Mīrā was Raidās's disciple is widespread, especially in the oral traditions of low-caste groups in Rajasthan.[13] Such a connection brings the element of caste specifically into the narrative as Mīrā suffers not only because she flaunts gender-related social expectations but also because she has embraced a low-caste guru. Further this association takes care of the perceived need for everyone to have a guru (even as the assignment of Raidās to Rāmānand does), though other tellings specifically deny that Mīrā had any human guru.

Further details turn up in various stories. The cup of poison sent by the rāṇā becomes but one method of trying to kill her. A venomous snake in a basket is sent but becomes a diamond necklace or a *śālagrām*. Scorpions become diamond toe rings, and a hungry lion responds as Narasiṁh to Mīrā's offerings rather than devouring her. The encounter with Akbar and Tānsen is "corrected" by one commentator who makes it clear that they came only for *darśan* of Mīrā's Lord.[14] Elsewhere the story is expanded with Akbar coming in disguise and then giving Mīrā a diamond necklace to adorn the image. Her acceptance of the necklace and the discovery that it came from the Muslim ruler then becomes the reason for attempts on her life or her being driven out of Chittor.[15] Who actually attempts to kill her is also explored. Is it her husband, his older brother or her father-in-law who is the ruler, or his younger brother who comes to power after her husband's death?

Mahīpati tells a quite different story of Mīrā in the eighteenth century in Maharashtra, rejecting Nābhādās and Priyādās's accounts.[16] Mīrā's poisoner becomes her own father in response to her refusal to marry. Kṛṣṇa as Viṭṭhal in Vārkari tradition is more often equated with a parental figure than a lover, and the contrast between him and the familial antagonist in Mīrā's story is preserved in this alternate telling. In his *Mīrā rī Paracī*, Sukhasāraṇ adds details about Mīrā's previous life, equating her with a Brahmin woman of Barsana who is mentioned but unnamed in the *Bhāgavata Purāṇa*.[17] Nāgrīdās (1699-1756) in his *Padaprasangmālā* joins her songs with narrative to give the context of their composition.[18] He places the attempts on her life and her abandonment of Chittor after the time of her husband's death and shows her adamantly refusing to burn on her earthly husband's funeral pyre in an act of *sati.* He is highly critical of the rāṇā, as one might expect from a Rathor Rajput who has renounced his own kingdom to become a follower of Vallabhācārya and a great saint.[19]

Beyond the Bounds: Exemplar or Exception?

Many other tellings of Mīrā's story emerge in the hagiographic traditions, each colored in part by the author's sectarian affiliation and background. Mīrā comes to belong to the general lineage of devotion, whether to Kṛṣṇa, Rām, or the *nirguṇ* Lord, but she does not become officially incorporated into any *sampradāy* nor do her songs enter any formal liturgical repertoire as do those of Kabīr, Raidās, or Sūrdās, for example. Explicit rejection of Mīrā is also voiced not once but three times in the *Caurāsī Vaiṣṇavan kī Vārtā* (1620) of the Vallabha Sampradāy.[20] The reason is clear: Mīrā does not accept Vallabhācārya as her guru and as an incarnation of Kṛṣṇa and thus stands outside of the community of the Puṣṭimārg. The existence of such renunciations suggest that Mīrā was extremely popular—why else would the followers of Vallabhācārya have to denounce her three times? Within these stories she appears to practice an eclectic devotion, considering all those who are devoted to God to be a part of her community and living surrounded by sādhus and saints. She is a beloved member of this wider devotional community, yet she also clearly belongs to no specific *sampradāy,* and her tradition has resisted any such formal incorporation.

Why is this the case? Mīrā is the perfect example of absolute devotion in the face of seemingly insurmountable opposition. As such she is universally admired, and many try to draw on the power of her example. Such absolute devotion, however, leads her to disregard social expectations based on gender and caste and supersedes human gurus or social and familial authority. The admired resistance to any and every obstruction to her devotion may lead to a rejection of social restrictions and expectations that institutionalized sects generally uphold and may undercut their authority by privileging the individual relationship with the divine. Mīrā is not interested in human or institutional intermediaries; she longs for the direct experience of union with her divine husband and Lord. Though the language of the Braj *līlā* enters the tradition of her poetry, she also speaks directly of experiencing Kṛṣṇa, bypassing the eternal realm of Vrindavan and the institutional structures that ordinarily facilitate one's entry into it. Hers is *pati bhāv,* the love of Kṛṣṇa as one's husband and Lord. For her there are not two realms—one ruled by social propriety and the other by the desire for divine union. Though a few tellings of her story suggest that social propriety and devotion can be reconciled, most allow for no such compromise. In the latter, Mīrā will bow to no other, human or divine—not husband, rāṇā, or guru. She will serve the saints and delights in this, but such service is clearly different from and secondary to her devotion to Kṛṣṇa.

Though Mīrā and her songs are extremely popular, an ambivalence runs beneath the surface of admiration for her. Many times people said to me, "Mīrā was Mīrā," implying that no one could approximate her depth of devotion today but also that what is admirable in the life of a great saint has no place in the lives of ordinary people. Is Mīrā the exception that proves the rule, or does she represent a model to be followed for devotees, especially women, within Vaiṣṇava traditions? Does she open up real possibilities for a religious life of independence outside of marriage or not?

Mīrā has been criticized for merely transposing the relationship of husband and wife into the divine-human realm, thus reinforcing it rather than radically challenging it. As such she becomes a figure of resistance perhaps but not of real liberation, as Kumkum Sangari concludes:

> Mīrā's bhakti is contradictory: it protests and assists in its appropriations, has both a radicalising potential and compensatory character. A product of social change, aspiring to level certain forms of inequality, it also participates in making a vocabulary and structures of feeling which can *compensate* for the absence of those desired freedoms. It traverses the perilous paths of brahminical injunction, salvation schemas and feudal relations in medieval Rajasthan, negotiates the webbed terrain of oral traditions and of overlapping patriarchies, but neither finds nor creates an unsullied space. Her bhakti is internally poised to lose the ground it sets out to gain. For us Mīrā represents a struggle, not a victory.[21]

Thus there is danger in suggesting that Mīrā may be an example for women. That example may be used as easily to convince women to accept social oppression as to fight it.

A widow may be called Mīrā to suggest that the life of renunciation and devotion allowed to her is a laudable one and that she should not demand or expect anything else, a usage perhaps most clearly seen in the comparison drawn between the saint and widows chanting Śrī Caitanya's *mahāmantra* eight hours each day in the *bhajan* ashrams of Vrindavan in exchange for rice and salt and a small monetary remuneration.[22] What little meaning such a life may have can be drawn from the example of Mīrā, but the crucial link between Mīrā's experience of oppression and her devotion is severed. These women suffer because of systems of social inequality, and their devotion arises out of economic necessity rather than strictly inner conviction. Without other resources, they make their way to Vrindavan in the hopes of eking out some meager living. As "Mīrābāīs" they are objects of charity but not liberative social change, and they are both given a place and kept in it through the example of Mīrā. The potential appropriation of Mīrā for the maintenance of social inequality and the danger of Mīrā's playing a compensatory role are clear. Yet this space is not the only one opened up for women by Mīrā, nor is it the final word on Mīrā's possible exemplary power.

Finding definite resources for the development of women's leadership in Śaiva and Śākta traditions, Sanjukta Gupta has suggested that Vaiṣṇava traditions do not contain such potential. A comparison between Kāraikkāl Ammaiyār, Mahādeviakkā, and Lallā Dèd on the one hand and Āṇṭāḷ, Mīrābāī, and Bahiṇabāī on the other provides the basis for her assessment. She gives a quite negative reading of Mīrā, choosing a particular telling of Mīrā's tale that supports her argument, including the claim that Mīrā never really moved out of the control of her family, being supported in later years by her natal kin even when she was living in Dwaraka.[23] Other tellings would radically contradict her conclusions, and there is no justification for surrendering Mīrā's story and her liberative potential to those who would portray her as a good wife whose devotion flowers in widowhood. Though perhaps we must concede with Gupta that examples of women's leadership and independence are more easily found in Śākta and Śaiva traditions, we need not accept her low estimation of the possibilities inherent in Vaiṣṇava traditions.[24]

June McDaniel reports that when she attempted to study women saints in Bengal, it was impossible for her to locate any Vaiṣṇava holy women to interview. Those she asked always steered her toward men.[25] In my field research focusing on Mīrā in Rajasthan and Vrindavan, however, I was able to find such women. Perhaps if I, too, had asked for holy women or *sādhikās,* my search would have been less fruitful. But I asked instead about women who lived like Mīrā. Because Mīrā's name itself has entered the cultural vocabulary of India as a category for classifying women who reflect particular characteristics exemplified by this sixteenth-century saint, my question elicited positive responses.

As an appelation, "Mīrā" carries both general and specific meanings. In its most generic usage, any woman who shows a religious inclination of any kind may be called Mīrā, even as Sūrdās's name is given to blind singers.[26] Mīrā's name is applied with increasing specificity to women who sing, dance, or compose poetry; to widows who live lives of devotion and renunciation (especially if they are high caste); to women who renounce marriage to become full-time devotees; and to many others who demonstrate qualities associated with Mīrā.[27] These qualities are not always admired, and her name also becomes a term of abuse in Rajasthan for a woman who is out of control, refusing to listen to her family, not interested enough in domestic affairs, inattentive to the expected behavior for a woman, or excessively religious or independently minded.[28] An underlying ambivalence associated with Mīrā again emerges. She is a great devotee, but her behavior as a woman remains problematic.

Mīrā's name becomes attached with the greatest specificity and tenacity to women who, like Mīrā, refuse to accept an identity based on being a wife and mother and instead embrace lives of devotion to Kṛṣṇa. For such women the identification with Mīrā is more comprehensive. People begin to talk of Mīrā's being reincarnated, and the women's individual birth names recede to be replaced by that of Mīrā. Their identities become deeply entwined with the character of Mīrā as social expectations for Mīrā-like women are imposed on them, and they consciously conform their lives to hers. Early childhood comparisons to Mīrā made by parents and religious leaders are elicited by their own precocious religiosity, emerging in the context of actively religious families. These young girls then seem to internalize this identification as they struggled to construct adult female selves not built around definitions of woman as wife and mother. The selves and lives they take on are decidedly religious.

After hearing of many such women, I was able to track down and interview four who now reside at least part of the year in Mathurā and Vrindavan in the Braj region (although I first heard about three of them from people in Rajasthan). These women compose songs for Kṛṣṇa, sing and dance in temples, have refused marriage and renounced social status and material wealth, and are called Mother Kṛṣṇa, Mīrājī, Mīrābāī, and Mother Mīrā by devotees who gather around them. The sixteenth-century Mīrā plays an integral role in their self-understanding as well as providing a way for families, society, and religious institutions to come to terms with their behavior. By examining their life stories and ways of living, we can see more clearly the kind of model provided by Mīrā and the real option for women opened up by her example.

Mother Kṛṣṇa of Mathurā

Some forty years ago a young Brahmin woman became famous for dancing and singing to Kṛṣṇa in the temples of Vrindavan and Mathurā. She came to be known as Mother Kṛṣṇa or Kṛṣṇa Mā.[29] From the age of two and a half she manifested devotion to God. Her mother was a great devotee, and sādhus and saints regularly came to their home. One sādhu gave the tiny child an image of Kṛṣṇa and told her to do *pūjā* even at this young age. Dancing and singing among the devotees filled her childhood days, and she would dress alternately as Kṛṣṇa and Rādhā for *līlās* portraying Kṛṣṇa's youthful adventures in Vrindavan. She did everything with Kṛṣṇa, even carrying his image to school with her.

As a child she also exhibited unusual knowledge that seemingly could only have come from previous lives. Using very specific names, she demanded Rajasthani clothing to wear, even though she had never seen or heard of this type of clothing before. This insistence together with her dancing and singing led others (including highly respected sādhus) to say that she was an incarnation of Mīrābāī. She also began to write treatises on religious topics when she was still quite young. The material came to her almost as automatic writing, and all agreed that it was not the work of a child her age but of a soul with the wisdom of past lives. Clearly she was an extraordinary child and young woman, and her gifts were acknowledged and encouraged.

Her great beauty, beautiful voice, and graceful dancing are remembered and praised by many in Vrindavan still, though she seldom goes to the temples now. When she came of age, she refused to marry. Her mother supported her in this but said that, if she would not marry, then she must remain within the confines of the family home. She readily agreed, and for 12 years she did not leave. To her this isolation seemed a gift because she could focus solely on God. She had no desires, no hopes. Kṛṣṇa was all in all. During this period people called her mad because she was so lost in devotion.

Over the years she has composed a great number of poems, three volumes of which have been published by her brother in whose home she resides. Two of these contain traditional rhyming *pads* while the third consists of a collection of "prose-poems," written in the style of prayers or letters to her Lord and Lover or sometimes as exhortations to fellow travelers on the path or to her own discouraged heart-mind (*man*).[30] For long periods she composed a song every day, and most are in *mādhurya bhāv* (the emotional stance of erotic love that marks the relationship of the *gopīs* and Rādhā with Kṛṣṇa), although she sings also of *vātsalya* (parental love), celebrating Kṛṣṇa's childhood. Expressions of *viraha* (love in separation) predominate, but she sings also of meeting and of Kṛṣṇa's *līlā* in Braj. She complains and begs her Lord to come in the traditional style of *vinaya* as well, or addresses her own mind with warnings to hold fast to devotion. Full of alliteration and internal rhyming, her *pads* are skillfully constructed. She works her name "Kṛṣṇa" into the final line of each *pad* in the usual way and clearly speaks in her own voice out of her own experience, although she draws on images and vocabulary common to Kṛṣṇa devotion and to Mīrā. She does not take on the persona of Mīrā in her poetry at any point, and Mīrā is not mentioned in any of the published verses.

The depth of her devotion becomes clear with every word. In one prose-poem she writes:

> Oh Lord!
> You alone are my foundation. Mother, father, brother, sister, guru, companion, best friend—all are bound up in you.
> You are my riches, my harvest, my dwelling place, my duty, my goal.
> My desire, affection, arousal, attachment, sulking are only for you.
> Only you enchant me, only you cause me irritation.
> My ambition, discipline, and inner strength I dedicate to you.
> My body, mind, and breath cry out as one...
> You are mine! You are mine![31]

In conversation also Kṛṣṇa Mā said again and again that Kṛṣṇa is everything to her, and her life at every level revolves around him. She has had few other friends, and her devotion is for the most part practiced in solitude, although she assured me that she was neither lonely nor alone.

When I asked her whether she had a guru, she said that she did not have a life-long one. In some sense the sādhu who gave her the image of Kṛṣṇa when she was a child fulfilled this role, but no lasting relationship developed between them. Though her family belongs to the *sampradāy* of Rāmānuja, she professes no institutional affiliation. Instead, she treats teachers of all lineages as her gurus, learning from each but becoming the disciple of none.

In the role of a teacher herself, she has numerous supporters who gather for a great celebration on her birthday every year. It was clear when she talked with me that she was a practiced speaker, weaving lines of songs (her own and Mīrā's) through her speech in a lively way and able to speak spontaneously and at length on religious matters. She moved her body as she sang, her hands taking up the gestures of dance though she remained seated. Dance and song merged with speech in her oratory.

At the time I interviewed Kṛṣṇa Mā in 1993, she was 50 years old. She lives in her brother's home in Mathurā with her own rooms on the second floor. Another small room off the courtyard serves as a temple and contains an image and pictures of Kṛṣṇa as well as a number of paintings of Mīrā and photographs of Kṛṣṇa Mā herself dressed as both Kṛṣṇa and Rādhā. Much of her day is spent in recitation and prayer. She has always lived with her family, and clearly they have great respect for her and make her devotional life possible.

Her life is a secluded one. She seldom goes far from home alone, although she clearly would have enjoyed a trip with me to the temples of Vrindavan (only a short tempo ride away but rain prevented our going) or a visit to a disciple in Delhi. She spoke of how difficult it was for women in India to choose, as she had done, not to marry. As a young woman, she must have felt the very real weight of social pressure to conform, and her present dependence on her brother's family and his authority over her are clear. Still she did not complain about her life. Instead she told me a number of times of the great inner peace that Kṛṣṇa brought to her. This was evident in her clear eyes and beautiful countenance and the peacefulness that seemed to radiate from her. In her, others had found the presence of Mīrā and called her an incarnation. For her part, she always directed the focus back to Kṛṣṇa. "It is as easy to meet Kṛṣṇa as to meet me," she said. "One need only ask and go looking."

Mīrājī of Mewar

In a small village in southern Rajasthan, the daughter of the *ṭhākur* (the traditional ruler of the area) has also taken up a life of devotion. So deeply is she identified with the sixteenth-century saint that she is known as Mīrājī. She is a Shaktawat Rajput who refused to marry and has composed *bhajans* in the name of Mīrā. Even in the heat of the summer, she dresses modestly in a saffron *sari* and long blouse with long sleeves pleated to fit closely at the wrist. She lives sometimes with her parents and her married brother in her own village; at other times she travels with family members to stay with relatives in Jaipur and Ahmedabad. Increasingly, however, she spends her time in Vrindavan. In the past she stayed at a small temple associated with the Nimbārka Sampradāy together with one of her female relatives, but she is now building a place of her own. She was thirty-six years old when I first met her in 1993.

In response to my questions, Mīrājī told the following story of her life.[32] From childhood she was religiously inclined, and her household was a meeting place for saints and sādhus. Mīrābāī's songs were sung in her home from her earliest memories, and she recalls a small book of Mīrābāī's life being in the house as well. She would play games of worship, creating imaginary temples and images of Kṛṣṇa (even as Mīrā is said to have done), and her parents took her on many pilgrimages. When she was six or seven years old, she began to recite the *Gītā* in Hindi as people gathered around to hear her. She had no real understanding of the text, however—it was like a story to her. A girl living in a small village, she had limited educational opportunities but did learn to read and write in Hindi.[33]

When she was 13 or 14, she entered a period of crisis. She found no pleasure in the world, and a great restlessness filled her. Her health became poor, and she had difficulty eating and sleeping. She wept constantly but did not know what was wrong. During this time her understanding of the *Gītā* increased, but it brought her no solace. Singing Mīrā's *bhajans* with others did offer some comfort, and the words of Mīrābāī seemed to give voice to her own feelings. This restlessness lasted four to six years, and she came to understand it as an experience of *viraha,* of longing for a divine lover who seemed far away, unreachable, even perhaps uncaring. During this same time period, the issue of her marriage came up. She refused to marry. Her parents were not happy about this, especially her father. Eventually they came to terms with it, and her mother or her aunt often accompanied her in later years when she traveled. She emerged from this period of darkness and confusion with her devotion firmly established.

At twenty one, she met her guru, Caturbhūjdās of the Nimbārka Sampradāy, while on a pilgrimage in Vrindavan. He gave her a mantra then, but for the next 15 years, she seldom met him because he did not remain in one place for more than a few days. He lived in the vicinity of Govardhan but moved whenever his location was discovered and people began to interrupt his devotional practice with their own devotion to him. By December of 1994, however, he had changed his ways. He had taken up *sakhī bhāv*—the emotional identity of a *gopī* lover of Kṛṣṇa and companion to Rādhā. He no longer wanders but has settled on the outskirts of Vrindavan with Mīrājī where they are now building an ashram together. Mīrājī has come to stay in Vrindavan, for the first time unaccompanied by female relatives. She says that though Mīrā Rathor may not have needed a guru, she is not the sixteenth-century saint's equal and does requires spiritual guidance.

Mīrājī used to compose songs of devotion to Kṛṣṇa. She always used Mīrā's name in the signature line, demonstrating clearly one way in which women devotees have added to the works attributed to Mīrābāī over the centuries. She is said to have composed four or five hundred songs, although when I asked her directly, she would not specify.[34] She is literate, but no text of her songs exists (with the exception of the one given below). At one point, she did write down a few songs. When she showed them to her guru, he told her to throw them into the Yamunā River. Unlike Tukārām's manuscripts (miraculously preserved beneath a river's surface when he received similar instructions), Mīrājī's remain only in her memory and that of her devotees of earlier years.[35] After some time, she concluded that Mīrābāī, Sūrdās, Tulsīdās, and others had already perfectly expressed what was in her heart, and she ceased composing. These days she sings few of her own compositions, drawing instead on songs from the wider Mīrābāī tradition and those of other saints.

She sang only one original composition for me, an adaptation of a popular *ghazal* (a Muslim Urdu song form) that also bears a resemblance to a popular Mīrābāī *pad*.[36] The text of the song goes as follows:

The one who does not come into love's lane,
  How will that one know the Beloved's whereabouts?
  How will that one know Mohan's house?

The one who has never been loved,
  How will that one know how to love?

The one who studies the vedas and perceives distinctions,
That one will never be pure in heart.

No matter how wisely a person may preach,
Who knows how to obtain God?

This world is a labyrinth and
everyone is blinded by illusion.

The one who, in the darkness, cannot see the Lord,
How can that one describe His beautiful form?

The one in whose heart pain has not been born,
How can that one know another's pain?

Mīrā is mad for Mohan,
how could anyone be crazy for this world?

Some of the words of the song are taken straight from the *ghazal* while other lines are adapted or introduced by Mīrājī. With the addition of the final stanza, the *ghazal* becomes a song attributed to Mīrā, but clearly its overall tone and structure are already compatible with songs of the Mīrā tradition. Such creative appropriation gives a vivid example of the way in which the compositions of others have been brought under Mīrā's name as the *ghazal* is transformed into Mīrāji's composition and Mīrā's *chāp* is attached to it.

As far as I know, Mīrājī has had no formal musical training. She sang for me without accompaniment although she generally plays the harmonium when she sings. According to Komal Kothari, her style of singing in this song and in her renditions of traditional Mīrā *bhajans* reflects the influences of professional caste musicians and classical traditions rather than the style of *bhajan* singing accompanied by *tanpura* in village Rajasthan. *Ghazals* are commonly sung by the low-caste Dholi women who traditionally sing for Rajput families in the region where Mīrājī was born, and she may have been influenced by them as well as by classical commercial recordings.[37]

Mīrājī embodies a particular image of Mīrābāī, one that is pure and sweet, without the dimensions of abandon and madness that sometimes mark representations of this saint. She is perhaps precisely the kind of woman many hagiographers and upper caste devotees might imagine Mīrā to be. Like Mīrā, she is a Rajput. When she sings, her voice is sweet and clear, filled with a tangible devotion and longing. As she speaks her eyes often move out to some distant place and are filled with the clarity and watery depth that mark those who have spent much time in prayer and meditation. She laughs easily. As she describes to me the things Kṛṣṇa likes (songs, good food, and beautiful ornaments) and makes sparkling decorations for his temple, she seems childlike in her innocence.

Shy and modest, she would never dance in a temple. Mīrā Rathor may have done so, dancing only for her Lord even in such a public space, but her namesake, Mīrājī, is not so free. She does not call attention to herself, although she accepts it when it comes because of her devotion. In other places she organizes and leads *bhajan* gatherings, but in Vrindavan where many such events occur regularly, she is generally a participant rather than a leader. Hers is a quiet life, but one which is filled with the company of other devotees and which gives her great satisfaction.

Mīrājī is supported by devotees in addition to her family. She has purchased land, or perhaps more correctly it has been purchased for her by her supporters. She spoke to me in August of 1993 of her desire to have a place of her own. In the village she lived under her brother and father's roof and authority, and in Vrindavan, under a Nimbārka sādhu's care. Although she expressed only gratitude for this support, she also articulated a clear desire to be on her own. Funding does not seem to be a problem. Her needs (financial and otherwise), she said clearly, are and will be taken care of by Kṛṣṇa. She had in mind a building that would include a living space for her above and a space below for devotees to gather for singing and other devotional practices. Construction was beginning in October 1993.

In the year following this conversation, her guru turned to *sakhī bhāv* and decided to settle in one place with her. It is interesting to note that he made this radical shift at precisely the time when Mīrājī was beginning to gain independence and to build "a room of her own." By December 1994, construction of the ashram was well underway but on a larger scale than Mīrājī had originally suggested. The main building will include a small kitchen, a room for devotional gatherings, storage space, two bathrooms, an enclosed verandah, and a room for her guru with a separate outside entrance. Only the kitchen was finished in December, and Mīrājī was living there. She also showed me where she planned to plant a *tulasī* garden and to have a large hall constructed in the future. Her vision for the ashram suggests that she and her guru may become the locus for the formation of a community of disciples, and she is clearly establishing herself as a permanent part of the Vrindavan community.

Although her designation as Mīrājī preceded such a development, there are other female primary disciples of male gurus who also bear this name. Sometimes they are foreigners, the most famous example being Gandhi's British disciple Madeleine Slade whom he called Mirabehn or Sister Mīrā, but there are others as well, including the Belgian disciple of a Śaivite guru.[38] The latter expressed surprise herself at being called "Mīrābāī;" after all, she is not even a devotee of Kṛṣṇa. Seemingly, "Mīrā" signifies not only the quintessential woman devotee (regardless of chosen deity) but also perhaps one who renounces a life of privilege, whether in a royal palace or a foreign land.

Indian women who are the primary disciples of male gurus also sometimes become particularly identified as "Mīrā." Such an identification suggests that a woman embodies the highest devotion both to God and guru and reflects also her guru's respect and devotion for her. Certainly Indira Devi became equated with Mīrābāī for Dilip Kumar Roy (himself a disciple of Sri Aurobindo), and she became his guru (even as he was hers) through her ability to meet Mīrābāī in meditative trance and to invoke the saint when her guru desired spiritual advise.[39] It is also said that the prolific writer and philosopher Bankey Behari spoke of his sole disciple Kṛṣṇa Mā as Mīrābāī even as he embodied Kṛṣṇa for her.[40] Here Mīrā's name implies not only that a woman's spiritual state is advanced but also that she is a companion of sādhus or holy men. Mīrā's tendency to sit among sādhus provides a precedent for a chaste relationship between male and female devotees and more specifically a model for a woman's devotion to holy men. Even as Mīrā was suspect for such behavior in the minds of some, however, so are those who receive her name in the context of primary relationships between male gurus and female disciples, especially when they live together. The *sakhī bhāv* of Mīrājī's guru will probably help to dissipate any such talk about them, but the question is still likely to arise for some. A woman who chooses to have an intimate relationship with a man outside of marriage can hardly escape this, and sādhus equally fall under suspicion in their relationships with women.

Mīrābāī of the Śālagrām Temple

In a small temple housing an immense *śālagrām* off one of the main bazaars in Vrindavan lives another woman called "Mīrābāī." When I met her in the summer of 1993, she had been living there for ten years and was about thirty-five years old.[41] She lives with a number of other women in the temple complex. Women live on one side, men on the other, with cloth partitions providing a measure of privacy. Her possessions consist of little more than bedding, an electric fan, a flute, the necessary things for *pūjā*, and a very elaborate altar with many pictures in addition to several images of Kṛṣṇa for her personal devotion. She apparently has no contact with her family, not having seen them for fifteen years. For her, as for other "Mīrās," Kṛṣṇa is all in all. When I first arrived at her temple home during the quiet hours of the early afternoon, she and another woman were reading aloud stories of saints from the *Bhaktamāl*. As we talked, a young girl came to bring her an offering of fruit, a gesture that suggests she is considered a spiritual teacher by others as well.

She, too, told me the story of her life, interspersing the narrative with songs. She was born into a Brahmin family in a village outside of Banaras. They moved many times during her childhood, and she lived in cities across the subcontinent including Calcutta, Lucknow, and Madras. When she was seven years old, her school mates asked her what she wanted to be when she grew up. To everyone's surprise she answered without hesitation, "When I am big, I will become Mīrābāī and be devoted to God." Restless as a young woman, she roamed and wandered in search of God, unable to keep her mind focused on studies or domestic work. Her parents worried that she would get into trouble and that her reputation and thus her future prospects would be ruined.

Kṛṣṇa came to her in her dreams, and she began to receive his *darśan* regularly in this way. The spirits of her ancestors (*kul ke pitar*) also appeared in her dreams and offered reassurance with regard to her spiritual calling. Her wanderings led her to Gayā, but unable to find work, she moved on to Banaras where she began working in a nursery school in order to survive. Despairing in her search for God, she decided to throw herself into the Ganges River and end it all. The Gaṅgā, however, seemed to throw her back on the shore. She had absolutely nothing but pulled herself together and called upon the Lord of Kashi for protection. This world of *saṁsār* had no meaning for her, and she vowed to go to Vrindavan where she would spend her days singing *bhajans.*

She felt compelled first to go to Ayodhyā. When she arrived, she met her guru who took her hand and, examining her palm, said that she had been a devotee through three lifetimes and that she must go immediately to Vrindavan where she would finally meet her Lord. She set off without delay, but the way was difficult. She was accosted by thieves and scoundrels as well as a train ticket collector who wanted to throw her in jail for traveling without a ticket. In both cases she was released when she began to sing devotional songs and to call on Kṛṣṇa. She reached Vrindavan and eventually made her way to the temple where she now resides.

This is a dramatic story of a restless and troubled young woman, who found peace finally by becoming (or acknowledging that she was) a Mīrā figure. Her ancestors, the goddess Gaṅgā, her guru, and Kṛṣṇa himself all confirmed her calling as she narrates her journey. Having reached Vrindavan, she took up a life of devotion. Her daily routine begins with a bath in the Yamunā, followed by personal devotion and by *darśan* and *satsang* in various temples. Her late afternoons and evenings are spent at any one of the many activities always happening in Vrindavan—talks given by famous storytellers or preachers, *līlās* of Kṛṣṇa's life, *bhajan* gatherings, special events around various holidays, etc.

Mīrābāī of the Śālagrām Temple is a public figure in the landscape of Vrindavan, often dressed in sparkling golden clothes as Kṛṣṇa and always carrying a flute which she plays on occasion. When she is not attired in this way, she wears the saffron of a renunciant. Her public persona is one of strength and independence rather than sweetness and modesty. Though relaxed and open in the private space of her temple home, outside she is more distant, her eyes seemingly on some far shore—a necessary distancing perhaps for a woman making her way in the streets alone even as a renunciant and a holy woman in Vrindavan. I often saw her alone outside the temple, although she also moved about in the company of other women devotees.

Some wonder at her ways of drawing attention to herself, and one sees in her behavior perhaps more of the madness associated with saints—that tendency to act against the grain or without regard for social norms that disturbs the complacency and self-satisfaction of others. Clearly she has a flare for the dramatic, but her dressing as Kṛṣṇa might also be read as a sign that she has entered the *līlā* fully, becoming completely absorbed in him or even losing, at times, the distinction between herself and her Beloved. If Caitanya could be the embodiment of Kṛṣṇa or of both Rādhā and Kṛṣṇa together, is it impossible that a woman should embody Kṛṣṇa alone or Mīrā and Kṛṣṇa in one form? In her dress, Mīrābāī of the Śālagrām Temple raises this question, whether or not such a comparison to Caitanya is warranted.

On one occasion, during a celebration at Rādhā Ramaṇ Maṇḍir, she rose to dance momentarily with a group of Bengali drummers.[42] They were all men, and no other women stepped up to join them except much later in the evening when large numbers of people danced. Mīrābāī of the Śālagrām Temple challenged the gender limitations of this space. After all, everyone is essentially female in the presence of Kṛṣṇa—all are *gopīs*. The male drummers, too, at times put on scarves and danced with clay pots, becoming Rādhā and her companions as well as Kṛṣṇa. Mīrābāī of the Śālagrām Temple, dressed as Kṛṣṇa, entered the dance, and pushed this fluid boundary between genders one more step toward dissolution. Yet even she did not dare to cross this threshold for long and moved out of the space after a short time. The challenges she offers seem to be taken in stride by the community, and she is clearly well respected in Vrindavan in spite of, or perhaps because of, her unusual behavior.

The Community of Mīrā Mātājī

Yet another "Mīrā" lives quietly in another part of Vrindavan. Sant Lakṣmī Bāī is called Mīrā Mātājī by those who revere her and her disciples.[43] She is now an old woman, perhaps 70 or 80—not long for this world she tells me with a twinkle in her eye. She was born into a Brahmin family in Madhya Pradesh. From childhood she, too, loved God, and in her home Hari's name was repeated. She did not want to marry, but her parents were afraid and insisted. She married into a fine family, and her husband was a good man, but her heart was not attached to him. She had one son (who is now a lawyer), but she did not remain long in her marital household. Her in-laws opposed what they considered her excessive devotion, yet she could not restrain herself. One night a golden flute appeared between husband and wife, and after this miracle, they stopped trying to interfere. She left home eventually and made her way to Vrindavan. As before but now without opposition, she sang and danced and played in the *līlā* of her Lord.

Vrindavan became her new home, but Mīrā Mātājī traveled extensively and soon developed a considerable following in a number of places. Devotees collected money and built temples and *satsang bhavans* in her name in many towns and villages. These *satsang bhavans* serve as gathering places for worship and devotional singing where the sectarian divisions of *sampradāys* and the distinctions of caste hierarchies have no place, and they also provide accommodations for Mīrā Mātājī and her primary disciples when they visit. As she herself said, it is not appropriate for such renunciants to live in the homes of householders. Mīrā Mātājī and her closest disciples are very dearly loved in all of these places and are known for their great devotion and the beautiful *bhajan* singing which is their vocation.

One such place is the Mīrā Satsang Bhavan in Salumbar, Rajasthan. When Mīrā Mātājī is not there, women meet daily for worship and singing, primarily of her songs. *Ārati* is offered to a beautifully painted and adorned picture of Kṛṣṇa and also before a grainy photograph of a woman with thick glasses who looks about forty years old—a reproduction of a portion of the only photograph that Mīrā Mātājī ever allowed to be taken of her.[44] The space is used for other *satsang* gatherings as well, particularly when singers come from out-of-town. Men and women attend, especially night gatherings, but only women may spend the night there.

These days Mīrā Mātājī herself does not travel much. She lives in Vrindavan in a community consisting of herself and four women disciples. Other women and men come to offer service to them, bringing provisions and assisting with practical chores. Her four direct disciples vary in age, the youngest seemingly in her late teens or early twenties and the oldest perhaps fifty years old. All are clearly educated. They live a life of prayer and peace, holding *ārati* and attending to Kṛṣṇa's needs at the appropriate hours; singing *bhajans;* making ornaments for Kṛṣṇa; going for *darśan* in the temples; completing the daily tasks of life; reading aloud and discussing the *Bhāgavata Purāṇa,* the stories of the saints, and a few other religious works; and speaking with those who come for their *darśan* and teaching. Her disciples also continue the work of traveling to sing devotional songs in the many communities where Mīrā Mātājī's devotees live.

In Salumbar, a sister of one of the disciples was very careful to point out that Mīrā Mātājī treats her disciples as equals. My own observations within the community confirmed this. Mīrā Mātājī is accorded great respect and devotion, but she seldom acts in an authoritarian manner. Only once did she stop some line of my questioning, when I wanted to know about the lives of each of her disciples and we had already been talking for some hours. These details she said are not important—Kṛṣṇa is the only thing that really matters. She also did not tell me her own story; I learned it from devotees in Udaipur. Her disciples clearly respected her wish, but there was a gentleness and a peacefulness to their acceptance of what she said rather than obedience. Mīrā Mātājī's appreciation and love for them is also very evident. She calls each "Bhagwān" or "Lord," and laughter and affection mark their interaction with each other and others. When they sang for me, her eldest disciple sat beside her on a raised platform, and another woman from outside sat at the same level. Mīrā Mātājī obviously did not think of herself as above them and did not demand the traditional guru-disciple etiquette that would require them to sit below her.

Their community has no ties to any formal religious institution. Mīrā Mātājī told me directly that a guru was unnecessary. She said that though one reads in many books of the importance of a guru, this is simply not true. There is a guru of the body who might give one a mantra, but the only guru of the *ātma* or true self is Paramātma, the Supreme Soul. Kṛṣṇa is everything—father, mother, husband, brother, son, and guru.

In mundane matters also there appears to be no outside male authority over this community. When I visited them in October of 1993, they were living in a place that had been built for them by devotees in the style of a small *satsang bhavan*, nestled deep within the interior lanes of Prem Gully. By December of 1994 they had moved to a new, more spacious place on a main road near Bankey Behari Mandir, and this, too, was provided by a devotee. Neither Mīrā Mātājī nor her primary disciples generally handle money directly. They are supported by offerings from many sources and ultimately by Kṛṣṇa and are not dependent on or beholden to any particular person. They live the life for which they feel they have taken birth—a life of ecstatic love of God, of religious study, and of travel for the purpose of communion with other devotees and of furthering devotion.

Mīrā Mātājī is the composer among them, and they regularly sing her songs. Three hundred and five of her compositions are printed in a small bhajan book entitled *Śrī Rādhā Kṛṣṇa Bhajanāvalī.*[45] Stylistically the songs are simple and repetitive, making them very good for group singing and *kīrtan*. Most do not contain Mīrā's name or *chāp*, but they are full of similar images and the common language of Kṛṣṇa devotion. Among her compositions are five that mention Mīrābāī specifically and several others which clearly relate to the narrative of Mīrā Rathor.

In one such song she sings of Mīrā:

Wonderful is the devotion you gave, Fluteplayer;
  totally intoxicated, your Mīrā was mad.
Wonderful is the devotion you gave, Fluteplayer;
  you made her very rich, fulfilled her greatest desires.
Wonderful is the devotion you gave, Fluteplayer;
  She had lost but still she won, clever Mīrā.
Amazing! You gave being itself, Fluteplayer.

The singer marvels at the devotion exhibited by Mira and the graciousness of God who gives that capacity for love as well as existence itself. In another song she clearly identifies with Mīrā, singing "Make your Mīrā a diamond, Manmohan-ji, Enchanter of the Heart." She would be close to Kṛṣṇa—a diamond in his crown, a sash at his waist, even a small strip of cloth or leather touching his feet. In a third she calls on the "Enchanter of Mīrā's Heart" to come to his devotees and to bring forth true devotion among them, like that of the Bhil woman who offered Rām tasted sweet fruit.[46] In a fourth she declares that Kṛṣṇa is known as the Protector because he protected Mīrā Rathor.

The one who enchanted Mīrā's heart has clearly stolen Mīrā Mātājī's as well. In an extended fifth song, lacking the repetitive half lines of the others and telling more of Mīrā's own story, she asks how he managed such a feat:

Enchanter, in what manner did you meet and join with Mīrā?

She always sang your name, that crazy woman renouncer!
Say how you taught her to love you so sincerely from her very birth.

She was a daughter of the Rathors who had married a Sisodiya.
Raṇchoḍ, tell me how you got the Rathor lady to sit beside you!

The mahārāja's mahārāṇī in the royal palace of Chittor!
Tell me how you revealed your own matchless beauty.
Upholder of the humble, kind and affectionate to the poor,
  refuge of the unsheltered.
Say how you fulfilled your true vow.

Your servant's true Lord, tell me the whole truth.
Having changed the poison to nectar, say how you got her to drink it.

When the dreadful injustice happened to your loving worshipper,
Then how did you cause her to triumph over this world,
O Lord of the World?

Your Vedas and mysteries cannot be fathomed; you are the far shore,
Brahman, the Almighty Lord.
Enchanter, in what manner did you meet and join with Mīrā?[47]

Though the song has a playful quality, the demands are serious. A teasing appreciation for Kṛṣṇa's ability to seduce even one who seemed to have it all interweaves with a longing to meet Kṛṣṇa even as Mīrā did and wonder at the possibility of love between a human being and the unfathomable divine.

Elsewhere Mīrā's story and songs are also invoked though her name is not mentioned directly. The rāṇā is addressed and the singer speaks in Mīrā's voice, saying she will play the drum and will not cease singing *bhajans* to Hari or wearing the saffron of renunciation. If the rāṇā becomes angry, so be it.[48] Kṛṣṇa is said to dwell in the singer's eyes and called to come quickly to her home, and she speaks also of being Kṛṣṇa's servant, of staying awake the whole night waiting for *darśan*, and of tying bells to her ankles and dancing.[49] Mīrā Rathor's songs and life story provide inspiration and much of the language used by Mīrā Mātājī in these songs, and these compositions suggest that she identifies deeply with Mīrā.

Other songs move away from the characteristic themes and language of the Mīrā tradition and more fully into mainstream Vaiṣṇava devotion with a number mentioning Rādhā and Yaśodā. There are also hymns of praise to Gaṇesh, Śiva, and Umā—themes not characteristically associated with Mīrā that place Mīrā Mātājī in a wider devotional context. Mīrā Mātājī's songs are sung by her primary disciples and their wider circle of devotees largely to the exclusion of most other *bhajans* and are in some sense definitive of the larger community.[50]

That Mīrā plays a part in the self-identity of Mīrā Mātājī and her disciples became even clearer when I visited them for a second time in 1994. As we sat around talking casually in the early afternoon after sharing the one meal they eat each day, they asked if I had seen a Mīrā *līlā*.[51] Yes, I responded, but I was assured that in fact I had not really seen one because I had not seen theirs. They had composed their own drama which they perform periodically, and they proposed to perform it for me the next day. The two youngest disciples acted as Mīrā and Kṛṣṇa while the other two played harmonium and dholak and some additional women took up rhythm instruments. A handwritten copy of the songs was used to spur memory as they all sang.

The story was a simple one with only the two characters. The rāṇā was absent as were all the other familial figures who are an essential part of so many dramas of Mīrā's life.[52] Instead the performance focused on Mīrā's longing for Kṛṣṇa and his appearance to her in meditation. The frame story, not dramatized, takes place in the eternal world of Vrindavan. At a meeting it is decided that the *sakhī* Lalitā should take birth as Mīrā in order to increase devotion in the world. Lalitā asks Rādhā, "Would you be able to live without Kṛṣṇa?" Rādhā answers, "No, but you also will not have to live without him. Kṛṣṇa will always be within. Whenever you meditate, you will see him." Because of this, however, Mīrā seldom experiences external *darśan,* and her life is marked by *viraha,* by longing and love in separation. Accordingly, in the drama Mīrā never encounters Kṛṣṇa in her normal state. He appears only when she is deep in meditative trance.

The disciple playing Mīrā appeared dressed in saffron, her hair loose, Mīrā's characteristic *ektāra* (a one-stringed instrument) and a rosary in her hands. She wept constantly, sang with great sorrow of her longing for *darśan* of her Lord, and danced in whirling circles. When the pain of *viraha* reached a peak and tears filled the eyes of the audience, Mīrā sat down to meditate, immediately radiating inner peace and stillness. At this time Kṛṣṇa appeared to stand before her, signifying her inner experience of his presence and offering *darśan* to the audience. Always he departed before she came out of trance, however. Three times this sequence was re-enacted. The third time when Kṛṣṇa came to her in meditation, he sprinkled her with holy water. (In fact, the disciple playing Kṛṣṇa splashed rather more water on her than intended, and everyone had to stifle laughter.) Kṛṣṇa answered her thirst, though even after this she awakened to separation.

The drama was not meant to tell a story per se but to call the audience into the sweet pain of separated love. Mīrā and Kṛṣṇa formed a tableau of great beauty, and the peaceful moments of their meditative unity contrasted sharply with the sorrow of its impossibility in the world of multiplicity. Clearly this *līlā* speaks of the experience of Mīrā Mātāji and her disciples. The separation so necessary for love to be experienced generates a longing for union that would end all distinction. Those who would love Kṛṣṇa with all that they are cannot but suffer this paradox. The intensity of such love leaves no room for any other drama or any other concerns. The reality of the world fades, and only the devotee and the Divine Lover remain.

In conversation also Mīrā Mātājī continually returned to Kṛṣṇa. She wept much of the time as she spoke of his kindness. Speaking to me as a guru, she stressed that Kṛṣṇa is everything and that we can do nothing without the grace and kindness of God. He protects our every step. God has given us birth so it is good, and every part of the body is created for the service of God—the eyes are for *darśan,* the voice for singing *bhajans.* The mind-heart and consciousness are for contemplation of God. In life after life we come into this world to sing to Rām. Bankey Behari resides within our own eyes; we need not go anywhere for *darśan.* Mīrā Mātājī's love for Kṛṣṇa poured forth as she spoke. In her youth she had often sung and danced for hours and days on end, and her devotees reported that she might go into *samādhi* in the midst of singing and not return to everyday consciousness for four days.[53] Although I tried to shift the conversation to her own life and that of her disciples, she would turn it back again and again to Kṛṣṇa.

Is it possible that the community of Mīrā Mātājī may lead to the formation of a religious institution centered around Mīrābāī, along the lines of the Kabīr Panth or the followers of Raidās? It is perhaps to such a community that H. H. Wilson referred in 1862 when he spoke of a sect dedicated to Mīrā and Kṛṣṇa as Raṇchoḍjī within the Vallabha Sampradāy.[54] He could also have had in mind a group like the Dādūpanthī nuns in Nagaur, Rajasthan, about whom Monika Thiel-Horstmann writes.[55] These women have a special dedication to Mīrā, singing her songs and drawing parallels between her devotion and that of their sect's founder Dādū, but they do not constitute an independent *panth.* Wilson offers few details, and other corroborating evidence of a true Mīrābāī sect has not been found. G.N. Sharma's reference to a Mīrābāī cult of widows in Mewar can also be dismissed, as he referred not to a formal sect but to a number of unrelated widows living lives of renunciation and devotion in villages across the landscape of Rajasthan.[56]

Mīrā Mātājī's community does have a physical infrastructure of temples and *satsang bhavans* across several states and a practice of singing her compositions that sets her followers off from other groups of devotees. Her four disciples of varying ages offer the possibility of continuity in leadership, and Mīrā Mātājī has shared both the community's devotion and her authority with them. That authority is based on their perceptible devotion and personal charisma as in seemingly all nascent movements, but clearly other sources of authority and allegiance will be necessary for the formation of a formal Mīrābāī sect.

Caste identity seems an unlikely candidate. Kabīr and Raidās are perceived as champions of low-caste people, and this identity is fundamental in the formation of *panths* around them. Although Mīrā renounces her caste privilege and plays a lively part in the non-institutionalized religious milieu of low-caste people in Rajasthan, she herself is a Rajput. The Rajputs, however, would not necessarily rally around her in large numbers as a religious figure because her behavior fundamentally undermines ideals of Rajput honor.[57] She may have an emergent place in a developing Rajput and Rajasthani identity but not as the leader of a religious institution.[58]

Gender equality might offer another basis for institutional formation, even as it did for the Brahmā Kumārīs. Mīrā is not said explicitly to have championed women's causes or to have advocated a devotional community strictly made up of women. In fact it was her association with holy men that got her into trouble in many stories of her life, and the community in which she lived according to the *Caurāsī Vaiṣṇavan kī Vārtā* was a radically inclusive one. Such an egalitarian community might provide a vision for a new *panth*, although initial ideals are often compromised in institutional development. Other historical and social factors would need to converge to generate an ongoing institution. In the case of the Brahmā Kumārīs, a millenarian vision with a rapidly approaching apocalypse was required to make gender hierarchy expendible, and even so the movement generated considerable hostility. The sect also took shape within a particular community and under the prophetic direction and almost militaristic discipline of its male visionary founder Dada Lekhraj. In his teachings, a rejection of physicality and sexuality is wedded to a critique of social restrictions for women, but other issues such a world peace, perhaps more attractive to male adherents of the sect, have become part of the group's transnational agenda as well.[59]

Only time will tell whether similar forces and agendas will come into play to transform communities like Mīrā Mātājī's into a formal Mīrābāī sect. Mīrā Mātājī herself seems an unlikely figure to be at the center of an emerging institution both because her sole focus seems to be devotion to Kṛṣṇa and because neither she nor her disciples show any interest in enhancing their own power or authority. Her willingness to speak with me seemed to come from her desire to propagate the love of Kṛṣṇa and her curiosity about life in other lands rather than any desire for self-promotion. As a loosely based community, however, they seem likely to flourish as long as other "Mīrās" continue to emerge to take the place of those who pass on, and similar communities may in all likelihood form around other such women.

The place of the sixteenth-century saint Mīrā at the center of a formal sect is also problematic because at the heart of her story is a fundamental refusal to accept any authority but God, whether it be social, familial, political, or religious. Such a stance poses a potential threat to any centralized institutional authority as well to hierarchical social structures defined by caste, gender, and economic inequalities. Her direct refusal of the role of wife and mother continues to generate ambivalence and even hostility. In the past conditions seemingly have not been right for the formation of a Mīrābāī sect. It is possible that in the future they may be, especially with increased awareness of the oppression of women, but there is certainly no guarantee that this will be the case.

The Followers of Mīrābāī

Having briefly looked at the lives of these living "Mīrābāīs," we are now in a position to define more clearly the meanings carried by the name of Mīrā and to delineate the contours of the religious space for women that her example opens up. While devotion to Kṛṣṇa is the central fact in all these women's lives, it is not the only thing they have in common. Their stories are not formal hagiographies—they are, after all, living women who themselves told me of their own lives. Even so, their narratives share common elements with those of other women saints, and they are clearly familiar with such stories and draw on them as patterns to make sense of their own lives.[60] Each of these women exhibits a devotion that begins in childhood and must find some way to escape the trap of marriage. Three out of four simply refuse to marry, and the fourth marries against her will but is able to leave her husband and child through Kṛṣṇa's miraculous intervention. All consider themselves married to Kṛṣṇa rather than to any human husband. Unlike other women saints, their own stories do not include episodes of direct challenge to gender and caste hierarchies or of testing by religious authorities, although their lifestyles and religious practices implicitly question them all. Whether the final chapter in their tales will include a physical merger with the divine remains to be seen.

There are other more specific characteristics of these "Mīrābāīs" that set them apart from women saints more generally and reveal their identification with the sixteenth-century Rajput saint. They all sing, three out of four dance, and three out of four compose in a manner much like their namesake. They sing Mīrā's songs and compose songs about her or in her name. All dress in a way consistent with the portrayal of Mīrābāī as well, in the colors of renunciation (saffron), of widowhood (white), or of marriage (red). All are high-caste women—Rajputs and Brahmins.

Another element that appears in three out of the four stories (though it is not a part of the sixteenth-century saint's tale) is a period of isolation or spiritual confusion and searching. In her study of ecstatic saints in Bengal, June McDaniel notes that the lives of such saints are often marked by a similar period of spiritual crisis, and the saint Mīrābāī herself seems to have more in common with ecstatic saints than with the bhakta carefully guided under the direction of a guru as described by McDaniel.[61] Mīrābāī of the Śālagrām Temple seems closest to this ecstatic model of sainthood, for it is she who speaks of experiencing *darśan* in her dreams as well as meeting the spirits of her ancestors who serve as her guides. She takes up a life of distracted wandering totally inappropriate to the daughter of a Brahmin household and seems to embody the dimension of Mīrā that is *pāgal* or mad more directly. Kṛṣṇa Mā is also called mad during her years of isolation and ecstasy, however, and Mīrājī exhibits symptoms during her adolescence which must have led her parents to consult physicians and to wonder about her sanity. Mīrā Mātājī reports no such specific period, but she says clearly that she was involved in devotion day and night. This would have created a de facto isolation, and she is later reported to go into *samādhi* or meditative trance for days at a time:

Although detailed information about Mīrā Mātājī's childhood and adolescence is unavailable and Kṛṣṇa Mā seemed to have totally immersed herself in love of Kṛṣṇa and an identification with Mīrā during this period, both Mīrājī and Mīrābāī of the Śālagrām Temple clearly describe spiritual crises of meaning coinciding with the onset of puberty. For Mīrājī, the trouble began when she reached the age of thirteen or fourteen and ended when she was eighteen or twenty; for Mīrābāī of the Śālagrām Temple a similar period of restlessness finally ended when she reached Vrindavan at the age of twenty-five. Both seemed to be struggling to find voice and identity in a world that offered very few options, and discussion of marriage either precipitated or exacerbated the crisis. The narrative and songs of the saint Mīrābāī appear to have played an essential role in the resolution of this inner turmoil. Mīrājī emerged from her period of struggle singing the songs of Mīrā and her own songs composed in Mīrā's name and with the acceptance of her family that she would not marry but live a life of devotion. Mīrābāī of the Śālagrām Temple speaks also of her despair at the meaninglessness of existence during her time of wandering, leading her to the brink of suicide. If she would not accept the identity of wife and mother, then who would she be? Mīrā seemed to provide the answer, and she found peace only when she came to Vrindavan and took on fully the persona of the sixteenth-century saint.

Mīrābāī of the Śālagrām Temple has not seen her family in almost fifteen years, suggesting that she must have left home for the last time at about the age of twenty. Why? Were there other factors in addition to a spiritual restlessness? I do not know, and I was also unable to corroborate her story with any outside sources (except the tacit agreement of another woman present when she recounted it to me). It is possible that this is not the whole story. Other factors may have been operative in the formation of the identities of these twentieth-century "Mīrās," but at this time I do not have access to such information. It is significant, however, that the narrative and character of Mīrābāī provided a way to make sense of both the crisis (whatever its causes may be) and its resolution for the women, their families, and the larger society. Further, a period of social isolation—through illness, wandering, or absorption—seemed necessary in order for these women to shape alternative identities and to find a voice at odds with dominant cultural expectations. Mīrā's narrative provided an interpretive framework for that identity, and her songs a vehicle to express resistance, longing, and love and a model for self-expression.

The space which these woman have come to occupy is a decidedly religious one, and in this sense is interior to society—"allowable" behavior for woman provided they remain chaste. Their relationships with religious authorities and gurus vary, however. Mīrājī of Mewar is devoted to her guru, but previously they seldom met. His exercise of authority over her is clear and appears to be increasing. She destroyed manuscripts of some of her compositions at his command, and together they are now building an ashram with explicit connections to the Nimbārka

Sampradāy, although her initial vision had been for a place of her own. Mīrābāī of the Śālagrām temple also acknowledges her guru with gratitude but without the familiarity that one might expect if they had a close teacher-disciple relationship, and he seems to have no direct control over her. She lives within a temple compound but voices no sectarian affiliation and participates freely in the activities of multiple sampradāys. Kṛṣṇa Mā advocates devotion to all and none at the same time, and Mīrā Mātājī emphatically denies the necessity of a human guru. Thus these women embody a range of possible relationships, even as the saint Mīrā does in various stories told about her. For the most part, however, they reside outside the formal boundaries of sampradāys and the control of male gurus.

Locating these women was not easy; they live lives of relative obscurity. Steadfast supporters provide for their needs, but they are not well-known gurus residing in large ashrams. Instead, they are quiet saints, leading radical lives in a world that might not accept them if they were more vocal. They have tried to built independent lives beyond the range of familial and institutional control with varying success. Only Kṛṣṇa Mā continues to live under her family's roof full time and under the authority of her brother. Her independence manifests itself primarily in her refusal to marry, her leadership of a large number of followers, and her deeply interior religious life. Mīrābāī of the Śālagrām Temple lives apart from her family (though within a temple compound) and moves around Vrindavan with considerable freedom.

Mīrājī of Mewar has also stepped out of her family's circle of control increasingly in the last year, but her guru's direct authority over her has increased during the same period, perhaps not coincidentally. She may eventually have disciples as Mīrā Mātājī does, although her guru's presence may limit the development of her own leadership. Mīrā Mātājī has managed to move fully beyond the control not only of family but also of human gurus and sampradāys. She is mother to an ongoing tradition of living Mīrās in a kind of women's monastic community run on a very egalitarian basis without institutional rigidity or male authority. Hers is perhaps the most truly independent life among the four.

The obscurity of their lives may be partly a result of saintly humility, but it may also be out of social necessity. These women practice *pati bhāv*—the worship of Kṛṣṇa as husband and Lord. This is not one of the relationships with the divine generally sanctioned by sects devoted to Kṛṣṇa. Taking on the role of a servant, friend, parent, or lover of God or of a *mañjarī* or *sakhī* of Rādhā, facilitating her relationship with Kṛṣṇa, is encouraged but not taking on the role of a wife to a divine husband.[62] Kṛṣṇa does not marry until he leaves Vrindavan, allowing no place for a marital relationship in the Braj *līlā*. Further, devotion to Kṛṣṇa as *pati* or husband makes Kṛṣṇa all in all; there is no room in the final analysis for human gurus or mortal husbands. Though in one sense these women have taken a socially sanctioned relationship and transferred it to the human-divine realm even as Mīrā is said to have done, in another sense it is clear that such a relationship radically challenges the norm and that their way of living is decidedly against the grain of social and religious expectation.

If the *pati bhāv* practiced by these "Mīrābāīs" were compatible with existing institutions, then it seems that they and their followers would be incorporated into formal sects and *pati bhāv* officially affirmed as another path to the divine. The sixteenth-century saint Mīrā has not been incorporated in this way, and her twentieth-century counterparts also are not fully integrated into sampradāys (although Mīrājī is being pushed in this direction). Their devotion and spiritual power are affirmed, but perhaps they, too, constitute some kind of danger even as Mīrā seemed to have done for the Vallabha Sampradāy. Perhaps they themselves also opt not to fight this battle either for institutional recognition or against appropriation, choosing instead to follow an inner calling and to live, together with others, lives of their own choosing purposefully outside such formal structures. It is not insignificant that they all reside at least part of the time in Mathurā and Vrindavan. Seemingly these holy cities offer a greater degree of latitude for women's religious behavior as well as an environment conducive to the cultivation of devotion.

As Kumkum Sangari has suggested in reference to Mīrā herself, the language of human-divine marriage can be used in compensatory ways or to uphold gender hierarchies.[63] Further, the space opened up by Mīrā's example is limited to the religious realm. Nevertheless, it is a significant space when these women are viewed as seeking an independent life outside of traditional *pativratā* ideals for women. They have none of things that society says provide fulfillment to women (or they have renounced them if they do), and yet they are living lives of seemingly great satisfaction and joy. These particular women expressed a religious inclination from a young age, and the high value placed on devotion by their families provided a nurturing environment for their developing religiosity. No direct commitment to social activism on behalf of women was voiced by any of the four, although they are willing to challenge all types of social restrictions and inequalities in the name of devotion.

It is also possible that Mīrā exemplifies a religious option particularly for high-caste women. All four of these women are Rajputs or Brahmins. I do not have sufficient data to conclude that low-caste women religious leaders of this type are not called Mīrā, but preliminary investigation suggests that they may not be. It is conceivable that "Mīrā" is an interpretive category and quintessential model for high-caste Vaiṣṇava women, while low-caste women leaders are not so strictly identified with her. Even as it did for foreign women, her example in this context seems to imply renunciation as well as devotion. High-caste women in Śākta traditions may have other options; possession by the Devī offers a possible avenue to religious leadership, as Kathleen Erndl reports.[64] Such a route is unavailable in Vaiṣṇava traditions, however. Instead, the model of Mīrābāī seems to prevail.

The possibilities inherent in Mīrā's example are not limited to individual women's religious callings. Mīrā Mātājī has established a women's community and *satsang bhavans* which are gathering places principally for women in a multitude of villages. Men are welcomed as devotees and equals within this community but not as religious, social, or economic superiors. Mīrā Mātājī is not a revolutionary in a wider social sense, but she has established an alternate communal life. Mīrājī, Kṛṣṇa Mā, and to a lesser extent Mīrābāī of the Śālagrām Temple also have their followers. The possibility of the development of a full-scale panth remains as does that of the proliferation of loosely structured communities like Mīrā Mātājī's.

Embodied by these women, Mīrābāī is not merely a long dead saint to be admired but not emulated; she becomes a living presence in the religious landscape of India, offering a viable (though perhaps not revolutionary) option for women outside of marriage. In her past and present incarnations, devotion to God is at the very center of Mīrā's identity and in some ways excludes or reduces all other concerns. By her example, Mīrā offers the possibility of a life lived for God and not for men and a way to approach the divine directly. Through her narrative she offers an interpretive framework for women's self-understanding and for social acceptance or at least tolerance of women who choose to live as she did. Though decidedly religious and circumscribed within the bounds of existing social structures, this space created by Mīrābāī allows for spiritual and personal growth; for the cultivation of talents, education, and leadership; and for the creation of a life beyond that of wife and mother for women. The lives of Kṛṣṇa Mā, Mīrājī, Mīrābāī of the Śālagrām Temple, and Mīrā Mātājī attest to the significance of this space and to the ongoing and lively presence of Mīrābāī in the imagination and lives of twentieth-century devotees.

NOTES

[1]This paper draws on field research carried out from August 1992 to October 1993 in Rajasthan and Vrindavan supported by the American Institute of Indian Studies, supplemented with additional data collected in Vrindavan in December 1994. It is a portion of a larger ongoing project on Mīrā—my doctoral dissertation entitled "Dyed in the Color of Her Lord, Multiple Representations in the Mīrābāī Tradition" to be completed June 1, 1995. I wish to express my gratitude not only to the American Institute of Indian Studies but also to Dr. Linda Hess for insightful comments on earlier drafts. I am especially grateful to the "Mīrās" whose stories are recounted here and who so graciously shared their lives and devotion with me as well as those who led me to them.

[2]This is a popular *bhajan* book form of this Mīrābāī *pad*. The translation is my own.

[3]The date and name of her husband are given by the seventeenth-century historian Muhatā Naiṇsī in his *Khyāt*, and noted by Munshī Devī Prasād in his *Mīrābāī kā Jīvancaritra* (Calcutta: Bangīya Hindī-Pariṣad, 1898, reprinted 1954), p.10, as well as many other scholars after him.

[4]Nābhādās, *Śrī Bhaktamāl*, with the *Bhaktirasabodhinī* commentary of Priyādās (Lucknow: Tejkumār Press, 1969), pp.712-713.

[5]This name for Kṛṣṇa is derived from the story in which he lifts Mt. Govardhan above the people of Braj to shield them from the torrential rains of Indra's anger after he has told the people to shift their worship of Indra to Mt. Govardhan and ultimately to himself.

[6]Dhruvdās, *Bhaktanāmāvalī*, text given by Vrajaratnadās, *Mīrā Madhurī* (Varāṇāsi: Hindī Sāhitya Kutir, 1948), pp.32-33. For a discussion of Dhruvdās, see Rupert Snell, "Bhakti in the Poetry of Dhruvdās," in Ronald Stuart McGregor, ed., *Devotional Literature in South Asia* (Cambridge: Cambridge University Press, 1992), p.248. Winand M. Callewaert and Peter G. Friedlander give Dhruvdās's dates as 1538-1623 CE in *The Life and Works of Raidās* (New Delhi: Manohar, 1992), p.16. McGregor dates his works from 1593 to 1641 in his *Hindi Literature from its Beginnings to the Nineteenth Century* (Weisbaden: Otto Harrassowitz, 1984), p.160, and Vrajaratnadās gives the time of the creation of this work as between 1623 and 1643 (p.32). *Kartāls* are hand-held rhythm instruments of wood with metal discs on wires in openings cut in the wood (resembling the edge of a tambourine in structure and also making a similar sound.) The translations of phrases from Dhruvdās's passage are my own.

[7]Rāghavdās, *Bhaktamāla* (Jodhpur: Rajasthan Oriental Research Institute, 1965), p.99. The text is also given by Vrajaratnadās, *Mīrā Madhurī*, pp.40-41; Prabhāt, *Mīrābāī* (Bombay: Hindī Granth Ratnākar, 1965), pp.50-51; and others. The date of 1713 CE for the completion of the text given by W.G. Orr, *A Sixteenth-Century Indian Mystic* (London: Lutterworth Press, 1947), p.213.

[8]Vrajaratnadās, *Mīrā Madhurī*, pp.39-40. Hukam Singh Bhāṭī, *Mīrābāī: Itihāsik va Sāmājik Vivechan* (Jodhpur: Rājasthanī Sāhitya Sansthān, 1987), pp.44-45.

[9]Priyādās, *Bhaktirasabodhinī Tīkā* in Nābhādās, *Śrī Bhaktamāl*, with the *Bhaktirasabodhinī* commentary of Priyādās, pp.713-723.

[10]A.K. Ramanujan, "On Women Saints," in John Stratton Hawley and Donna Marie Wulff, eds., *The Divine Consort: Rādhā and the Goddesses of India* (Boston: Beacon Press, 1982) pp.316-324. Ramanujan identifies five stages: "early dedication to God," "denial of marriage," "defying societal norms," "initiation," and "marrying the Lord."

[11]Priyādās is reported as both a disciple of Nābhādās of the Rāmānandī sect and as a disciple of Caitanya. See McGregor, *Hindi Literature*, p.163 and Friedlander and Callaweart, *The Life and Works of Raidās*, p.15.

[12]Cited by Callewaert and Friedlander, *The Life and Works of Raidās*, p.13, drawing on J.S. Sabar, *Bhagat Ravida's Srodha Pustak* (Amritsar: Guru Nānak Dev University Press, 1984), pp.69-81. The only detail about the story of Mira in the *Pothīpremabodh* which is related by Callewaert and Friedlander is that Mīrābāī (rather than the Jhālī Rāṇī) is mentioned as Raidās's disciple (see p.26, footnote 113.) Called Ravidās in the Punjab, this saint is called Raidās in other parts of north India (pp.21-22), and Friedlander and Callewaert discuss his dates in detail, concluding that he probably lived in the period from 1450 to 1550 CE (pp.28-30). Even if he lived in the first half of this period, he would have been seventy years old in 1520, as Callewaert and Friedlander point out, and could certainly have met Mīrā in the first decades of her life.

[13]Callewaert and Friendlander, *The Life and Works of Raidās*, pp.30, 32.

[14]Vaiṣṇavdās, Priyādās's grandson and a member of the Nimbārka Sampradāy who lived in Vrindavan, made this correction in his *Bhaktamāl kā Dṛṣtant* in the latter half of the eighteenth century (ca.1750 CE.) Prabhāt identifies this text for the first time in the Hindi literature and reads it as the correct interpretation of Priyādās's text. See his extended discussion in *Mīrābāī*, pp.42-50.

[15]For an example, see Dilip Kumar Roy and Indira Devi, *The Beggar Princess: A Historical Drama in Five Acts* (Allahabad: Kitab Mahal, 1955).

[16]Mahīpati, *Bhaktivijaya* (1762 CE) translated by Dr.Justin E. Abbott and Paṇḍit N.R. Godbole in *Stories of Indian Saints* (Delhi: Motilal Banarsidass, 1988, fourth edition published 1933),volume 2, pp.66-77.

[17]Nārāyaṇ Singh Bhāṭī, ed., *Mīrābāī rī Paracī va Paracī Kāvya* (Jodhpur: Rājasthānī Shodh Sansthān, 1984). The text is also discussed by Prabhāt, *Mīrābāī*, pp.77-80 and Hukum Singh Bhāṭī, *Mīrābāī: Itihāsak va Samājik Vivechan*, pp.48-51. Based on textual evidence, Prabhāt reports that Sukhasāraṇ may have been a member of the Rāmsnehī Sampradāy writing in the early half of the eighteenth century CE, but he admits that the text may have been composed at a later date. Vikram Singh Gundoj says nothing is known about Sukhsāraṇ ("Rājasthānī Paracī Kavya - Ek Paricay," in *Mīrābāī rī Paracī va Paracī Kāvya*, p.87), while H.S. Bhāṭī follows Prabhāt (p.48). The dates on the two manuscripts used for the version published by Rājasthānī Shodh Sansthān are 1877 CE and 1882 CE.

[18]Nāgrīdās, *Padaprasangmālā*, text given by Vrajaratnadās, *Mīrā Madhurī*, pp.44-45. For a discussion of the text, see Vrajaratnadās, pp.42-48 and Bhāṭī, *Mīrābāī: Itihāsik va Sāmājik Vivechan*, pp.45-47. For background information on Nāgrīdās, see also McGregor, *Hindi Literature*, pp.158-59.

[19]He was a well educated member of the Rathors, who as Sāvant Singh had ruled in Kishangarh (Ajmer, Rajasthan) but renounced his kingdom and settled in Vrindavan.

[20]The *Vārtās* are traditionally said to have been composed by Gokulnāth (the fourth son of Vallabha's son Viṭṭalnāth) and then compiled and commented on by Harirāy. A paraphrase of the stories involving Mira and Govind Dube, Rāmdās, and Kṛṣṇadās is offered by Vrajaratnadās, *Mīrā Madhurī*, pp.33-34 and Bhāṭī, *Mīrābāī: Itihāsik va Sāmājik Vivechan*, p.52. The texts are also given by Prabhāt, *Mīrābāī*, pp.63-64 and discussed by Hiralāl Maheshvari, *Rājasthānī Bhāṣā aura Sāhitya* (Calcutta: Adhunik Pustak Bhavan, 1960), p.303. A full translation of the the story of Kṛṣṇadās with Harirāy's commentary can be found in Richard Barz, *The Bhakti Sect of Vallabhācārya* (New Delhi: Munshiram Manoharlal, 1992, originally published 1976), pp.213-214. For a detailed discussion of the text as a whole, see Barz, "The *Caurāsī Vaiṣṇavan kī Vārtā* and the Hagiography of the Puṣṭimārg" in Winand Callewaert and Rupert Snell, eds., *According to Tradition, Hagiographical Writing in India* (Wiesbaden: Otto Harrassowitz, 1994), pp.43-64.

[21]Kumkum Sangari, "Mira and the Spiritual Economy of Bhakti," *Economic and Political Weekly* (July 7 &14, 1990), p.1551.

[22]Explicit connections have been drawn between these widows and Mīrā by the women themselves and people coming to the ashram. Punjal Butalia has documented this in the film he directed about them entitled *Moksha* (film copyright held by Jane Balfour Limited, London) and affirmed it in more detail in personal communication, May 8, 1994. See also John Stratton Hawley's description of their life in *At Play with Krishna: Pilgrimage Dramas from Brindavan* (Princeton: Princeton University Press, 1981), pp.45-48.

[23]Sanjukta Gupta, "Women in the Śaiva/Śākta Ethos," in Julia Leslie, ed., *Roles*

and Rituals for Hindu Women (Delhi: Motilal Banarsidass, 1991); pp.202-204, 209.

[24]For examples of non-Vaiṣṇava women religious leaders, see June McDaniel, *The Madness of the Saints: Ecstatic Religion in Bengal* (Chicago: University of Chicago Press, 1989), pp.191-240 and Kathleen M. Erndl, *Victory to the Mother: The Hindu Goddess of Northwest India in Myth, Ritual, and Symbol* (Oxford: Oxford University Press, 1993), pp.105-134.

[25]June McDaniel, *The Madness of the Saints*, pp.192, 315 (note 3).

[26]Philip Lutengdorf gives the example of a Rāmāyaṇī (reciter of the *Rāmāyaṇa*) of Kanak Bhavan Temple in Ayodhyā called Ramsahay Sūrdās ("Sūrdās" having been added to his name as a sign of respect.) Lutgendorf, *The Life of a Text: Performing the Rāmcaritmānas of Tulsidas* (Berkeley: University of California Press, 1991), p.70. Edward O. Henry identifies "blind itinerant singers" as a particular classification of singers and notes that they are generally addressed as Sūrdās. Henry, *Chant the Names of God: Musical Culture in Bhojpuri-speaking India* (San Diego: San Diego State University Press, 1988), pp.159-160.

[27]See Karine Schomer's discussion of Mahadevi Varma as a modern Mira in *Mahadevi Varma and the Chhayavad Age of Modern Hindi Poetry* (Berkeley: Univerisy of California Press, 1983). For specific examples of widows called Mīrā, see Ann Grodzins Gold, *Fruitful Journeys: The Ways of Rajasthani Pilgrims* (Berkeley: University of California Press, 1988), pp.270, 288.and Hiralal Maheshwari, *History of Rajasthani Literature* (Delhi: Sahitya Akademi, 1980), p.152.

[28]A Reghar man in the village of Nagri, district Chittor, Rajasthan gave this as the primary reason why he would not name his daughter Mīrā; though he himself admired the saint, for others her name is a term of abuse (interview, May 18, 1993). This use of Mīrā's name in Mewar is commonly reported.

[29]The following account is drawn from three conversations with Kṛṣṇa Mā on February 26, 1993; August 14, 1993, and October 9, 1993. Her brother was present and guided the first conversation, but I talked with her alone on the other two ocassions. I was able to locate her only through the long-time friend of her family who first told me about her, although many other people remembered her from earlier years.

[30]Kṛṣṇa Mā, *Śrī Jugal Pad Bandan* (1980), *Ātmajā: Gadya Kāvya* (1983), and *Archnā: Brajbhāṣā Pad Sangrah* (1991), published by Janhit Prakashan, Mathura. *Ātmajā* is "prose-poetry" written in the style of prayers or letters to her Beloved while the other volumes contain traditional *pads*.

[31]Kṛṣṇa Mā, *Ātmajā*. p.3. In most lines all the terms begin with the same letter, but this alliteration could not be easily duplicated in translation, and I chose to privilege meaning over form in this instance.

[32]This account is drawn from several meetings with Mīrājī. The first was a for-

mal audience on June 30, 1993 in a village outside of Udaipur in the company of many other people including K. C. Shastri, the research director of Mīrā Kalā Mandir in Udaipur to whom I am deeply grateful for first introducing me to Mīrājī. He had learned of her from her brother who contacted him specifically about his sister. I spoke with Miraji again on August 17, 1993 and October 8, 1993 in Vrindavan at a Nimbārka temple in the company of her aunt. More recently I spoke with her alone on December 29, 1994 at her new ashram which is under construction on the outskirts of Vrindavan.

[33]K.C. Shastri reported to me that she had completed up to the fifth class based on earlier conversations he had had with her and her family. Personal Communication, June 30, 1993.

[34]The number of four to five hundred was given to me by K.C. Shastri, Personal Communication, June 30, 1993.

[35]Justin E. Abbott, trans., *Life of Tukaram: Translation from Mahipati's Bhaktalilamrita Chapters 25-40* (Delhi: Motilal Banarsidass, 1930, reprinted 1986), pp. 204-214.

[36]I was unfamiliar with the popular *ghazal* from which this song had been adapted and owe this observation to Komal Kothari, director of the Folklore Institute of Rajasthan (Rupayam Sansthan) in Jodhpur. Personal Communication, January 10, 1995. Unfortunately I do not have the full text of the *ghazal* for comparison. The well-known *pad* "*Hari mai tu prem diwānī*" ("Hari, I am mad for love") has a similar structure. Mīrā speaks of being mad for love and of only the one who has suffered the pain of injury knowing the pain of the wounded and only the jeweler knowing the value of the jewel. See *pad* 571 in Padmāvatī Shabnam, *Mīrā Bṛhat Pad Saṅgrah* (Banaras: Lok Sevak Prakāśan, 1952), p. 1952 and *pad* 70 in Paraṣurām Caturvedī, *Mīrābāī kī Padāvali* (Prayāg: Hindī Sāhitya Sammelan, 1989), p. 120.

[37]Komal Kothari provided the musical analysis of Mīrājī's song in this paragraph. Personal Communication, January 10, 1995.

[38]Mahatma Gandhi, *Bapu's Letters to Mira, 1924-1948* (Ahmedabad: Navajivan Trust, 1949); *Mirabehn* (Madeleine Slade), *The Spirit's Pilgrimage* (London: Orient Longmans, 1960). The Śaivite Mīrābāī was reported by Asīm Kṛṣṇadās, Personal Communication, October 10, 1993. Sri Aurobindo's primary female disciple was a French woman also by the name of Mira (Mira Paul Richards), although she apparently came to him already with this name and with time became known as the Mother. See Ashis Nandy, *The Intimate Enemy* (Delhi: Oxford University Press, 1983), pp. 36, 94-95.

[39]Indira Devi is an extraordinary example of an individual woman's encounter with Mīrā, and I have written extensively about her and the way that Mīrā's narrative functions as a transformative *līlā* for her in another chapter of my dissertation. She met Mīrābāī regularly in her meditative trances, bringing back songs, stories,

and teachings from the sixteenth-century saint. Her identity and that of Mīrā merged with time, and she emerged as a composer and religious leader in her own right. For an introduction to her life, see Dilip Kumar Roy and Indira Devi, *Pilgrims of the Stars: Autobiography of Two Yogis* (Porthill, ID: Timeless Books, 1973, reprinted 1985).

[40]Gopal Chundra Ghosh, librarian, Vrindavan Research Institute, Personal Communication, October 8, 1993.

[41]The following account is drawn from conversations with "Mīrābāī" on August 3, 1993 and August 15, 1993 in the presence of one of her female companions within their temple home. I also observed her on a number of ocassions at various public functions in Vrindavan.

[42]Robyn Beech, Personal Communication, December 28, 1994.

[43]Mīrā Mātājī's story was first told to me by devotees in Udaipur in May of 1993. I learned more about her and her community from devotees in Salumbar at Mīrā Satsang Bhavan on September 23, 1993 and finally met Mīrā Mātājī herself and her primary disciples in Vrindavan on October 9-10, 1993. She confirmed the story I had previously been told. I met these women again on December 29-30, 1994.

[44]Ārati is a form of worship in which candles or lamps are waved in front of the object of veneration.

[45]Srī Pujya Mātājī Mahārāj Lakṣmī Bāī, *Śrī Rādhā Kṛṣṇa Bhajanāvalī*, n.d. This text was published before 1982 because I was shown a copy by people who had not seen Mīrā Mātājī since then. At least one more collection has been published more recently, but I have not yet been able to obtain a copy.

[46]The Bhil woman's devotion is also celebrated in a *pad* of Mīrābāī, translated beautifully into English by John Stratton Hawley and Mark Juergensmeyer, *The Songs of the Saints of India* (Oxford: Oxford University Press, 1988), p.137.

[47]Lakṣmī Bāī, *Śrī Rādhā Kṛṣṇa Bhajanāvalī*, #126, p.30.

[48]Ibid., #45, p.11

[49]Ibid., *bhajans* 21, 203; 118, 300, 14, 273; 36; 46, 125, 268.

[50]I was told by devotees in Salumbar that this was so (September 23, 1993). I did not spend enough time with them to see whether or not other *bhajans* are in fact sometimes included when people gather to sing. Certainly singing only Mīrā Mātājī's songs was a part of their self-identity as her followers.

[51]Mīrā's story has entered the *līlā* performance tradition in Vrindavan, and I have written about this in more detail within my dissertation.

[52]Such dramas include not only līlās but also folk dramas such as the Marwari *khyāls* of Lacchirām and Punim Chand Sikhwāl both entitled *Mīrā Mangal* or

"Mira's Marriage."

[53]Reported by devotees in Salumbar, September 23, 1993.

[54]H. H. Wilson, *Religious Sects of the Hindus* (Calcutta: Susil Gupta, 1861, reprinted 1958), pp.78-79. The editor of the volume, Ernest R. Rost, points out in a preface that most of Wilson's sources were textual (p. vii). Wilson gives no reference for his statements about this Mīrābāī sect, and elsewhere he uses the term "sect" rather loosely. He suggests that Sūrdās is "almost entitled to be considered as the founder of a sect, as blind beggars carrying about musical instruments, to which they chant stanzas in honour of Vishnu, are generally called Sur Dasis" (p.32). He also writes of "Sena Panthis," although he acknowledges that only the name of this break-away sect remains.

[55]Monika Thiel-Horstmann, "The Bhajan Repertiore of the Present-day Dādūpanth", Thiel-Horstmann, ed., *Bhakti in Current Research, 1979-1982* (Berlin: Dietrich Reimer, 1983), pp.395-396.

[56]G. N. Sharma, *Bhakta Mīrābāī* (Udaipur: Mīrā Kalā Mandir, 1990), p.52; and Sharma, Personal Communication, April 30, 1993.

[57]This has been discussed in detail by Lindsey Harlan, *Religion and Rajput Women: The Ethic of Protection in Contemporary Narratives* (Berkeley: University of California Press, 1992) and Parita Mukta, *Upholding the Common Life: The Community of Mirabai* (Delhi: Oxford University Press, 1994).

[58]The proliferation of Mīrā parks, Mīrā statues, and Mīrā festivals in Udaipur and Chittor in recent years attests to the incorporation of Mīrā into an emerging Rajput/Rajasthani identity.

[59]Lawrence A. Babb, *Redemptive Encounters: Three Modern Styles in the Hindu Tradition* (Berkeley: University of California Press, 1986), pp.93-155.

[60]Ramanujan, "On Women Saints." See note 10.

[61]June McDaniel, *The Madness of the Saints*, p.265.

[62]See Donna M. Wulff, *Drama as a Mode of Religious Realization: The Vidagdhamādhava of Rūpa Gosvāmī* (Chico: Scholars Press, 1984); David Haberman, *Acting as a Way of Salvation: A Study of Rāgānugā Bhakti Sādhana* (Oxford: Oxford University Press, 1988); and the *Journal of Vaiṣṇava Studies 1, 3* (Spring 1993) focusing on "Rāgānugā Bhakti/Visualization." Āṇṭāḷ might be cited as a counter example from Vaiṣṇava tradition, but her marriage to Viṣṇu at a young age also marked the end of her physical life as she merged with his image at Śrīraṅgam.

[63]Kumkum Sangari, "Mirabai and the Spiritual Economy of Bhakti," p.1551.

[64]Kathleen M. Erndl, *Victory to the Mother*, pp.105-134.

"WHERE'S MY BELOVED?" MĪRĀBĀĪ'S PREM BHAKTI MĀRG

Andrew Schelling

I.

Two poets linked across centuries by the act of translation develop a perilous intimacy. I want to speak a word about this intimacy, about the intricate wildness, about the unpredictable responses poets provoke from each other. I want to consider why the song of a poet from a far distant time or culture sings to contemporary ears, and how this kinship called translation, forged across centuries, can only imperfectly be explained by scholarly expertise. I am not being vague or mystical. It is with gravity and reverence I bow my head to the task of scholarship. Any act of translation should be founded on as much discipline as possible in the language, culture, biography, hagiography, poetics and prosody of the poet you would work at. Every book you arm yourself with, every shop-talk you engage a colleague in, plays its indispensible role. Knowing your facts—basis for the tough task ahead. But beyond all the tools of the scholar's trade, beyond the expertise acquired through long hours of difficult labor, lies the adventurous realm to which few maps or guidebooks can lead you.

Expanding on a term the Sanskrit poets once used, I call this the realm of "twilight speech." A place in language where two poets divided by centuries meet, and between them conceive something new. An extreme statement? The translator as much as the artist shares with the archaic figure of the shaman an ability to cross boundaries that ordinarily seem impermeable. Boundaries between cultures, boundaries between languages, between oral and written literatures, between this world and the other, between life and death. This is the field. And still, there is a further crossing a few of us take—between genders. In many archaic cultures this was considered qualification enough to endow you with shamanic vestments.

I had known the name Mīrābāī for some years but hadn't given her much thought. It was 1985, a year our nation declared "Festival of India." Cultural magazines ran regular features on India, and in Washington a massive event moved into full swing—concerts, camels, traveling museum shows, jugglers and craftspeople flown in for the occasion, storytellers and dancers. My friends at the metaphysical bookstore in Berkeley asked me if I knew any good translations of Mīrābāī. They were besieged with requests for Kabīr and Sister Mīrā—the two Indian poets with any reputation among American readers. But upon hearing the singer Lakshmi Shankar perform two Mīrā bhajans that year, I wrote a sharp essay, arguing that if you wanted the art of Mīrābāī you should go direct to the singers—they are the ones, not the scholars and theologians (though these have performed fine and indispensible work), who risk themselves on each song. They are the ones negotiating the delicate griefs and savage ecstasies you arrive at through Mīrābāī's music. In Lakshmi Shankar's renditions, later in those by M.S. Subhalakshmi, Kishori Amoonkar and others, I came to a flash of recognition no translated bhajan on the page had delivered.

Then a few years ago a publisher asked me to translate several Mīrābāī poems—to accompany one of my essays. I was dubious, afraid Mīrā's words once laid out on the page would turn cold, inert, like the printed lyrics of a great blues singer divorced from a singer's voice. But something intrigued me—I sought out a cultured acquaintance whose business interests had made him adept in contemporary Hindi. I armed myself with my Sanskrit books, every available Hindi dictionary, and the recordings of Mīrā I could track down. We set to work, in every instance going to the singers to get a cue to the song, listening in particular to the weave of their lyrics.

After a few weeks of work together my friend withdrew—something in my demeanor alarmed him? But he had provided me a working knowledge of Mīrā's old Rajasthani. With that elemental grounding, a Mīrā *kosha* (wordbook), a battery of research material, and the expertise I carried in Sanskrit, I went into the music, into the books, began to live and breathe and eat and sleep with Mīrābāī. I would wake up with her words and my words mixed in my head. The shape of a poem that at the writing desk seems grey and obtuse, will often display itself clearly in sleep. One night I had a particularly explosive dream in which Mīrā appeared, her figure luminously merged with the woman I'd recently fallen in love with. The next day I recorded the dream in a notebook. To a traditional artisan from India, such a dream would come as a sign that the work had the gods' approval.

> And dream'd my friend L, her hair feathered raven—
> shifted from frame to frame of the dream,
>   or was it from room to room drifted,
> dancing, striking both ends of an earthenware drum.
> *Pakhaavajam mirdang*—
> slung by a sash over the shoulder, its skins sensitized
> with a paste of wet flour.
> The same as Mīrābāī carried, whose thin *nagari* letters and abductive
>   melodies
> for weeks had consumed
>   the waking hours—
>
> Then awoke to bright snow, ice over the mountains....

From the Agni Purāṇa: *O Lord of gods, teach me in dreams how to carry out the work I hold in my mind.*

And from Ananda Coomaraswamy: *The artist* (sādhaka, mantrin, or yogin, as he is variously—and significantly—called), *after ceremonial purification, is to proceed to a solitary place...on pronouncing the dhyanam mantram, in which the attributes are defined, the divinity appears visibly, "like a reflection," or "as in a dream" and this brilliant image is the artist's model.*

II.

Most accounts agree Mīrābāī was born about 1498 into a Rajput clan, the Rathors, who ruled the city of Merta and it surrounding villages. Her great grandfather on her father's side, Jodhaji, had founded the city of Jodhpur, still one of Rajasthan's centers of handcraft and trade. Her grandfather, Dudaji, had conquered the city of Merta along with 360 surrounding villages, and gave Mīrā's father, Ratnasingh, twelve of them, including Kudki where Mīrā was born into a small but lavishly equipped fortress.

It was a troubled time politically. Ruthless warrior clans battled each other over territory and trade. They regarded each other with too much suspicion to unite against the Moghul rulers who kept their seat of Empire in Delhi. But they could forge a rough temporary alliance, and fight fiercely, when threatened by foreign armies. Unsteady alliances kept everyone edgy. If you visit any of the old Rajput palaces, ask to see its armory of inventive and gruesome weapons—blades and cudgels, cutters and impalers, enormous scissor-like slashers—you'll get some idea how warfare and battlefield honor gripped the imaginations of the powerful ruling families, and with what fervor those families carved up the available territories among themselves.

The Rajputs exact a strict loyalty from their wives and sisters. Between the exogamous Rajput clans, that pride themselves on the sexual virtue and exaggerated modesty of their women, marriage had one principal objective—the securing of military alliances. So, following the day's custom, Mīrā's family prepared to marry her into a neighboring clan, the Sisodiya Rajputs of Mewar, in order to stabilize the local politics and perhaps avert a blood feud. Yet as a princess, born to privilege and being readied for a politically consequential marriage, Mīrā would have been exactingly tutored in a variety of arts. She studied music, poetry, dance; perhaps theatre and painting. Judging by the savviness of her poetry and how it rings with the verse of the past, I suspect a good deal of the old Sanskrit language with its classical poetry got into her ear. She could ride and probably shoot a bow. As for the martial arts, she would have known them intimately—if only by observing the far-out arrogant swagger of the family warriors she grew up with. These were wild-minded people.

Legend has it that as a small child Mīrā answered the palace gate to give food to a *sādhu*—a wandering religious beggar—who whispered a few words in her ear and pushed into her fist a tiny statue of Krishna which she treasured for the rest of her life. In a few of her songs she announces receiving "the words" of a guru. Since there exists no account of her having ever taken a teacher, or undergoing formal instruction, tradition ascribes to those few whispered words all the teaching she ever required. Who was the *sādhu*? Nobody knows. But one day Mīrā in girlish curiosity pestered her mother about who she'd be married to. (Every Rajasthani girl knows this is the great event her childhood prepares her for.) Her mother in jest or exasperation swept her hand toward the little Krishna image. "To him. Krishna will be your groom." From that moment on Mīrā considered herself married to Krishna, whom she addressed by the tender name Shyam—the Dark One.

When Mīrā arrived at the fortress of her new family by marriage, wed to Bhojraj, son of the fearsome warrior Rana Sanga, she ran into immediate trouble. By customary law the bride belonged to the Sisodiyas—Mīrā was in effect their property. In her songs when she twists things around and speaks of being sold off at the market, it's no simple metaphor. She felt the raw humiliation that arranged marriages can mean for a woman. She had a reputation for beauty, for the poise and elegance she'd cultivated, for her learning, her pride. But no one was prepared for the uncompromising independence she could show, the demands for artistic, spiritual, sensual freedom.

The equally proud members of the Sisodiya clan were Shaktas—worshippers of the Goddess—and by tradition Mīrā was expected to assume their style of worship. More precisely, by the old institution of *suhag*, her religious duties were to be discharged in unquestioning service to her husband. She simply refused to carry them out. One account tells how she dutifully touched her mother-in-law's feet but lightly walked past their Goddess image, saying she'd been sold into the hands of the true god and couldn't bow to a lump of stone.

Compounding the indignity, Mīrā insisted that Shyam, pledged to her lifetimes ago, was her true husband—Shyam, the dark-skinned mischievously seductive, adolescent flute-playing form of Krishna. Mīrā, the stories say, refused to sleep with her husband. Details about her Bhojraj remain sketchy—only in recent years have scholars managed to get clear who he was. Probably a bit weak-minded for a warrior he scarcely figures in the Mīrābāī legends. It's likely he died on the battlefield shortly after their wedding.

Mīrā refused to wear widow's weeds though, and rejected every convention of widowhood. She took to singing and dancing, dedicating these acts to Shyam—who she addressed in the most intimate terms—her songs plead and adore, badger, scold, weep. Overstepping all propriety she would regularly descend from the Sisodiya palace into town, where she consorted with sādhus and low-caste bhaktas (worshippers) in local temples. Her in-laws were enraged. Vikram Singh, a brother-in-law who had succeeded his father as clan leader and prince, suspected her sādhu compatriots as spies—engaged by rival clans or hostile military powers. He saw Mīrā as their contact in Mewar. And in a reflex of paranoia he imagined her songs to be coded messages detailing vital military secrets. Legend holds that after failing to subdue Mīrā by posting a guard at her door in the palace, Vikram Singh and his mother attempted on three occasions to kill her.

First they offered her consecrated water, saying it had been used to wash the feet of an image of Krishna; they'd in fact laced it with lethal poison. In one of her most famous songs—*pad gunghru bandh*—Mīrā declares she "drained the cup without missing a step." Her in-laws then sent her a wicker-basket of fruit, a deadly black cobra hidden under its lid. But when Mīrā opened the basket she found a *shālgram*—one of the black fossilized ammonites found along the Gandaki River which worshippers recognize as a form of Vishnu. Her in-laws in a final attempt on her life forced her to lie on a bed of razor-sharp spikes. Somehow the spikes as she lay on them turned into flower petals. Three attempts on her life, three times, say her admirers, Mīrā's god had interceded to save her. Or as the more cold-eyed among us suspect, secret allies in the palace replaced each lethal substance with an inert substitute. Certainly the day's politics were complex—agents and counter-agents threaded the countryside. And Mīrābāī would have been a precarious target—her songs, her blatant disregard for convention, her razor-tongued defense of the downtrodden—these had earned her some notoriety as a quite reckless saint who treated the poor and outcaste with memorable tenderness. One also suspects her old Rathor family ties remained considerable.

Trust in god but keep your powder dry. Mīrā's god might keep a close eye out for her, but Mīrā knew the next step. She quickly fled the Sisodiya territories, took to the road on foot, fled the excessive pride and wealth that shackled her, the calculating in-laws, the mediocre religion and the subservient widow's role expected of her. And she spent the rest of her life wandering the forests, villages, highways and temples of north India, pursuing a phosphorescent love affair with her god. A god that seems always a few villages out ahead of her pursuit—flirting or sleeping with some other woman.

III.

At this point even legend gets hazy. Accounts of Mīrā's wanderings take her through much of Rajasthan and Gujarat, and into the Vaishnavite grounds known as Madhuban, "Forest of Sweet Delights." According to reliable accounts, her brave and tender songs passed like quicksilver among bhaktas, and fame followed her wanderings. Cycles of legend grew up around her. Unlike most of the renowned bhaktas who sing their devotion to some form of the god Vishnu—men like Sūrdās and Tulsīdās come to mind—Mīrā's songs hold no subtle theological arguments, are decked out in no ornamentation. They cut to the quick—amorous, hungry, full of ecstasy or tossed with despair. This is her wildest contribution, to my mind what sets her apart from the well-known men of her era—in her song she reanimates India's old tradition of love poetry, and recklessly sweeps it up into religious conviction.

Mīrā reaches some indescribably elemental point in each of her songs. She speaks as a lover reduced to wreckage from the passion she feels. That she reached such a condition, and sustained it for years, without eliminating her human intelligence—this is what makes her song so explosive. She condemns injustice, pride, power. In her concern for the downtrodden she argues for what in the West we call an "intentional community"—a communalist, idealist, antinomian, deliberately poor family of religious beggars, the bhaktas. Yet her most conscious artistic device was not to fit political vision to song—she simply rekindled the old literary genre at which India had excelled for centuries—the love poem.

The earliest classical poetry appeared in India nearly 1500 years before Mīrā's birth. The Prakrit *Gatha-Sattasai*, compiled by King Hala of the Satavahana Dynasty, contains 700 two-line poems, most of them amorous. Cited by Indian scholars and poets over the centuries, the *Sattasai* poets established the tones, rehearsed the gestures, and set forth the passions every generation of poets in India has renewed.

> "The nearly intolerable longing for an absent lover; the thrill of braving perilous weather and animals, or the censure of neighbors and relatives, in order to meet the beloved in some wild trysting place; the appearance of rain clouds marking the end of India's insufferably hot, dusty 'riot' season; the quickening of parched vegetation and sluggish wildlife by monsoon rain."

The season of rain—from the start it's the season of love in India's poetry. Add to it all the peacock's shrill scream, the far off clashing of thunder, a fragrance of blossoms stirred and then torn by the wind, and the haunting song of the Indian cuckoo (*papaiya*: *Cucculus nelanoleucus*). With these Mīrābāī sets out her scene.

bādlā re the jal bharāṁ ājyo

Come to me, cloud
bursting with water—
O secret friends
a drumming of rain, but listen,
the cuckoo is crying!
Thunderbolt music—
fresh wind—
ply after ply of cloud in the heavens.
Today my lover arrives
and I beg you to sing for him....

But the feral passion she sings of, from which nothing can block her, is a state almost unknown to the older secular tradition. The Sanskrit poets stayed coy and evasive. An anguished woman, awaiting her lover's arrival, appears in so many old poems! But those women suffer on their cots, or secretly weep to an intimate friend. A few anthologized verses toy with a parallel between the woman parted from her lover (*viyogini*), and the female ascetic (*yogini*). But Mīrā took the charming old trope and spit poetic fire into it—nothing like this had occurred—

Karṇāṁ suni śyām meri

Hear my plea, Dark One, I am
your servant—
a vision of you has driven me mad,
separation eats at my limbs.
Because of you
I'll become a yogini and ramble
from city to city
scouring the hidden quarters—
pasted with ash, clad in a deerskin,
my body wasting
to cinder.
I'll circle from forest to forest,
wretched and howling—

O Unborn, Indestructible,
come to your beggar!
Finish her pain and touch her
with pleasure!
This coming and going will end,
says Mīrā,
with me clasping your
feet forever.

Vipralambha—the separation of lovers. Conjuring desertion, desolation, intolerable anguish. In the hands of the old Sanskrit poets hundreds of tiny scenes raise this mood, enough to make you weep—the fevers and sweating, thin pale limbs, desperate dreams, even a feverish ramble under the moon. But nothing that approaches the spiritual ruin Mīrābāī voices. One of her finest songs—

Jogi mata jāa, mata jāa

Yogin, don't go—
at your feet a slave girl has fallen
She lost herself
on the devious path of romance and
worship,
no one to guide her.
Now she's built
an incense and sandalwood pyre
and begs you to light it.
Dark One, don't go—
when only cinder remains,
rub my ash over your body.
Mīrā asks: Dark One,
can flame twist upon flame?

Mīrā's rebelliousness, her swift condemnation of injustice towards women, her mockery of institutionalized religion, these brought notoriety to her. But in some songs she mocks even the complete outsider—the yogin, who has renounced all the attachments of sexual love. She saw her beloved Shyam as a wandering yogin, off on a journey part pilgrimage, part infidelity—and herself as a yogini—or hopeful bride—born again and again, tracking him through the ages, to consummate their love. She shows something girlish and coy—until the desolation we call reality strikes—

jogiyārī prītṇī hai dukhṇā re mūl

Take a yogin
for lover, get nothing but grief.
He beguiles you with intimate whispers—
    all worthless.
Sister, he plucks your flower
like a sprig of jasmine,
then pulls on his robe and is gone.
Mīrā says, Dark One,
I saw you once,
    but tonight I'm an utter wreck.

Driven mad by her longing—in the songs that's how she puts it—but overstepping all modesty, to take up a drum and sing her madness aloud to the world. To herself she applies the word *bavri*—(etymologically the same word as *Baul*, taken by noted "crazy wisdom" singers of Bengal several centuries later).

Mad, raked by separation—
drifting from country to country—
look at Mīrā's black hair
    it's turned white.

This is the madness of the *prem bhakti mārg*—the path of romance and worship she calls devious (*nyaro*). A wild path, a pathless path to a place no map can show you. Not a path to salvation, it seems the farther you travel it, the more hopeless your station, the more pointed the anguish, the deeper the desolation.

By her fiftieth birthday, Mīrā had come to reside in the coastal Gujurat city of Dwarka. In Dwarka stands the Ranchorrji temple, one of India's four cardinal destinations of pilgrimage, the sea beating against its rear doors. At least one biographer suggests Mīrā set up a soup kitchen and hospice at the temple where she could attend to the poor. Back in her homeland the Sisodiya clan meanwhile had suffered a series of devastating military reversals—one account says 13,000 women in Sisodiya territory immolated themselves on a pyre to keep from falling into the hands of the enemy. Rumor flared through the region's population, saying the defeats had come as divine retribution for Sisodiya mistreatment of Mīrā. Confronted with a possible revolt in their domains, Mīrā's in-laws decided to bring home their princess, to manipulate Mīrābāī's reputation in order to stabilize their rule. They sent an envoy of civic officials and priests off to fetch her.

Confronted with a return to the life she'd rejected years ago, Mīrā requested a final night alone in the temple of her god. In the morning the envoy broke down the doors which had been locked from within. All that remained—draped across the feet of the deity—were Mīrā's robe and her hair.

IV.

I have cast the work of translating Mīrābāī's song into religious terms. But I doubt for a North American it is Mīrābāī's religion that will keep her verse vivid. The bhakti she assumed so unquestioningly, so lightly, with such dignity and fervor—to most North Americans these would be a crabbed, cumbersome affair—a flash of historical emotion, exotic and deeply dependent on specifics to the culture of India. So what sends us back to her songs? Mīrā's ferocious indictment of inequity wherever she met it? Our own brand of secularism with its hunger for heroic personages? Not these alone. What survives, what will carry into the next millenium, is Mīrābāī's passion—and her art. The poetry. Five hundred years after her birth, on a continent half a world away, the notion of pursuing a raven-skinned god through the forests (now mostly turned desert) of north India could only appeal to a few. The poetry remains. The intelligence that animates her song and keeps non-Hindus responsive is something I can't give any other term than *poetry*.

I'll say it again. To listen to Mīrābāī's song and understand it as simply an expression of Indian religion is to fence in some terribly wild thing. Those songs reach through bhakti, reach back through medieval India, stretching into paleolithic times and even across species, back to the same impulse that makes every mammal and songbird cry out its instinctual urges in a voice half woven of ecstasy, half of grief. A religion of birds and mammals? My friend Carole Koda, an expert birdwatcher, tells me that most every birdsong takes as its theme, "Where's my beloved?" This was Mīrā's theme. It is the wildness in her—the cricket, the cuckoo, the alley-cat. Maybe this is why no major religious cult has developed out of her bhajans. Hers is the wildness of forest and field, backlane and market, and from an excess of affection I'd hate seeing it tamed, isolated into some sectarian religion. The religion of forest and field is older than Varanasi—older than Jerusalem or Mecca—older than Mesopotamia. It is the creed held by every lover who wakes to the first cold light of dawn. The oldest religion, the most irreducible, one that in a saner world would be self-evident. Passion, heat, amusement, intelligence, song.

Mīrā walks with those who've composed the world's durable poetry. Her song is like Dante's—readers do not go to him, year after year, out of any particular liking for his Christian cosmology or crippling sense of damnation. We read Dante for the poetic spark, the sharply etched detail, the incorruptible song.

ch'io ho veduto tutto il verno prima
il prun mostrarsi rigido e feroce,
poscia portar la rosa in su la cima; *(Paradiso xiii: 133)*

for I have seen first, all the winter through, the
thorn display itself hard and forbidding, and
then upon its summit bear the rose;

Americans who carry no more than a distant anthropological interest in raven-hued Krishna nonetheless take to Mīrābāī's verse like a religious man to scripture—or a horse to water. Each of her songs carries at least one detail freighted with musical emotion. And the burden, heard or only half heard in each, is the old one—"*Where's my beloved?*" The wildest cry of every species on earth. This is the primary religion—Mīrā herself heard it—she suffered its heat—she gave it durable song—

papaiyā mhārī kab rau

Why this impulse
to hurt me, O cuckoo?
I was in my own
hut asleep
when you cried out a love song—
rubbing salt in the wound.
There you sat,
high on a tree branch,
singing from deep
in your throat—

WOMEN SAINTS IN GAUḌĪYA VAIṢṆAVISM

Jan Brzezinski

According to eminent Bengali historian, Ramakanta Chakravarti, "One of the positive results of the Caitanya movement was the elevation of the social and religious status of women in Bengal. This remarkable development was first seen in the assumption of ecclesiastical leadership by Jāṇhavā Devī, second daughter of Sūryadāsa Sarkhel and second wife of Nityānanda,"[1] This is only one view—a respected one, to be sure—but there are other perspectives as well. In fact, it has become something of a cliché amongst feminist analysts to state that the worship of goddesses has no proven relation to any amelioration in the status of women in the society in which such worship is conducted. In a cross-cultural study of women in religion, it has been observed that, "Quite frequently, the very aspects of women glorified in a religious system are used as justification for the social and political denigration of women. Different ideological definitions and perceptions of men and women further the separation and isolation of women. Seldom does this work to women's advantage. Even when women are seen as spiritual, as in the nineteenth-century cult of true womanhood, the expression of such spirituality was believed best confined to the privacy of the domestic world."[2]

In its origins, it might be said that the Caitanyaite Gauḍīya tradition is no exception to this rule. In spite of the exalted place which it gives to a female deity, Rādhā, and to the feminine virtues, the Caitanyaite sect, at least in the vision of it presented by the Vrindavan Gosvāmīs and their followers, with its strong emphasis on asceticism, appears to have followed the Purāṇic traditions regarding women found in the *Bhāgavata*. However, a closer examination of the *Caitanya-caritāmṛta* shows that though women are clearly not given the status that men have, there is no overt misogyny. The heavy emphasis on the renunciation of sexuality and the dangers of involvement with women when engaged in the exercise of spiritual practices do not enjoin the hatred or denigration of women.

The case of Junior Haridās, described by Kṛṣṇadās Kavirāj in the *Caitanya-caritāmṛta*, is perhaps the most outstanding example of the strict standard of sexual segregation Caitanya expected of his renunciate disciples. The young renunciate Haridās was ostracized by Caitanya for having begged rice from an old woman, Mādhavī Devī, the sister of one of his most intimate associates, Śikhī Mahiti. Caitanya's adherence to a principle, to an ascetic standard irrespective of all extenuating circumstance, is highlighted by Kavirāj when he glorifies Mādhavī Devī for her own devotional achievements; he states that she is a member of Caitanya's most exclusive inner circle: the half of the three and a half most worthy recipients of his mercy in the universe.[3] Even so, of the various *Bhāgavata* verses which might have been chosen as authorities for such a strict standard, Kavirāj envisions Caitanya as quoting BhP ix.19.17, which places emphasis on the strength of the senses and the weakness of man rather than on the insidious sexuality of women:

> One should not sit alone with one's mother, sister or daughter.
> The senses are so strong that they can distract even a wise man.

On the other hand, that Mādhavī Devī is known as only "half a worthy" indicates rather clearly the sexual-political position taken by Kavirāj and the Vrindavan school of Caitanya Vaiṣṇavism. It should be noted, however, that Mādhavī Devī is unique in the biographies of Caitanya as a woman who is given credit for personal spiritual achievement—even though neither her devotion nor her age could rid her of the curse of being a danger to men who wish to free themselves of sexual desire.

Another comparable incident is found in the same biography: Caitanya is described as being overwhelmed emotionally upon hearing verses from the *Gītagovinda* being sung by a woman. He runs to embrace the singer, oblivious of her sex. Only when he is tackled by his servant Govinda Dās does he come to his senses and realize the magnitude of what he had been about to do.[4]

The exception which proves the rule is also given by Kavirāj. On one occasion in his later life, while Caitanya was taking darshan of Jagannāth in the midst of a crowd, an Orissan woman placed her feet on his back as she strained to get a look at the deity, entirely unaware of the impropriety of her action. Rather than condemning the woman, as his own disciples wished, Caitanya told them to leave her alone and let her drink in the vision of the Lord to her heart's content. He furthermore expressed a wish for a similar intensity of desire, saying, "Oh that fortunate woman! I worship her feet. By her grace may I also have such eagerness [to see Jagannāth]." It is significant, though, that Caitanya does not speak to her directly.[5]

In principle, however, it would be a mistake to judge the Caitanyaite attitude to women on the basis of the strict standards of behaviour shown by the ascetics who modelled themselves on Caitanya. The medieval bhakti movements in general showed a more democratic attitude to the practices of religion, giving equal rights to low castes, untouchables and women. Thus Balarāma Dās could sing that women of respectable lineage (to whom such a public display would have been anathema) danced publicly in the *saṅkīrtan* procession.[6] Quite in contrast to the findings of Sinclair cited above, Donna Wulff, based on her experience of modern feminist singers of *kīrtan* like Rādhārāṇī, has concluded that women in Bengal have always enjoyed a comparatively higher status than elsewhere in India and that this fact is both reflected in and supported by the existence of cults of feminine deities.[7] Nevertheless, the women whose biographies (or legends) are described briefly in this article are exceptional: women have only rarely exercised leadership roles for large numbers of Gauḍīya devotees of both sexes.

It is no doubt true that women of sahajiyā sects have higher status within their groupings (the above-mentioned Rādhārāṇī belongs to such a sampradāya), while the orthodoxy preserves a more conservative attitude to sexual relations. Even so, I believe it would be a mistake to attribute the elevated position and reputation of some of the women in orthodox Gauḍīya Vaiṣṇavism to the widespread influence of sahajiyā doctrines on orthodoxy. Indeed, orthodox Gauḍīya Vaiṣṇava women have excelled on their own, with little or no outside influence.

The history of women saints in the Gauḍīya tradition can be divided into roughly three periods which we shall call for convenience's sake, the early, middle and modern periods. The early period covers those women who were contemporary with Caitanya and whose stories are found in his biographies; the middle, those whose lives were described in the histories of the early post-Caitanya period, such as *Bhaktiratnākara, Premavilās, Anurāgavallī, Vaṁśīśikṣā, Muralīvilās,* etc. Finally, by the modern period I refer to the the 19th and 20th centuries. Despite the limited amount of information available, it is tentatively concluded that the status of women reached a high point in the middle period, when Jāhnavā Devī and others exercised considerable leadership.

I. Women in Caitanya's Life

Few of the women who figure in the Caitanya biographies are there as Vaiṣṇavas in their own right. They are devotees of Caitanya rather than Kṛṣṇa, and their high status in the hierarchy of Caitanya's associates is due primarily to the relation which they have to him. The category to which their affection belongs, seen in the light of Rūpa Gosvāmī's divine aesthetic, is that of *sambandhānuga;* they possess a love which though not without glory, is of an inferior variety because mundane relationships have not had to be sacrificed in order to achieve it. Caitanya's wives or mother are not renunciates of their social roles; it is rather through their relationship to Caitanya, their natural, human love for him, and indeed, the adherence to the ideal role as mother or wife, that they have come to be revered by Caitanya's devotees. In orthodox Gauḍīya Vaiṣṇavism, which is dominated by the Vrindavan spirit of erotic devotion for Kṛṣṇa, there is little or no devotion to Caitanya modelled on the love of Śacī, Lakṣmīpriyā or Viṣṇupriyā.[8]

In contrast to this relative lack of interest in the lives of Caitanya's wives and mother on the part of the Vrindavan-oriented Vaiṣṇava community, the Bengali people as a whole show an enduring attachment to them as the main *āśrayas* or "vessels" of emotion in dramatizations of his life, which traditionally end with his renunciation, "Nimāi-sannyās." The telling of this story in the *Caitanya-bhāgavata* of Vṛndāvan Dās, and even more so in the influential Gaura-nāgara tradition of Vāsu Ghosh, Locan Dās and others, in many ways self-consciously parallels the tale of Kṛṣṇa's abandonment of his family and the *gopīs* in Vrindavan: Caitanya's departure is final—though he is alive, he is lost forever as a son and lover. Thus, as with Māthura-līlā, the dominant sentiment is that of separation and pity for those wounded by the departure of the object of love.

The primary difference, then, between these women and those who follow in the later periods, is in their emphasis on the human person of Caitanya himself rather than the god Kṛṣṇa, and their human love rather than the practice of asceticism and ritual devotion.

1. Śacī Devī

The stage for Caitanya's dramatic departure is set by describing Śacī Devī as an ideal mother, the worthy bearer of the incarnation. She is everywhere recognized to be identical to both Yaśodā and Devakī, the foster-mother and mother of Kṛṣṇa, respectively. Her glories are extensively described in the *Caitanya-bhāgavata,* where she is said to be devotion incarnate, mother of the universe, etc.[9]

Śacī was an educated woman, the daughter, wife and mother of scholars, and she demonstrated her learning in the metaphysical arguments she had with her precocious son. According to the biographers, she was privileged on several occasions to experience evidence of Caitanya's divine status. Vṛndāvan Dās describes her hearing the sound of the flute coming from the child Nimāi's mouth and then having a vision of his divine power.[10] In true *Bhāgavata* fashion, Śacī is not swayed from her purely maternal affection by any display of divinity on the part of her son. As he grew older, however, she was prepared to take instruction from him in the matter of religious practice, particularly when he told her to take up the Ekādaśī fast[11] and to accept his metaphysical explanations when he consoled her after his first wife Lakṣmīpriyā's death by snakebite.[12]

A rather significant incident is described in *Caitanya-bhāgavata,* when Caitanya, sitting on the seat of Viṣṇu as he was wont to do during his early ecstatic moments of identification with the god, states bluntly that Śacī has not achieved *premabhakti,* the ultimate goal of devotional practice and that which he had descended to earth expressly to distribute freely. Śacī had apparently committed an offense to Advaita Ācārya and was admonished by her son, who used the occasion to show the gravity of offenses to the Vaiṣṇavas. She again accepted her son's admonitions with good grace and according to Vṛndāvan Dās was given *prema* after having followed his instruction and having asked forgiveness of Advaita.[13]

After Caitanya's departure for Puri, Śacī is described in the *Caitanya-caritāmṛta* making offerings to her deity. Rather than meditating on her Gopāl deity, she thought of how she used to feed her own son, Nimāi. She would then have most realistic visions of him eating the offering. When she arose from her meditation, she would observe that the plates on which the food had been offered were empty and would become confused thinking that she had fallen asleep and simply dreamt of her son's coming and that she had not made any offering at all. Her sense of reality completely distorted by the overwhelming absorption in love in separation, she would return to the kitchen to start her offering all over again. Caitanya sent messages on several occasions through associates of his travelling to Nabadwip to assure her that she was not going mad, but that he had indeed been going to Nabadwip to accept her offerings.[14] Kavirāj Gosvāmī follows Jīva in his use of the term *āvirbhāva* to refer to these objective manifestations of the Lord in his physical absence. Śacī's home was one of four places where such manifestations took place.[15]

2. Caitanya's wives

Caitanya's first wife Lakṣmīpriyā died young, while he was travelling in East Bengal. Not much more is said about her other than that she was a devoted wife who fulfilled her household duties on one occasion by herself cooking for a large group of monks who had been invited to eat at their house.[16] She is identified with Rukmiṇī in the *Gaura-gaṇoddeśa-dīpikā* (45-6).

Caitanya's second wife Viṣṇupriyā is given a more important place in the biographies as she was the wife who witnessed his transformation into an ecstatic. She is described as a devastated woman who had been helplessly losing her husband to a progressive obsession with the life of devotional commitment to Kṛṣṇa. Prior to her marriage, she led an exemplary life, bathing three times daily in the Ganges, but overall her character is not particularly well-developed in any of the Caitanya biographies, understandable in that she was probably not much more than twelve or thirteen years old at the time of her marriage and her separation from him not long thereafter. The wedding itself is described in a stereotypical fashion, with the usual hyperbole surrounding the opulence, etc., of the ritual. The pivotal event in her life was of course Caitanya's departure for a life of renunciation. Of Caitanya's biographers only Locan Dās in the *Caitanyamaṅgal* describes the couple as having spent the last night of their life together in the same bed.[17]

Several descriptions have been given of Viṣṇupriyā in the years which followed Caitanya's departure. Primarily the image is that of the ideal widow, carefully leading a pious life as was and is still generally expected of Bengali widows.[18] Though it does not seem as though she took an active leadership role in the devotional movement inaugurated by her husband, she nevertheless remained an icon and living place of pilgrimage during that time. Continuing to live and serve her mother-in-law Śacī, she adhered to a high standard of austerity which impressed the devotees of the movement. In the *Advaitaprakāśa* (Chapter 21), Caitanya's disciple Jagadānanda describes to him the daily activities of Viṣṇupriyā: She rose early each morning before daybreak with Śacī to bathe in the Ganges, but then remained indoors the entire day, never letting either the sun nor the moon shine upon her. The devotees would never see her face except when she came to eat, and no one heard her speak. She would only eat Śacī's remnants and spent all her time absorbed in the repetition of the Holy Names while looking at a picture of Caitanya as he looked before taking the renounced order of life.

Viṣṇupriyā Devī seems to have taken the *bhajan* path designated by Caitanya seriously. One of the most often repeated descriptions of her recounts that she counted each completion of the sixteen names of Kṛṣṇa by placing a grain of rice in a clay pot. When she had completed her daily meditation sometime in the early afternoon, she would cook, offer and then eat only those grains.[19] In the later histories of the movement, these descriptions show that her prestige amongst the followers of Caitanya had expanded beyond merely that of being his wife. She seems to have had a close friendship with Jāhnavā and was complicit in the adoption of Rāmacandra described below.

Moreover, Viṣṇupriyā inaugurated the worship of a Caitanya image around which numerous legends arose. It is said in the 17th century *Vaṁśīśikṣā*, a history of the Bāghnāpāḍā Gosvāmīs, that after Caitanya's renunciation, Viṣṇupriyā had abandoned food and drink until he appeared to her (and Vaṁśīvadanānanda Ṭhākur) in a dream, telling her to have an image of himself carved in the margosa tree under which Śacī had sat to suckle him. When the *mūrti* had been finished, Viṣṇupriyā sang the verse of Caṇḍī Dās: "Here is the lord of my life. I am finally able to see him for whom the arrows of desire have caused me to burn and come to the point of dying."[20] This same deity, known as Mahāprabhu, is still worshipped by the descendents of Viṣṇupriyā's cousin, Mādhava Ācārya, in Nabadwip where it remains the central focus of pilgrimage. Whatever worship of Caitanya in the mood of Viṣṇupriyā exists, such as that of Caitanya Dās Bābājī in the early part of this century, centers around the Mahāprabhu deity.

3. Sītā Ṭhākurāṇī[21]

The wife of Advaita, Sītā Ṭhākurāṇī, was a woman who, like her husband, lived a long life. It appears that after marrying Sītā, Advaita moved to Śāntipur. Nevertheless, most biographies of Caitanya tell that she was present at his birth ceremonies, and was even responsible for giving him the nickname, "Nimāi." It is said that she took some leadership responsibility after the death of her husband, but not much detail can be given about how she conducted herself in such a role.

According to the *Premavilās*, Sītā had a woman disciple, Jaṅgalī, about whom it recounts an interesting legend. It seems that she was fearless and engaged in solitary devotional practice in a jungle which was filled with wild animals like bears and tigers (hence her name). On one occasion the Shāh of Bengal was hunting in that area and saw her and was attracted by her beauty. When he attempted to rape her,[22] he was surprised to find that she had transformed into a man. The astonished king asked her whether she was a man or a woman. She answered cryptically, "Women see a woman, men see a man. But at no time ever have I been a man." The king remained confused. He sent a woman to examine Jaṅgalī and was told that she was indeed a woman, but when he sent a man, he was told she was a man. The astonished king realized that Jaṅgalī possessed some extraordinary powers and he fell at her feet and asked for forgiveness. After she forgave and blessed him, he built a large residence for her there in the woods which was known as Jaṅgalī Ṭoṭā.[23]

4. Other women contemporary to Caitanya

Only a few other women contemporary to Caitanya can be considered as having hagiological status in their own right. Mālatī Devī was the wife of Caitanya's associate Śrīvās Paṇḍit. She had an extraordinary relationship with Nityānanda, who treated her like his mother. Though she was past child-bearing age, her dried up breasts brought forth milk when the full-grown Nityānanda sat on her lap.[24]

Another woman worthy of mention is Nārāyaṇī, the mother of Vṛndāvan Dās (author of *Caitanya-bhāgavata*). She was Śrīvās Ṭhākur's niece, only a little girl at the time, who was present there on the occasion of Caitanya's *mahāprakāśa*, or great epiphany (CBh ii.10.229-235) and was given special attention by him. Another of Śrīvās's servants, Dukhī ("unhappy"), was privileged to observe Caitanya's nightly *kīrtan;* she would bring Ganges water for the Vaiṣṇavas to drink. She thus earned blessings from Caitanya and was given the name Sukhī ("happy") in place of her original name (CBh ii. 25. 11-23).

II. Second generation women

Though some of these women are junior contemporaries to the women associates of Caitanya, they are distinguishable from them by their personal charisma, their knowledge and practice of the religion founded by Caitanya and his inner circle, and the leadership roles they took in the proselytization of that religion.

1. Śrī Jāhnavā Īśvarī (16th century)

Karen Sinclair has observed that though women have attained great prominence in Hindu sects, it is generally as "Holy Mothers" or consorts of male religous adepts, and she gives Sarada Devi, the consort of Ramakrishna, and Aurobindo's "The Mother" as modern examples. In her view, in such circumstances, women are nominally venerated but their role is circumscribed, as is the case with the Virgin Mary in Christianity.[25]

In modern South Asia, as indeed elsewhere in the world, widows, daughters and sisters of martyred political leaders have risen to political prominence. Most of the early generations of Gauḍīya Vaiṣṇava women leaders are similarly related to earlier charismatic leaders of the movement. Of all these women, who are nevertheless not all that numerous, Jāhnavā, the wife of Caitanya's chief associate Nityānanda, stands out. A number of reasons might be conjectured for her rise to prominence. She was widowed, it would seem, when still fairly young. She had no children herself, but her nephew and stepson, Nityānanda's son Vīrabhadra (born of Vasudhā), was not yet of an age where he could exercise leadership in the dynastic system which was apparently envisioned as appropriate for the continuation of the movement. In the absence of another appropriate leader, Jāhnavā stepped in to fill the leadership void. Mary Katzenstein, in her analysis of the causes of the political prominence of women in India, has concluded that in societies where kinship plays an important role, in the absence of a regularized, stable system whereby succession of political leaders is assured, daughters, widows, or sisters are often called upon to lead.[26] Nevertheless, for any woman to succeed in a role of leadership in such circumstances, it would be necessary that she show qualifications of a more practical sort; simple relationship could only play a temporary role. It is quite clear that Jāhnavā won respect throughout the Vaiṣṇava community as well as constituting a strong influence on her two principle disciples, Vīrabhadra and Rāmacandra. She was known as Īśvarī, the feminine form of the commonly used word for God, Īśvara. At the very least, the term implies a great mastery over others. Narahari recounts in his *Bhaktiratnākara* that Yadunandan Dās and the other devotees gathered in Katwa as Jāhnavā made her way to Kheturi out of respect ate only after she had finished her repast.

Jāhnavā and Vasudhā were sisters, daughters of a brāhmaṇa scholar, Sūryadās Sarkhel, and nieces of Gaurīdās Paṇḍit, both of which brothers were significant devotees of Nityānanda and Caitanya in their own right. The two girls were given in marriage to Nityānanda, but Jāhnavā remained without issue while Vasudhā gave birth to two children: a girl, Gaṅgā, and a boy, Vīrabhadra. Though Jāhnavā was Vīrabhadra's stepmother, she played a more significant role in his spiritual development than did his natural mother. One legend is recounted in the *Nityānanda Vaṁśavistāra*[27] in which it is said that Vīrabhadra was seeking a spiritual master (having been orphaned before receiving initiation from his own father). In the course of his search, he approached Sītā Ṭhākurāṇī, the wife of Advaita, the third member of the Gauḍīya Vaiṣṇava divine triumvirate. She told him that he should seek closer to home, but Vīrabhadra was not convinced that Jāhnavā was sufficiently qualified to be his guru. On his return home, however, he saw his stepmother as she was completing her bath. While drying her hair, her wet sari slipped and in order to conceal her nakedness, she sprouted two extra arms to hold up the falling cloth. Vīrabhadra was impressed by this show of divinity and asked Jāhnavā to initiate him.[28]

Though some comparable epiphanies are related in legends about Nityānanda, there is a proliferation of such simplistic attempts at legitimizing the divine character of personalities in the later hagiographical histories of Caitanya Vaiṣṇavism. The *Nityānanda Vaṁśavistāra* also recounts that Vīrabhadra (identified as *īśvara* by Kṛṣṇadās [CC i.11.8] and as Kṣīrodakaśāyī Viṣṇu in the *Gaura-gaṇoddeśa-dīpikā*) manifested divine forms of this nature on various occasions during his preaching career.

Jāhnavā is not the only woman to have manifested a four-armed form. Stories similar to the one recounted above are also told about two other women in Gauḍīya Vaiṣṇava history. Nityānanda's powerful disciple Abhirāma Ṭhākur married a Muslim girl, an act which met with considerable criticism. Though some devotees were prepared to accept her presence in the church, they were certainly not ready to take food, not even *prasād*, from her hand. They were quieted when Rāmī sprouted extra arms to hold up the cloth covering her head which slipped as she was serving. Again, a similar story is told by Haridās Dās (*Gauḍīya-Vaiṣṇava Abhidhāna*, 1422) about Hemalatā Ṭhākurāṇī, the daughter of the important third generation Gauḍīya Vaiṣṇava leader Śrīnivāsa Ācārya. The legend about Hemalatā is particularly significant, not so much in its details, but rather in that, as with Jāhnavā, it confirms her personal authority as guru.

Vīrabhadra was not Jāhnavā's only important disciple. Other disciples of distinction begin with Rāmacandra Gosvāmī. Grandson of Vaṁśīvadanānanda Ṭhākur (mentioned above in connection with Viṣṇupriyā Devī), Rāmacandra was adopted by Jāhnavā after she gave the benediction to his father that he would have two sons. After the second son was born, when Rāmacandra was 11 or 12 years old (ca. 1545), Jāhnavā took him to live with her. Rāmacandra was given special treatment by his stepmother and guru, and to some extent became a rival to Vīrabhadra for her favours, accompanying her on her last trip to Braj. He later founded the Bāghnāpāḍā branch of Gosvāmīs through his nephew Rājavallabh's family; he himself never married.[29]

It would appear that Jāhnavā had imbibed some of the scholarship of her father and uncle, and it stood her in good stead when she began to take on the role of Nityānanda's successor. In *Muralīvilās*, Jāhnavā instructs Rāmacandra Gosvāmī in the details of the path of worship (*mañjarībhāve bhajan*) outlined by Rūpa Gosvāmī. Nevertheless, despite her personal scholarship, she does not seem to have given public discourses on scripture and was even self-effacing when in the association of male devotees. For instance, in Kheturi, she did not ascend to the podium with the associates of Caitanya and Nityānanda who were present there.[30]

Nor did she do anything more than act as an audience for *kīrtan*. On the other hand, she appears to have liked to cook for large numbers of devotees, herself serving them, and participated directly in deity worship, at least by offering foodstuffs. At Kheturi, she orchestrated many of the activities, such as the greeting (*satkār*) of the guests (BRK 10.511), the playing of *phāgukhelā*, etc.[31]

Perhaps Jāhnavā's most significant contribution was to the organization and character of Bengali Vaiṣṇavism as it endeavoured to deal with the theological sophistication of the Vrindavan Gosvāmīs. The event at which this took place was the famous Kheturi festival already mentioned above, the date of which is still a matter of conjecture, but likely took place in the 1570s. Her role there was to lend approval to the innovations in the practice of *kīrtan* as well as the theological formulations on the nature of Caitanya and his incarnation that Narottama and Śrīnivās Ācārya had brought with them from Vrindavan.[32]

Jāhnavā, doubtless impressed by the culture of the new leaders of the movement and the learning they had received at the hands of Jīva Gosvāmī, decided to go herself to Braj and witness firsthand the developments which had taken place there. Travelling with a large group of Vaiṣṇavas and being carried in a palanquin which protected her modesty, she led the undoubtedly rather impressive group which made the lengthy pilgrimage, taking between five and six months to make the trip. Narahari describes an incident which took place in a village en route. The residents of the village were Caṇḍī worshippers who mocked the group of Vaiṣṇavas when they saw them bowing to and touching the feet of Jāhnavā. Considering that by offering respect to Jāhnavā rather than to their local deity of Caṇḍī, the Vaiṣṇavas had committed a great offense, they vowed to slaughter the whole group of travellers. Caṇḍī, however, found this proposal unacceptable and appeared in an angry form to her worshippers in a dream and revealed to them the glories of Jāhnavā, saying,

> You rascals! You do not know the truth about her whom you look down upon and whom you have called a *brāhmaṇa* woman. She is the wife of Nityānanda-Balarāma, an object of respect even to me and worshipable by all. Her name, Jāhnavā Īśvarī, is exceedingly sweet. Simply by uttering this name, one can be freed from life's worries. She is the beloved of Nityānanda, the incarnation of compassion; she voluntarily distributes loving devotion to Kṛṣṇa to the living beings. Whoever worships her lotus feet and sings her glories will be delivered from the threefold sufferings.[33]

Caṇḍī concludes by telling the villagers to beg Jāhnavā for forgiveness; which they did. Jāhnavā converted them all to Vaiṣṇavism and stayed for several days in the village before moving on. Similarly, another miraculous event took place at another village where robbers thought to attack the group. They were unable to find Jāhnavā and her party of travellers despite knowing clearly their location. They too converted to Vaiṣṇavism when they realized that Jāhnavā was divinely protected.

On her way back home from Braj, she stopped with her entourage at the birthplace of Nityānanda in Birbhum. She made a second and perhaps even a third trip to Braj before the end of her life, ultimately dying there. It is said that while still alive, she had an image of Rādhā made and placed on the right-hand side of Gopīnāth in Braj, where an image of Rādhā already stood on the left. When she died, she is said to have entered into that deity, thenceforth known as Anaṅga Mañjarī.

Jāhnavā's apotheosis as Anaṅga Mañjarī, the sister of Rādhā, is perhaps what sets her apart from most other woman saints in Gauḍīya Vaiṣṇavism. The *Gaura-gaṇoddeśa-dīpikā* of Kavi Karṇapūra identifies her first with Revatī by virtue of her being the wife of Nityānanda [Nityānanda is identified with Balarāma whose wife is Revatī.], but recognizes the Anaṅga Mañjarī identification as well. Though Viṣṇupriyā is identified with Satyabhāmā, the wife of Kṛṣṇa in Dvārakā,[34] this identification is far less prestigious in the heavily Vṛndāvana-influenced Gauḍīya Vaiṣṇavism of later days than that of Jāhnavā with Anaṅga Mañjarī.

It was Jāhnavā's adopted son and disciple Rāmacandra Gosvāmī who developed the theology of Anaṅga Mañjarī in his short work *Anaṅga-mañjarī-sampuṭikā*.[35] Anaṅga Mañjarī has an ontologically special status in that she is both *mañjarī*, or maidservant to Rādhā, and *sakhī*, who enjoys dalliances with Kṛṣṇa in her own right. Furthermore, she is the consort of Balarāma on one hand, and identical with him in that metaphysical slight of hand known to Vaiṣṇava theologians which states that a power and its possessor are non separable.[36] Thus, Balarāma (= Nityānanda), who enjoys his own *rāsalīlā* with gopīs attached erotically to him, also enjoys access to the superior *rāsalīlā* enjoyed by Kṛṣṇa through his presence there in the form of Anaṅga Mañjarī. This bit of theological contortionism arises directly out of Jāhnavā's "conversion" to the higher standards of devotion established by the Vrindavan gosvāmīs. In order to give legitimacy to his line, it was now necessary to show that Nityānanda, who had always been understood to possess the friendly mood (*sakhyabhāva*), was also privy to the erotic mood as well (*madhurabhāva*). If Caitanya had come to distribute this type of love to all humans who had never before had access to it, then how could his most intimate associate and primary distributory agent be deprived of it?

Jāhnavā's exceptional status no doubt led to the common occurrence of maternal initiation in many Nityānanda-dynasty families. In some cases, such as the family of Prāṇ Gopāl Gosvāmī of Nabadwip, the tradition is that the sons are always initiated by their mother. Prāṇ Gopāl would say that when the power of the mercy of the guru was coupled with maternal love, an extremely powerful spiritual force was created.[37] The Gauḍīya Maṭh movement directed by Bhaktisiddhānta Sarasvatī fought strongly against the principle of disciplic succession from fathers to sons and even more vehement in its criticism of such inherited succession which involved female members. Even so, they too accepted Jāhnavā's legitimacy as a spiritual master in the line.[38]

Whatever the attitude of neo-orthodoxy to Jāhnavā, there is little to support Edward Dimock's contention that she was a sahajiyā, or in any way influenced by sahajiyās, nor that her adopted son was one. Nor is it necessarily true that the increased influence of women in Gauḍīya Vaiṣṇavism is a result of increased sahajiyā influence. It shows rather the potential power of women that was given the opportunity to develop when Caitanya instructed his chief lieutenant Nityānanda to return to Bengal and get married, thus giving increased legitimacy to the householder life. The Gauḍīya movement has always held that the renunciates and householders operate in separate spheres with different rules.

2. Gaṅgā Devī

Nityānanda's daughter. It is said that when she was born, Abhirām Ṭhākur came to prostrate himself before her. This, rather than being a sign of respect, was a test. Abhirām's prostrations were dangerous, and had nefarious results. Indeed, several of Vasudhā's other babies had died after Abhirām had made such shows of devotion. Gaṅgā, however, survived the test and was thus declared a greatly powerful woman and Abhirām even pronounced her to be the incarnation of the Ganges, writing a twenty-verse poem in her honour. According to *Gaura-gaṇoddeśa-dīpikā*, her husband Mādhava Chaṭṭopadhyāy was Śantānu in a previous incarnation. Their family took up residence in the village of Jīrāṭ on the western bank of the Bhagīrathī and their descendents continue to function as initiating gurus of Vaiṣṇavism.[39]

3. Hemalatā Ṭhākurāṇī

There is unfortunately an insufficient amount of information about Hemalatā Ṭhākurāṇī, the daughter of Śrīnivās Ācārya, one of the principle leaders of the second generation of Gauḍīya Vaiṣṇavism and contemporary of Jāhnavā. Hemalatā initiated many disciples, most important amongst whom is Yadunandan, a prolific poet and author, and she is best known for her role in ostracizing the leader of the early 18th-century sahajiyā challenge to Gauḍīya orthodoxy, Rūpa Kavirāj. It is said that she tore his *tulasī* beads from his neck to indicate that he was no longer eligible for commensality. Yadunandan writes about her exercise of authority in *Karṇānanda,* primarily a life of Śrīnivās Ācārya, which he wrote on her order.[40] Śrīnivās Ācārya's second wife Gaurāṅgapriyā also initiated several disciples.[41]

4. Kṛṣṇapriyā and Viṣṇupriyā

These two sisters represent a new type of woman in Gauḍīya Vaiṣṇava history: they were renunciates who practiced a life of intense asceticism and devotion comparable to those of the male monks in whose contact they themselves lived. Daughters of Narottama Dās's chief disciple Gaṅgānārāyaṇ Cakravartī, they were told by Narottam himself to take initiation from their father. They lived for some time at Rādhā Kuṇḍ in Braj. Their reputation was sufficient that Raghunāth Dās's Govardhanaśilā, which had been given to him personally by Caitanya, was entrusted to their care by Mukunda, the disciple of Kṛṣṇadās Kavirāj (who had received it from Raghunāth). This in itself was a highly unorthodox act which resulted in a certain amount of dissent in the conservative community.

According to the *Narottama-vilās* of Narahari, Kṛṣṇapriyā took a number of disciples, but ultimately had to disown one of them, Rūpa Kavirāj, who, for whatever motive, took the side of those who felt that her sex restricted her role in certain public religious acts. In particular, he objected to her presence in the assembly of men at the reading of *Bhāgavata.* The Vaiṣṇavas present all offered obeisance to her in the assembly with the exception of Rūpa Kavirāj who asked her how she, being a woman, could listen to the *Bhāgavata* reading, to which she answered, "It is the wagging of tongues that makes listening to the reading difficult, not my presence." This made Rūpa Kavirāj furious, but the result of his offensive behaviour was that *he* was forced to leave Vrindavan and return to Orissa, where he ultimately died a leper.[42]

5. Gaṅgā Mātā Gosvāminī

Again, little information can be found regarding this extraordinary 18th-century figure. Gaṅgā Mātā Gosvāminī was probably the first woman in

Caitanya Vaiṣṇavism who built a reputation as a devotee purely on the basis of her own learning and spiritual achievements and who founded her own spiritual "family."

Her original name was Śacī. Legend has it that she was a daughter of a rich landowner in Puntia in Orissa, and that she took initiation from Haridās Gosvāmī of Vrindavan.[43] On the orders of her spiritual master she went to Rādhā Kuṇḍ, where she lived for several years with her God-sister Lakṣmīpriyā. Afterward, she was again instructed by her spiritual master to establish herself in Jagannāth Purī, taking the so-called *kṣetrasannyās*. She took up residence at the home of Sārvabhauma Bhaṭṭācārya, an important disciple of Caitanya during his years in Purī. When she came there, there was only a *śālagrāmaśīla* named Rādhā-Dāmodara being served at this house. She gradually expanded the service.

Śacī gave discourses on the *Bhāgavatapurāṇa* which attracted large audiences. The king of Orissa, Mukundadeva, had a dream of Jagannāth who told him to make a donation of land for the service of the deity. Prior to this, Śacī had begged in order to maintain this service. Near the home of Sārvabhauma is a tank which is known as the white Ganges (Śvetagaṅgā) into which the water from the Jagannāth temple, including the water which is used for bathing Jagannāth, is drained. Once, on the auspicious occasion for bathing of Mahāvāruṇī, which takes place in the middle of the night, she was washed by the currents of the Ganges up to the gate of the Jagannāth temple. The temple guards thought that she was a thief and had her arrested. King Mukundadeva once again had a dream of Jagannāth who told him that he should set her free. Mukundadeva and many of the *sevayats* of Jagannāth eventually took initiation from her. Because she had been washed by the Ganges water which springs from the feet of Lord Jagannāth, Śacī became known by the name of Gaṅgā Mātā Gosvāminī.

The house of Sārvabhauma Bhaṭṭācārya is now more commonly known as Gaṅgā Mātā's Maṭh and is one of the major houses of Vaiṣṇavism in Purī. Several siddha-bābājīs were initiated in her line which traces its lineage back to Gadādhar Paṇḍit and wears the distinctive *nūpur* style *tilak*.[44]

III. Women saints in the modern era

The primary source of information for women saints of the modern period is O.B.L. Kapoor's Hindi *Braj ke bhakta*.[45] Altogether, there are only twelve woman saints described in *Braj ke bhakta*, of which five can be considered Gauḍīya. Though these women are respected for their saintliness, only one (Sādhu Mā) is a leader in the sense of being an initiating guru. It is no coincidence that she was born into one of the great Gauḍīya initiating families, that of Advaita Ācārya. Otherwise, the others were all also born in well-to-do families. Of the three women who were Bengali, all were *brāhmaṇas.*

All twelve women whose biographies appear in Kapoor's book are renunciates, showing perhaps more the bias of what that author expected a "saint" to be like, and thus are not necessarily representative of true saintliness. Taken as a whole, the women of *Braj ke bhakta* show, as might be expected, a decided tendency to the *vātsalya* or parental type of devotion. One outstanding exception to this is, of course, that of Śrīmatī Devī, whose taste leaned to the *sakhya* or "the friendly mood," as described below.

1. Piśimā Gosvāminī

Candraśaśī Mukhopadhyāy, later known as Piśimā Gosvāminī, is the only woman mentioned in Haridās Dās's Gauḍīya Vaiṣṇava Jīvanī.[46] Her story centers around the Gaur-Nitāi deities who are found today in Vrindavan in Banakhaṇḍī near Loy Bazaar. These deities belonged at one time to the childhood companion of Caitanya, Murāri Gupta, whose name is carved on the base of one of the statues. They were apparently lost at one time and later rediscovered in Siūri in Birbhum district in Northwestern Bengal. A wandering Orissan monk, Balarām Dās Bābājī, while passing through Siūri had a dream in which he was instructed to take over the service of the deities. Not long thereafter, the daughter of a wealthy landowner in Nadia district, Candraśaśi, at the time 20 years old, came to Siūri for business reasons. She became attracted to the deities and attended services regularly in the temple while there. One night she had a dream in which Gaur-Nitāi came to her in the form of young boys and said that they were very hungry and wanted her to feed them *khir.* Because she had not been initiated, Balarām Dās was not prepared to give food prepared by her to the deities, so she took initiation from him so that she could comply with Gaur-Nitāi's request.

A few days later, when she was about to leave Siūri for home, she had another dream in which Gaur-Nitāi begged her not to leave, for otherwise who would give them such good things to eat? Like children, they tugged on her skirts and even tore off a piece of her cloth. Candraśaśi awoke with a start and saw that her cloth was indeed torn. She went to Balarām Dās who found the missing bit of cloth in the hands of the deity of Gaur. From that day on, she abandoned any intention of returning home to her village and decided to stay on in the service of Gaur-Nitāi.

Not long thereafter, however, speculations about the nature of her relation with the monk Balarām Dās started in the town. Balarām Dās and Candraśaśi decided, again on the basis of instructions given to them in a dream, to take Gaur-Nitāi with them to live in Vrindavan. They placed the deities on a boat and made the 1600 km. trip along the Ganges and Jamuna to Braj. Candraśaśi, known in Braj as Piśimā ("aunt") managed to build a new temple in Bankhandi for the deities who became known locally as Piśimā's Gaur-Nitāi.

One of the interesting legends concerning Piśimā Gosvāminī is the following. One day, while preparing a meal for Gaur-Nitāi, whom she treated as her own children, her menses started, rendering her ritually impure for service to the deities. This interruption greatly distressed her. When she nodded off to sleep, Gaur-Nitāi came to her and told her that just as an ordinary mother does not interrupt her service to her own children while menstruating, neither should she. Furthermore, they assured her, she would be liberated from this discomfort from that day on. She bathed and made the food offering to the deities and never again experienced the female cycle.

Piśimā Gosvāminī led a strict life according to the Vaiṣṇava regulations, bathing in the Jumna three times a day, chanting on her rosary daily, etc., but her real focus was on *arcanā*, deity worship. She was engaged in a quasi-constant conversation with Gaur-Nitāi, who also appeared occasionally to other people to demand various types of service, etc. Later, when she was old and no longer personally bathed the deities or rendered other types of service, she still was able to know whether things were going in the desired manner by this personal communication. In a typical account, when on one cold winter morning Piśimā's successor, Gopīśvar Gosvāmī, bathed Gaur-Nitāi with cold water, she divined the blunder when she saw that the deities had running noses. To Gopīśvar Gosvāmī's amazement, she ran a handkerchief over their noses to show him the moisture which demonstrated that they had caught colds due to his carelessness.

Haridās Dās recounts that Gopīśvar Gosvāmī personally told him that when Piśimā Gosvāminī first asked him to take over the service of Gaur-Nitāi, he complained that he felt no pleasure in serving such small deities as he did not have the same type of parental affection as she, but was rather moved by the sentiment of friendship. He said that Piśimā then went to the deities, pulled on their chins and they changed size to take on their present form.[47]

2. Ma Yaśodā (d. 1944)[48]

Mā Yaśodā is known more through her relationship with her disciple, Krishna Prem, than for her own achievements. Sri Krishna Prem, or Ronald Nixon (b.1898), was a British pilot in the First World War who felt that he had been miraculously saved in the course of a mission in Germany. After the war, Nixon undertook a spiritual search which led him to India. A degree holder from Cambridge, he taught English at Lucknow University while staying in the home of the Vice-Chancellor, Jnanendranath Chakravarty, a leader of the Theosophist movement. Manika Devi, the wife of the Vice-Chancellor, was also a highly educated woman and had maternal feelings for Nixon, calling him Gopal, as many Bengali mothers call their sons. As Nixon recounted to the Bengali singer and bhakta Dilip Ray, Mrs. Chakravarty was heavily involved in her husband's rather busy Western-style social life. As he himself took an increasing interest in Buddhism and Hinduism, studying Sanskrit and Pali, Nixon observed that even within her superficially mundane life, she exuded a spiritual peace. He noticed that she disappeared from the scene during parties and returned rejuvenated. Curious, he followed her on one such occasion and saw her absorbed in a deep meditation. Upon being questioned, she explained to him that she and her husband had developed an interest in Vaiṣṇavism and had been initiated by Bālakṛṣṇa Gosvāmī of the Rādhāramaṇ family in Vrindavan. Impressed, Nixon then asked to be initiated by her. Eventually he asked to take *sannyās* from her, and in order to be able to do so, she herself went to Vrindavan and there took *sannyās* so that she could give him this initiation too. The name Yaśodā Mā was given to her on this occasion, while Krishna Prem was the *sannyās* name given to Nixon.

Abandoning academic life, the two of them went to Mirtola, near Almora in the Himalayan foothills, where they founded an ashram which they called "Uttara-Vrindavan." They installed a Rādhā-Kṛṣṇa *mūrti*. She taught local children to read and write and opened a dispensary, while Krishna Prem wrote several books and attracted a number of Englishmen as well as Indians to become his disciples.

In her childhood, while living at Ghazipur, Yaśodā Mā had had several formative experiences with holy men. As a girl of twelve or thirteen, she was chosen as a representative of the goddess at a Kumārī-pūjā in which Swami Vivekananda himself offered flowers to her feet. On another occasion she had heard that a local yogi, Pawhari Baba was giving a free cloth and *kamandalu* to all monks who came to his cave. Wondering how he could fit the large amounts of cloth, etc., which would be required to make this gift, she disguised herself as a boy and stood in line as the goods were handed out. When it came her turn, she jumped into the small space of his grotto and saw that it was empty. This act of daring resulted in a strong belief in miracles.

Yaśodā Mā had a deep emotional attachment to her deities in the parental mood and had a number of extraordinary experiences with her Gopāl deity which she recounted to Dilip Ray.

3. Siddheśvarī Devī, Sādhu Mā (d. 1944)[49]

The daughter of Govindacandra Goswami in Pabna district of Bangla Desh, she was a descendant of Caitanya's associate Advaita Ācārya. Born during the festival of Durgāpūjā, her father considered her to be an incarnation of Yogamāyā. From her childhood, she showed a devotional propensity and studied the scriptures under her father who also initiated her. She took *sannyās* after the death of her father (wearing saffron cloth like Prabodhananda Saraswatī). Although still a young girl, she wandered throughout India visiting all the major places of pilgrimage, depending on God alone for her protection. She met the famous Śākta Bama Khepa at Tarapith, who told her to spend some time at Belur and then to go to Vrindavan. It is said that Bama Khepa also recognized her as an incarnation of Yogamāyā.

When she finally came and settled in Vrindavan, she eventually built a large ashram dedicated to Rādhā Kuñjakiśorī near the Rangaji temple gardens. She had hundreds of Punjabi and Bengali disciples, including many who were prominent and wealthy citizens, and eventually built other temples and ashrams in Puri, Belur, Govardhan, Bhuvanesvar, Cakratirtha, etc.

In the tradition of the Advaita family, she strictly followed the *Haribhakti-vilāsa*, even instituting regular performances of fire sacrifices in all her temples except in Braj where she supposedly had a vision of Rādhā who prohibited such rituals as unnecessary. She loved *rāsalīlā* performances, but is said to have fainted once on hearing Mahāprabhu's *sannyās* being sung.

Like many of the other powerful women devotees of Braj, she placed a lot of emphasis on service to the devotees who all called her mother. She had dealings with some of the stranger characters of Braj such as Gwāriyā Bābā.

4. Śrīmatī Devī[50]

Interesting in view of the accepted wisdom that women saints in Indian religions are comfortable in their sexual identity in contrast with men who often, and particularly in Rādhā-Kṛṣṇa worship, seek a female identification,[51] is the story of Śrīmatī Devī. O.B.L. Kapoor recounts the legend in connection with Kṛṣṇānanda Svāmī, a Punjabi disciple of the Nityānanda family descendent Prāṇ Gopāl Gosvāmī (d. 1955). Though initiated in the Gauḍīya tradition by a staunch promoter of the *mañjarī* mood of devotion, Kṛṣṇānanda worshipped Kṛṣṇa in the friendly mood (*sakhya*). Though his guru wanted him to take disciples and preach devotion to Kṛṣṇa, Kṛṣṇānanda Svāmī was reluctant to do so because he wished to avoid the association of women. For years he had kept the vow that he would not look upon the face of a woman and this continued until he came in contact with an eleven-year old girl named Śrīmatī Devī.

Śrīmatī Devī lived in the Braj area in the village of Nagla Lakṣmaṇpur. After becoming widowed at the age of eleven, she devoted herself fully to the worship of her Kṛṣṇa deity. She herself had a tendency to the friendly mood of devotion and had hear of Kṛṣṇānanda Svāmī and had become attached to the idea of becoming his disciple. Eventually, at the insistence of some of her relatives, Kṛṣṇānanda Svāmī wrote the *mahāmantra* on a piece of paper and some instructions in how to worship Kṛṣṇa.

Śrīmatī Devī still wished to see her guru and she vowed that until she saw him, she would not go outside in the light of day. She would rise at four in the morning and bathe, then sit indoors, chanting the holy names until sunset. She kept this up for three years, but still she was not given the opportunity to see her guru. Finally, she stopped all food and drink and had thus been fasting for nine days when Kṛṣṇānanda had a vision in which Balarām told him that he could break his vow.

After making this breakthrough and receiving personal contact with her guru, Śrīmatī Devī quickly attained perfection in the friendly mood. She began to dress like a boy; her behaviour, her language all took on the characteristics of a cowherd boyfriend of Kṛṣṇa and people began to call her *bhaiyā* ("brother"). She became progressively absorbed in a total consciousness of Kṛṣṇa's presence.

Her health was poor and she did not live much longer after this. One day, when her guru came to visit her, he took her head in his lap and she said, "Buddy, let's go. Look, Balarām and Kṛṣṇa are calling their friends to come." Kṛṣṇānanda Svāmī replied, overcome with emotion, "Go ahead, buddy. I'll be right along." Having received this permission from her guru, she entered the eternal world of Braj.

5. Girijā Devī[52]

Girijā Devī was the wife of a rich landowner in Jamīrā in the state of Bihār who was habituated to a life of great luxury. She started to lose her interest in family life when her oldest son died at the age of eighteen, followed shortly afterward by the death of her second son. In her grief she became indifferent to food and drink. Her husband asked his family guru for advice, and he began to read *Bhāgavatapurāṇa* to her with the result that she began to develop an interest in devotion to Kṛṣṇa and she started to desire to move to Braj. Despite the family tradition which kept strict purdah on its women, her husband eventually gave her permission to go.

In Vrindavan she rented a room in the Rādhāramaṇagheṛā and quickly began to experience visions of Rādhāramaṇ. Rādhārāṇī would appear to her to complain about imperfections in the service which an ordinary person would have been unable to know anything about. On occasion, Rādhāramaṇ spoke to her by possessing one of the temple gosvāmīs and speaking through him.

Girijā Devī smoked tobacco from a hookah and maintained other habits from her days in Bihār and so was not always looked upon with faith, but eventually such inexplicable events caused the *sevāyats* of Rādhāramaṇ to revere her. Even so, Nīlamaṇi Gosvāmī, her landlord, once decided to evict her in order to rent out the house at a higher rent. Before he could carry out his plan, on that very day when he returned to his own home, he found that neither he nor any of his companions was able to open the locked door, even though he had the key. Another neighbour, a woman devotee, suggested to him that he had perhaps offended Girijā Devī and that if she gave permission he would be able to open the door. Nīlamaṇi went to her and asked her to open the door. Much to her own astonishment, she was able to unlock the padlock and the door opened. They attributed the mysterious event to the workings of Rādhāramaṇ himself.

After the death of her husband she spent the remainder of her days in Jamīrā, maintaining her devotional practices while running the family estate through agents.

Conclusions

June McDaniel notes in a recent study of Bengali religion that during her fieldwork it was virtually impossible for her to find a Vaiṣṇava holy woman.[53] This suggests that a certain disdain of women continues to exist in orthodox Vaiṣṇava circles today, despite the achievements of a few exceptional women at various points in Gauḍīya Vaiṣṇava history. The fear of sahajiyāism has something to do with this. The ascetic community endeavours to maintain its purity by following the principles of sexual segregation standardized by Caitanya as far as possible. Vaiṣṇavas who allow women of any age or marital status to stay in their ashrams at night are called *kuñjavāsīs* and have the lowest status. Those who speak to women in daytime are called *thoṛavāsīs*, while those who refuse to have anything at all to do with women are known as *vanavāsīs*. These latter Vaiṣṇavas are given the highest status in the renunciate community. *Kuñjavāsīs* are routinely suspected of sahajiyā practice. The problems faced by Piśimā Gosvāminī in the early part of her relationship with Balarām Dās are typical of those which face any women who wish to practice a life of asceticism. Outside the realm of the ascetics, in the entirely different world of the gosvāmīs and householder Vaiṣṇavas, the wives of the Prabhusantāns have always been strong leaders amongst the women of their communities, occasionally stepping in, like Jāhnavā, to exercise greater influence.

As a final word, however, it should be stated that here, as elsewhere, history is generally written by men about men. How many thousands of women in every religious tradition have led quiet lives of simple sanctity and asceticism, and been passed over by the few historians who have written about these matters only by virtue of their sex?

NOTES

1. Ramakanta Chakravarti, *Vaiṣṇavism in Bengal* (Calcutta: Sanskrit Pustak Bhandar, 1985), p. 174.

2. Cf. Sinclair, Karen, "Women and Religion" in *The Cross-Cultural Study of Women*, (ed.) Margot I. Duley and Mary I. Edwards (New York: The Feminist Press, 1986), 107-124. Particularly, pp. 110-2.

3. *Mahitir bhaginī sei nām mādhavī devī/ vṛddha tapasvinī ār paramā vaiṣṇavī// prabhu lekhā kare jāre rādhikār gaṇ/ jagater madhye pātra sāṛe tin jan// svarūp gosāñi ār rāy rāmānanda/ śikhi mahiti tin, tar bhaginī ārdha jan//*(iii.2.104-6).

4. *Caitanya-caritāmṛta,* iii.13.77-87. See also iii.3.75.

5. *Caitanya-caritāmṛta,* iii.14.24-31.

6. Cited in Sankar Sen Gupta, *A Study of Women of Bengal,* Calcutta: Indian Publications, 1970, 179. *saṅkīrtana mājhe nāce kulera bauhārī.* Caitanya's early *kīrtans* in the house of Śrīvās Paṇḍit, however, were not open to women. Vṛndāvan Dās tells that Śrīvās's mother-in-law tried to hide in order to witness Caitanya's dancing, but that her presence, even though not visible, interfered with his experiencing the usual ecstasy. *Caitanya-Bhāgavata,* ii.16.1-18.

7. "Images and Roles of Women in Bengali Vaiṣṇava Padāvalī Kīrtan," in (ed.) Joseph O'Connell, *Bengal Vaiṣṇavism, Orientalism, Society and the Arts* (East Lansing, Michigan: Asian Studies Centre, 1985), 11-27.

8. Haridās Goswāmī of Nabadwip is an exception to the rule. A prolific and able writer, he produced a number of works in the early second half of this century glorifying Caitanya through the eyes of Viṣṇupriyā, and established deities of Caitanya with Viṣṇupriyā throughout Bengal. This model of Caitanya devotion is, however, of relatively recent date and of relatively limited following. The Gaurāṅganāgaras who followed Narahari did not follow in the footsteps of Viṣṇupriyā, but rather an imaginary extramarital relation with Caitanya. They did not thus model their devotion on that of Viṣṇupriyā, nor did they conceive of themselves as handmaids of Viṣṇupriyā on the pattern of mañjarībhāva in the way that Haridās Goswāmī did. Even so, there is a deity of Viṣṇupriyā worshipped at Śrīkhaṇḍa, the home of Narahari and centre of the Gaurāṅganāgara sect, which was installed by Kānāi Khuṭiyā, an Orissan contemporary of Caitanya.

9. *viṣṇubhaktisvarūpinī, Caitanya-bhāgavata,* ii.22.40; *mūrtimatī bhakti, ibid.,* ii.22.45.

10. *Caitanya-bhāgavata,* i.10.225-31. This, as many of the other stories of Caitanya's childhood, is a pastiche of the original *Bhāgavata* stories of Kṛṣṇa's childhood.

11. *Caitanya-caritāmṛta,* i.15.10-11.

12. *Caitanya-caritāmṛta,* i.16.22-23; *Caitanya-bhāgavata,* i.12.183-8.

13. *Caitanya-bhāgavata* ii.22. What Vṛndāvan Dās means by *premabhakti* in this context appears to be the ecstatic symptoms which Caitanya himself and his associates manifested in their singing of the holy names. Vṛndāvan Dās makes no reference to the devotional sentiments which later were made current in the thought of Rūpa Gosvāmī. Nothing would indicate that Śacī was ever expected to "rise above" her parental relationship with Caitanya.

14. Jīva Gosvāmī tells a similar story about Kṛṣṇa's mother Yaśodā having such experiences during her son's absence in Mathurā. Kṛṣṇa similarly sends her assurances that it is he who is in fact coming in a divine form to receive her offerings. The writing of the *Gopālacampū* precedes that of the *Caitanya-caritāmṛta,* so it is likely that Kṛṣṇadāsa Kavirāj

took his inspiration from Jīva. Cf. *Gopālacampū*, ii.12.

15. *śacīr mandire ār nityānanda-nartane/ śrīvās-kīrtane ār rāghava-bhavane// ei cāri-ṭhāñi prabhur satata āvirbhāv/ premākṛṣṭa haye prabhur sahaj svabhāv// Caitanya-caritāmṛta* iii.2.35-6. The more detailed account of Caitanya's appearance in Śacī's house is found in CC iii.12.86-94.

16. *Caitanya-bhāgavata*, i.14.

17. *Caitanyamaṅgala*, ii.12.1-40. Vṛndāvan Dās envisions Caitanya spending the last night with his friend Gadādhar Paṇḍit.

18. A sannyāsin's wife would be expected to act as though her husband were legally dead.

19. This can be found in *Premavilāsa*, chapter 5, *Bhaktiratnākara*, 4.48-52, *Vaṁśīśikṣā*, p. 161.

20. Prem Dās, *Vaṁśīśikṣā* (Nabadwip: Nimai Chand Goswami, n.d.), 161-2.

21. There is a work named *Sītācaritra*, by Lokanāth Dās.

22. The word used is *dharmanāś karā*.

23. *Gauḍīya Vaiṣṇava Abhidhān*, (ed.) Haridās Dās (Nabadwip: Haribol Kutir, 471 Caitanyābda [1964]), 1243. Apparently, other sources say that Jaṅgalīpriyā was the name of a male disciple of Sītā's who took the feminine name after initiation. Cross dressing in the Vaiṣṇava tradition is not unknown, though it is not considered to be orthodox. Those following this aberrant tradition are given the name Sakhībhekhī. Lalitā Sakhī, a disciple of Caraṇ Dās Bābājī, is a fairly recent example of a male who considered it an essential part of his devotional life to dress like a *gopī*. The unambiguous statement of Jaṅgalī that "at no time have I ever been a man" could be nothing more than the firm conviction of the possession of an eternal feminine identity in relation to the eternal male, Kṛṣṇa.

24. *Caitanya-bhāgavata*, ii.11.8-10.

25. *op. cit.*, 112.

26. "Towards equality? Cause and consequence of the political prominence of women in India," in *Asian Survey* xviii, 5 (May, 1978), 480.

27. The same story is told in a somewhat different fashion in the 24th chapter of some editions of the *Premavilāsa*.

28. Four-armed human forms are the prerogative of denizens of the planets of Viṣṇu, though they have no particular theological relevance for followers of Rādhā and Kṛṣṇa, where they are specifically relegated to that category of manifestation of divine power held in disdain by the worshippers of the *madhura* sentiment. Even so, Caitanya himself is said to have displayed a number of unusual forms in the *Caitanya-bhāgavata* and *Caitanya-caritāmṛta*, particularly in the early part of his career when perhaps it was felt that some concrete evidence of his divinity was needed.

29. Other important disciples of Jāhnavā were Jñāna Dās, one of the greatest writers of Vaiṣṇava padāvalī kīrtan, and Nityānanda Dās, writer of the *Premavilās*.

30. *Bhaktiratnākara* 10.477. *maner ullāse sabe baise divyāsane/ śrīJāhnavā īśvarī baisaye saṁgopane//*.

31. BRK 10.633-5. *Phāgukhelā* is the Bengali term for the throwing of coloured and scented powders on one another on the occasion of Holi. The Kheturi festival took place to commemorate the birth of Caitanya, which took place on Holi, the full-moon day of the month of Phālgun.

32. BRK 10.628. *śrī Jāhnavā īśvarī kahaye mṛdubhāṣe/ pūrṇa anugraha narottam-śrīnivāse//.*

33. BRK 11.45-51.

34. *Gaura-gaṇoddeśa-dīpikā,* 48.

35. ed. Sundarānanda Vidyāvinoda, (Calcutta: Sripat Parag, 1964).

36. *śakti-śaktimator abhedatvāt.*

37. Personal communication from Madan Gopāl Gosvāmī, current guru in the line. There is, of course, another reason for this practice: this family of Gosvāmīs is not descended from Nityānanda through males alone.

38. Viz. Bhakti Rakṣak Śrīdhar Mahārāj's statement in connection with the disciplic succession accepted by Bhaktivinoda Ṭhākur "We have to follow the spirit; otherwise after Jahnava devī, the wife of Lord Nityānanda, up to Vipina Gosvāmī...so many unknown lady gurus. Through them, the mantra came to Vipina Goswami, and from him Bhaktivinoda Thakura received the mantra. We accept Bhaktivinoda Thakura, but should we count all those ladies in our disciplic succession? What was their realization?" *Śrī Guru and His Grace,* (San Jose, CA.: Guardian of Devotion Press, 1983), 23. Further, when A.C. Bhaktivedānta Swāmī was asked if a woman can become a guru in disciplic succession, he responded: "Yes. Jahnava Devi was. Nityananda's wife. She became. If she's able to go to the highest perfection of life, why it is not possible, to become guru?" in *Conversations with Śrīla Prabhupāda* (Los Angeles: Bhaktivedanta Book Trust, 1990), Volume 22, Toronto, 6.18.76, pp.19-20.

39. *Śrī Gauḍīya-Vaiṣṇava-Abhidhān,* 1196.

40. *Karṇānanda,* (ed.) Rāmanārāyaṇ Vidyāratna (Berhampore: Radha Raman Press, 1929), 122.

41. According to Sukumār Sen in *Bāṅglā Sahityer Itihās* (Calcutta: Modern Book Agency, 1940), Gurucaraṇadās wrote his *Premāmṛta* on the order of Gaurāṅgapriyā (p.409).

42. *Narottam Vilās,* 204. Cited in Edward C. Dimock, *Place of the Hidden Moon* (Chicago: University of Chicago Press, 1966), 100-1. See also *Gauḍīya Vaiṣṇava Abhidhān,* 1191.

43. This Haridās was the *sevāyat* of the Govinda temple and is mentioned in the *Caitanya-caritāmṛta* as the leader of the Vrindavan Vaiṣṇava community after the death of Jīva Gosvāmī (d.1610).

44. *Gauḍīya Vaiṣṇava Abhidhān,* 1197-8.

45. 5 volumes, Mathura: Sri Krishna Janmasthān Sevā Saṁsthān, 1981-2.

46. pp. 163-171. Haridās Dās credits Haridās Goswami's *Nitāi-Gaura-vigraha-līlā-kāhinī* for most of the data used in his account. O.B.L. Kapoor (*op. cit.,* Vol. 1, 193-212) has based his story primarily on that of Haridās Dās.

47. *Gauḍīya Vaiṣṇava Jīvanī*, 169.

48. The main source for the information given here is *Yogi Sri Krishna Prem*, by Dilip Kumar Ray (Bombay: Bharatiya Vidya Bhavan, 1968). Also, O.B.L. Kapoor, *op.cit.*, Vol. 2, 124-169.

49. *Braj ke bhakta*, Vol. 4, 133-140.

50. *Braj ke Bhakta*, vol. 3, 132-3.

51. Cf. A. K. Ramanujan, "On Women Saints" in (ed.) J.S. Hawley and Donna Marie Wulff, *The Divine Consort* (Delhi: Motilal Banarsidass, 1984[1982]), 316.

52. *ibid.*, 210-221.

53. *The Madness of the Saints* (Chicago: University of Chicago Press, 1989), 192. In a footnote to this comment, she writes, "The general response of Vaiṣṇava practitioners was a look of amazement, followed by, 'A holy woman (*sādhikā*)? Why would you want to speak to one of them? Look at all the holy men who are here—they are much better to speak with.' None could or would suggest specific women to interview."

THE DEBATE ABOUT WOMEN IN THE HARE KRISHNA MOVEMENT

Kim Knott

The issue of women in this well-known Western Vaiṣṇava movement has been troublesome for many years both within its boundaries and in the depictions of those outside it. For large numbers of devotees, predominately women but some men, it has been a deeply painful matter, and it has been perhaps second only to the issue of the status and role of the guru in threatening the future of the movement. I first considered and wrote about the issue in 1987 in Ursula King's edited collection, *Women in the World's Religions, Past and Present.*[1] The account which appears below is based loosely upon that earlier article, to which I have added new material and arguments and updated references. In the eight years since 1987 consideration of this issue has benefited both from the rise of more sophisticated feminist analyses and from studied reflection and debate within the International Society for Krishna Consciousness (ISKCON) of the history, philosophy and sociology of their problems. Despite beginning my account in the same graphic way, I hope that the changes in later sections do justice to these developments.

An Introductory Scenario

It is central Boston, and it is early morning.[2] A day breaks in the service of Śrī Krishna. For the *brahmacharis*—the young, celibate male devotees—the early hours are spent in ablutions, in worshipping Krishna in the first of the day's religious services, and in chanting the Hare Krishna mantra, the holy names of God. As most of Boston is thinking of rising for work, the *brahmacharis* gather in the temple to greet the Deities.[3]

The curtains open. Lying prostrate on the floor in homage, the *brahmacharis* pay their obeisance to Rādhā and Krishna. The music begins, and the devotees, standing close to the Deities, admire their Lordships' clothes, and the jewels and garlands with which they are adorned. Some of the *brahmacharis* are swaying, others standing quite still, all transfixed by the beauty of Rādhā and Krishna. Then, with the beat of the *mṛdanga* and the clash of the *kartālas*, *guru-pūjā* begins. The guru or spiritual master is honoured with offerings of incense, light, cloth, water and flowers. Each *brahmachari* offers a handful of petals at his feet. Songs of praise are sung, and the peaceful and reverent mood gradually changes to a mood of ecstatic celebration: The swaying turns to energetic dancing; the slow tempo accelerates to a fast and lively rhythm. Everyone is fully involved, happy to be worshipping and serving Krishna and His representative. The *pūjā* is followed by a class—a reading and discourse on a passage from scripture. As time is precious, hearing the class is combined with other activities: The young *brahmacharis* prepare vegetables for the day's meals or make garlands, carefully selecting and sewing together the carnations, roses and lilies for tomorrow's offering. After class, and a vegetarian breakfast, the day's work begins, the *brahmacharis* dispersing to the kitchens, the living quarters or the streets, to cook, to clean or to distribute literature.

The devotional life of Krishna Consciousness is not a life for *brahmacharis* alone. These acts of worship and service are also performed by married men, and by women, both married and single. It might seem odd then for me to have begun an account about women and their place in this religious movement with a description of men and what they do. The reason for this, as I hope to show, is that we can learn a great deal about the spiritual position of women in the Hare Krishna movement if we start by looking at the men. In this case it can help us to appreciate the perspective from which the issue of gender is approached within the movement itself. Looking back to the description of the morning program at the Boston temple, we can see that the activities of a *brahmachari* are hardly what might be connoted traditionally "masculine" in type. *Brahmacharis* engage in singing and dancing, sewing and cooking, dressing the Deities, praising and admiring clothes and flowers, all in a spirit of submission and obedience. Roles which, in society at large, have been commonly assigned to women are here adopted as a spiritual discipline by those of both sexes.

Devotees on the theory of gender equality in Krishna Consciousness

According to accounts by women in the Hare Krishna movement, their role is not restricted to the above-mentioned activities. When asked about this, one devotee replied,

> Some [women] are designers, writers, accountants, teachers, housewives, secretaries, cinematographers. I know one who's a landscape architect, one who runs an art gallery. Their roles are no different from women outside the movement. The difference is their consciousness.[4]

Another woman commented,

> There are no exclusively female vocations in the movement. Both men and women cook, clean, and raise children. And rather than remain homebound, our women are strongly encouraged to be assertive as missionaries and preachers.[5]

Women devotees have also been eager to stress other aspects of their equality with men: "The scriptures do describe women as a cause of material entanglement for men, and that's true. But scripture balances that out by describing that men are also a material entanglement for women"; "unmarried women...live as celibates within the protection of the temple community, living the same ascetic, devotional life as the male disciples."[6]

Technically, at least, there is no reason why women should not have the highest religious authority in the movement, as *guru*—though, as yet, none have achieved this—or the highest managerial responsibility, as temple president. A few act in this capacity. Women, like men, were granted by Prabhupāda (the movement's founder) the opportunity for initiation as Krishna devotees. Like men, they may be celibate *brahmachari(ni)s;* they may be married in the service of Krishna. Against orthodox Hindu tradition, they may be initiated as *brāhmaṇs* and may act as *pūjarī,* servants of the temple Deities. And, although the stage of *sannyāsa* or renunciation is not open to them for reasons I will explain later, as spirit-souls they are afforded complete *spiritual* equality with male devotees. What then accounts for "the women issue" in ISKCON, the great debate both outside and inside the movement on the roles and treatment of women?

Sociologists on the role of women in the Hare Krishna movement

The promise of equality does not readily conform to the picture of ISKCON presented to us in scholarly accounts. In 1974 in the earliest book on the Hare Krishna movement, J. Stillson Judah described the place of women as follows:

> The position of women in the Society may not appeal to Americans interested in women's liberation. Swami Bhaktivedānta says that all women other than one's wife are to be considered as one's mother, and yet he regards them as prone to degradation, of little intelligence, and untrustworthy. They should not be given as much freedom as men, but should be treated like children; they should be protected all during their lives, by their fathers when young, later by their husbands, and in their old age, by their sons...This view is largely consonant with the traditional one found in the ancient Indian law books. Females may not become presidents of any temple, nor occupy positions of authority. They may do the cooking, help with the devotional services and maintenance of the temple and prepare the flower offerings for Krishna.[7]

This view was reiterated in the late 1970s and early 1980s by several scholars: Francine Daner, "Ideally, the woman must be completely submissive and a constant servant to her husband"; Vishal Mangalvadi, "The strongest opposition to it [the Hare Krishna movement] has come from the feminist movements, because of the low position it gives to women"; and John Whitworth and Martin Shiels, "Women are regarded as being at once childlike and dangerous as it is their nature to tempt men from the paths of virtue, and are felt to be less intelligent than men and hence less reliable."[8] In later, more thorough accounts the movement is aligned with traditional, private and feminine virtues, particularly for women,[9] and with the Indian dictum of "male protection" for women.[10]

Situating the debate about women in ISKCON

Is it possible to square the account given by the devotees themselves about gender equality with this damning sociological critique? How can these seemingly contrary positions be explained? And how can internal wrangles on the nature of women devotees and their treatment by their male colleagues be understood?

To understand these differences of opinion we need to evaluate the beliefs and practices of Krishna Consciousness concerning the issue of gender. Moreover, to comprehend the debate more fully we must gain some insight into the problems of interpretation which revolve around the issue of women both inside and outside the movement. To fulfil these aims I will begin by investigating the claim of spiritual equality and will then discuss ISKCON's view of the gendered body and the way in which this view is conditioned by its theology of nature and society (*dharma*). This, as I hope to show, explains some of the hermeneutical difficulties which exist within the movement on the question of women. From there I will examine the problems of interpreting the issue from a position outside the theological framework of Krishna Consciousness. In the final sections, I will move from a theological consideration of ISKCON's understanding of gender, via the founder's attitudes to women, to a brief history of women's experiences in the movement.

The Hare Krishna movement, established in the United States in 1966, aims to spread the teachings and practices of love and service to Krishna popularized in India in the sixteenth century by Chaitanya Mahāprabhu and his followers. As such it is part of the Indian tradition of Vaiṣṇava bhakti.[11] Although it is new to the West, it is familiar to Indians and seen by many as a legitimate form of 'Hinduism.' In the early days of the movement those who became involved were nearly all young.[12] It is helpful to remember that, although they were eager and quick to learn, they did not at first have a sophisticated understanding of the philosophy of the movement or its founder, A. C. Bhaktivedānta Swāmī Prabhupāda. This resulted in a number of disputes and misunderstandings, not least of all in relation to this question of gender, some of which are reflected in the testimonies of devotees reproduced in the sociological and anthropological literature. Judah, for example, cites one female devotee, interviewed in the early 1970s:

> Well, spiritually, we have an equal position...We're subordinate now in Kali Yuga, but it doesn't mean we're inferior necessarily. Actually we are...I can see that women tend to flip out a lot more than men. They are more emotional. Women's lib tries to gloss over all of the very obvious differences...and it's non-

> sense...On the whole we are less intelligent, our attention is not so good...So we take our orders from the men and it's nice. They're very nice. It's no problem. You're protected and you're given instruction, and you don't have to make the decision; it's really pleasant...The boys really have propensities for administration...that we just don't have. So it must be my female body, but I'm very pleased not to have to make very many decisions anymore.[13]

Although there are undoubtedly many different views held by devotees concerning the different strengths and characteristics of women and men, there are now very few who would go as far as this devotee. The issues of 'protection' and the nature of male and female continue to be discussed in the movement, but generally speaking the tenor of her comments is rejected, at least in public. The movement's leadership teaches a view of equality-in-difference (to which I will return shortly), and practical opportunities for advancement are supposedly made available for people according to their propensities and abilities. As in society at large, the practical outworkings of these theories and intentions are conditioned by a range of local social, historical and psychological circumstances. It is here, of course, that inequality of opportunity and actual discrimination against women generally arise.

Equality and the soul: The starting point

> Women themselves have to transcend the bodily conception of life and become liberated from the mundane social sexual rat race. And of course men have to raise *their* consciousness. Spiritual life begins with the realisation that one is not the material body but an eternal spiritual soul and the designations "male" and "female" refer only to the material body. So ultimately they have nothing to do with the soul or self.[14]

Devotees may differ on other matters regarding the women issue, but no one dissents from this view. Many articles written on the subject of women in Krishna Consciousness by devotees make this their focus of attention.[15] Judah also mentions this: "Regardless of their social positions, the souls of female devotees are to be considered of equal value with their male counterparts."[16] While this priority can be confusing to those outside the movement who are not acquainted with Krishna Consciousness philosophy or its language, it is central to those within it. Like many religions, then, this movement teaches spiritual equality. All the souls (*jīva*) are distinct from one another, and are both of the same quality and nature yet separate from the supreme soul, Krishna.[17]

The self-realization sought in Krishna Consciousness is not primarily the liberation of the soul from the round of rebirth (*saṁsāra*), although this is a by-product of the process, but the attainment and perfection of a relationship of loving service to God. Bhakti or devotional service is both the path and the goal. It is a path open to anyone. It is a path whose success is dependent not just on keeping the regulative principles (abstention from meat and other unacceptable foodstuffs, alcohol and drugs, illicit sex and gambling), but particularly on a "service attitude," a position of surrender to Krishna, the spiritual master or guru, and all the other devotees. Egoism, pride, envy and greed, whether they are directed to material or spiritual attainments, are signs of deviation from the realization that one is by nature a servant. In Krishna Consciousness it is essential to recognize the dutiful nature (*dharma*) of the soul as well as the body. While the latter is dependent on one's social position, stage of life and gender, the former is eternal (*sanātana*). It is the constitutional nature of the soul to be a servant of God. The perfection of this natural role is exemplified by Rādhā, the beloved consort of Krishna, and it is only through Her that devotees ultimately can approach Him.

This then explains why devotees writing on the subject of women return again and again to this philosophical starting point. This is where their concept of equality has its roots. What is more, the success of the self-realization of the soul is measured against the "service attitude" of Rādhā. Therefore, in theory, it is not that the women on the path of Krishna Consciousness must aspire to or imitate male spiritual practice, but that all devotees, whether female or male in body, must adopt what might be called a "feminine" approach to spirituality.[18] This "feminine" approach is essentially an attitude—spiritual, mental and physical—of surrender and service to others, and ultimately to Krishna who manifests a "masculine" approach. Femininity and masculinity, as manifested transcendentally in Rādhā and Krishna, are eternal values, not merely cultural constructions.

This is important for several reasons. First, the spiritual role model for devotees is apparently "female" (though her transcendental form is nonmaterial). Secondly, the "feminine" approach of surrender and service is recommended for all. We see it manifested by Arjuna in the *Bhagavad-gītā* as well as by Rādhā. Thirdly, women, by virtue of their social and cultural conditioning in Indian and Western societies, are better practiced in this attitude or approach than men. Many men—and some women—have found it difficult, for example, to surrender to a spiritual master, and there have been battles in the history of ISKCON over the issue of serving God through his representative, the guru. Most women, it is said, seem to have less problem accepting this aspect of the philosophy or the practical consequences of obedient and submissive behavior. There are, naturally, a number of women who, while attracted to Krishna, find the notion of submission initially objectionable on the grounds that it reminds them of the oppression from which as intelligent women they are trying to escape. It will be pointed out to them, however, that there is a world of difference between material submission and spiritual submission, the one leading to oppression, the other to liberation.

The basic philosophy of Krishna Consciousness concerning the soul is one of spiritual equality. At this level, the woman problem is largely irrelevant. Devotees are the first to admit, however, that they are *aspiring* to live on what they call "the spiritual platform"; they have not achieved it yet. Equality may exist on this ideal level, but, at the level of conventional experience, it is threatened by all the circumstances of material and social embodiment.

Equality and the body: A can of worms?

Although in the philosophy of Krishna Consciousness the soul is eternal and the body merely impermanent, it cannot and should not be ignored. The body is there to enable the soul to experience service to God. The opportunity of human embodiment is to be treasured for providing the soul with the occasion for liberation. Human beings may respond to God's call in a way that other living beings may not, and they may experience, albeit in a qualified way, the pastimes of Krishna. But human embodiment also provides many opportunities for entrapment. Living out a spiritual path in which the body is used with care as a vehicle for liberation is extremely difficult. The way is full of material temptations. It might be easier if all bodies were the same, like all souls, but they are not. They are different, each one having a unique *dharma* or dutiful nature. This *dharma* differs according to one's social situation (*varṇa*) and stage of life (*āśrama*).

And, traditionally, both of these differ according to gender.[19] Formally, according to scripture, women are excluded from the requirements of *Varṇāśramadharma* and have their own *dharma*. Various women in the texts exemplify different aspects of this, e.g. Kuntī, Draupadī, Devahutī, and Sītā. Although all these women were strong and devoted, their roles were essentially supportive. They expected to serve their husbands (though difficulties arose in this even for these women) and to find spiritual fulfillment and material protection in doing so. These roles derived from an understanding of women's nature. It was associated with *prakṛti*, matter, and *māyā*, illusion. Their bodies were formed for procreation, and this process bound them to material nature to a greater degree than men. What is more, the beauty of their form made them potentially dangerous both to men on the spiritual path (hence they were perceived to be a problem to be avoided) and to the honor of families (as a result of which they were to be protected at all times by male relatives). As we will see, this traditional view of women's nature and roles, *strīdharma*, has been influential in the women issue in ISKCON.

Although devotees come across these ideas in scripture regularly, the teachings of the movement focus more on the problems of dealing with our material bodies while striving to live on "the spiritual platform". As all *jīvas* or souls are embodied materially until spiritual realization is attained, this is a problem for women and men. But different bodies are differently problematic, and there does seem to be a common view among devotees that the woman's body is the more entrapping for a soul in search of liberation for the reasons given above.

It is in relation to this issue of the body that confusion arises in critical circles outside the movement and also within the movement itself. The disparity of views on the issue of material, as opposed to spiritual, equality arises in relation to two areas, conflicting approaches to understanding how devotees, particularly women, should live, and the practical problems of interpreting the subject of gender from inside and outside the movement. I will now try to give some account of these.

Women and *dharma*: three levels of meaning

The first area of difficulty stems directly from the teachings of the movement on *dharma* as they relate to women, and concerns the use of three distinct levels of meaning. These are not always clearly distinguished and, as a result, have led to a certain amount of confusion both inside and outside ISKCON.[20] For example, devotees speak of participating both in *Varṇāśramadharma*, social nature and its attendent responsibilities, and in *bhāgavatdharma*, divine nature.[21] In fact, Krishna Consciousness, as a radical Vaiṣṇava bhakti movement offers the latter as a challenge to the old, brahminical orthodoxies. Devotees remind us frequently of the promise in the *Bhagavad-gītā* of spiritual realization to women and *śūdras* as well as those from twice-born groups. Surely, it is the teaching on humanity's divine nature and duty in service to Krishna, on *bhāgavatdharma*, that is of greatest importance in Krishna Consciousness. Or is it? There is certainly a recognition of *āśrama*, the different stages of life, in the movement. And, although Prabhupāda initiated male and female devotees as *brāhmaṇs*, there is a common parlance of *varṇadharma* at work in the movement, devotees seeing themselves as engaged according to their nature in *śūdra* or *kṣatriya* activities and so on. And how do women fit into all of this? Should they obey the classical legal prescriptions laid down in *Manusmṛti* on a woman's duty (*strīdharma*) which place them outside the conventions of *Varṇāśramadharma*, or does their position in ISKCON's *bhāgavatdharma* leave them immune to these? Such difficulties are compounded by references made by devotees to "Vedic" culture and ideals. Are devotees trying to live out a philosophy and practice derived centuries previously in a different social and cultural context? Should women devotees try to live in a "Vedic" manner, and what would that mean in practice?

What is ISKCON's understanding of *dharma*, particularly as it applies to women? To answer this, it is helpful to distinguish between three distinct understandings of *dharma* which might best be designated "Vedic," "Hindu" and "Krishna Conscious."[22] Although devotees frequently refer to their aspiration to live according to "Vedic" prescriptions, at the theological level a distinction is made between the Vedic way of life per se and the ideal, "Krishna Conscious" way of life or *bhāgavatdharma*. The account that follows, particularly with regard to the concept of "Vedic" culture and ideals, conforms with a devotional scholarly view and not necessarily with any view held by scholars outside the movement.[23]

The "Vedic" way of life was specific to a particular period of time and a particular people, who lived out their relation to God in a particular social form.[24] In India, "Vedic" *Varṇāśramadharma* men served God through their spiritual masters, and women served God through the men who protected them: their fathers, husbands, or sons. Because they understand this social system to have been operated in a different time and place, and by a people who knew perfectly how best to serve God, the devotees do not see this arrangement as unequal or oppressive. The men did not abuse their positions by using them as mechanisms for the pursuit of power over women, and women served God by supporting the male members of their family. In this arrangment, the husband was the wife's spiritual master, *patidev*.[25] This view of social life has a mythic and historical reality for devotees to which I will return shortly.

The "Hindu" system of *Varṇāśramadharma* also has an historical reality, but it relates to a different period, that of the dark age of Kali yuga. The "Hindu" social system, according to devotees, is a function of this age. During this period Indians have continued to live by the social rules of Vedic *Varṇāśramadharma*, but these have become distorted in practice. In Kali yuga the path of spiritual life has been obscured, and people resort to the lesser goals of material and sensual gratification. What was once a spiritually legitimized system of social organization has become a means of oppression. Women are still expected to serve, but, instead of offering spiritual guidance and protection, men exploit and oppress them. Similarly, although *Varṇāśramadharma* is not indigenous to the West, Europe and America in Kali yuga have experienced a similar period of social and moral degradation in which the distortion of old social structures and principles has led to the exploitation of women. This, as devotees see it, has led to the rise of feminism: Women have been oppressed by the very people who they were told were supposed to protect them and their interests, and their natural response has been to attempt to take control of their own lives, to protect themselves. When such women come into ISKCON, unsurprisingly, they wish to resist any hint of male protection. They want to take charge of their own bodily needs and spiritual advancement.

And difficulties may certainly arise as a result of this. The Hare Krishna movement is not a "feminist" movement. As we saw earlier, it understands the essential nature of masculinity and femininity to be different, and believes, *ideally*, that men and women should have separate and different natures and roles while being spiritually equal. The recognition that women and men cannot be expected to behave in conformity with their ideal "Vedic" types, is conceded unwillingly in the cold reality of Kali yuga. And this brings us to the "Krishna Conscious" view of *dharma*, or *bhāgavat-dharma*.

The "Krishna Conscious" view is an attempt to apply the Vedic "service attitude" to Kali yuga. The aim is not to copy the Vedic system of *Varṇāśramadharma*, but to use it for guidance in a troubled period. This cannot be achieved by introducing the system wholesale and expecting it to work. This, as the devotees see it, is the failing of the "Hindu" system. For this reason, in the "Krishna Conscious" system, men and women are seen not only as spiritually alike but also as materially alike in the sense that they are ultimately responsible for their own spiritual welfare with guidance from a guru. Both men and women take gurus, and when they marry, although the women are responsible for bearing and raising children and the men for supporting them in this, both are expected to serve Krishna and the spiritual master in the best way they can, be this cooking, gardening, teaching, sewing, managing, writing or whatever. Women are not seen as less intelligent or less able. Kali yuga has changed the ground rules.

Following the Vedic ideal in this dark and dangerous age of Kali yuga, then, does not mean that women should submit to the whims of their husbands but that both parties should do whatever is best for serving Krishna. In the Vedic period this would naturally have meant service through the husband; in Kali yuga it means service through the spiritual master by whatever means is most conducive. If a woman feels, in consultation with her guru, that her spiritual life is best practiced through serving her husband, she may focus on this; if she feels that she can serve best through cooperative independence, she may cultivate her career in conjunction with sharing the care of her family with her husband.

The changing demands of the contemporary situation are illustrated with reference to the thought-provoking comments of two male devotees:

> We had to become friends in Krishna Consciousness, because I couldn't become that *varṇashrama* husband—the one that is so respectable that the wife would automatically do everything, as soon as I come home she would wash my feet and whisper pleasantries in my ears. That's not real life for ISKCON devotees today.

> I'd like to challenge the supremacy of the male body for realisation...It seems to me that that concept actually belongs to *Varṇāśramadharma*. *Bhāgavatdharma* doesn't actually place a stress on male or female. When you go to any place of worship, there's always more women than men there—church,

> temple, mosque, even...Vṛndāvana, even in Rādhākuṇḍ, there's at least as many women as men there. So I really wonder if it's true, on the *bhāgavatdharma* platform, that women can't make progress as easily as men.[26]

In the first we see the welcome recognition by a male devotee that it is not only women but men who are affected by the changes brought about in Kali yuga. A relationship of equality and partnership came about as a result of the impossibility of either party living up to the Vedic ideal. In the second, in a powerful challenge to the common assumption that the female body is unsuited to the path of spiritual realization, the speaker affirms the radical nature of the "Krishna Conscious" system or *bhāgavatdharma* for overturning the problems of material embodiment. Together these examples confirm that, for devotees, Kali yuga demands changing strategies from both women and men, and that the most appropriate strategies are those which conform not to "Vedic" ideals (impossible to achieve in Kali yuga) or "Hindu" practice (the failure of Vedic *Varṇāśramadharma*) but to *bhāgavatdharma*, the Krishna Conscious spiritual path.

Needless to say these complex levels of interpretation have led to many misunderstandings among both commentators and devotees. Devotees continue to strive for clarification about Prabhupāda's own view of the relationship of *Varṇāśramadharma* and *bhāgavatdharma*. My view is that the ambiguities of this relationship are not likely to be resolved in a movement which accepts as fundamentally authoritative both scripture and guru. Ancient texts speak of philosophical ideals and social principles which were worked out for distant places and times; living teachers have to interpret these in the light of contemporary circumstances while not losing the impetus for real spiritual revolution. The need to balance a commitment to ideals and the wisdom of a spiritual tradition situated in real time and place inevitably elicits mixed messages, those spoken out of an appreciation of ideals and those framed in the experience of the hard realities. It is commendable in the face of this tension that the founder of the Hare Krishna movement made a philosophy and practice available to women that had once been largely closed to them, allowing them effective material equality with men and the opportunity to serve in the same ways *despite* his own cultural background and the ideal prescriptions of his tradition. He acted in accordance with the spirit of *bhāgavatdharma*, in the manner of Chaitanya, and in the specific context of Kali yuga as it manifested itself in the West.

What happened in ISKCON subsequent to the initial positive opportunities for women is a matter to which I will return later.

Representing the gender issue: Rhetoric and context

I want briefly to discuss several practical matters which compound differences of opinion on the subject of women in the movement. These apply particularly to views expressed from either side of the ISKCON boundary. Chief among these matters is the misuse of comparative examples. Commentators outside the movement and exponents inside it make frequent use of the device of comparison in order to underline the differences between the relative situations of women. Sometimes a writer seeks only to observe a difference; at other times he or she may seek to show that one situation is superior to the other. Both intentions are legitimate, when and where appropriate, if and when they compare like with like. This is not always the case.

In the early sociological accounts attention was frequently given to the practical restrictions placed on women in the movement. Judah, for example, stated that,

> The position of women in the society may not appeal to Americans interested in women's liberation...Females may not become presidents of any temple, nor occupy positions of authority. They may do the cooking, help with the devotional services and maintenance of the temple, and prepare flower offerings for Krishna.[27]

Reading this now, we feel that women in the Hare Krishna movement in the early 1970s faced many restrictions. However, if we think of women in American society as a whole in the early seventies, we remember that the situation was not so different. Few women were in important managerial positions or were engaged in activities other than those traditionally assigned to women. There were welcome ideals concerning the equality of women and their career entitlements, but these had not filtered through to the practice of working life in general.

A common reading of Judah's words, I surmise, is that the practice of gender roles in the Hare Krishna movement differed considerably from the ideal of gender roles in liberated American society. This is true, but is it a fair point of comparison? Devotees writing on this subject are equally prone to the rhetorical device of comparing like with unlike.

> When Krishna, or God, is at the center of our relationships, we can live in perfect harmony with those around us. This principle is basic to the entire Krishna Consciousness Movement. Without a spiritual foundation a marriage stands a good chance of deteriorating into the 50 percent of recent U. S. marriages ending in divorce.[28]

Here, the "principle" of Krishna Conscious marriage is compared favorably with the "empirical observation" of the poor success rate of American marriages in general. But are Krishna Conscious marriages always true to the ideal? Do they never fail? Are their not laudable sentiments concerning love and marriage even in secular society which, if they could be adhered to, would provide the basis for a higher rate of success?

These mistaken, and I am sure unconscious, comparisons of principles or ideals with practices or empirical observations tend to exacerbate the disparity between the views of women inside and outside the movement. The "life" of women in the movement, therefore, can seem and has seemed restrictive by the "standards" of those outside. The same kind of problem can arise from a further practical problem, the failure to contextualise statements on the subject of gender.

"Ideally, the woman must be completely submissive and a constant servant to her husband."[29] This was how Daner described the theoretical role of women in the Hare Krishna movement in the mid-1970s. From what we have seen of the philosophy of Krishna Consciousness there is some truth in this. However, it would be true also to say that the man must be submissive and a servant to his wife. (The suffix *dāsa* or *dāsī*, which all devotees take after their names, denotes "servant.") The important point, of course, is that everyone is a servant of God, and must be submissive, particularly to the spiritual master, but also to all other Vaiṣṇava devotees.[30] Daner's comment is not incorrect, but, by making no reference to the philosophy which produces this ideal, it suggests that women are subordinate.[31]

The teachings of Krishna Consciousness concerning the body and material life have produced a number of problems of interpretation. As we have seen some of these have resulted from the complexity of the teachings themselves. This has been compounded by the fact that, as a young movement with an old theology, its members are still learning the task of articulation. The other problems are related not to the teachings directly but to the way in which they have been expressed by those describing the movement. In some ways they are only minor points but they have had an important effect on our understanding of the women issue in the Hare Krishna movement. Whereas the souls are equal and the same, in Krishna Consciousness or *bhāgavatdharma*, bodies are to be viewed as equally useful for liberation but clearly materially different. The souls have the same nature (*dharma*); bodies have different natures, depending on their social situation and gender. It is not the case, however, that women's bodies and minds are of intrinsically lower status than the bodies and minds of men. Neither is it the case that the souls which inhabit women's bodies must be born again in men's bodies in order to achieve liberation. As far as it is possible to tell, the philosophy of Krishna Consciousness attributes spiritual and material equality—not to ordinary men and women—but to devotees, to those in *bhāgavatdharma*. This is not to say, however, that female and male devotees use or have been allowed to use this potential in the same way.

Women in the Hare Krishna movement: A short history

What have been the experiences of women in the movement? Are the teachings on the soul, the body and gender safeguards for the treatment of women or mere platitudes? After all, although provisions were made by the founder, Prabhupāda, for women in the movement, in *Kṛṣṇa: The Supreme Personality of Godhead*, he wrote, "never put your trust in a diplomat or a woman" and referred to women as "less intelligent."[32] In order to understand why someone who upheld such an apparently sexist view should choose to open his movement to women, we must again return to the focal point of the philosophy, the equality of the souls. Early disciples frequently point out that Prabhupāda saw and treated his disciples as equals regardless of gender. He did not, however, see those outside the Hare Krishna movement as necessarily equal, although they had the potential to be so once they saw themselves as spiritual rather than material entities. To put it another way—using Hare Krishna terminology—according to the "bodily conception" of life there were men and women; according to the "spiritual conception," *bhāgavatdharma*, there were only souls. When two female devotees asked Śrīla Prabhupāda if they would make slower progress than the male devotees, he replied, "Yes...if you think of yourselves as women, how will you make any advancement? You must see yourself as spirit-soul, eternal servant of Kṛṣṇa."[33]

Until the arrival of Prabhupāda—Bhaktivedānta Swāmī as he was then known—in the United States in 1966, his religious training and his empirical experience had provided him with little reason to take women seriously except as home-makers. In the Gauḍīya Vaiṣṇava tradition of which he was a part, the emphasis had previously been placed on the spiritual progress of men. Certain women, renowned for their great spirituality and leadership, were mentioned favorably in the texts, but they had at that time no place in the ritual practices or the *āśramas* of this tradition.[34] In addition, the normal role of women in Indian society was one of domestic subservience, with few women given the opportunity to attain higher material or spiritual positions. When Bhaktivedānta Swāmī came to the United States, however, his empirical experience altered. In a talk to the residents of Vṛndāvana, India, several years after his arrival in America, he reported, "...in the Western countries there is no distinction. They [boys and girls] are given equal liberty. In our country there is still discrimination."[35] Because of this he saw it as appropriate to allow both men and women to enter his movement, to become disciples on the path of Krishna Consciousness with the same opportunities for advancement and responsibilities for service.

Women were involved in Krishna Consciousness from the earliest days of the movement.[36] A woman devotee named Janaki was one of the first initiates and was married shortly after in the first ISKCON marriage ceremony. With two other couples, she and her husband, Mukunda, travelled to England to preach Krishna Consciousness under instruction from "Swamiji." Other early female disciples were given special responsibilities too, like Yamuna, who sang and cared for the Deities, and Vishakha, who received encouragement in her vocation as a photographer. Women and men were enjoined to start centers for the movement, "Krishna does not make distinction—female dress or male dress...Krishna gives intelligence."[37] They participated actively in worship, in cooking, in serving Krishna and the spiritual master. Prabhupāda made the women responsible for more traditional feminine activities, but did not bar them from stepping out of these into other roles if those suited them better. After the setting up of the Governing Body Commission (GBC), women were included in its membership. Women also gave scripture classes. Like the men, they travelled freely with Prabhupāda and served him personally, even in India where Hindu women were generally denied equal participation in religious movements and close involvement with a spiritual teacher.[38]

But, as a number of female and male devotees attest, the situation began to change in the mid-1970s.[39] For it was at this time that several male devotees had been initiated as *sannyāsīs*, celibate renunciates.[40] They worked closely with Prabhupāda, particularly on various projects in India where they were exposed to very different cultural circumstances to those operating in the West. Looking back to this time, older devotees now see this situation as causal in the devaluation of women within the movement. With a desire to protect their own *āśrama* and their individual spiritual advancement, they saw the involvement of women as a problem. The householder or *gṛhastha āśrama* as a whole was criticized, with women in particular targetted.[41] Some *sannyāsīs*, it is said, wanted to see the initiation of women stopped, presumably in line with much Indian religious practice. One practical effect of their preaching was the reorganization of worship such that women were made to stand at the back of the temple behind the male devotees.

Prabhupāda was certainly aware of some of the things which took place in this period. Most devotees, however, in evaluating the changes in relation to Prabhupāda's original openness and equal treatment of women, believe that he allowed such things to happen "to allay the fears of...[his] newly celibate male population,"[42] and perhaps to help them with the difficulties that the renunciate lifestyle inevitably engendered. The female devotees close to Prabhupāda were able to appeal to him in some of these matters, with some success, until he passed away in 1977. Following this, while the management of ISKCON was in the hands of the Governing Body Commission (GBC), spiritual authority was taken on by a group of male initiating gurus, all *sannyāsīs*, who were not sympathetic to calls for the reinstatement of opportunities for women.

Although some devotees in the early 1980s wrote about the position of women in the movement in response to feminist developments in the wider society, it was not until the mid to late-1980s, with the rise of a more vocal group of women in the movement and with pressures for reform growing in relation to a number of matters, that real calls for change began to resonate throughout ISKCON. Female and male devotees began to acknowledge the degree of damage that was being done through a failure to tackle the issue of women's second-class status.

> [S]houldn't women be taken seriously? If they aren't, our move-

> ment may survive, but will it prosper? Not only will we be turning away half of the world's population, but we will be neglecting those who are strong enough to stay. We will exploit them, hurt them, and not allow them to reach their full potential. And in the process of doing this, we will be exploiting, hurting, and denying ourselves. We will not progress, nor will we understand even the simplest things about the Krsna conscious view of women.[43]

Women started to propose changes and to write about the problems they faced. One devotee, suggesting that women devotees organise to place a referendum of their views before the GBC, drew fellow devotees' attention to the violation of,

> ...one of the main objectives of Vaiṣṇava culture which is to inculcate in its adherents an enlightened, broad-visioned and compassionate attitude, thereby creating a socially just, non-repressive, God-centered society.[44]

And changes began slowly to take place. In the mid-1990s, the issue has by no means disappeared completely, but there is a little more reason for optimism. Some positive European examples include the changes in Ireland which brought women and men side by side for worship and entitled women to give classes to all devotees, and the situation in Germany where three out of eleven temple presidencies and one-third of National Council seats are held by women.[45] Similar progress is gradually occurring elsewhere.

With regard to spiritual advancement as opposed to these important managerial changes, all devotees are reminded that there are no scriptural grounds and no GBC rulings which deny advanced women devotees the possibility of leading classes or taking on the role of guru. The latter has not yet occurred in ISKCON.[46] Perhaps it is only when it does that women devotees will feel fully affirmed as equal spirit-souls in Krishna Consciousness. Principles of equality are all to the good, but if they are never practically enacted, it is all too easy to doubt the sincerity of those who proclaim them.

As it remains the case that few women are given the public opportunity of speaking prophetically about ISKCON, it is left to two men, one a devotee and the other a sympathetic outsider, to invite the movement to proceed further and faster down the road to reform. Ravīndra Svarūpa dāsa, a leading commentator within ISKCON, was not referring explicitly to the women issue when he wrote the following, but his comments elsewhere lead me to believe he would include it in his hopes for the future:

> Our work of reform and renewal continues. It has to be perpetual. As part of that work, ISKCON is beginning to look back at itself, engaging in its own process of honestly coming to terms with its past. Only by so doing can it have a viable and progressive future.[47]

This sentiment is echoed by a British scholar of Hindu studies, Julius Lipner, who calls with great sincerity for a serious commitment to change on the issue of women's participation in the Hare Krishna movement:

> ISKCON needs all the help it can get in the years ahead. Unless it succeeds in convincing the female devotees that they have an equally important role to play—not only physically, but also intellectually and spiritually if they so desire— an immense resource will be wasted; more important, ISKCON's prospects for the future will be seriously undermined. It seems to me... that the role of women must be reconstructed in ISKCON.[48]

I would suggest, on the basis of this account, that the philosophy and scripture of ISKCON need provide no significant barrier for women's progress in ISKCON. Moreover, its history provides examples—if comparatively few in number—of great women devotees. Prabhupāda's own writings—which need some explanation and commentary for new devotees and outsiders—when set alongside his radical actions in opening up a previously male movement to substantial female participation should provide no obstacle for women's spiritual advancement and material involvement in ISKCON. As Vṛndā devī dāsī points out in her plea for change, "[We do] a terrible disservice to His Divine Grace [Prabhupāda] and his mission. These points should be cleared up for the sake of our own interpersonal dealings, and secondarily for our appearance in the eyes of the public."[49]

While those in new religious movements may always be misunderstood, even misrepresented, by outsiders, the primary responsibility, for cleaning the ISKCON house and the hearts of devotees on the subject of women, falls squarely to those inside the movement.[50] It is only once this has been achieved that the movement will rightfully shake off the stigma of sexism.

Notes

[1] Published by Paragon House, New York, pp. 111-128. The work was reprinted in a new edition in 1994.

[2] The main sources for this account were interviews in the 1980s with devotees in Boston, Mass., and Watford, UK, and ISKCON's own discussions and writings, principally from *Back to Godhead, Priti-lakshanam, ISKCON Communications Journal* and the tapes of the first ISKCON European Communications Seminar, 1992 (entitled "The position of women in ISKCON today", parts 1 and 2).

[3] The Hare Krishna devotees refer to the temple forms of Rādhā and Krishna as "Deities," these being actual incarnational forms of the divine. I have used this and other devotional terms in the text because it is my intention to convey—to the best of my "outsider" ability—a sense of the women's issue as it is discussed and experienced within the movement. ISKCON members have had few opportunities in the scholarly literature to explain the philosophical and historical perspectives of the movement on the woman question. Whilst not ignoring the mounting discontent among many women devotees in the late 1980s and 1990s (which I will discuss later in the article), I wish to present these perspectives, in the context of external, sociological criticisms, in order to render explicable the apparent diversity of views about gender and equality in ISKCON.

[4] Satarūpa dāsī, "I am not this body," interview in *Who Are They?* (Los Angeles, Bhaktivedanta Book Trust, 1982), 16.

[5] Sītārāṇī dāsī, "What's the role of women in Kṛṣṇa Consciousness? A Kṛṣṇa Conscious woman explains." interview in *Back to Godhead* 17, no. 12 (1982), 26.

[6] Ibid, 26. The first of these points was also reiterated by a senior male devotee in 1991 in a paper presented to European devotees involved in communications work. Referring to scriptural references for sexual entrapment, Ravīndra Svarūpa dāsa said, "For a man, woman is the woman; for a woman, man is the woman." He confirmed that this was how Śrīla Prabhupāda had explained passages in śāstra which cited woman as the lure for a man engaged in spiritual life. ("The Position of Women in ISKCON Today," part 2, *ISKCON European Communications Seminar*)

[7] J. Stillson Judah, *Hare Krishna and the Counterculture* (New York, Wiley, 1974), 86.

[8] Francine Daner, *The American Children of Kṛṣṇa* (New York, Holt, Rinehart and Winston, 1976), 68. Vishal Mangalvadi, *The World of the Gurus* (Delhi, Vikas,

1977), 98. John Whitworth and Martin Shiels, "From across the black waters two imported varieties of Hinduism—the Hare Krishnas and the Ramakrishna Vedānta Society," 161 in Eileen Barker, ed., *New Religious Movements: A Perspective for Understanding Society* (New York, Edwin Mellen, 1982), 155-72.

9 Burke E. Rochford, *Hare Krishna in America*, (New Brunswick, Rutgers University Press, 1985), 130.

10 Larry D. Shinn, *The Dark Lord: Cult Images and the Hare Krishnas in America* (Philadelphia, Westminster Press, 1987), 114.

11 ISKCON's relationship to Vaiṣṇava bhakti is important when evaluating the question of gender. The bhakti movements in North and, particularly, South India provided liberatory path for groups normally excluded from brahminical orthopraxis, notably for low castes and women. A useful account of the teachings about and opportunities for women in a similar Vaiṣṇava movement is provided by Katherine Young, "Śrīvaiṣṇava feminism: Intention or effect?," *Sciences Religieuses/Studies in Religion* 12, No. 2 (1983), 183-90. See also her paper in this issue of JVS.

12 For more information on this early period see Judah, *Hare Krishna and the Counterculture*; Satsvarūpa dāsa Goswāmī, *Śrila Prabhupāda-līlāmṛta*, 6 vols (Los Angeles, Bhaktivedanta Book Trust, 1980-3) and *Prabhupāda* (Los Angeles, Bhaktivedanta Book Trust, 1983).

13 Judah, *Hare Krishna and the Counterculture*, 87.

14 Sītārāṇī dāsī, "What's the role of women," 11-12.

15 See also Satarūpa dāsī, "I am not this body," 17; Vishakha dāsī, "Women in Kṛṣṇa Consciousness: Questions and Answers," *Back to Godhead* 16, No. 3-4 (1981), 6.

16 Judah, *Hare Krishna and the Counterculture*, 86.

17 This philosophical stance of identity-in-difference is known as *achintya-bhedābheda*. See O. B. L. Kapoor, *The Philosophy and Religion of Śrī Caitanya* (Delhi, Munshiram Manoharlal, 1977), Steven J. Gelberg, ed., *Hare Krishna, Hare Krishna: Five Distinguished Scholars on the Krishna Movement in the West* (New York, Grove press, 1983), and Shrivatsa Goswami, "Acintya Bhedābheda" in Steven J. Rosen ed., *Vaiṣṇavism: Contemporary Scholars Discuss the Gauḍīya Tradition* (New York, Folk Books, 1992), 249-60.

18 Satyarāja dāsa cautiously comments on this in a critique of the treatment of women in ISKCON: "Gauḍīya Vaiṣṇavism...exalts the feminine side of reality as supreme...[But] This emphasis of feminine spirituality...is something that we've yet to explore [in ISKCON]." (*Priti-laksanam* 4 (1992), 11).

19 The Krishna Consciousness view of *Varṇāśramadharma* is described by A. C. Bhaktivedānta Swāmī Prabhupāda in his purports to chapters 3 and 4, *Bhagavad-gītā As It Is* (Los Angeles, Bhaktivedanta Book Trust, 1983) and to canto 7,

Śrīmad Bhāgavatam (Los Angeles, Bhaktivedanta Book Trust, 1987). A contemporary view is that of Krishna Dharma dāsa, "Towards Varnashrama Dharma: A Constitution for ISKCON," *ISKCON Communications Journal* 4 (1994), 69-79.

20 Among those who have written about the movement there is an awareness that the teachings of Krishna Consciousness are related to the traditions and philosophies of India, but an uncertainly about the extent to which these are normative for devotees. Both Judah and Whitworth and Shiels mention "Hindu theology," and Daner uses the phrase "Vedic ideals." The difficulty is that these terms, to a reader unfamiliar with Krishna Consciousness, may signal something rather different to that perceived by Hare Krishna devotees. Their perspective on such terms, and on *dharma* itself, has to be understood in relation to their status as a Vaiṣṇava bhakti movement, a part of the Gauḍīya tradition rooted in the experience of Chaitanya.

21 The tension between *Varṇāśramadharma* and *bhāgavatdharma* was explored by devotees at a European communications seminar. The lecturer, Ravīndra Svarūpa dāsa pointed out that both are mentioned in the writings of Śrīla Prabhupāda and it is difficult to see how the two should fit together in practice ("The position of women in ISKCON today").

22 These particular designations were explained to me in an interview with Garuḍa dāsa who also discussed this issue in "Dharma: nature, duty, and divine service," *Back to Godhead* 15, no. 12 (1980), 7-13. The distinctions between these different perspectives are further alluded to, though not described explicitly, by Satsvarūpa dāsa Goswāmī, *Living with Scripture*, vol. 1 (Philadelphia, Gita Nagari Press, 1984), 61, and Sītārāṇī dāsī, "What's the role of women?," 26. See also Ravīndra Svarūpa dāsa, "The position of women in ISKCON today."

23 I have discussed the relationship between these perspectives in "Problems in the interpretation of 'Vedic' literature: The perennial battle between the scholar and the devotee," *ISKCON Communications Journal*, No 2 (1994).

24 The Vedic period is held by devotees to form the latter part of the age previous to this one, Dvāpara yuga (about 5000 years ago).

25 This ideal "Vedic" view of *Varṇāśramadharma* and *stridharma* conforms with that which is presented in the classical Hindu lawbook, *Manusmṛti*. However, devotees would see the practical attempt to live out the prescriptions of Manu in India in the last 2,000 years as "Hindu" rather than "Vedic" and as representing the distortion of the ideal system of *Varṇāśramadharma* in the dark age of Kali yuga.

26 These reflections formed part of the discussion about the situation of women in the Hare Krishna movement at the European communications seminar ("The position of women in ISKCON today," part 2).

27 Judah, *Hare Krishna and the Counterculture*, 86.

[28] Satarūpa dāsī, "I am not this body," 17.

[29] Daner, *The American Children of Kṛṣṇa*, 68.

[30] Hare Krishna devotees regularly pay their obeisances, not only to Krishna and the spiritual master, but also to the other devotees.

[31] Both this problem and the one of implicit comparison are well illustrated in Janet Jacobs' article, "The economy of love in religious commitment: the deconversion of women from nontraditional religious movements," *Journal for the Scientific Study of Religion* 23, no. 2 (1984), 155-71. She not only uses those who have left New Religious Movements (de-converts) to illustrate the attitudes of these movements to women's roles, but she also neglects to give any consideration to the religious beliefs held by the groups. The inevitable result is that Jacobs concludes that for women in "nontraditional" religious movements "a submissive self image also becomes inseparable from the goals of spiritual growth" (158). This is certainly true for Krishna Consciousness, yet we read it without realizing that this goal, and the image attached to it, is shared by both men and women.

[32] A. C. Bhaktivedānta Swāmī Prabhupāda, *Kṛṣṇa: The Supreme Personality of Godhead*, 3 vols (Los Angeles, Bhaktivedanta Book Trust, 1970), 7, 21.

[33] Satsvarūpa dāsa Goswāmī, *Śrīla Prabhupāda-līlāmṛta*, Vol 3: *Only he Could Lead Them, San Francisco/India 1967* (Los Angeles: Bhaktivedanta Book Trust, 1981), 150.

[34] In addition to the undeniably high position afforded to great Vaiṣṇava queens and other female epic figures (see Nandarāṇī dāsī, "How a Krsna Conscious woman achieved liberation: A queen of Vedic India found freedom in dependence," *Back To Godhead* 15, No. 12 (1980)), the Chaitanya movement itself provides good examples in Jāhnavā, the wife of Nityānanda and a guru in her own right, and Gaṅgāmātā Goswāmī, a celibate devotee from the following generation who inspired many Vaiṣṇavas in Orissa (See Satyarāja dāsa, "Great Vaiṣṇava women," *Back to Godhead* 24, no. 10 (1989), 8-12).

[35] Satsvarūpa dāsa Goswāmī, *Śrīla Prabhupāda-līlāmṛta*, Vol 5: *Let There Be a Temple, 1971-5* (Los Angeles, Bhaktivedanta Book Trust, 1983), 21-22.

[36] The sources for this account of the early years are Satsvarūpa dāsa Goswāmī, *Śrīla Prabhupāda-līlāmṛta*, *Prabhupāda,* and taped conversations with devotees.

[37] Satsvarūpa dāsa Goswāmī, *Prabhupāda,* 147.

[38] There are some other neo-Hindu movements in India which allow the active participation of women, e.g. the Brahma Kumaris (led entirely by women), the Sarada Devi Math (exclusively for women), the Swaminarayan Sampradāya (in which women are segregated from men but are actively involved) (Lawrence

Babb, *Redemptive Encounters: Three Modern Styles in the Hindu Tradition*, Berkeley, University of California Press (1986); Lynn Teskey Denton, "Varieties of Hindu female asceticism" in Julia Leslie, ed., *Roles and Rituals for Hindu Women*, Delhi, Motilal Banarsidass (1992), 211-32; Nirmala Pancholi, "The role and contribution of women in the Hindu Swaminarayan Sampradāya," MPhil thesis, University of Leeds (1993); Ursula King, "The effect of social change on religious self-understanding: women ascetics in modern Hinduism" in K. Ballhatchet and D. Taylor, eds., *Changing South Asian: Religion and Society*, London, Centre of South Asian Studies (1984), 69-83).

39 The sources for this discussion are taped conversations, and Vṛndā-devī-dāsī, "Change ourselves, then the world," *Priti-Laksanam* 4 (1992), 8-10.

40 This was one role which women were unable to take on. Whereas Prabhupāda had initiated them, giving them *brahmacharini* status, allowed them to become *brāhmaṇs* (though they did not where the sacred thread) and *pūjāris*, they were not formally allowed to renounce the world and wander as *sannyāsinis*. The explanation given for this is that renunciation would separate a woman devotee from the sources of her protection, e.g. a husband or temple authorities, and this would expose her to danger and exploitation.

41 Ravīndra Svarūpa dāsa, "Cleaning house and cleaning hearts: Reform and renewal in ISKCON, Part One," *ISKCON Communications Journal* 3 (1994), 52.

42 Vṛndā devī dāsī, "Change ourselves, then the world," 9.

43 Satyarāja dāsa, "As we learn our tradition, deep things will unfold," *Priti-laksanam* 4 (1992), 11.

44 Vṛndā devī dāsī, "Change ourselves, then the world," 10.

45 Taped discussion, "The position of women in ISKCON today," and Dayā devī dāsī, "ISKCON Germany: Perspectives on the past and lessons for the future," *ISKCON Communications Journal* 3 (1994), 37-42.

46 Unfortunately, this accords with the findings of June McDaniel in Bengal where, in her study of women spiritual leaders, she concluded that no Vaiṣṇava holy women were to be found (Chapter 5, *The Madness of the Saints: Ecstatic Religion in Bengal*, Chicago, Chicago University Press (1989), 192).

47 Ravīndra Svarūpa dāsa, "Cleaning house and cleaning hearts: Reform and renewal in ISKCON, Part two," *ISKCON Communications Journal* 4 (1994), 33.

48 Julius J. Lipner, "ISKCON at the crossroads?," *ISKCON Communications Journal* 3 (1994), 24.

49 Vṛndā devī dāsī, "Change ourselves, then the world," 9.

50 Phrase borrowed from Ravīndra Svarūpa dāsa, "Cleaning house and cleaning hearts."

RĀGĀNUGĀ BHAKTI: BRINGING OUT THE INNER WOMAN IN GAUḌĪYA VAIṢṆAVA SĀDHANĀ

Steven J. Rosen

If one studies the mystical texts of the Gauḍīya Vaiṣṇava tradition—and by this I mean the massive theological literature left by the Six Gosvāmins of Vṛndāvana and their followers—one sees that the ultimate goal of Caitanyaite Vaiṣṇavism is to realize one's inner identity as the servant of the servant of Rādhārāṇī's maidservants, and by so doing develop love for God in the feminine mood of the well-known *gopīs* of Braj.

Similar descriptions of divine romanticism are found in the mystical literature of other traditions: the Kabbalah speaks of approaching the Absolute with the intense passion of a lover, and St. John of the Cross and other Christian mystics write of becoming a "Bride of Christ," reserving one's love and passion only for the Lord. It is my opinion, however, that such amorous imagery, especially in relation to the Divine, is nowhere as developed as in the writings of the Gauḍīya Vaiṣṇava theologians mentioned above.

It is interesting that most of the literature about "*gopī*-love" is written by men, i.e., by those who are not privy to distinctly feminine emotions while in their present body. What's more, the bulk of this literature was composed in a culture where men had much to lose if they were to adopt the role of a woman, even if just in their inner, meditative lives. Such a meditation was, in a sense, a humbling experience, one that would lead to inner realization of the highest order. As John Stratton Hawley, Professor of Religion at Barnard College, Columbia University, insightfully writes:

> Most of the poetry and all of the theology describing this miraculous union of human and divine have been fashioned by men. For them, to assume the role of a *gopi* as a technique for gaining access to Krishna is to undergo a social devaluation in two ways. First, they must shed the pretentions of learning, literacy, and caste to become cowherds; second, they must leave behind their maleness—in Indian society a superior social station—and become women. Vaishnava theologians have generally agreed, moreover, that men suffer another loss when they recognize this female identity within themselves. As *gopis* they are not Krishna's wives—a socially acceptable role—but women who are tied to him by an illicit liaison (*parakīyā*). Most of the *gopīs* who are attracted to Krishna, it is said, already have husbands, whom they leave behind when they hear his call. In doing so they abandon the measure of status that society has accorded them, all of it conferred through marriage. To become one of Krishna's *gopīs*, then, is to become not merely a low-caste, rural person and a woman but an adulterous as well—or at best an unmarried young girl living a life that in worldly terms must be seen as irredeemably profligate. When one recognizes that one is a *gopī* in relation to Krishna—for these cowherd women symbolize the soul in relation to God—one embraces, in the religious realm, not only humility but social opprobrium as well.[1]

But there is more here than meets the eye. Gauḍīya Vaiṣṇava theology, again, recognizes the mood of the *gopīs* as the highest spiritual achievement for both men and women. To understand just why this is so, however, one must first understand the mission of the founder of Gauḍīya Vaiṣṇavism, Śrī Caitanya Mahāprabhu, who is accepted by his followers as an *avatāra* of Rādhā and Krishna in one form. He is said to be the personification of Lord Krishna's internal desire to experience the spiritual love of his greatest devotees (particularly that of Śrī Rādhā, the Lord's divine pleasure potency, or *hlādinī-śakti*). This, it is said, is the confidential reason for Mahāprabhu's descent, and it impacts greatly upon the male/female imagery described above: by personally taking on the mood and complexion of Śrī Rādhā—by virtually taking on her divine persona—Krishna desired to taste the intensely passionate love that Rādhā has for him. Gauḍīya Vaiṣṇava theology teaches that Caitanya Mahāprabhu embodies the highest expression of this experience.

This internal reason for Mahāprabhu's descent is traditionally broken down into three related subdivisions:

> (1) Krishna wanted to experience the greatness or depth of Rādhārāṇī's love for him.
> (2) He wanted to experience the sweetness of this love from Rādhārāṇī's perspective.
> (3) He wanted to experience the distinct bliss that Rādhārāṇī achieves by virtue of engaging in his service.

These three internal reasons for Mahāprabhu's descent reflect three unfulfilled desires that were previously experienced by Krishna when he descended to Vṛndāvana. (1) In Krishna-*līlā*, Krishna was the subject and Rādhā was the object. Although their love was unfathomable, they were still "separated," that is to say, they were in two distinct bodies. Consequently, Krishna's intense desire to fully taste (*āsvadā*) Rādhā's love for him (*prema*) remained unfulfilled. The only way in which Krishna could fully taste this love was to himself become Rādhā. This he did as Caitanya Mahāprabhu. (2) A subtle variation on this is seen in the second unfulfilled desire: Krishna wanted to experience the untold sweetness of Rādhā's love for him. Again, this required amalgamating himself into Rādhā's essential personhood (*rādhikā svarūpa*). If he were able to see things from her inconceivable perspective, he would perhaps be able to understand her unmotivated and unending love for him. (3) Krishna appreciated that her love was essentially embodied in her service to him, and so his third unfulfilled desire was to fully engage in such spontaneous service (*krishna-prema-sevā*). In order to fulfill his three desires, Krishna would have to experience the emotional reality of a devotee (*bhakta bhāva*). In particular, again, he would have to *become* Śrī Rādhā, who tastes the highest essence of a devotee's love (*mahābhāva*). Gauḍīya tradition teaches that these unfulfilled desires are perfectly fulfilled in the manifestation of Caitanya Mahāprabhu.

It may be argued that God (Krishna) is already omniscient, and if this is so then he should not have to make some extraneous endeavor to realize these internal truths about his own self-existent nature. The Vaiṣṇava response to this, however, is that Mahāprabhu is *not* an extraneous manifestation. Rather, he is an alternate feature of the original Personality of Godhead. Thus, Krishna's descent as Mahāprabhu is merely an expression of the methodology by which he realizes the sweetness of his devotee's love. It is not that the Lord has to make an external endeavor—Mahāprabhu is that eternal form of the Lord by which he internally experiences these esoteric truths about himself. In essence, the manifestation of Caitanya Mahāprabhu teaches us something confidential about nothing less than the nature of God's experience.

But Kṛṣṇadāsa Kavirāja Goswāmin takes us even further. In his *Śrī Caitanya-caritāmṛta,* he adds another dimension to the Lord's internal reason for descending upon our earthly realm, and this brings us to the central point of our paper:

> *prema-rasa-niryāsa karite āsvādana*
> *rāga-mārg bhakti loke karite pracāraṇa*
>
> *rasika-śekhara kṛṣṇa parama-karuṇa*
> *ei dui hetu haite icchāra udgama*

"The Lord's desire to appear was born from two reasons," says Kavirāja Goswāmin. "He wanted to taste the sweet essence of the mellows of love of God (as exhibited by Śrī Rādhā), and he wanted to propagate devotional service in the world on the platform of spontaneous attraction (*rāgānugā*). Thus he is known as supremely jubilant and as the most merciful of all."[2]

These two internal reasons are described as the *mūla-kāraṇa* or the "main causes" of Śrī Caitanya's descent. Having described something of Krishna's desire to experience the love of Rādhārāṇī, I will now focus on the second, more confidential reason for his descent, namely, to establish "the glorious path of *rāgānugā-bhakti.*" For sincere practitioners of devotional service, this path is approached with as much caution as enthusiasm, since its coveted and difficult-to-achieve goal is to reawaken our lost relationship with Krishna by emulating a *rāgātmikā-bhakta,* or "an eternally perfected being in the Kingdom of God." Consequently, a prudent word of caution should be offered at this point: few in this day and age have the honesty and spiritual acumen to execute this path properly. Therefore, great contemporary Gauḍīya *ācāryas,* such as Bhaktisiddhānta Sarasvatī Ṭhākura and A.C. Bhaktivedānta Swāmī Prabhupāda, have recommended a slow, methodical progression, following the rules and regulations of scripture (*vaidhī-bhakti*), as the path most suitable for the mass of people.

Such guidelines protect the sincere practitioner from the propensity to cheat (which may manifest in subtle and inadvertent ways), for this is a problem in many people's spiritual lives. The desire to be known as a great renunciant, *yogī,* or devotee can become quite alluring, and some give in to this last snare on the path of God realization. This being the case, the common accoutrements of *rāgānugā-bhakti*, such as the *siddha-praṇālī* process of initiation and living near Rādhā-kuṇḍa, are generally discouraged by the wise representatives of the genuine disciplic lineages. This is not because these elements of *rāgānugā-bhakti* are necessarily wrong—They are not wrong!—but because they are generally embraced by those who are not ready for such an advanced stage of spiritual life. In fact, sages have declared that those who prematurely live near the blissful Rādhā-kuṇḍa, or the "lake of Rādhā," will instead experience the terrible Nāraka-kuṇḍa, or the dreaded "lake of hell."[3] Nonetheless, when one actually reaches a level whereby he/she can honestly practice *rāgānugā*, the real *mano-bhīṣṭam*, or internal desire, of Caitanya Mahāprabhu, is fulfilled.

In A.C. Bhaktivedānta Swāmī Prabhupāda's gloss to the above verse from *Caitanya-caritāmṛta*, he says, "Lord Krishna wants to make known to all the conditioned souls that He is more attracted by *rāga-bhakti* than *viddhī-bhakti*, or devotional service under scheduled regulations." Here, Śrīla Prabhupāda makes clear that although *rāga-bhakti* is indeed confidential, "*all conditioned souls*" (italics added) should be taught of its practice and purpose. In this way, they will be aware of "the ultimate goal of life." Moreover, Prabhupāda's comment is not meant to minimize the importance of *viddhī-bhakti*, which consists of rigid discipline, rules, regulations, and worship of the Lord in awe and reverence. Although the path of *rāgānugā* is not dependent on any prerequisite, a *rāgānugā-bhakta* will not neglect *viddhī*, as exemplified by the Six Goswāmins of Vṛndāvana. But the ultimate goal should be clear as well.

Some, in fact, are eternal *viddhī-bhaktas*, but their destination is Vaikuṇṭha-*dhāma*. They do not go to Krishna's supreme abode, Goloka, where spontaneity, sweetness, and love reign supreme. Because they are inclined to awe and reverence, they go to the transcendental kingdom where the Lord is lovingly worshipped in that particular way.

To emphasize this point, the Lord says, "All the universe is filled with the conception of my majesty, but love weakened by that sense of majesty does not satisfy me. If one regards me as the Supreme Lord and himself as a subordinate, I do not become subservient to his love, nor can it control me. According to the transcendental emotion (*bhāva*) in which my devotee worships me, I reciprocate with him. That is my natural behavior."[4]

The goal is to become aware of our eternal relationship with the Lord—re-enter that relationship—and please him in that way. This is done through the process of Krishna consciousness. According to Rūpa Gosvāmin [*Bhakti-rasāmṛta-sindhu,* 1.2.1], Krishna consciousness evolves through three steps: (1) *Sādhana-bhakti,* devotion in practice; (2) *bhāva-bhakti,* devotion in ecstasy; and (3) *prema-bhakti,* devotion in pure love of God. It should be noted that *sādhana-bhakti* is further divided into *viddhī* and *rāgānugā,* and it is often said that unless one graduates to the *rāgānuga* part of *sādhana-bhakti,* as stated earlier, the highest level of Krishna consciousness is not generally attained.

It should perhaps be stated here that it is not simply a question of "graduation" or "evolution," as some may think. Most of the classical texts on the subject deny the sequential nature of *vaidhī* and *rāgānugā,* saying that they are two separate if also parallel paths. As evidence of this latter perspective, one can point to the fact that Rūpa Goswāmin deals with them as separate phenomena, addressing *vaidhī* in *Bhakti-rasāmṛta-sindhu* 1.2.6-269 and *rāgānugā* in verses 270-309. Rūpa also claims that the two paths give rise to completely different emotions or *bhāvas* (1.3.7-14) and to totally divergent kinds of sacred love or *prema* (1.4.5-8) as well. The love that arises from *rāgānugā* is termed by him kevala ("pure"), whereas the love that arises from *vaidhī* he calls *mahimāyukta* ("mixed with a sense of awe").

When (and if) one does develop a taste for *rāgānuga,* then the "*bhāva*" referred to earlier has an opportunity to fully manifest and one's direct relationship (*rasa*) with Krishna becomes clear. This relationship may be one of the following: (1) *śānta-rasa,* a relationship of tranquility or neutrality; (2) *dāsya-rasa,* servitude; (3) *sākhya-rasa,* friendship; (4) *vātsalya-rasa,* parental affection; and (5) *mādhurya-rasa,* or amorousness: the intimate relationship of conjugal love. These are all based on the *sthāyi-bhāva,* or permanent relationship, of love for Krishna.

But Caitanya Mahāprabhu specifically descended to introduce what may be called "a unique" *sthāyi-bhāva:* In addition to the above *rasas,* he revealed *Bhāvollāsa-rati,* or that state wherein one's love for Rādhārāṇī supersedes one's love for Krishna [see *Bhakti-rasāmṛta-sindhu,* 2.5.128]. This, indeed, is the "inner woman" that Gauḍīya Vaiṣṇavas seek to get in touch with. Many prominent Vaiṣṇava authorities—such as Gopāla Guru Goswāmin (Mahāprabhu's intimate associate), Dhyāncandra Goswāmin (Śrī Gopāla Guru's disciple) and Narottama Dāsa Ṭhākura—brought out the special significance of *Bhāvollāsa-rati,* which they described as *Mañjarī-bhāva,* or the mood of a very special class of *gopī.*

To clarify *Bhāvollāsa-rati,* or Mañjarī-bhāva, I will make a brief survey of these most confidential devotees—the *gopīs*—and then explicitly identify the particular class who are especially given to this Mañjarī-bhāva.

First, we have the *parama-preṣṭa-sakhīs* ("most dear friends"). These are Rādhārāṇī's most intimate associates—the eight principle *gopīs*. They are Lalitā, Viśākhā, Chitrā, Champakalatā, Raṅgadevī, Sudevī, Indulekhā, and Tuṅgavidyā. These eight *gopīs*, though friends of Rādhā, also have intimacy with Krishna, and sometimes Radharani herself arranges their pastimes with the Lord of her heart.

Next are the *priya-sakhīs*, who are subordinate to the primary eight *gopīs* and serve their every need. There are sixty-four of these particular kinds of *sakhīs*, and they are divided into eight groups of eight—one group for each primary *gopī*. But they also have their own encounters with Krishna. There are innumerable other *gopīs*, too, known generally as the *sakhīs*, who have similar experience. Either they love Krishna intensely (*Krishna-snehādhikā*), or they love Rādhā and Krishna equally (*sama-snehādhikā*).

The *prāṇa-sakhīs* and the *nitya-sakhīs*, however, are an extraordinary group of *gopīs*. They savor an emotion known as *Rādhā-snehādhikā:* their love for Rādhārāṇī stands supreme (*Bhāvollāsa-rati*), and it is so intense that they desire only to push her toward Krishna, with no consideration for their own relationship with him. This is Mañjarī-bhāva. Even if Rādhārāṇī insists, such a *mañjarī* will not go to Krishna. This is her determination. She is selfless. Krishna belongs only to Radha! And a *mañjarī* will do whatever is necessary to bring Rādhā and Krishna together. Her primary concern, over and above her own self-interest, is Rādhikā's pleasure.

According to David Haberman, Associate Professor of Religion at Indiana University, the word *mañjarī* is itself something of a mystery.[5] Monier-Williams, author of *A Sanskrit-English Dictionary*, defines it as "a flower, bud, or shoot."[6] More accurately, however, a *mañjarī* is a stamen—the part of a flower that is closest to its center. If Vṛndāvana is compared to a lotus flower, and Rādhā and Krishna are acknowledged as the center, then the *sakhīs* may be compared to the petals and the *mañjarīs* to the stamens.

The *mañjarī* is a beautiful young *gopī* who is resplendent with all charming qualities. She is always pre-pubescent or, at most, she is thirteen years old. This is so because, according to Vaiṣṇava canon, this age is one of innocence and emotional intensity. Being young, the *mañjarī* is invariably characterized as an apprentice to primary *sakhīs* such as Lalitā or Viśākhā.

In some ways, however, *mañjarīs* are considered superior to regular *sakhīs*. For example, when Rādhā and Krishna desire to engage in their most intimate transcendental *līlā*, the regular *sakhīs* cannot gain entrance. They are required to leave. The *mañjarīs*, on the other hand, are allowed to stay due to the worldly naivete and purity associated with their young age. In these private moments, the *mañjarīs* serve the needs of the divine couple. The types of service rendered by the *mañjarīs* include fetching water, serving betel nut, fanning Rādhā and Krishna, combing and braiding the divine couple's hair, decorating their bodies, massaging their limbs, and entertaining them with food and dance.[7] Thus, only the *mañjarī* witnesses and relishes the most intimate *līlā* of the Lord. The *mañjarīs* are ultimately the most fortunate of all *gopīs*. As stated by Śrīla Prabhupāda:

> It is very difficult to express their [the *mañjarīs'*] dealings with Krishna because they have no desire to mix with Krishna or to enjoy Him personally. Rather, they are always ready to help Rādhārāṇī associate with Krishna. Their affection for Krishna and Rādhārāṇī is so pure that they are simply satisfied when Rādhā and Krishna are together. Indeed, their transcendental pleasure is in seeing Rādhā and Krishna united. The actual form of Rādhārāṇī is just like a creeper embracing the tree of Krishna, and the damsels of Vraja, the associates of Rādhārāṇī, are just like the leaves and flowers of that creeper. When a creeper embraces a tree, the leaves and flowers as well as the creeper automatically embrace it. *Govinda-līlāmṛta* (10.16) confirms that Rādhārāṇī is the expansion of the pleasure potency of Krishna and is compared with a creeper, and Her associates, the damsels of Vraja, are compared to the flowers and leaves of that creeper. When Rādhārāṇī and Krishna enjoy Themselves, the damsels of Vraja relish the pleasure more than Śrīmatī Rādhārāṇī Herself...[8]

Thus, Gauḍīya Vaiṣṇavism teaches that Caitanya Mahāprabhu came to give all living entities the opportunity to experience Mañjarī-bhāva, the state of selfless service to Śrī Rādhā (*Rādha-dāsyam*) in the mood of a cowherd girl. The ecstasy associated with such spiritual selflessness exceeds that of Rādhārāṇī herself, as stated above. This, it is said, is Śrī Caitanya's greatest and most confidential gift to humanity.

And Rādhārāṇī herself is not devoid of this pleasure. In fact, her chief ecstasies come from trying to arrange meetings between Krishna and the primary *gopīs*. As Śrīla Prabhupāda says:

> Although the associates of Rādhārāṇī do not expect any personal attention from Krishna, Rādhārāṇī is so pleased with them that She arranges individual meetings between Krishna and the damsels of Vraja. Indeed, Rādhārāṇī tries to combine or unite Her associates with Krishna by

> many transcendental maneuvers, and She takes much more pleasure in these meetings than in Her own meetings with Him. When Krishna sees that both Rādhārāṇī and Her associates are pleased by His association, He becomes more satisfied. Such association and loving reciprocation have nothing to to with material lust, although it resembles the material union between man and woman. It is only because that similarity is there that such reciprocation is sometimes called, in transcendental language, transcendental lust. As explained in *Gautamīya-tantra* (B.r.s., 1.2.285): 'Lust means attachment to one's personal sense gratification. But as far as Rādhārāṇī and Her associates are concerned, they did not desire personal sense gratification. They only wanted to satisfy Krishna.'[9]

In this context, "transcendental lust" chiefly refers to the love of the primary *gopīs*, which, obviously, is totally devoid of prurient interest; the *mañjarīs* assist those who are given to this spiritual lust. *Rāgānugā-bhakti*, being modeled on *rāgātmikā*, is generally divided into two categories: the followers of those with "transcendental lust" (*kāmānugā*), who are solely in *mādhurya-rasa,* and the followers of those who relish "relational bhakti" (*sambandhānugā*), who may be engaged in any of the five *rasas* but who are not given to the special "lustful" brand of *mādhurya* under discussion. This is elaborately explained in Śrīla Rūpa Goswāmin's *Bhakti-rasāmṛta-sindhu* (1.2.290). The highest level, says Śrī Rūpa, is the path of *kāmānugā*, the path of the *gopīs*, and this topmost path is actually facilitated by those in Mañjarī-bhāva —the *gopīs* are indebted to the *mañjarīs* for assisting them in their relationship with Krishna. Consequently, Mañjarī-bhāva is seen as the preeminent position in Gauḍīya Vaiṣṇavism.

Gauḍīya Vaiṣṇavas are distinct among Vaiṣṇavas of the other *sampradāyas* in their pursuance of Mañjarī-bhāva, although the Nimbārkas, Vallabhites, and Harivaṁśas also have some interest in the subject. Following in the footsteps of exemplary *mañjarīs* is natural for those in the line of Mahāprabhu, for this was the mood exhibited by Lord Caitanya's closest associates. The original Six Goswāmins were themselves manifestations of six primary *mañjarīs*, as were Lokanātha Goswāmin, Kṛṣṇadāsa Kavirāja Goswāmin, and virtually every prominent *ācārya* in the Gauḍīya line. This means that, throughout history, the greatest teachers of Gauḍīya Vaiṣṇavism—who were predominantly male—labored to bring out "the inner woman" (albeit in an extremely spiritual sense) through meditation on their spiritual form as *mañjarīs*.

The scriptural basis alluding to Mañjarī-*sādhana* can be traced to the *Padma Purāṇa,* while more explicit instructions can be found in Raghunātha Dāsa Goswāmin's *Vilāpa-kusumāñjali.* It is also referred to in Rūpa Goswāmin's *Stavamālā.* Dhyāncandra's *Smaraṇa-padhati* elaborates on this theme, and Narottama Dāsa Ṭhākura develops it in a systematic sense. Viśvanātha Cakravartī Ṭhākura, too, in both his *Kṛṣṇa-bhāvanāmṛta* and his *Rāgavartma-candrikā,* deals with the subject at some length.

Bhaktivinoda Ṭhākura wrote about it extensively: Chapter Fifteen of *Harināma Cintāmaṇi* (entitled "*Bhajan Praṇālī*") gives details about the fundamental basis of Mañjarī-*sādhana,* i.e., *rāgānugā-bhakti*; in Bhaktivinoda's novel, *Jaiva Dharma,* the two heroes of the story meet with Gopāla Guru Goswāmin and Dhyāncandra, who in Chapter Twenty-six give preliminary details about *rāgānugā bhakti* and allude to Mañjarī-*sādhana.* Further, in Bhaktivinoda's "*Siddhi-lālasā*" (which is part of his lengthier work entitled *Gīta-Mālā*), he specifically deals with Mañjarī-bhāva and mentions his own spiritual form by name: he is the young girl Kamala Mañjarī. So there is ample literature on the subject in the orthodox Gauḍīya Vaiṣṇava line.

June McDaniel, assistant professor in the Department of Philosophy and Religious Studies at the College of Charleston in South Carolina, elaborates on the nature of Mañjari-*sādhana,* or the practice of those who desire to follow in the footsteps of the *mañjarīs*:

> In the Vṛndāvana-*lilā,* the person visualizes himself as inwardly female, a handmaiden (*mañjarī*) to Rādhā. This body is twelve or thirteen years old, wearing a certain color *sari,* in a certain residence, with a particular type of service, following the guidance of a handmaiden who is already a part of the paradise. This more experienced woman explains the details of service to Rādhā and Krishna to the newcomer. In addition to this information, the disciple must memorize the layout of the heavenly Vṛndāvana: he must learn the location of Rādhā's house, her village, Krishna's house and village, Rādhā-kuṇḍa (the pond in the forest where Rādhā and Krishna meet), and the locale of the various bowers around Rādhā-kuṇḍa. Elaborate diagrams of all these localities are kept by Vaiṣṇava gurus who specialize in teaching such visualization. Once this is learned, the disciple must learn the eternal activities of Rādhā and Krishna. This set of activities is divided into the eight times that divide the twenty-four-hour day. At each of these times, Rādhā and Krishna have a specific action which the disciple must visualize in his spiritual body. He must fit himself, with his visualized body and service, into the appropriate scene.[10]

The "eight times that divide a twenty-four-hour day" concept, known as *aṣṭa-kālīya-līlā*, will be addressed later. Before discussing this, it would be prudent to note that Mahāprabhu was himself given to Mañjarī-bhāva, and there is evidence of this in several episodes depicted in *Caitanya-caritāmṛta*. In *Antya* 4, for instance, Mahāprabhu says to Svarūpa Dāmodara: "Who has brought Me here from Govardhana Hill? I was seeing Lord Krishna's pastimes, but now I cannot see them...Hearing the vibration of Krishna's flute, Śrīmatī Rādhārāṇī and all Her *gopī* friends came there to meet Him. They were all very nicely dressed. When Krishna and Śrīmatī Rādhārāṇī entered a cave together, the other *gopīs* asked Me to pick some flowers..." Here, Mahāprabhu is not acting as Rādhā or Krishna, but, rather, he is experiencing the ecstasy of Mañjarī-bhāva.

This is also seen in *Antya* 5, where Mahāprabhu, again talking to Svarūpa Dāmodara, says: "After hearing the vibration of the flute, I went to Vṛndāvana, and there I saw that Krishna, the son of Mahārāja Nanda, was playing on His flute in the pasturing grounds. He brought Śrīmatī Rādhārāṇī to a bower by signalling with His flute. Then He entered that bower to perform pastimes with Her. I entered the bower just behind Krishna, My ears captivated by the sound of His ornaments. I saw Krishna and the *gopīs* enjoying all kinds of *līlā* while laughing and joking together. Hearing their vocal expressions enhanced the joy of My ears..." This, too, is in the mood of Mañjarī-bhāva, for Mahāprabhu is acting as neither Rādhikā nor Krishna but rather as one who is merely delighted to see them enjoying together. Finally, Narottama Ṭhākura has concluded in his *Rāgamālā* that Mahāprabhu, in more confidential moments, experiences the emotional reality of a *mañjarī*.

Having established that *rāgānugā-bhakti*—and its concomitant Mañjarī-bhāva—was a central reason for Śrī Caitanya's descent, there is an urgent point that needs to be addressed. If *rāgānugā-bhakti* is integral to the process of Gauḍīya Vaiṣṇavism, why is it apparently denigrated by stalwart followers of the tradition? As mentioned earlier, great *sādhus* warn practitioners away from it, claiming that one is better safe than sorry. Recommended instead is *vaidhī-bhakti*, especially for neophytes on the path. How, then, does one find entrance into *rāgānugā-bhakti-sādhana*? What are the dangers and pitfalls? Where does one begin?

Very simply, one must begin by approaching a bona-fide spiritual master and inquiring from him submissively. One should also render menial service to the spiritual master according to the rules and regulations of scripture. This is called *viddhī* (or *vaidhī*)-*bhakti.* One must learn to hear and chant Krishna's name—Hare Krishna, Hare Krishna, Krishna Krishna, Hare Hare/ Hare Rāma, Hare Rāma, Rāma Rāma, Hare Hare—under the guidance of this spiritual master as well. In the beginning, especially, it is the holy name—and not remembrance of Krishna-*līlā* per se—that leads to perfection.

In *viddhī-bhakti,* the devotee is called upon to submit to higher authority and to perform various acts of service to Krishna. Although the process of surrender begins at this stage, one is still largely functioning according to one's bodily identity and has not yet modeled himself (or herself) after an inhabitant of Vraja. Through prescribed devotional activity and association, however, the practitioner becomes familiar with Vaiṣṇava behavior and scripture, including the pastimes of Krishna and his associates. By prolonged exposure, one begins to remember his eternal constitutional position and gradually becomes re-established in his real identity, divorced from the illusions associated with the body and mind of this world. The practitioner becomes cured of "amnesia," as it were, and begins to recollect his original life in the kingdom of God. David Haberman elaborates:

> The Vaidhī Bhakti practitioner is required to frequently listen to (*caritra-śravaṇa*), remember (*smaraṇa*), sing about (*līlā-kīrtana*), meditate on (*krīḍa-dhyāna*), and otherwise celebrate the stories of the Vraja-*līlā.* These excercises familiarize the practitioner with the world of Vraja and the characters who inhabit it. Staged dramas (such as the *rāsa-līlās*) are also a favorite means of making the world of Vraja-*līlā* objectively available to the interested community. Here the *bhakta* [devotee] as spectator is presented with a vivid expression of the ultimate world of Vraja, which can provide an aesthetic foretaste of and a powerful incentive for further pursuit of that world. The practitioner of Vaidhī Bhakti, continually studying the Vaiṣṇava scriptures that narrate the Vraja-*līlā,* moreover, is like an actor learning the script of a drama to be enacted...A study of *Rāgānugā-bhakti-sādhana* will demonstrate that there is in fact such a formula, and that it is as follows: one enters the religious reality by assuming, via role-taking, an identity located within that reality. The new identity is the vehicle to the new reality. Close attention, then, should be given to role-systems and the ritual structures devised by religious traditions to construct new identities for concerned individuals, thereby transporting them to a new concomitant reality...Gauḍīya Vaiṣṇavas claim that a new identity is the entrance pass to the highest reality of Krishna's play.[11]

The follower of *vaidhī-bhakti* may gradually develop *lobha* ("internal desire") or *laulyam* ("greediness") for higher attainments, and this is the beginning of *rāgānugā-bhakti-sādhana.* Having passed through the levels of *śraddhā* ("firm faith"), *sādhu-saṅgha* ("the desire to associate with like-minded devotees"), *bhajana-kriyā* ("the point of serious meditation, commitment, and usually of initiation"), and *anartha-nivṛtti* ("the slow demise of one's unwanted habits"), one can achieve the state of *lobha* or *laulyam* at the stage of *niṣṭhā,* or "transcendental steadiness," and one may even achieve it prior to this level. For example, Śrīla Viśvanātha Cakravartī Ṭhākura implies in his *Rāgavartma-candrikā* that it can occur from the stage prior to *anartha-nivṛtti* (i.e., *bhajana-kriyā*), or whenever intense longing for the Lord arises in one's heart. He does say, however, that more often than not it will begin at the level of *niṣṭha.* For evidence, see Viśvanātha's *Bhakti-sāra-pradarśinī,* 1.3.7. The thing to remember is that it is a form of *sādhana,* "practice," not perfection, and thus the desire to engage in it can develop at any time.

Jīva Gosvāmin (in *Bhakti-sandarbha*) distinguishes two kinds of *rāgānugā-bhaktas*: *jāta-ruci* ("those who already have a taste") and *ajāta-ruci* ("those who do not yet have a taste but still desire to follow in the footsteps of those who do"). Most will fall into this latter category. Jīva clearly says that those who do not have a developed taste must follow all the rules and regulations of *vaidhī,* whereas those who are *jāta-ruci* do not. Sometimes it is hard to distinguish between these two kinds of devotees. Thus, at whatever stage one feels *rāgānugā*-like spiritual longing, one would do well to approach his spiritual master and ask for pertinent instructions in how to pursue the path of *rāga.* If one is indeed ready, the guru will give specific information in regard to a disciple's *siddha-rūpa,* or one's perfected form in the spiritual world. This may reflect any number of relationships, but for Gauḍīya Vaiṣṇavas, especially, this generally refers to Mañjarī-bhāva. It should be noted that Gauḍīyas are also inclined to *sākhya-rasa,* the mood of friendship, perhaps as a result of Nityānanda's predilection in this area.[12] Bhaktivinoda Ṭhākura has further said, quoting Dhyāncandra's famous *padhati,* that Gauḍīya Vaiṣṇavas tend to have two spiritual forms: a male form in the eternal Caitanya-*līlā* and a female form (as a *mañjarī*) in Krishna-*līlā.* The female form, however, is a central focus for meditation among followers in this tradition.

There is an inherent danger, of course, for those who are not truly ready to meditate on their spiritual form, and I have alluded to this earlier. Thus, in India, there is a preponderance of *prakṛta-sahajiyās,* or those who take the practice cheaply (making a trite imitative show).[13] It is easy to cheat, but one will then miss the benefits of true spiritual life. Vaiṣṇava theologians are quick to point out that in such a case one is only cheating oneself. Naturally, they say, the safest path is *vaidhī-bhakti-sādhana,* only moving forward when one has the blessings of the guru. Even then, it must be practiced cautiously and in strict confidence, since it is, even fundamentally, an esoteric and deeply internal process.

In fact, contrary to popular belief, it is clearly meant to be an inner meditation. *Rāgānugā-bhakti* does not require one to dress as a *gopī,* for instance, and to externally show signs of ecstasy,[14] although this is the hallmark sign of a *prakṛta-sahajiyā.* A true *rāgānugā-bhakta,* as stated earlier, would strictly continue his discipline as if he were an ideal *vaidhī-bhakta.*

But his inner meditation would be different, and to practice genuine meditation in this way on one's *siddha-rūpa,* especially if one is in *mādhurya-rati,* there are eleven items (*ekādaśa bhāva*) of which one must be aware: name, relationship, age, body color, group, dress, order, residence, service, highest desire or expectation, and under whom one serves. Again, this does not refer to one's outer bodily appearance but to one's actual spiritual existence in the kingdom of God. The minutiae of this existence is revealed by the guru and is enhanced by inner meditation.

The mental *sādhana* of the *rāgānugā-bhakta* chiefly involves a meditative technique called *līlā-smaraṇam.* This *smaraṇam,* or "remembrance" (or even "visualization") is at the heart of *rāgānugā-bhakti-sādhana.* Śrīla Prabhupāda comments on *līlā-smaraṇam* in his summary of the *Bhāgavata Purāṇa*'s tenth canto, ***Krishna** Book*:

> They [the residents of Vṛndāvana] were thinking "Krishna was playing in this way. Krishna was blowing His flute. Krishna was joking with us, and Krishna was embracing us." This is called *līlā-smaraṇa,* and it is the process of association with Krishna most recommended by great devotees; even Lord Chaitanya enjoyed *līlā-smaraṇa* association of Krishna when He was at Purī. Those who are in the most exalted position of devotional service and ecstasy can live with Krishna always by remembering His pastimes. Śrīla Viśvanātha Cakravartī Ṭhākura has given us a transcendental literature entitled *Kṛṣṇa-bhāvanāmṛta,* which is full with Krishna's pastimes. Devotees can remain absorbed in Krishna thought by reading such books. Any book of Krishna-*līlā,* even this book, *Krishna,* and our *Teachings of Lord Chaitanya,* is actually a solace for devotees who are feeling separation from Krishna.[15]

The *Kṛṣṇa-bhāvanāmṛtam,* among other books referred to by Śrīla Prabhupāda and other Gauḍīya *ācāryas,* is meant to take the practitioner beyond a general remembrance of Krishna's pastimes, and it outlines *līlā-smaraṇam* more specifically, with special attention to the remembrance of the eight-part-day division in Vṛndāvana (*aṣṭa-kālīya-līlā*), which was mentioned earlier. Śrīla Prabhupāda directly mentions this phenomenon in his translation to Text 10 of Rūpa Gosvāmin's *Upadeśāmṛta,* although the words "*aṣṭa-kālīya-līlā*" are not found in the Sanskrit text itself. By this cryptic reference in Prabhupāda's translation, he is obviously attempting to bring out the internal meaning of the text, which promotes *līlā-smaraṇam.* Although Prabhupāda rarely mentions this sort of thing directly, references to it can be found peppered throughout his books and recorded conversations. Implicitly, then, it *is* a part of the Gauḍīya tradition, and it is endorsed even by an otherwise *vaidhī*-oriented movement like ISKCON, at least for advanced disciples.

This *aṣṭa-kālīya-līlā* is presented as a short poem by Rūpa Goswāmin in his *Aṣṭa-kālīya-līlā-smaraṇa-maṅgala-stotraṁ* ("Auspicious Praise of the Remembrance of Divine Activity Divided into Eight Time Periods") and it is directly based on the *Paṭala-khaṇḍa* of the *Padma Purāṇa.* Viśvanātha Cakravartī Ṭhākura revealed an inner meaning to *aṣṭa-kālīya-līlā* wherein the practice could be applied to the remembrance of Mahāprabhu's pastimes in Navadvīp as well. Bhaktivinoda Ṭhākura also elaborated upon the eight-times-of-the-day principle to include Śrī Caitanya in his classic work *Śrīman Mahāprabhu Aṣṭa-kālīya-līlā smaraṇa-maṅgala-stotraṁ.* This concept has been popularized in modern times by Siddha Kṛṣṇadāsa Bābājī of Govardhana's work, *Gaura-Govinda-līlāmṛta-guṭikā.*

To practice *līlā-smaraṇam* in the fullest sense of the term, one must know his *siddha-deha* and be able to envision this original spiritual form as it interacts with the denizens of the spiritual world. As stated earlier, the day in Goloka Vṛndāvana is divided into eight parts, and according to the details of scripture and the predecessor *ācāryas,* one enters into a particular meditation according to an average day in Vraja. The meditation is quite complex and requires the level of concentration that only an accomplished devotee could achieve. There are three practical guidebooks in this regard: *Kṛṣṇa-bhāvanāmṛta,* which has already been mentioned, Kavi Karṇapūra's *Kṛṣṇāhnika-kaumudī,* and, most significantly, Kṛṣṇadāsa Kavirāja Goswāmin's *Govinda-līlāmṛta.*

Using *Govinda-līlāmṛta,* Vṛndāvana historian Alan Entwistle offers an extremely abbreviated if also eloquent summarization of *aṣṭa-kālīya-līlā*:

> In his *Govinda-līlāmṛta*, Kṛṣṇadāsa Kavirāja declares that the purpose of the work is to inspire devotees to contemplate the various pastimes of Krishna and Rādhā as they take place throughout the day. He begins the cycle with the first watch (*prātaḥ*) when Vrinda [a prominent *gopī*] calls upon the birds to wake Krishna and Rādhā, who have been sleeping together after meeting at night to dance the *rāsa*. They emerge dishevelled from the bower, return to their respective homes, and creep into bed before the rest of the household awakes. During the second watch (*pūrvāhna*) Paurṇamāsī [She is the saintly go-between and the grandmother of Krishna's brahmin friend and confidante, Madhu-maṅgala] visits Nanda's house in order to see Krishna wake up. She notices the marks caused by his love-play with Rādhā, but assumes that they are the result of his having wrestled playfully with Balarāma [Krishna's elder brother] before falling asleep. Krishna gets up, plays with the other boys, and goes to milk the cows, while Rādhā is woken by her mother-in-law [Jaṭilā, Abhimanyu's mother] and begins her daily routine. During the third watch (*madhyāhna*) Krishna goes out into the forest to graze the cattle while Rādhā and the Sakhīs go to worship Surya. Rādhā's mother-in-law had encouraged the Sakhīs to take her with them in order to keep her occupied because she suspected that Krishna would attempt to meet her. Nevertheless, they do meet each other in the forest and during the fourth watch (*aparāhna*) amuse themselves on the banks of the Rādhā-kuṇḍa. After playing in a swing and frolicking in the water of the lake, Rādhā returns home, and Krishna, during the fifth watch (*sāyāhna*), brings the cattle back to the village while playing his flute. During the sixth watch (*pradoṣa*) Krishna and Rādhā eat their evening meal and look at each other from the gazebos of their respective homes. During the seventh watch (*naiśa/madhyarātri*) everyone goes to sleep and Krishna and Rādhā steal away for their tryst in Vṛndāvana. During the eighth watch (*niśānta*) they dance on the banks of the Yamunā, frolic in the water, and finally retire to the bower.[16]

The experienced Vaiṣṇava reader will notice several technical problems in Entwistle's synopsis. *Niśānta* is actually the first watch, and so the list of watches is slightly off. And Paurṇamāsī is not the one who notices the marks on Krishna's body—it is Mother Yaśodā. But these points are minor, and, to be fair, they are cited differently in different places. As a general overview, with specifics deleted, Entwistle's work is fine, at least as an introduction. Moreover, learned and observant devotees will notice the correlation between the "eight-times-of-the-day" concept and the *āratī* ceremony, or Deity worship in the temple. This is meant to give the contemplative practitioner of *vaidhī-bhakti-sādhana* a foretaste for the desired goal of his practice: to enter into spontaneous service and love (by the process of *rāg-ānugā-sādhana*). The eight periods in the daily life of the Deity may be compared and contrasted with *aṣṭa-kālīya-līlā* meditation for deeper understanding of each *āratī* ceremony.

(1) **Maṅgala āratī.** The Deities of Śrī Śrī Rādhā and Krishna are awakened from their transcendental sleep, usually at about 4:00 A.M., and they are offered various items for their pleasure.

(2) **Śṛṅgāra āratī.** Krishna is fully and elaborately dressed for his day's activities, as is Śrī Rādhā. They are offered a morning snack as well.

(3) **Rāja Bhoga āratī.** The Deities are then offered a large midday meal and are prepared to take a short nap.

(4) **Utthapana āratī.** They are awakened from their nap in order to continue their daily activities.

(5) **Saṁdhyā āratī.** During a specific twilight hour, the Deities return home—Krishna from grazing his cows and Rādhā from her activity—to rest from an active day.

(6) **Vyalu Bhoga āratī.** At this time, the Deities are served their large evening meal.

(7) **Śayan āratī.** The last offering takes place between 9:00 and 10:30 P.M., and devotees can see the Deities for the last time of the day before the altar doors close. At this time the Deities are dressed for bed and they retire for the evening.

(8) **Rāsa-līlā.** After the Deities take rest, they should not be disturbed, for at this time they sneak out to enjoy their transcendental *rāsa* dance (only to return in the early morning hours just before *maṅgala āratī*).

There are some variations on this theme—*āratīs* are sometimes referred to by different names, etc.—but in essence this is how the Lord and his associates spend their day. This is the inner secret of the Gauḍīya *sampradāya,* and it can be experienced on the spiritual platform by strict adherence to the process of Krishna consciousness. That all conditioned and even liberated souls benefit from this experience is the internal desire (*mano-bhīṣṭam*) of Śrī Caitanya Mahāprabhu.

I have attempted here to briefly outline this esoteric revelation—the main contribution of Caitanya Mahāprabhu—called Mañjari-bhāva (in relation to *rāgānugā-bhakti-sādhana*), because many sincere devotees and scholars have asked me to do so. I have complied with their wishes for my own purification as well as for the benefit of all interested readers. It is an elaborate subject and due to propriety and lack of space I have chosen to cut short my analysis. It is a confidential aspect of the Gauḍīya tradition, and even this much has only been revealed in the good faith that it will entice readers to study more closely the profound subject of Gauḍīya Vaiṣṇavism, and to not take it cheaply.

At least this much can be said: in the life and teachings of Caitanya Mahāprabhu we have an extraordinary revelation of theological aesthetics, one that is full of color, vitality, and emotion. By contrast, in the West, God is often perceived as a colorless, somber personality—if a person at all!—and this has prompted contemporary philosophers to declare that "God is dead!"

Frederick Nietzsche, the well-known German philosopher who was initially bold enough to make this claim, would have sung a different song if he had known about Caitanya Mahāprabhu. But, like many Western philosophers, Nietzsche's conception of God was beleaguered by Teutonic myths and negative theology. The God of the Bible was for them a vengeful and static God, not a dancing cowherd and his lovable Rādhikā. Consequently, Nietzsche was once known to have facetiously exclaimed: "I should believe only in a God who understood how to dance."[17] Alas, Nietzsche never knew of Mahāprabhu, the divine golden dancer, a God in whose eternal dance the highest aspects of divine love, culminating in *rāgānugā-bhakti-sādhana* and the bliss of a faithful *mañjarī*, are revealed. The inner, innocent girl in us all is waiting to emerge, and to play with our friendly cowherd in an exhange of love. This, indeed, is the God for whom everyone is searching.

Notes

1. John Stratton Hawley, "Images of Gender in the Poetry of Krishna," in eds., Caroline Walker Bynum, Stevan Harrell, and Paula Richman, *Gender and Religion: On the Complexity of Symbols* (Boston: Beacon Press, 1986), pp. 231-232. Hawley explores the interesting question of whether women would tend to have less difficulty visualizing their spiritual female bodies than men. He does this by analyzing the work of Sūrdās and Mīrābāī.

2. His Divine Grace A. C. Bhaktivedanta Swami Prabhupada (trans.), 17 Volumes, *Caitanya-caritāmṛta* (Los Angeles: Bhaktivedanta Book Trust, 1974), *Ādi-līlā* 1, ch. 4, texts 14-16, pp. 237-8.

3. See His Divine Grace A. C. Bhaktivedanta Swami Prabhupada, *Conversations With Śrīla Prabhupāda* (Los Angeles: Bhaktivedanta Book Trust, 1990), Volume 21, pp. 1-17, and Volume 22, p. 95. Also see *Nectar of Devotion* (Los Angeles: Bhaktivedanta Book Trust, 1982), p. 127.

4. *Caitanya-caritāmṛta,* op. cit., *Ādi-līlā* 1, ch. 4, texts 17-19, pp. 238-40.

5. David Haberman, *Acting as a Way of Salvation: A Study of Rāgānugā Bhakti Sādhana* (New York: Oxford University Press, 1988), p. 189.

6. Sir Monier Monier-Williams, *A Sanskrit-English Dictionary* (Oxford, 1899), p. 589.

7. The specific services rendered by *mañjarīs* are discussed by Narottama Dāsa Ṭhākura. See Niradprasad Nath (in Bengali) *Narottama Dāsa O Tāhār Racanāvali* (Calcutta: Calcutta University Press, 1975), pp. 307-53.

8. His Divine Grace A.C. Bhaktivedanta Swami Prabhupada, *Teachings of Lord Chaitanya* (Los Angeles: Bhaktivedanta Book Trust, reprint, 1974), pp. 331-2.

9. Ibid.

10. June McDaniel, *The Madness of the Saints: Ecstatic Religion in Bengal* (Chicago: University of Chicago Press, 1989), p. 49.

11. David Haberman, op. cit., pp. 7 & 66.

12. Nityānanda Prabhu is Śrī Caitanya's chief associate and he is an incarnation of Balarāma. Gauḍīya Vaiṣṇava literature is replete with stories of his predilection for the friendship *rasa,* which especially comes out in his relationship with his twelve "gopālas." See also Śrī Nayanānanda Ṭhākura, *Śrī Śrī Preyo-Bhakti-Rasārṇava,* circa 1713 A.D., trans., Daśarath Suta Dās (Union City: Nectar Books, 1994).

13. For an elaborate survey of bizarre groups that may be generally classified as *prakṛta-sahajiyā,* see Suhotra Svāmī's four-part article, "Deviant Vaiṣṇava Sects," in *Back to Godhead,* Vol. 25, Nos. 3-6, June-November 1991.

14. The subject of whether Vaiṣṇavas should dress as *gopīs* was laid to rest by Viśvanātha Cakravartī, who defeated the ideas of Rūpa Kavirāja (not to be confused with Rūpa Gosvāmin), saying that the "practitioner body" should behave as the Six Gosvāmins of Vṛndāvana (i.e., as ascetics) while the "internal meditative body" may emulate a *mañjarī.* Rūpa Kavirāja, it seems, would have it that male practitioners dress externally according to their internal meditation, a tactic that can and has led to troublesome consequences. For an extensive discussion of whether male Vaiṣṇavas should externally dress as *gopīs* and how this practice was rejected by the tradition, see David Haberman, "Imitating the Masters: Problems in Incongruity," in *Journal of the American Academy of Religion* 53, No. 1 (March 1985) pp. 41-49 and Neal Delmonico, "Trouble in Paradise: A Seventeenth-Century Conflict in the Caitanya Vaiṣṇava Tradition," an unpublished paper delivered at the 21st Bengal Studies Conference, Oshkosh, Wisconsin, May 1987.

15. His Divine Grace A. C. Bhaktivedanta Swami Prabhupada, *Krishna Book,* Three Volumes (Los Angeles: Bhaktivedanta Book Trust, reprint, 1982), Vol. 1, p. 291.

16. A.W. Entwistle, *Braj: Centre of Krishna Pilgrimage* (Groningen, the Nether-

lands: Egbert Forsten, 1987), pp. 55-6.

17. Walter Kaufman (trans.), Frederick Nietzsche, *Thus Spoke Zarathustra* (New York: Penguin Books, 1961), p. 68.

BAHIṆĀBĀĪ: THE ORDINARY LIFE OF AN EXCEPTIONAL WOMAN, OR, THE EXCEPTIONAL LIFE OF AN ORDINARY WOMAN*

Mary McGee

Blessed is she who knows herself as a dutiful wife. She carries along at the same time her household duties, and her religious duties. (Abhaṅga 467.3-4)

The life of Bahiṇābāī, the seventeenth-century Vaiṣṇava bhakta from Maharashtra, seems quite ordinary when compared with the life stories of other women bhaktas. She did not discard her clothing along with other marks of distinction like the Vīraśaiva saint Mahādevī. Nor did she dramatically merge with God, as did the Tamil āḻvār Āṇṭāḷ at Śrīraṅgam. Unlike Mīrābāī, the Rajput princess married to a Mewari prince, whose songs reveal her obsession with her beloved Giridhar Gopāl (Krishna), Bahiṇābāī did not claim her beloved God to be her true husband, shunning all advances from her worldly and legal husband. Yet, Bahiṇābāī's life stands out, in some sense, because of its ordinariness. In several ways Bahiṇābāī withstands the pattern of many women bhaktas who are notable for, among other things, their defiance of societal norms as they "invert and even subvert the traditional ideals of womanhood" in the name of their devotion to God (Ramanujan 1986, 317). She renounced neither marriage nor motherhood, and indeed, she even composed a number of

*I would like to thank Steven Rosen, Anne Feldhaus, and especially Gary A. Tubb for helping me at various stages in the research and composition of this essay.

verses focused on *pativratādharma*, in which she instructs, praises, and blesses the dutiful wife. However, these hymns must be considered alongside her autobiographical hymns, which, among other things, reveal her anguish and uncertainty as she experiences the conflict between her duties as a wife and her desire to focus her devotions exclusively on her guru and God. It is also in these *abhaṅgas* about the early period of her life that we learn that the conflict Bahiṇābāī experienced was not just internal and emotional, but physical as well: Bahiṇābāī, one of Maharashtra's most honored women saints, was a victim of domestic violence.

To better understand how Bahiṇābāī dealt with these different types of conflict in her life and how her spirituality and theological imagination played a key role in her ability to survive these difficulties, we must look more closely at the larger context of her life—the religious, social, and political climate—as well as at the specifics of her own life as detailed in her autobiography.

The Religious, Social, and Political Context of Bahiṇābāī's Life

Bahiṇābāī was born in 1628 in the town of Devagaon, located near Verula, not far from the now-famous caves of Ellora. At the time of her birth, the Mughal Empire, under the reign of Aurangzeb, was in power in the Deccan; yet it was also during her lifetime that the Mughal Empire experienced its decline. While Bahiṇābāī's autobiographical *abhaṅgas* make no reference to the political climate, another very well-known Marathi Vaiṣṇava bhakta of her time, Rāmdās (1608-1681), makes these observations in his famous work *Dāsabodha* (R. D. Ranade, 419-20):

> Many people have now become Mahomedans; some have fallen on the field of battle; many have lost touch with their native language, and have become proficient in foreign tongues. The bounds of Mahārāshtra have been curtailed. People are engaging themselves in politics. They do not find time even to take their food. Many engage themselves in a life of warfare, and by the pride natural to that life, they engage themselves day and night in war topics. The merchant is carrying on his commerce, and cares for nothing but his belly. Various sorts of philosophical opinions have prevailed. Many kinds of atheistic schools have sprung up.

> Wherever you go, you find false teachers. Others have divided themselves as followers of either Śankara or Vishṇu. Confusion reigns everywhere. People are merely following the best of their desires. They cannot distinguish right from wrong.

Rāmdās was one of several influential religious teachers in Bahiṇābāī's life.[1] As the spiritual advisor of the great Maratha leader Śivājī, Rāmdās also played a key role in shaping the future of Maharashtrian dharma under the leadership of the Marathas. However, though Rāmdās became Bahiṇābāī's spiritual guide late in her life, it was the *sant* Tukārām who led her through the more critical stages of her spiritual development. The first hymn in the collection of the *Bahiṇābāīcā Gāthā*[2] traces her spiritual lineage (*ādiparam-parā*) through several gurus, beginning with Ādināth (Śiva), and eventually coming to Jñāneśvar and finally Tukārām, from whom she received her spiritual initiation. Jñāneśvar and Tukārām, along with Rāmdās, are two of the most well-known *sants* in the Maratha bhakti tradition, which brought a religious revival to Maratha people during a period in which the Mughal Empire dominated. As Balkrishna Govind Gokhale observes (Gokhale, 176):

> The Bhakti movement, with its egalitarian ethos, was the inspiration behind the early Maratha movement for independence. Its creators and exemplars were that bond of earnest devotees of a simple theistic creed called the Saints (*Santa*), from Dny[a]neshwar (1275-96) to Tukaram (1607-1649) and Ramdas (1608-81). Its deity was Vitthala, a regional form of Vishnu, and its centre was Pandharpur. Its leadership transcended caste, and its invidious progeny untouchability, for it included Brahmans as well as Shudras and Untouchables alike. It set little store by ritual and preached a universal ethic for man.

The religious revival which Bahiṇābāī herself was swept up in was influential in bringing the Marathas together and back into power after the death of Aurangzeb in 1707. Bahiṇābāī was one of several Vaiṣṇava women saints from Maharashtra[3] whose compositions, primarily in the form of *abhaṅgas* or devotional hymns, are known to us. Indeed, many of her *abhangas* are still part of the devotional repertoire of the *Vārakarī panth* or *sampradāya,* which to this day has a strong and visible presence in Maharashtra. Sudha Desai notes that "the *Varakari sampradaya* slightly differed from other Vaishnava schools in that it maintained exclusive devotion to Lord Vithoba of Pandharpur" (Desai, 115). The *sant* Jñāneśvar played a significant role in the development of the Vārakarī tradition, which conceived of God more as a friend, companion, or parent, rather than God as lover, a theme that is characteristic in many other Vaiṣṇava traditions. Thus we find little use of erotic or bridal metaphors in Vārakarī bhakti literature, as compared to bhakti literature in other regions of India (Vanita, 47). The Vārakarī tradition, which greatly influenced Bahiṇābāī's own articulation of her spirituality, emphasizes the caring, affectionate, and protective nature of God; thus Viṭṭhaḷ is often addressed by Bahiṇābāī and other Vārakarī poets as a caring friend, a helpful brother, or a nurturing mother (in which case God is addressed in the feminine as Viṭhāī).

In the Vārakarī tradition, the guru is often identified with God, and this is certainly the case with Bahiṇābāī, who does not make much of a distinction between her *sadguru* Tukārām and the Lord Viṭṭhaḷ;[4] "A saint," she says, "is very God in visible form" [232.4]. The Vārakarī sect also stresses the benefits of pilgrimage (*vārī*) to Pandharpur, *nāmasmaraṇa* (the remembrance and recitation of the names of God), *bhajanas* and *kīrtanas* in praise of the Lord, and vegetarianism. Though the Vārakarī sect challenged the elitism of the Brahmanical tradition and stressed egalitarianism, it accepts and respects many traditional ideas such as the authority of the Vedas and the importance of *varṇāśramadharma,* recognizing that it is not necessary (or responsible) to renounce one's duties or lifestyle in order to become a devotee. These are themes echoed in the compositions of all the Vārakarī poet-saints, including Bahiṇābāī.

Despite her significant literary contributions in the forms of *abhangas,* including her autobiography, Bahiṇābāī is not mentioned in Mahīpati's eighteenth-century text, the *Bhaktavijaya,* which is a compendium of biographies of notable saints, primarily from the area of Maharashtra. In fact, Mahīpati does not give much attention to any women saints, with the exception of Mīrābāī, though he does briefly mention two other very well-known Marathi women saints with whom Bahiṇābāī is often grouped, namely Muktābāī and Janābāī.[5] Muktābāī (14th cent.), was the younger sister of the great poet-saint Jñāneśvar. Along with their brothers Nivṛtti and Sopāndeva, Muktābāī and Jñāneśvar suffered ostracization, as they were offspring of a *sannyāsī*. Muktābāī, like her brothers, devoted herself to the religious life and spent her short life living and moving about with her brothers, never marrying. She died during adolescence, leaving poems that "illustrate the intellectual rather than the emotional side of bhakti" (MacNicol, 27). Janābāī (1298-1350), born into a Śūdra family, was given in service to the family of the saint Nāmdev around the age of seven, and thus grew up with and was deeply influenced by Nāmdev as well as by his spiritual teacher Jñāneśvar. As far as we know, Janābāī never married, but spent her whole life in service to the Dāmāśeṭī family as a maid and to Lord Viṭṭhal as a devotee. Her compositions reflect her absorption with God to the point of distraction, and God often comes to her aid to help her complete forgotten household chores.

Both Jaṇābāī and Muktābāī more readily fit the pattern of the female bhakta as schematized by A. K. Ramanujan in his essay "On Women Saints." Neither of them enters the traditional life of wife and householder, the norm for Hindu women of their times; each is allowed to devote herself exclusively and emotionally to developing a relationship with God.[6] Neither of them faces the strife that distresses Bahiṇābāī and which is so poignantly captured in this single verse from *Abhaṅga* 73.5: "I could not make [Tukārām] a *namaskār*, for fear of my husband." Bahiṇābāī is clearly aware of the source of the tension, and articulates the two conflicting sides of her position in *Abhaṅga* 62:

> To leave a husband is against the teachings of the Vedas, and thereby one can never acquire the supreme spiritual riches. [3]
>
> At my door there seemed a great serpent hissing at me. How could I live under such conditions? [4]
>
> It is the teaching of the Vedas, that one should not neglect one's duty, but my love was for the worship of God (Hari). [5]
>
> Says Bahiṇī, "I was in a sea of troubles. How can I describe the increasing anguish of my heart!" [6]

Bahiṇābāī's life as a woman was shaped both socially and psychologically by the Brahmanical and patriarchal ideal of the obedient wife (*patīvratā*).

Her verses above reflect how difficult it would be to defy this dominant authority represented by the Vedas. In the culture of her time, wives were looked upon more as property than as companions, and husbands ruled the household as lord (*pati*) and master (*svāmī*). Society was patriarchal and stratified, though the bhakti saints and leaders made great efforts to live (and provide examples for) a more democratic and egalitarian lifestyle. From other socio-historical evidence, we know that child marriage was prevalent in Maharashtra during the seventeenth century, and thus it is not surprising that Bahiṇābāī herself was married around the age of five. Bahiṇābāī's life and writings must be considered within the context of this social, political, and religious landscape.

Ordinary Life, Exceptional Woman

Madhu Kishwar, in an introduction to a special issue of *Manushi* devoted to women bhakta saints, remarks (echoing A. K. Ramanujan's thesis) that "the vast majority of women bhakta poets in one way or another opted out of married and domestic life, and remained childless" (Kishwar, 5). In this sense, most women bhakta saints were rather extraordinary, as they defied the model of the traditional Hindu woman and housewife. Bahiṇābāī is the exception to this female bhakta paradigm. Her life was rather ordinary, as it followed the pattern of most Hindu women. As Anne Feldhaus points out, "Bahiṇā's is not a radical bhakti like that of Āṇṭāḷ, Mahādevī, Lallā, or Mīrā, but it is a bhakti much better suited than theirs to the life of the average Indian woman" (Feldhaus 1985, vii). Unlike other notable women bhaktas, Bahiṇābāī not only married, but remained with her husband even after undergoing spiritual initiation, giving birth to two children. She is also exceptional in that she has provided us with autobiographical writings which give both details and insights into her experiences as a woman and a bhakta.

The corpus of Bahiṇābāī's compositions consists of some 473 *abhaṅgas*, seventy-eight of which constitute her autobiography (*Ātmanivedana*),[7] with an additional thirty-six (the *Niryāṇapara Abhaṅgas*) composed as a deathbed recitation of her previous thirteen lives which she narrates to her son. Other *abhaṅgas* deal with such themes as the duties of Brahmans and good wives, the glorification of Pandharpur and Pundalika, the virtues of saints, the glories of God's name, the significance of bhakti, and the importance of a sadguru. For the purposes of this essay, I am most interested in exploring what is most unique among her compositions, namely her autobiography. We already know from A. K. Ramanujan's study of the life-style patterns of over one hundred women saints that Bahiṇābāī's life does not fit the pattern of the typical woman saint. Does this suggest that the life of a bhakta and that of a housewife and mother are incompatible? What problems does Bahiṇābāī encounter as a housewife trying to lead a life of spiritual devotion, and how does she address them? What insights does Bahiṇābāī's life offer on the life of devotion and the life of female householder? Is she to be looked upon as a role model for other women? Given her experience as a battered wife, do her life and writings suggest ways for dealing with abuse?

The first-born of her family, Bahiṇābāī was conceived after a series of austerities and devotions were performed by her long-childless parents, Jānakībāī and Āūjī Kuḷkarṇī. These austerities were performed at the Lakshatirtha on the banks of the nearby Shiva River made famous by the sage Agastya who, according to legend, lived for four months in Devagaon and bathed daily in the Shiva river. When leaving the area, Agastya blessed the Lakshatirtha so that the prayers of whoever performed austerities and devotions there were answered. However, Bahiṇābāī was not to spend much of her life in this auspicious and tranquil setting. At the age of four or five, she was married to a thirty-year-old widowed relative from Shivapura. His name was Gaṅgādhar Pāṭhak. Her earliest memories of her husband-to-be were of "an intelligent *purāṇik*, an excellent jewel of a man" [5.3] who was "the astrologer of Shivapura" [6.2] and a reciter of the Vedas (*vaidika*) [59.1]. Yet, subsequent verses reveal that Bahiṇābāī's deep faith was not shared by her husband. Bahiṇābāī recalls that as a child, while other girls played with dolls she enjoyed reciting the names of God [56.1].

> I did not enjoy childish plays. I do not know how,
> but a strong faith early manifested itself. [56.2]
>
> I did not enjoy the games of *phugadi*, or of *tipari*. I
> felt I wanted my mind fixed (on God). [56.3]

In stark contrast to her own spiritual values, she remembers that her husband acted as if the name of God were something defiling [65.1]. She elaborates in *Abhaṅga* 65:

> ...The *Bhagavadgītā* and *Shāstras* were considered as
> enemies in our family. [1]

> No one cared for God, for sacred bathing places, for pilgrimages, for Hari himself. It was into such a home that I was given in marriage. [2]
>
> They did not like the communion of saints, nor the bhakti of Rāma.... [3]

In *Abhaṅga* 59 she explains that while her husband recited the Vedas for his profession, he had no love of God, no sense of bhakti. Out of respect for the Vedas, she served him, but her spirits were depressed [59.4]. Bahiṇābāī's *abhaṅgas* often reveal the tension between empty Brahmanical elitism (symbolized by her husband) and the emotion-filled bhakti tradition (represented by herself). Just as the Brahman elite felt threatened by the vigor and independence of the bhakti movement, so Bahiṇābāī's husband experienced his wife's growing devotion as a threat to his authority as master of the household.

Four years after her marriage, Bahiṇābāī left her home town rather abruptly; at her father's request, her husband Gaṅgādhar helped them to escape in the middle of the night, as Bahiṇābāī's father was threatened with bankruptcy and jail. Bahiṇābāī and her husband joined her parents and younger brother on this flight, and together they took up lives like hunted criminals, wandering from place to place, not lingering long enough to be identified. Of this difficult period, Bahiṇābāī writes: "We journeyed, begging as we went along; we had to suffer many hard experiences" [9.1].

Their journeys took them to many holy shrines and *tīrthas,* but Bahiṇābāī's husband kept them moving. As Bahiṇābāī recounts their peregrinations around Maharashtra, we get glimpses into her deepening spirituality. She speaks especially lovingly of her experiences at the Pravara Sangam, where she bathed in the holy Godavari river and listened to *kīrtanas* and stories from the *purāṇas.* We sense her longing for the religious life in her laments each time she is wrenched away from another center of spirituality: "We were exceedingly sorry to leave the place. What is this that wretched Fate has done to us?" [8.5] Her soul is most deeply moved by her experiences at Pandharpur (the center of Vārakarī devotion), and she uses such words as *mahāsaukhya* (great joy; 9.7), *santoṣa* (contentment; 9.8) and *mahāharṣa* (ecstasy; 9.9) to describe her *darana* of Pāṇḍuraṅg. Her heart is rent by the conflict brought about by her desire to stay at the foot of Viṭhobā and the need of her family to move on.

> Even though it might mean death to us, yet Paṇḍharī was the place we would be in. We felt as though we could not leave its river-water. [9.11]

This conflict between family responsibility and allegiance and her personal, religious feelings was to become even more acute once Bahiṇābāī's family settled down, first in Rahimatpur and then in Kolhapur. In Rahimatpur, Bahiṇābāī's husband temporarily took on the responsibilities of town priest (*upādhyāya*) and astrologer (*jyotiṣa*) while the local priest took a year's leave to journey to Benares. It is during this time that Bahiṇābāī most clearly experienced her own call to a life of devotion: "I was now eleven years of age, and felt a strong desire to be in the company of saints" [12.9]. This eleventh year of Bahiṇābāī's life was to be a most pivotal and difficult one.

The Spiritual and Domestic Ordeals of Bahiṇābāī

During her eleventh year, Bahiṇābāī's family moved again and settled for a prolonged period in the holy city of Kolhapur. It was here that Bahiṇābāī came under the influence of Jayarām Gosāvī, a great bhakta well known for his *harikīrtanas*, while her family lived in the home of a Yajurvedī Vedāntin by the name of Bahiraṁbhaṭ (also called Hiraṁbhaṭ by Bahiṇābāī). On a particular festival occasion, Hiraṁbhaṭ was presented with a milch cow as dakṣiṇā, and he in turn presented it to Bahiṇābāī's husband. After the cow had calved, Bahiṇābāī took responsibility for the calf and very soon she and the calf were inseparable. Bahiṇābāī recounts how the calf would follow her everywhere: to prayers, to *kīrtanas*, for bathing—"At night it slept on my bedding" [14.19]. And she expresses her own attachment to this calf: "If the calf was not in sight, I was troubled; I felt like a fish out of water. Whether I was grinding, or pounding grain or carrying water, I was unhappy, though with others, without the calf" [14.26-27]. Within the Vārakarī tradition, the cow and calf are a frequently-used metaphor for the relationship between Viṭṭhaḷ and his devotees. The intensity of Bahiṇābāī's affection for the calf and her virtual inseparability from it reflect her great spiritual advancement as she approached the ultimate stage of enlightenment, namely oneness with God.

Though an eleven-year-old girl tending a calf would seem routine in 17th-century Maharashtra, the unusual relationship between Bahiṇābāī and the calf (who would eat and drink only from Bahiṇī's hand) made for rich gossip in town. This unwanted attention to his wife initially angered her husband Gaṅgādhar, until he rationalized her attachment to the calf as an expression of Bahiṇābāī's longing for a child of her own [20.28-30].[8] His remedy to this, which also allowed him to assert his control and manlihood, was to impregnate Bahiṇābāī. Bahiṇābāī, still only a child herself at age eleven, would soon become a mother.

Despite her age, Bahiṇābāī was unusual in her spiritual acumen, as observed by Svāmī Jayarām Gosāvī, who recognized in this young girl the purity of heart and great *vairāgya* [18.4; 14.64] of a true *yogabhraṣṭa* [17.8], that is, one who has been a yogī in a previous life. Jayarām Gosāvī further discerned that her intimate relationship with the cow and calf was significant to her own spiritual development (see especially *Abhaṅgas* 17 and 18). He explained to a crowd that had gathered to hear his *harikīrtanas:*

> The calf is her guru; the calf is her means of salvation,
> for it destroys the cord that binds it. [17.12]

Jayarām Gosāvī's public recognition of Bahiṇābāī's spiritual advancement and the attention it focused on her and the calf was too much for her husband to bear, and in a rage fueled by jealousy and humiliation,

> He seized me [Bahiṇābāī] by the braids of my hair,
> and beat me to his heart's content. [15.12]

No one restrained him: "My mother, father, and brother kept quiet, until my husband gradually restrained his rage" [15.15]. However, the cow and calf, in distress over the beating of Bahiṇābāī, mourned loudly [15.12-13].

This was not the first time that Bahiṇābāī had suffered at the hands of her husband. In one *abhaṅga* she describes him as "a man of very angry disposition" [15.11]; in another she reports that

> ...I was in constant terror of my husband. I had heard
> of the anger of Jamadagni.[9] My husband showed the
> same characteristic in his dealings with people. [58.2-3]

In *abhaṅga* 16.1a she states quite solemnly, "when it came to his mind to do so he beat me violently." *Abhaṅgas* 60-73 are particularly wrenching, depicting the most desperate longings and depression of a battered wife. Symptomatic of much domestic violence throughout the world and history is the victim's assumption that she somehow is at fault. Bahiṇābāī is no exception to this, though the blame she assigns to herself is colored by particular orthodox Hindu religious beliefs and cultural attitudes. After describing one episode of being beaten, Bahiṇābāī asks, in *abhaṅga* 15.14, "In what duty to my husband had I failed?"

It is clear from the verses in *Abhaṅgas* 60-73 that Bahiṇābāī prayed to Lord Viṭṭhaḷ many times to rescue her from the abuse of her husband. Wondering why God did not feel compassion for her and come to her aid, she contemplated suicide as a way to end her misery [*Abhaṅgas* 66 and 67]. She also questioned how much longer her body could endure her husband's abuse [67.3, 7]. Yet, Bahiṇābāī did not give up her faith in God, but rather rationalized that the abuse she suffered at her husband's hand either must be some kind of test that God was putting her through [*abhaṅga* 67] or else was due to some sin she had committed in a former birth [64.1]. She was reluctant to place any blame on God, but rather tried to comfort herself with the thought "that all this suffering has come because of deeds in a former birth....It is my fate to have to suffer. What can even God [Govinda] do to help me?" [70.2, 4; cf. 71.4]. Her devotion to God was so strong that she insisted "I will not leave the worship of God, even if it should mean the losing of my life" [67.2], referring to the beatings that resulted from her husband's jealousy of her devotions.

In these same *abhaṅgas* [60-73], we find references to the gender bias of the dominant Brahmanical culture which had influenced Bahiṇābāī's own thinking. Bahiṇābāī initially deduced that being born in the form of a woman was a kind of punishment she must endure. She was raised within a religious culture that denied women access not only to many spiritual aids (such as the Vedas, the *Gāyatrī mantra*), ascetic lifestyles, and philosophical texts [see *Abhaṅgas* 60 and 64]), but also denied women direct access to *mokṣa*. The orthodox Brahmanical tradition of her time stressed that *mokṣa* was attainable only by twice-born men and therefore a woman would have to be born as a man to achieve this ultimate goal. This is one of the Brahmanical ideologies that the bhakti tradition challenged by teaching that *mokṣa* was available to people of all walks of life and was dependent on the love of God, not on such things as caste, gender, wealth, or ritual. Bahiṇābāī eventually comes to realize this, but in the meantime she suffers under the dominant hegemony, which confuses and frustrates her, for while she experiences the love of God she is conditioned to believe that she cannot pursue or realize her spiritual goal in this lifetime because she is a woman:

> Possessing a woman's body, and myself being subject to others, I was not able to carry out my desire to discard all worldly things [*vairāgya*]. [60.1]
>
> ...
>
> The Vedas cry aloud and the *Purāṇs* shout that no good comes of a woman. [63.1]
>
> Now I in the natural way have a woman's body. What means then have I to acquire the supreme spiritual riches? [63.2]
>
> Says Bahiṇī: "If a woman's body brings disaster, what chance is there for her to acquire in this life the supreme spiritual riches?" [63.4]

The authoritative tradition, for her the Vedas and the Purāṇas, taught that her body was an impediment to *mokṣa*;[10] and her husband, professionally trained to recite those authoritative texts, abused that same body, taking out on Bahiṇābāī his jealousy, anger and frustrations. Surely Bahiṇābāī's deep faith came at a great cost.

The most intolerable instance of domestic violence that Bahiṇābāī describes follows Gosāvī's declaration of Bahiṇābāī's spiritual advancement. Her husband's fury was so great that he tied her up and beat her, throwing her helpless, battered body aside when his rage was spent (*abhaṅga* 16). Only then were Hiraṁbhaṭ and Bahiṇābāī's parents able to intervene, but by then the damage was done. Her devoted calf, greatly distressed at the treatment of Bahiṇābāī, refused to eat or drink, and within days the calf died. The combination of the severe beatings and her grief at the death of her beloved companion drove Bahiṇābāī into a deep coma.

While in this comatose state, Bahiṇābāī had a vision of Tukārām, whom she affectionately refers to as Tukobā. It was the words of Tukobā that bring her from the edge of death back to consciousness, though it took several more days for Bahiṇābāī to recover her physical strength: "My body is altogether feeble, but my soul is strong" [20.15]. Bahiṇābāī came through the worst of her physical ordeals spiritually strengthened, and at the age of eleven she was reborn as a devoted disciple of Tukārām.

The Spiritual Transformation of Bahiṇābāī

The religious experiences and spiritual initiation (*dīkṣā*) Bahiṇābāī underwent during this comatose period of some eight days are described in *Abhangas* 21-27. These *abhangas* are filled with Bahiṇābāī's longings to meet the great Tukārām, whose image and verses brought her joy and peace of mind. Tukārām's reputation was well-known in the areas in which Bahiṇābāī had traveled, and most likely his popular songs of praise and longing for God (Viṭṭhaḷ) were part of Bahiṇābāī's own repertoire of devotional hymns. Tukārām was as famous for his *abhangas* as he was for being a Śūdra *sant.* Bahiṇābāī described how Tukārām responded to her pleas to become his disciple and recounted a specific dream in which she takes *dīkṣā* from Tukārām and he becomes her *sadguru.*

> ...he placed his hand upon my head and whispered a mantra in my ear. [25.7]
>
> I then placed my head on his feet.... [25.8]
>
> My heart rejoiced. It fixed itself on Brahma, pure Intelligence. I sat up astonished. [25.10]

Bahiṇābāī's initiation is strikingly similar to that experienced by the Śūdra saint himself. Tukārām's initiation from his own guru, Bābājī Caitanya, was also received by way of a dream in which he was taught the same mantra revealed to Bahiṇābāī in her dream.

In these same *abhangas* [21-27] we can discern the emergence of Bahiṇābāī's theological stance. Her compositions show the influence of Vedānta and have a strong Advaitic streak in them. For her, Tukārām, her *sadguru,* and Viṭṭhaḷ, her God, are one and the same.

> Tukobā's eyes are also Pāṇḍurang. His ears are Pāṇḍurang in the form of the *Abhang.* [26.9]
>
> Whatever Tukobā's hand writes, that is clearly Pāṇḍurang. [26.10]

> All the actions of Tukobā are Hari, who makes him one with Himself, through the fact of non-duality. [26.11]

It is Lord Viṭṭhaḷ in the form of Tukārām who comes to Bahiṇābāī's rescue. In many of her *abhaṅgas*, Bahiṇābāī refers to Tukā and Viṭṭhaḷ as her brother (*sahodara*, e.g., 21.12; 67.2; 68.1). (Her own name, Bahiṇī or Bahiṇā, means "sister.") I find this particularly significant, because in Maharashtrian tradition and folklore it is the brother's responsibility to escort his sister from her in-laws' house to her parental home for family visits; he is his sister's protector and her link to the world outside her marital home. In a previous study I have done of Marathi religious folktales, it is the brother, not the husband, who comes to the rescue of a woman in her times of distress. While Bahiṇābāī does have an actual blood-brother some six years younger, it is Viṭṭhaḷ in the form of Tukārām whom she turns to for refuge and protection, as she seeks both solace and safety. Her sisterly affection for Tukārām is evident in the names by which she addresses him, Tukā and Tukobā. Imagining Tukā as her brother is very much in keeping with the Vārakarī tradition's theological imaginings of God as companion, friend, parent or relative.[11]

Bahiṇābāī's spiritual life changed significantly after her vision of Tukārām, yet her domestic life remained very much the same. While Bahiṇābāī's heart is absorbed in her intensified affection for Tukā/Viṭṭhaḷ, her husband's heart is hardened and he is filled with bitterness and rage by her new piety, and he resumes beating her. He called his wife's new obsession demonic, and he was especially humiliated that his wife had focused her mind and heart on a Śūdra, namely Tukārām. The words Bahiṇābāī attributes to her husband in *abhaṅga* 32 reveal a very live tension between the ideologies of the egalitarian bhakti movement and of the Brahman elite, a conflict certainly not restricted to Bahiṇābāī's household or to Maharashtra:

> We are Brāhmans. We should spend our time on the study of the Vedas. [32.1]
>
> What is all this! The *shudra* Tukā! Seeing him in a dream! My wife is ruined by all this! What am I to do? [32.2]

> Who cares for Jayarām and who for Pāṇḍuraṅg? My home has been destroyed! [32.3]
>
> What care I for singing the names and praises of Hari? Even in my dreams, I know not bhakti. [32.4]
>
> Who cares for saints and *sādhus*! Who cares for the feelings of bhakti! Let us always be found in the order of the religious mendicants. [32.5]

Gaṅgādhar denounces the bhakti impulse and stands by the systematic ordering of his Brahmanism.

Resolving the Conflict of Heart and Home

The domestic conflict within Bahiṇābāī's household reached a feverish pitch at this point in her life. Remember, she was only eleven, and, as we learn in *abhaṅga* 34, she was three months pregnant. How was she going to deal with this situation, this conflict? What were her choices? We know from an earlier verse that her parents were unsupportive, and that they basically stood in the shadows, choosing not to intervene in or mediate the differences between Bahiṇābāī and her husband. To be sure, her parents owed their son-in-law a debt, as it was he who had arranged their escape from Devagaon and led them to safe haven. It is clear that Gaṅgādhar was the master of his household, despite the unusual arrangement of a son-in-law's being in residence with his wife's family.

Abhaṅgas 33-35 provide insight into the very different ways in which Hindu culture prepared Bahiṇābāī and her husband to cope with the domestic conflict at hand. While Gaṅgādhar's response reveals his upbringing within a very structured, patriarchal, Brahmanical environment, Bahiṇābāī's decision reflects influence from both the teachings of Marathi bhaktas and the teachings of orthodox Hinduism on the expectations of gendered roles. Let us take a closer look at their different responses to their domestic situation at this critical period following Bahiṇābāī's spiritual awakening.

In response to the domestic conflict intensified by his wife's new status as a holy woman, Gaṅgādhar decided to leave his family to become a renunciant. We know from Bahiṇābāī's autobiography that her husband was a scholar trained in the Purāṇas and in astrology, and that he was from a

Brahman *gotra* (Gautama) more prestigious than that of Bahiṇābāī's father. Gaṅgādhar's behavior, as described by Bahiṇābāī throughout her autobiographical *abhaṅgas,* paints a portrait of a man who expects his authority to be respected and obeyed. He is the master of the household, who expects his wife to be deferential and obedient, submissive and unobtrusive. His cultural and social upbringing has inculcated in him these values and expectations of dominance and authority. We can imagine how his skin must have prickled when Svāmī Jayarām Gosāvī advised him as follows:

> Your wife is a *Yogabhrashta,* and the manner of life she must adopt is of a very austere kind. Now do not distress her any more. [17.8]
>
> By her special wifely duties she will do you service; and you will save your soul. [17.9]
>
> You must possess some good deed done in a former birth. By means of it you have become associated with her. [17.10]

This is surely not what a man of Gaṅgādhar Pāṭhak's upbringing expected to hear—that he should defer to the spiritual prowess of his wife, adjusting his expectations to her life-style. It is not surprising that he curses Jayarām, blaming him for playing a significant role in the destruction of his home [32.3] brought about by the spiritual conversion of his wife. Yet perhaps Gaṅgādhar should have heeded the advice found in one of the mainstays of Hindu Brahmanical authority, the *Mānava Dharmaśāstra* (Laws of Manu), in which it is written (Doniger 1991, 48):

> Fathers, brothers, husbands, and brothers-in-law who wish for great good fortune should revere these women and adorn them. [3.55]
>
> The deities delight in places where women are revered, but where women are not revered all rites are fruitless. [3.56]
>
> Where the women of the family are miserable, the family is soon destroyed, but it always thrives where women are not miserable. [3.57]

While Hindu law and tradition (though perhaps not the popular sentiment honoring Bahiṇābāī) would certainly have supported Gaṅgādhar in his decision to take another wife (had Bahiṇābāī been culpable in her duties as a wife), Gaṅgādhar chooses instead an option sanctioned within Brahmanical orthodoxy: mendicancy and retreat to the forest. In response to their domestic conflict, Gaṅgādhar chooses to withdraw from the complexities of the world and seeks solicitude and consolation in the forest. Here is a man whose role as husband and head of the household within a very patriarchal society has been threatened by his wife's devotions to Tukā/Viṭṭhaḷ. He was no longer the master, guru, or deity of the household, as his wife's attentions were now focused on her sadguru Tukārām. His wife, some twenty-five years younger than him, was no longer dependent on him. The intimacy of the marital relationship was now replaced, at least for Bahiṇābāī, by her intimate fellowship with Tukārām.

We have seen that Gaṅgādhar's initial response to dealing with the conflict of authority within his household was to beat his wife into submission. In their examination of violence against women, Neera Desai and Maithreyi Krishnaraj point out that "[v]iolence accompanies power; it is committed to prove or feel a sense of power; it is an instrument of coercion used to maintain power" (254). We can imagine that Gaṅgādhar, feeling his authority and power within the household being replaced or challenged, initially resorted to beating his wife to demonstrate and reassert his power. His decision to renounce the world, rather than either to take another wife or to continue taking out his frustrations on Bahiṇābāī, can be interpreted as a sign either of a weak man who "shrinks from trouble and anxiety by retiring from the world's conflict" (M. G. Ranade, 70) or of a prudent man realizing that his situation called for a period of withdrawal and reflection. Indeed, Gaṅgādhar's decision to follow the renunciant's path is the beginning of his own conversion experience, which, like that of Bahiṇābāī, comes after a period of life-threatening illness. We must recognize that Gaṅgādhar backed off from the track of domestic violence and at the same time maintained a monogamous path, even though both wife-beating and polygamy were tolerated within the culture of his time (both practices also having their opponents).

Bahiṇābāī's sustained devotion, sanctity, and popularity probably also contributed to Gaṅgādhar's decision to take up the life of a homeless wanderer. His domestic life was no longer private, and perhaps he felt there was more dignity in renouncing his householder life than in remaining in a household in which he felt humiliated by his wife:

> "for people are going to bow down to her, while she regards me as worth but a straw. [33.2]
>
> They will discuss with this woman the meaning of the *kathās*, but she herself will consider me a low fellow. [33.3]
>
> The people make regardful enquiries about *her* while I, who am a Brāhman, have become a fool!" [33.2-4].

To be sure, the traditional roles were reversed within Bahiṇābāī's household; whereas her husband should have been expected to be the superior authority as he was both a Brahman and a male,[12] the visions and inspiration that came to Bahiṇābāī and led to her being recognized as a *yogabhraṣṭa* and a *gosāvī* [33.5] placed her in a position of spiritual superiority and authority, leaving her husband unsure of his role, powerless, and humiliated.

In *Abhaṅgas* 33 and 34, Bahiṇābāī describes her husband as a very frustrated man who feels that his reputation, authority, and respect have been diminished. Her insight into his feelings, evident in the striking portrait she paints of his agony, reveals the great empathy she has for this man who is her husband. Despite her emotional attachment to Tukā and the abuse she has taken from her husband, she seems keenly aware of what her husband is going through. Her description of him is not a hostile one, but rather is mature and sympathetic in its tone. Bahiṇābāī is certainly aware, as other *abhaṅgas* show, of the traditional expectations of a wife. As I read and reread *Abhaṅgas* 33 and 34 as a prelude to *abhaṅgas* 35, in which Bahiṇābāī spells out her duties as a good wife, I began to sense that Bahiṇābāī's response to the domestic conflict, whether out of sympathy to her husband or a sense of her duty as a wife, would be to succumb to the dominant ideal of the submissive wife, prioritizing her husband's demands and desires over her own spiritual desires. While I am troubled by this propensity of Bahiṇābāī, at the same time I am concerned about why this troubles me, as it raises questions about how (and why) I am reading, interpreting and representing Bahiṇābāī, questions I will return to in my discussion below and in the conclusion.

The peaking of conflict within her household, and her husband's decision to leave the household and become an ascetic, cause Bahiṇābāī to reflect on her responsibilities as a wife; these reflections, found in *Abhaṅgas* 35-38, culminate in her decision to "give my body to the joy of rigorous service (for my husband), in accordance with the guidance of the Vedas" [38.2]. In *abhaṅga* 35 from her autobiography as well as in *abhaṅga* 467 from the hymns on *pativratādharma,* Bahiṇābāī reviews the duties and virtues of a good Hindu wife, reiterating the orthodox Brahmanical cliche that a woman's husband is her god. "My duty is to serve my husband," she says, "for he is God to me. My husband himself is the Supreme Brahma" [35.4].

My own initial response to her decision was one of disappointment; I wanted Bahiṇābāī to leave this abusive man and follow her heart in its devotions to Tukārām and Viṭṭhaḷ—I wanted her to follow the paradigm of other women bhakta saints. But she does not. What concerned me, though, was that Bahiṇābāī might fit into another, more disturbing paradigm: that of the battered wife who thinks herself to be at fault, and rather than leaving the abusive environment, takes more abuse, accepting it as a punishment due her. For example, in *abhaṅga* 35, Bahiṇābāī seems to be chastising herself for past behaviors:

> If I transgress my husband's commands, all the sins of the world will be on my head. [35.7]
>
> If I have any other God but my husband, I shall have committed in my heart a sin like that of the killing of a Brāhman. [35.10]

These are harsh condemnations: but are they the words of a repentant, remorseful woman, or are they the words of a woman aware of the cultural norms of her society, who chooses to compromise her own desires, preferencing the happiness of others over her own happiness? We should also consider to what extent her pregnancy influenced her decision to resume her role as a faithful obedient wife. Surely Bahiṇābāī is concerned with the future well-being of her child, and that well-being may be in jeopardy if her husband is to leave. In *abhaṅga* 36.1 she asks, "Supposing my husband should go away to live the ascetic's life, then, O Pāṇḍuraṅg, of what value would be my life among men?" Is Bahiṇābāī just trying to be practical and realistic? Should we fault her for that, or admire her courage? As she provides the litany of wifely duties in *Abhaṅgas* 35 and 467, I cannot help but imagine that Bahiṇābāī, in both composing and reciting these *abhaṅgas*, was trying in good faith to convince herself that this was the way she should behave—certainly the *pativratā* model was the dominant one that she was expected to follow as a Brahman Hindu woman. While Bahiṇābāī's heart and mind are focused on Tukārām, we witness her efforts to defy that emotional (and spiritual) impulse, for she has been taught that her salvation lies in her devotion to her husband:

> The Vedas in fact say that it is the husband who has the authority in matters of religious duties, earthly possessions, desires, and salvation. [35.7]
>
> This is then the determination, and the desire of my heart. I want my thought concentrated on my husband. [35.8]

And in *abhaṅga* 36.3-5, Bahiṇābāī reflects on the necessary complementarity of husband and wife:

> My husband is the life, I am the body....
> My husband is the water in which I am the fish....
> My husband is the sun and I its brightness.
> How can these two be separated?

It is significant that in *Abhaṅgas* 35-38, in which she reaffirms her duties as a wife, Bahiṇābāī uses the Marathi word '*bhratāra*' rather than '*pati*' for husband. The term '*pati*', meaning lord or master, can refer to one's husband but is also frequently used in bhakti circles to refer to one's spiritual lord and divine master, the God of one's desires (*iṣṭadevatā*). Had Bahiṇābāī used the term '*pati*' instead of '*bhratāra*,' we could consider interpreting these particular *abhaṅgas* metaphorically as expressing her longing for union and submission to her beloved Tukā/Viṭṭhal—yet this is not the case here.

By *abhaṅga* 38, Bahiṇābāī has convinced herself that serving her husband faithfully is not only her duty and responsibility, but is also a *sādhana*, "a means of saving both family lines." We could interpret her "saving of family lines" in two ways: first, as a reference to the progeny who both continue the family line and have the responsibility to perform the *śrāddha* (memorial) rites necessary to satisfy the deceased family ancestors as they progress from one life to the next. On a subtler level, Bahiṇābāī may be suggesting that just as the calf was her means to salvation, she, in her role as wife (and mother), may be the one fated to provide the means (*sādhana*) by which her own family achieves *mokṣa.* (Indeed, Bahiṇābāī herself fits her description of the virtues and attributes of a sadguru as found in her *sadguru abhaṅgas,* 162-178.) She recognizes that she has a specific purpose within that family which is related to both her fate and her future: "Says Bahiṇī, 'I shall find my rest of soul in my husband, and the final end to my succession of births and deaths' [38.4].

As it turned out, Bahiṇābāī did serve this purpose: her husband fell deathly ill just as he was about to leave his household to take up the life of a renunciant. While he is in a feverish state, a Brāhman appeared to him, chastising Gaṅgādhar for considering the abandonment of his wife. The elderly wise man advised him: "She is truly a bhakta of Hari. You should likewise be one also" [40.6]. Gaṅgādhar's fever broke and he came out of his illness a converted man; he said to his wife: "Whether it brings us good or evil, we are going to give ourselves fully to the worship of Hari" [41.8]. Together Bahiṇābāī and Gaṅgādhar traveled to Dehu to become disciples of Tukārām, who was in residence there. At last Bahiṇābāī was to lay eyes on the guru she had only seen in her dreams, and, as she reported it, "joy danced in my eyes" [45.4]. And it was here in Dehu that Bahiṇābāī became a mother, giving birth to a daughter by the name of Kāśībāī.

Lest we think that Bahiṇābāī's life was now full and happy, there is still evidence in her *abhaṅgas* that despite her husband's new-found devotion to Viṭṭhaḷ he still harbored a jealousy of her attentions to Tukārām. Bahiṇābāī had to wait until her husband left town before she could spend three days in complete meditation on God [*Abhaṅgas* 73-78]; as she tells us, she could not even bow before Tukārām for fear of her husband's reaction, much less spend days wrapped up in *kathās* in praise of Tukārām [see *Abhaṅgas* 73, 75, and 98].[13] Yet her faith gets her through these difficult times, as she thanks God for helping her to find a way to balance her devotion to God and her duty to her husband:

> In worshipping Thee I can still be true to my duty of devotion to my husband. Thou, O God [Meghashyāma], must thus think also. [68.2]

> The Supreme spiritual riches are surely not contrary to the Vedas. Therefore, think of this purpose of mine. [68.3]
>
> Says Bahiṇī: "O God [Hari], think at once of my longing, by which I can accomplish both." [68.4]

Towards an Understanding of Bahiṇābāī's Decision

In reading through numerous other *abhaṅgas* of Bahiṇābāī I have found clues which have helped me understand Bahiṇābāī's decision to refocus her life in service to her husband rather than in devotion to her God and guru. I have tried hard to understand her decision, for her history as a battered wife who remains in a relationship with an abusive husband is a story all too familiar to us even in contemporary times. Did Bahiṇābāī have a choice? Did she have options? As Gandhi and Shah point out in their discussion of contemporary domestic violence in India "The battered woman is really quite alone in trying to deal with a violent husband." (62). Since Bahiṇābāī's parents lived with her, she did not have the option of returning home, but even if she had, we know that within her culture at that time, for a wife to return to her parental home under such circumstances would have brought disgrace to her family. Shelters and counselling for victims of domestic violence were not an option either, for only in contemporary times have such resources been developed in response to the growing recognition that domestic violence is a widespread phenomenon not restricted to particular cultures or economic groups. Suicide was one option contemplated by Bahiṇābāī, as it is by many abused women in India today.[14]

Bahiṇābāī's spiritual awakening and subsequent devotion to Tukārām which followed her coma was obviously well-known to the community who flocked to her household to witness the change in her: was she possessed, demented, or blessed, people asked. The sant Jayarām Gosāvī declared her enlightened and blessed, and many accepted her new state as reflecting her great devotion and spiritual acumen. Perhaps Bahiṇābāī could have chosen to abandon her life as a householder and wife and become a full-time disciple of Tukārām or some other guru. But she did not. Why? Was it because she was pregnant with her first child? Or was it because her husband soon fell deathly ill and she chose to remain at his side as a good wife and nurse him back to health? Or did her decision have something to do with her new awareness of the essential unity of all things? I think that it was a combination of all these factors. Just as she had nowhere to turn as a battered wife, it is improbable that a pregnant woman would desert her husband and family to go sit at the feet of a guru—this would not only be socially unacceptable, but impractical. Furthermore, her autobiographical *abhaṅgas* reveal a woman who was loyal to her family, virtuous, empathetic, patient, and forgiving, a woman who would not desert someone in distress, least of all her husband. Yet her later, more philosophical *abhaṅgas* suggest that her decision to continue to fulfill her duties as a *pativratā* were based not so much on her obedience to convention as on a new, transformed view of the world in which Bahiṇābāī perceived that "the differences in our worldly life are done away with, through our knowledge of the fact of non-duality.... there is one substance alone; there is no other" [451.7-8].

The conflict between her duty as a wife and her desire to follow her spiritual longings does not surface outside the *ātmanivedana* series of *abhaṅgas*. Many of her other *abhaṅgas* are more philosophical in nature. Some emphasize the importance of fulfilling one's duty, while others sing of the path and realization of bhakti as a means of liberation. Bahiṇābāī understands bhakti as "at the root of indifference to worldly things" [152.4] and "the very highest means of salvation" [152.1]. Her own life choices suggest that it is possible to live in the world, fulfilling one's socially prescribed duties, while cultivating knowledge (*jñāna*), detachment (*vairāgya*), and discrimination (*viveka*), which Bahiṇābāī emphasizes as critical factors to the practice of bhakti. This is very much in line with the philosophy of the Vārakarī panth, which values family life and the fulfillment of one's social responsibilities (*varṇāśramadharma*). In *abhaṅga* 450.1 Bahiṇābāī gives this advice:

> The duties belonging to caste, and those of the *āshrams*...should be carried out perfectly, and God should be held in one's heart with singleness of devotion.

This verse, along with those that I quote below, while not from Bahiṇābāī's autobiographical *abhaṅgas*, nonetheless provides us with theological insight into how Bahiṇābāī was able to worship God while still being true to her duty of devotion to her husband.

> When in one's heart there arises indifference to worldly things, then he does not care for association with what appeals merely to the senses. [158.1]
>
> What can such an one lack of joy? He it is rather who is ever joyous. [158.2]
>
> ...
>
> He who has learned that this worldy life is not the true life, such an one cares not for the objects of sense. [161.1]
>
> While in the discharge of his worldly affairs he acts like one indifferent to them, having left all desires for them, [161.2]
>
> Such a one becomes a witness of the *mana[s]* with its characteristics of good and evil thoughts. [161.3]
>
> He witnesses also to the *buddhi* [reasoning faculty] with its will, the mind with its determination, and the self-consciousness with its purpose. [161.4]
>
> He recognizes all the relationships of this world as of *māyā* origin, his fixed principles being founded on the non-dual Brahma. [161.5]

What can we infer from these verses about how Bahiṇābāī coped with her own domestic situation? In her reading of Bahiṇābāī's situation, Tara Bhavalkar argues that Bahiṇābāī developed a fear and dislike of marriage and conjugal relations due to the fact that she was married as a child to a man six times older than her; indeed, it is evident that she was sexually active at a young age if she bore her first child at the age of eleven. Given this situation, explains Bhavalkar, it is not surprising that Bahiṇābāī writes about not caring for sensual pleasures and advocates detachment from the worldly and the egotistical. Bhavalkar's interpretation is a most feasible one and considers the psychological implications of Bahiṇābāī's domestic and marital situation. I would like to offer another reading, aware that my reading is influenced by my desire to portray Bahiṇābāī as a woman of great strength and moral courage who has transcended, by way of her spiritual awareness, the domestic and social ordeals and conflicts which continue to face her as she continues to live in the world. My more theologically-based interpretation borders on an apologetic of Bahiṇābāī's decision.

Bahiṇābāī fulfilled her social duties as a wife and mother. Her enlightened state, characterized by her recognition of the essential non-dual unity of the universe, allowed her to live and participate in the world. Bahiṇābāī advises:

> Identify your body with the universe, but stand aloof from it as Witnesser. [182.1]
>
> Become yourself the All, and yet be apart from the All. Learn this from the mouth of the sadguru. [182.2]
>
> ...
>
> Considering desire and longing, as Māyā, live happily among men. [182.4]
>
> Be yourself in everything, whether in men or in forests. [182.5]

Bahiṇābāī preaches a path of living in the world but not being of the world. She recognizes that while the body and all worldly things lack reality (*asatya*) [195.4], they also serve a purpose in helping one "to attain the essentials of the way of deliverance" [197.1]. In other words, there is a purpose to living in this world and fulfilling one's dharma that is conducive, given right-thinking (*viveka*), to attaining the "eternal peace in the intense love of Brahma" [196.3]. She recognized that "the life of business and the spiritual life [can] both go on happily together" [460.6] if one cultivates goodness, attention, and devotion. Indifference does not lead to withdrawal from the world, but rather to honest, good, exemplary living within the world. Having realized the unity of all things, Bahiṇābāī could easily shift her devotion from Tukārām to her husband, for they were essentially the same. Bahiṇābāī blended together her duties as a wife, including the worship of her husband, with her worship and devotion to Tukārām, realizing that they were different only in name, not in reality.

Bahiṇābāī's new awareness seemed to include an appreciation of the social realities of her time. She was born into a particular life with particular responsibilities that she was bound to assume. She came to realize that these duties need not, indeed should not conflict with her spiritual goals. In Bahiṇābāī's case, she was born as a woman, and in this final and "thirteenth birth this body has played its part" [98.1].[15] As a wife and mother, Bahiṇābāī served others as a spiritual guide and exemplar. Her role as a wife had a social as well as spiritual purpose. From this life as a woman, the devout Bahiṇābāī achieved *mokṣa:*

> I have set fire to the impression caused by illusion (*māyā*) on my heart, and my heart is now united to the term, "That thou art," and unity with Brahma has been attained. [109.17]
>
> ...my soul has attained its Brahmahood. [109.19]

While one might argue that Bahiṇābāī's enlightenment released her from having to fulfill the domestic duties and lifestyle of a *patīvratā,* it was this very realization of Brahman that allowed her to resume her domestic role as wife and mother. It is possible to become happy and freed from fear by following the path of devotion, but one needs to "put away your thought of self, and your self-consciousness," Bahiṇābāī advises [*abhaṅga* 138.2]. This opportunity is available to anyone and is not limited by caste or gender:

> And of how many more would you have me tell you, belonging to all the four castes, who have attained to happiness, even in this world of care? [139.5]
>
> Says Bahiṇī: "Oh *Mana[s],* by this same path, I have clung to the feet of God with devotion." [139.6]

Exceptional Life, Ordinary Woman

Sanjukta Gupta's and Ruth Vanita's readings of Bahiṇābāī's writings suggest that the circumstances of Bahiṇābāī's life caused her to internalize her devotions while externally going through the motions of the obedient and subservient wife. This would be in contrast to the 'normative' pattern of women bhaktas as outlined by A. K. Ramanujan in which women saints "dramatized their bhakti" (Feldhaus 1985, v), their external actions and social behavior embodying the passion of their spiritual devotions. Gupta explains that Bahiṇābāī had no choice but to internalize her religious activities, since her husband prohibited her from attending harikathā gatherings and going to temples (Gupta, 204-5). This internalization, in contrast to other women bhaktas, allowed her to stay at home "as a humble wife" playing the "role of a dutiful wife while mentally renouncing all attachment to life," including the mental (though not physical) rejection of her husband (Gupta, 205). Bhavalkar takes a similar position and even argues that Bahiṇābāī is like other women bhaktas (who may have left their husbands or been unmarried or widowed) in that she is separated from her husband in thought (though not in deed). While Muktābāī, Janābāī, Mīrābāī, Lallā, and Āṇṭāḷ represent women who followed a dramatic and exclusive path of bhakti, Bahiṇābāī, in the opinion of Sanjukta Gupta, represents a compromise "between her chosen exclusive path of devotion (*bhaktimārga*) and the will of society with its orthodox traditions" (Gupta, 205). Anne Feldhaus also describes Bahiṇābāī's path as one of reconciliation; she quite insightfully observes that Bahiṇābāī's writings and life provide not just an example for other Hindu women on the reconciliation of wifely duties and devotion to God, but also provide an important model for the "domestication of medieval bhakti, its reconciliation with the world and with the orthodox tradition" (Feldhaus 1985, vi). Thus, Bahiṇābāī should not just be studied for the perspective she offers as a woman, but also as an example of the how the tension between religious orthodoxy and bhakti was experienced and dealt with.

It is obvious that Bahiṇābāī's life and writings can be understood on many levels and from many perspectives. Madhu Kishwar has noted that the "specific social dimensions of the lives and work of women bhaktas, have, by and large, been neglected by scholars" (Kishwar, 4). Anne Feldhaus, Ruth Vanita, Sanjukta Gupta, Tara Bhavalkar, A. K. Ramanujan and Friedhelm Hardy are some of the scholars who have reflected on and written about the life of Bahiṇābāī, all of them emphasizing how she stands out from other women bhaktas as one who fulfilled her dharma as a woman (meaning that she became a wife and mother) and lived a deeply spiritual life in bhakti. Yet I cannot help but wonder how many other Bahiṇābāī(s) are out there, for surely there are many other Hindu women who have balanced the domestic life with the devotional life—saints within their own households and lifetimes; but perhaps they neither chose nor had the opportunity to record that experience. If we shone a light on the lives of these ordinary women, to be sure we would discover the exceptional and remarkable in their own lives as each woman confronts her particular domestic ordeals while drawing on the strength of her religious devotions. In this sense, Bahiṇābāī's compositions provide us with a view into one ordinary woman's particular experiences as a wife and bhakta.

In my study of Bahiṇābāī's life and writings, I have chosen to dwell more than my colleagues do in their essays on the aspect of domestic violence within Bahiṇābāī's life. I did not set out to do this, but it was an issue and image too strong for me to ignore the more I got into her writings. In particular I wanted to come to a better understanding of how Bahiṇābāī's spirituality helped her to cope with this situation. Is this why Bahiṇābāī wrote her *abhaṅgas*, particularly the autobiographical *abhaṅgas*, to provide some guidance to other women who found themselves in similar situations?

The rage and beatings of her husband were a reality for Bahiṇābāī, and her life and writings must be examined with an awareness of this domestic situation as a backdrop. While I do not want to overdramatize this aspect of Bahiṇābāī's life, I do not want to dismiss it either; though it is not a subject central to her writings, it is a matter pertinent to understanding her life and the development of her theological stance. While certainly many women of Bahiṇābāī's time suffered abusive husbands, just as many women in the world today do, not every housewife was a victim of domestic violence. Yet wife beating has been a very common form of violence against women, both in Bahiṇābāī's time and now, but it is a very difficult problem to address because of its invisibility. "Wife beating is invisible because it is hidden in the many intimate, intricate and complex layers of the relationship between a husband and wife with overtones of romanticism, sexuality and patriarchy" (Gandhi and Shah, 61). This invisibility is compounded by the fact that in India, as in most other countries, wife beating has been understood as a personal, domestic problem, and neighbors and family members are often afraid to intervene (cf. Gandhi and Shah, 62, 63; Desai and Krishnaraj, 271). This attitude is changing, but very slowly, through combined efforts of education, activism, and law.

Nonetheless, domestic violence is still very much a problem, and one that is often too readily tolerated. There is no doubt that Bahiṇābāī tolerated the rage and beatings of her husband, just as there is no doubt that her religious devotions gave her the strength to cope with this abuse. Her cultural upbringing raised her to expect masculine domination; this attitude prevails even today in India (as well as in other parts of the world). Gandhi and Shah (63) observed an attitude among contemporary Indian women who have suffered beatings from their husbands which is similar to one we have heard in some of the *abhaṅgas* of Bahiṇābāī: "There is also the 'something is wrong with me' feeling or that it is not the man's problem, but the woman's failure as a wife." Bahiṇābāī, as we have seen, initially thought the beatings of her husband were some test of God that she must endure, connected by causality to her past life, to her birth as a woman, and to her future achievements. She prayed to Tukārām for understanding, for solace, for strength. Some would say that Bahiṇābāī found an escape in religion from her difficult domestic situation. Gandhi and Shah (64) have observed that

> Wherever women have found alternatives [to domestic violence], reconciliation, divorce, escape in religion, etc., they have grasped them because the constant assault on the body and mind, with the inability to fight back, erodes self-confidence, respect and the will to live.

We see all of these things in Bahiṇābāī's autobiographical *abhaṅgas:* her self-doubt, her contemplation of suicide, her initial contempt for her female body which denied her access to union with God, and the lack of self-respect conditioned by a culture which viewed the characteristics of women as "foolishness, selfishness, seductiveness, and deception. All connection with a woman is disastrous" [*abhaṅga* 63.3]. But we also see that Bahiṇābāī overcame these obstacles once she looked into herself and knew herself, and this knowledge led Bahiṇābāī to proclaim with great confidence, "I am Brahma" [107.8]. The *abhaṅgas* that are not part of her autobiography, which for the most part reflect her experience of and teachings on the fullness of God, reveal a woman of great strength, wisdom, and insight—there is no lack of self-confidence or self-respect in these *abhaṅgas.*

To draw strength and wisdom from one's spiritual knowledge is quite different from escaping into religion, which implies weakness. To say that Bahiṇābāī escaped into religion would be to deny her the intellectual and spiritual wisdom which she obviously possessed. While Bahiṇābāī lived the life of an ordinary woman, she was no ordinary woman—she was a *yoga-bhraṣṭa,* an individual perched in this life on the edge of *mokṣa.*

According to Bahiṇābāī and the testimonies of others she includes in her compositions, at the time she was born into this particular historical life (her thirteenth rebirth) she was already far along the path of spiritual maturity. To have knowledge of previous lives is a sign of a great yogī. It is unclear at what stage of her life Bahiṇābāī became aware of her past lives (she narrates them to her son on her deathbed), but as her autobiography unfolds in her *abhaṅgas,* we witness her growing awareness and knowledge of herself, which in turns led her to an understanding of the world (and its essential non-dual nature) and her ultimate realization of God (*mokṣa*). The freedom that Bahiṇābāī experienced with this enlightenment allowed her to live fully and joyfully in the world, attending to the needs and desires of those, such as her husband, who were surely further down the spiritual ladder than her (though she herself would not make such a distinction). Thus "In body, speech and mind she submits herself to her husband, and the knowledge of Brahma plays at her door" [469.3].

Bahiṇābāī's spiritual wisdom was a strength that allowed her to live in her world and within the conditions of her household. As she says, "A saint performs all his duties while in the world, yet not of the world" [228.1]. It has not been easy for me to discern a particular path advocated by Bahiṇābāī. My own reading of her *abhaṅgas* is influenced by my own experiences, questions, and politics as a twentieth-century American woman who is a student of Indian religious traditions. I have worried that my interpretation of her theological resolution of her *strīdharma* and bhakti could be taken to imply that a battered woman should accept the abuses of her husband, as, according to Bahiṇābāī's theology, such worldly matters are essentially unreal. Bahiṇābāī herself said that the unreal leads to the real (Brahman), and, as we see in her own testimony, she had to work through many difficult layers to reach this level of understanding. But Bahiṇābāī also recognized that there are many different ways of coming to this awareness, so we should not conclude that Bahiṇābāī was advocating her own particular path or resolution for others. While her *pativratādharma abhaṅgas* seem to be preaching to women on how to be obedient and faithful wives, reiterating the classic stereotype of the submissive wife, if we look at these *abhaṅgas* in the context of her bhakti theology, a new layer of meaning is revealed which is reminiscent of the message Krishna conveys to Arjuna in the *Gītā*: perform wifely duties in the name and joy of God, cultivating detachment from worldly things (*vairāgya*). For Bahiṇābāī, a true bhakta is one so absorbed in God that one's duties (be they of a wife, a husband, a mother, a son) are done fully and perfectly out of devotion and in service to God.

I do not think that Bahiṇābāī's life represents a compromise any more than it represents a particular choice of lifestyles. Rather, I think that she comes to realize the complementary nature of her dharma (as a housewife) and her bhakti. Yet, why should this surprise us? The Vārakarī panth is known for its advocacy of integrating the life of bhakti into the household. And as Uma Chakravarty has pointed out in her study of South Indian bhakti movements, "there was no contradiction in the pursuit of bhakti and the life of the *grahastha*." Yet she goes on to point out that "In practice, however, the collapsing of such a boundary operated only in the case of men. For women, the dichotomy persisted and the tension between marriage and devotion to a personal god was never successfully resolved" (Chakravarty, 23). Chakravarty adds that in the South Indian bhakti tradition, "We have no equivalent among the bhaktins of the normal male bhakta, or someone like Tiruvalluvar, for example, who was a great devotee and a good householder at the same time" (23). The Marathi bhakti tradition does have such an example in Bahiṇābāī, who, in the words of Anne Feldhaus provides "a promise that [other Hindu women] too can remain faithful to their wifely duties and still participate fully in the bhakti tradition" (Feldhaus 1985, vi).

Bahiṇābāī's autobiographical *abhaṅgas* make us acutely aware of the tensions and ordeals a Hindu woman could experience trying to serve both a husband and a personal God. While these tensions do not completely subside, at least for her husband, Bahiṇābāī seems to have reached a personal resolution of this conflict, and she subsequently lives a full and peaceful life, her death coming at the age of seventy-two. This is not to suggest that Bahiṇābāī's life should be viewed as exemplary or paradigmatic, for I think that she recognized that each individual worked out her or his own good and path, depending on one's own particular circumstances; but her life story does provide an alternative to what has been represented as the normative pattern of female bhaktas, those women saints whose lifestyles often fly in the face of *pativratā* dharma as they follow their passionate longings for God. Perhaps the climate of medieval Marathi bhakti, which was characterized more by the feeling of *vātsalya* (tender affection) than the *rasa* of the erotic (*śṛṅgāra*) contributed to Bahiṇābāī's ability to be at home with her husband and her God. But to suggest that Bahiṇābāī is the exception is to overlook the lives of numerous other ordinary women (and men) who in the joy of their bhakti live good and righteous lives as they go about fulfilling their everyday duties and responsibilities.

> In this Kaliyuga there are sants (saints) to be found from house to house, just as plentiful as the cheapest vegetables. [114.2]
>
> Says Bahiṇī, "Right feelings will save you all. This is all I wish to say." [114.3]

ENDNOTES

[1]Rāmdās (1608-1681) was the founding guru of the Samartha sampradāya, a Vaiṣṇava sect focused on the worship of Rāma.

[2]There is no critical edition of Bahiṇābāī's *abhaṅgas,* and Anne Feldhaus, for one, has raised a question as to whether the *abhaṅgas* attributed to Bahiṇābāī are the work of a single author (Feldhaus 1985, vii). The *abhaṅgas* are composed in old Marathi, and Justin Abbot, in his preface to his edition and translation of Bahiṇābāī's *abhaṅgas,* discusses the difficulty in translating some of the compositions. The verses from Bahiṇābāī's *abhaṅgas* that I cite in this essay are from Justin Abbott's 1929 edition, *Bahiṇābāī: A Translation of Her Autobiography and Verses,* which includes both the Marathi text of her *abhaṅgas* and his own translations (although, as he notes in his preface, he has not translated all of her verses). Anne Feldhaus's article on Bahiṇābāī (Feldhaus 1982) contains some new and beautiful translations of Bahiṇābāī's work done by Feldhaus, among them some verses not included in the Abbott collection. See her bibliography for additional Marathi collections of Bahiṇābāī's *abhaṅgas.*

[3]Among other Marathi women saints of the medieval period are Mahadambā, Muktābāī, Janābāī, Kānhopātrā, Veṇubāī, Akkābāī, Bayābāī, and Aṃbābāī.

[4]Viṭṭhaḷ, Viṣṇu in his form at Pandharpur, is also referred to as Pāṇḍuraṅg and Viṭhobā—among other epithets—by Vārakarī devotees, including Bahiṇābāī.

[5]The recently published collection, *Women Writing in India,* edited by Susie Tharu and K. Lalita, includes selections from Janābāī and Bahiṇābāī, but not Muktābāī. Margaret Macnicol's 1923 edition of *Poems by Indian Women* includes verses from Muktābāī, Janābāī, Bahiṇābāī, and a verse from the wife of the Mahār saint Cokāmeḷā (14th cent.). Ranade's study, *Mysticism in Maharashtra,* regrettably pays little attention to the contribution of women saints in Maharashtra; however, in his introduction he recognizes Muktābāī, Janābāī, and Kānhopātrā as the three most conspicuous female bhaktas in Maharashtra, noting that they are comparable to Julian of Norwich, Catherine of Siena and St. Teresa (R. D. Ranade, 4). He does not mention Bahiṇābāī. A more contemporary essay on women saints in Maharashtra by

Ruth Vanita, published in the journal *Manushi,* focuses on Muktābāī, Janābāī, and Bahiṇābāī.

[6]Tara Bhavalkar, in her essay "Women Saint-Poets' Concept of Liberation," is of the opinion that the wishes of Muktābāī and Janābāī "did not play much of a role in the fact that they remained unmarried." She adds in a footnote that "in their times, it was not socially acceptable for Muktābāī, as the daughter of a renouncer, or for Kānhopātrā [another acclaimed female bhakta from Maharashtra who did not marry], as the daughter of a courtesan, to marry."

[7]"*Ātmanivedana,*" meaning autobiography, is a term used by the sant Rāmdās, one of Bahiṇābāī's spiritual guides, to refer to the surrendering of the Self to God. In his famous work *Dāsabodha,* Rāmdās explains that "Ātmanivedana is attained when we have properly investigated the nature of Self and God. When the Devotee realizes God, he becomes one with Him, and the distinction between God and Devotee vanishes" [VIII.8.9-24, quoted by R. D. Ranade, 406]. This passage is significant in understanding the title given to Bahiṇābāī's autobiographical *abhaṅgas,* for it is soon after she has experienced the nature and presence of God that Bahiṇābāī feels inspired to write. The words come to her, she says, "like the tide of the ocean or like the words of the Gods of Thunder [Indra] in the sky of my heart" [78.5].

[8]After giving birth to her first child, a daughter named Kāśībāī, Bahiṇābāī writes: "The feelings I had [towards the calf], I felt now in their fullness" [54.6]. This verse, as well as evidence in the *Niryāṇapara Abhaṅgas,* causes me to disagree with A. K. Ramanujan's assessment that Bahiṇābāī bitterly regretted having children (Ramanujan 1989, 14). The Vārakarī tradition, as I have already mentioned, values maternal attributes, and Viṭṭhal is often referred to in the feminine as Viṭhāī; Bahiṇābāī herself speaks of the motherly nature of the guru [180.5] and addresses God as "my mother" [*āī mājhā,* 235.1].

[9]Jamadagni is the name of a *ṛṣi* who was the son of Bhārgava Ṛṣika and his wife Satyavatī. One time his very devoted and perfect wife observed a couple in the throes of passion and was envious of their experience; Jamadagni became enraged at her feelings and thought them defiling. His anger and jealousy led him to command each of his sons in turn to kill his wife, their mother. The fifth son, Paraśurāma, was the only one to obey, and he cut off his mother's head. Jamadagni granted his son a wish in return for his obedience, and he asked that his mother's life be restored.

[10]While Bahiṇābāī cites the Vedas and Purāṇas as representative of the dominant authority on religious matters, it would be misleading to take her statement about the negative attitude toward women as applicable to all the Vedic corpus and Purāṇas, for there are plenty of examples from both these textual traditions that portray women in a positive and favorable light. Indeed, many of the Purāṇas come out of the spirit of bhakti and emphasize the accessibility of *mokṣa* (usually defined as some type of spiritual union with God) for all, regardless of caste and

gender. However, there is no doubt that the dominant cultural ethos in India and Maharashtra during Bahiṇābāī's time was one in which women were considered and treated as structurally inferior to men in legal as well as religious matters, and it was not difficult for a priest or a pandit to find verses in the scriptures to support the derogatory and negative attitudes toward women. For an example of how some scriptural passages are used to control and subordinate women, see the presentation and analysis of Tryambaka's eighteenth-century *nibandha* on *strīdharma* (the duties of women) in I. Julia Leslie's book *The Perfect Wife.*

[11]Of related interest here are *Abhaṅgas* 79-99, in which Bahiṇābāī looks back on her previous twelve lives. She addresses these particular *abhaṅgas* to her son, significantly named Viṭhobā, and points out that in all of her previous lives he acted in one capacity or another as a companion of hers. While I do not have the space in this particular essay to examine the significance and complexity of this relationship as represented in these *Niryāṇapara Abhaṅgas,* it is important to point out the various inversions of familial relationships that are at play in Bahiṇābāī's compositions and which underscore the Vārakarī emphasis on family, including the nurturing, familial relation of God and devotee.

[12]In orthodox or śāstric Hinduism, Brahmanhood is associated with birth, maleness, purity, learning, high status and rank, and privilege (and this is how it is used here in reference to Gaṅgādhar). Bahiṇābāī reviews some of the traditional characteristics of Brahmanhood in *Abhaṅgas* 404-410, but goes on to question many of these characteristics in *Abhaṅgas* 411-421 ("But who in reality is to be called a Brāhman?" [411.1]). For Bahiṇābāī, Brahmanhood is not determined by birth, bodily form, color (*varṇa*), learning, or social or religious duties, but by the knowledge of Brahman: "But the real Brāhman is the one who knows Brahma. Thereby he becomes in actuality God Himself." [434.2]. "Says Bahiṇī, 'He who lives his life in Brahma is a Brāhman. It is not a question here of caste.'" [427.4]

[13]I have read these particular *abhaṅgas* as reflecting a period after Gaṅgādhar's conversion and their move to Dehu. However, Bahiṇābāī's *abhaṅgas* are not necessarily in chronological order, and indeed *Abhaṅgas* 55-78 seem to be a revisiting and summary of some of the key moments in her life which she has already provided details on in *Abhaṅgas* 2-54. It is possible that Bahiṇābāī is referring to incidents of her husband's jealousy earlier in her life, but evidence in *abhaṅgas* 73.2 leads me to infer that Bahiṇābāī still had reason to fear the oppression of her husband even after his own conversion to a life of spiritual devotion.

[14]Gandhi and Shah (62) note that a battered woman "might go away to a neighbour's or relative's house, or make a desperate suicide attempt. In Maharashtra as many as 1725 young married women committed suicide from 1983 to 1986. Other states have reported a two-fold increase in women's suicide cases."

[15]In her previous twelve lives, as narrated in *Abhaṅgas* 90-96, Bahiṇābāī was also

born as a woman; in the first three she was unmarried; in her fourth through seventh rebirths, it is unclear from her narrative whether or not she was married; in her eighth life she was widowed at a young age, whereas in her ninth life she herself died young; she was married in all three of her rebirths leading up to her current life, and during her tenth life became the mother of three sons.

References

Abbott, Justin E., tr. *Bahiṇā Bāī: A Translation of Her Autobiography and Verses.* Poet-Saints of Maharashtra Series, No. 5. Poona: Scottish Mission Industries Co. Ltd., 1929; reprinted Delhi: Motilal Banarsidass, 1985.

Abbott, Justin E., and Pandit Narhar R. Godbole, trs. *Stories of Indian Saints: Translation of Mahipati's Marathi Bhaktavijaya.* Two volumes in one. Delhi: Motilal Banarsidass, 1982 (first printed Poona, 1933).

Bhavalkar, Tara. "Women Saint-Poets' Concept of Liberation," in *Images of Women in Maharashtrian Literature and Religion*, ed. Anne Feldhaus. Forthcoming from SUNY Press.

Chakravarty, Uma. "The World of the Bhaktin in South Indian Traditions—The Body and Beyond." *Manushi*, Nos. 50-52 (Jan.-June, 1989), 18-29.

Deleury, G. A. *The Cult of Viṭhobā.* Poona: Deccan College Postgraduate and Research Institute, 1960.

Desai, Neera and Maithreyi Krishnaraj. *Women and Society in India.* Ajanta Publications, 1987.

Desai, Sudha V. *Social Life in Maharashtra under the Peshwas.* Bombay: Popular Prakashan, 1980.

Deshpande, Kamalabai. "Great Hindu Women in Mahārāṣhṭra," in *Great Women of India,* ed. by Swami Madhavananda and Ramesh Chandra Majumdar, pp. 343-361. 2nd edition. Mayavati: Advaita Ashrama, 1982.

Doniger, Wendy with Brian K. Smith, tr. *The Laws of Manu.* London: Penguin Books, 1991.

Feldhaus, Anne. "Bahiṇābāī: Wife and Saint." *Journal of the American Academy of Religion,* 50 (1982), 591-604.

Feldhaus, Anne. "Foreword" in the 1985 republication of Abbott's *Bahiṇābāī,* q.v.

Gandhi, Nandita and Nandita Shah. *The Issues at Stake: Theory and Practice in the Contemporary Women's Movement in India.* New Delhi: Kali for Women, 1992.

Gokhale, Balkrishna Govind. *Poona in the Eighteenth Century: An Urban History.* Delhi: Oxford University Press, 1988.

Gupta, Sanjukta. "Women in the Śaiva/Śākta Ethos," in *Roles and Rituals for Hindu Women,* ed. Julie Leslie, pp. 193-209. London: Pinter Publishers, 1991.

Hardy, Friedhelm W. "Diary of an Unknown Girl." *Religion* 10, No. 2 (Autumn, 1980), 165-182.

Hawley, John Stratton and Mark Juergensmeyer. *Songs of the Saints of India.* New York: Oxford University Press, 1988.

Khanolkar, Savitribai. *Saints of Maharashtra.* Bombay: Bharatiya Vidya Bhavan, 1978.

Kishwar, Madhu. "Introduction" [to special issue on Women Bhakta Poets]. *Manushi,* Nos. 50-52 (Jan.-June 1989), 3-8.

Leslie, I. Julia. *The Perfect Wife: The Orthodox Hindu Woman according to the Strīdharmapaddhati of Tryambakayajvan.* Delhi: Oxford University Press, 1989.

Liddle, Joanna and Rama Joshi. *Daughters of Independence: Gender, Caste and Class in India.* London: Zed Books Ltd., 1986.

Macnicol, Margaret, ed. *Poems by Indian Women.* The Heritage of India Series. Calcutta: Association Press, 1923.

McGee, Mary. "Ties of Protection, Ties of Affection: Brother-Sister Festivals in Maharashtra," unpublished manuscript.

Raghavan, V. *The Great Integrators: The Saint-Singers of India.* 4th edition. New Delhi: Ministry of Information and Broadcasting, Government of India, 1979 (first published 1966).

Rajan, Rajeswari Sunder. *Real and Imagined Women: Gender, Culture and Postcolonialism.* London and New York: Routledge, 1993.

Ramanujan, A. K. "On Women Saints," in *The Divine Consort: Rādhā and the Goddesses of India*, edited by John Stratton Hawley and Donna Marie Wulff, pp. 316-324. Beacon Press, 1986 (first published 1982).

Ramanujan, A. K. "Talking to God in the Mother Tongue." *Manushi,* Nos. 50-52 (Jan.-June, 1989), 9-14.

Ranade, Mahadeo Govind. *Rise of the Maratha Power.* Classics of Indian History and Economics. New Delhi: Ministry of Information and Broadcasting, Government of India, 1974 (first published Bombay, 1900).

Ranade, R.D. *Mysticism in Maharashtra (Indian Mysticism).* History of Indian Phil., Vol. 7. Delhi: Motilal Banarsidass, 1982 (first published Poona, 1933).

Taves, Ann, ed. *Religion and Domestic Violence in Early New England: The Memoirs of Abigail Abbot Bailey.* Religion in North America Series. Bloomington and Indianapolis: Indiana University Press, 1989.

Tharu, Susie and K. Lalita, eds. *Women Writing in India: 600 B.C. to the Present.* Volume I: *600 B.C. to the Early Twentieth Century.* New York: The Feminist Press at CUNY, 1991.

Vanita, Ruth. "Three Women Sants of Maharashtra: Muktabai, Janabai, Bahinabai," in *Manushi,* Nos. 50-52 (Jan.-June, 1989), 45-61.

Women Saints East and West. London: Ramakrishna Vedanta Centre, 1955.

ĀṆṬĀḶ'S DESIRE

Dennis Hudson

According to the sacred stories of the Śrī Vaiṣṇavas of southern India, in the early years of the Kali Yuga, the Goddess Earth (Bhūdevī or Bhūmi) appeared as a baby girl under a basil plant. The basil (*tulasi*) was in the garden of the Śrīvilliputtūr temple forty miles southwest of Madurai, the Pāṇḍya capital. A great devotee of Kṛṣṇa named Viṣṇucitta found her there and raised her as his daughter named Godā. As she matured, her innate female passion focussed exclusively on Kṛṣṇa, whom she sought to marry. Out of her intensely passionate desire for him she composed fifteen Tamil poems, the single poem of thirty stanzas, *Tiruppāvai* (TP), and the set of fourteen sequential poems, *Nācciyār Tirumoḻi* (NT). Then, at the request of the Bhagavān himself, her father processed her northward to the Śrī Raṅgam temple where she entered the sanctum, climbed up onto the altar of the reclining Raṅganātha, and entered into his stone icon. She had returned to her origin in the Goddess Earth, the material "womb" of the Bhagavān's Śakti, Śrī Lakṣmī. Because of her extraordinary passion for Kṛṣṇa, Śrī Vaiṣṇavas know her now as Āṇṭāḷ, "she who rules." And for his own devotion to Kṛṣṇa, they know her father as Periyāḻvār, "the great Āḻvār."

The poems Āṇṭāḷ left behind now serve as a verbal means by which the ardent devotee may enter into the Goddess's own *viraha-bhakti* in her guise as Āṇṭāḷ, into her passionate attachment to the Supreme Male for whose pleasure she exists, and by means of whom she knows herself. Śrī Vaiṣṇavas believe that Āṇṭāḷ's experience of Kṛṣṇa reveals the Bhagavān's true nature, a revelation that confirms the wisdom of the Upaniṣads.[1]

The more a devotee shares in Āṇṭāḷ's enjoyment of him, the more truly the devotee knows the Bhagavān and his or her own self. Her pāvai poem, *Tiruppāvai,* is regarded as especially authoritative in this regard and is given special prominence in the daily liturgies of Śrī Vaiṣṇava temples and homes. Throughout the month of Mārgaḷi (December-January) it shares today a public prominence along with Māṇikkavācakar's Śaiva pāvai poem, *Tiruvempāvai.*

For Śrī Vaiṣṇavas, the Bhagavān Vāsudeva Kṛṣṇa is the absolutely transcendent Nārāyaṇa, the owner of spacetime, who revealed himself in space and time in various avatārs, but most fully as Kṛṣṇa. "Kṛṣṇa," *Bhāgavata Purāṇa* (BP) 1.3.4 says, "is the Bhagavān himself."[2] He also dwells in icons residing in temples and homes, and within the consciousness of every sentient being as its essential Self (*ātman*). Indeed, by means of the Goddess Earth he is the very material matrix of oneself and the world. Yet few know him, for the blindness of ignorance resides so deeply in consciousness that people normally assume that they and their world center in themselves, not in him. They thus cannot see him, living in a kind of sleep that they mistakenly assume is wakefulness. To counter that ignorance, the Bhagavān Nārāyaṇa, who is Vāsudeva, descends as avatār to awaken people to him, to stimulate a desire for he who is already within them. Intense desire for him is all that one needs to see him, the tradition insists—"He desires those who desire him" (NT 11.10)—but in the present Kali Yuga, even so simple a thing as desire for God who resides at the center of one's own consciousness is difficult to generate, and once generated, it is still difficult to pierce through the darkness of the ego to see him.

Nārāyaṇa's gracious response to that problem is to use the problem as the solution. Since desire to continue to be who one normally and ignorantly thinks oneself to be is the overwhelmingly dominent force in life, a propulsive thirst at the deepest levels of embodied consciousness in the soul (*jīva*), the Bhagavān does not destroy that desire, but uses it. He directs it to himself. By embodying himself so that people can experience him through their physical apprehensions—through touching, tasting, smelling, hearing, seeing, and thinking—he then stimulates in those bodies a desire for him. That sets up, of course, a conflict between the desire for him as a sensual object and the desire for any other.

Once he has "hooked" people through their bodies by means of his bodies, he proceeds to eradicate ignorance centered on the "I." Envisioned as battles against demons, he eradicates ignorance within consciousness until all competitive desires are either removed or put in their proper place. Desire for him then takes over as the only propulsive thirst; such purified people are now qualified to see God who had been present to them all along as their own Self. As Kṛṣṇa told Arjuna in *Bhagavad-gītā* (BG) 9.29, "I am the same in all existing beings, none is despised by me, none is favored, yet those who experience me because of attachment, they are in me and I am in them." Those who experience (*ye bhajanti*) Kṛṣṇa do so by means of attachment (*bhakti*) to him generated by a knowledge of themselves and of him that has overcome ordinary ignorant consciousness.

That exceptional and mysterious experience of being in Kṛṣṇa while Kṛṣṇa is in oneself is so subtle that no single metaphor can express it fully, though that of lovers gets close to its intimacy, as Āṇṭāḷ experienced. The devotee's side of the relationship—in the traditional stereotypes of gender—is the intense and innate desire (Sanskrit *kāma*; Tamil *māl*) of the dependent female that results in attachment (*bhakti*). It puts all ordinary desires of life aside in favor of seeing the only object that will satisfy every desire. The Bhagavān's side of it is the protective male's gracious and loving response, for Kṛṣṇa went on to tell Arjuna in BG 9.34: "Living with your mind on me, attached to me, sacrificing to me, prostrating to me, indeed you shall escape to me, having thus disciplined yourself as one who depends on me." In that teaching, Arjuna was to play the faithful wife (*pativratā*) in relation to Kṛṣṇa the husband (*pati*).

Stepping outside of Śrī Vaiṣṇava hagiography and theology, historical evidence indicates that Āṇṭāḷ and her father Periyāḻvār were poets and mystics who probably lived in the 9th century. The type of male-female relationship that Kṛṣṇa referred to in the *Bhagavad-gītā* had been highly developed in classical or Saṅgam Tamil poetry (c.lst-2nd centuries CE) and Āṇṭāḷ drew upon that literary tradition to expresss her own experience of Kṛṣṇa. Vidya Dehejia has made Āṇṭāḷ's entire work available in one volume, *Āṇṭāḷ and Her Path of Love* (Albany, N.Y.: SUNY Press, 1990), but in this study I will draw on my own prose translations.[3]

Since I have written about Āṇṭāḷ and the later story of her life in the *Journal of Vaiṣṇava Studies* ("Āṇṭāḷ Āḻvār: A Developing Hagiography," 1.2 (1993): 27-61), I would now like to touch on details not fully covered there. What follows will complement especially pages 27-42 of that article. My interest here is to place Āṇṭāḷ's desiring devotion into its historical context and to examine her development of it from the liturgies she used for worship, for she was a skilled religious poet within a specific liturgical tradition.

The few contemporaneous data about her appear in her poems and those of her father Viṣṇucitta anthologized as *Periyāḻvār Tirumoḻi*, but nowhere else.[4] As noted above, Śrī Vaiṣṇavas now tell a story of her that expresses their belief in her divine nature, but it developed later. It encodes a sophisticated theology developed within the liturgical system of the Pāñcarātra Āgama as I attempted to demonstrate in the above cited article. Here, however, I would like to explore her genius as a poet and mystic when she is regarded not as a divine being, but as a human of virtuoso accomplishments. The following brief summary of my interpretation attempts to put a reasonable body on the skeletal data now available.

An Interpretation of Her Life

The poet called herself Godā (Kotai in Tamil). She was born to a Brāhmin father, Viṣṇucitta, in a family long connected to the service of Kṛṣṇa. She and her father lived in Villi's New Town, some four hundred miles southwest of Kāñchipuram, the Pallava capital, and about forty miles southwest of Madurai, the Pāṇḍya capital. The geographical span between those two dynastic capitals, connected by Bhāgavata temples and liturgies, is where we must place Godā's cultural and religious context as one of the twelve Āḻvār poets (though from now on I shall refer to her by her later title of Āṇṭāḷ, "she who rules," given because of her aggressive longing for Kṛṣṇa).

Āṇṭāḷ's two sets of poems have been preserved in the canon of the Śrīvaiṣṇava sect, which follows the Pāñcarātra Āgama. In contrast to the six Nāyanār poets of the Śaiva canon, who spanned a period of two hundred or more years, the historian K. V. Raman has noted that the Āḻvārs appear to have lived within a span of three-generations in the 8th and 9th centuries.[5] If so, their period coincides with the sixty-five year reign (731-796) of Nandivarman II Pallavamalla at Kāñchipuram and with the reigns of his son and grandson. Pallavamalla was an initiated slave of Kṛṣṇa (a meaning of "Bhāgavata"), as probably were his son and grandson, and their influence appears to have extended into the deep south. The temple in Villi's New Town, for example, may be dated on stylistic grounds to c.775, during Pallavamalla's rule and after he had defeated the Pāṇḍyan in a struggle over control over the Kāveri river delta; it was perhaps a reflection of his Bhāgavata patronage.

In about 770, in the Pallava capital, Pallavamalla built a stunning temple with three floors in its mountainous tower (*tritala vimāna*). It was a

Viṣṇu-house for Vāsudeva Kṛṣṇa, a three-dimensional maṇḍala in stone that was the first of its kind as far as we know. As I have explained in a study of that temple published previously in the *Journal of Vaiṣṇava Studies* ("Vāsudeva Kṛṣṇa in Theology and Architecture: A Background to Śrīvaiṣṇavism," 2.1 (Winter 1993), pp.139-170), its fifty-six sculpted panels follow the Pāñcarātra Āgama and depict the *Bhāgavata Purāṇa*, a Sanskrit text that is inseparable from the Āḻvārs' Tamil poetry and a major component of Kṛṣṇa worship to this day.

Moreover, that temple appears to have spawned a sequence of seven or eight similar three-floor Viṣṇu-houses, some now in worship and others in ruins, that linked the entire Tamil region from the Pallava domain south through the Pāṇḍya domain and beyond to the Āy dynasty of modern Trivandram. It appears, then, that in some way the Pallava emperors at Kāñchipuram in the 8th and 9th centuries presided over a Bhāgavata sect widely spread among the Tamil elite.

It is significant, then, that the two most prolific Āḻvārs appear to have been provincial administrative officials. The non-Brahmin Kalikanri ("Tirumaṅgai") held the administrative position of "ruler of Mangalanāṭu."[6] He appears also to have functioned as a poet to the court, for he wrote two poems about his emperor's own dīkṣā (*Periya Tirumoḻi* 2.8 and 5.8), about his performance of a purification rite (5.1), about the Parameccura-viṇṇagaram he built in Kāñchipuram (2.9), and about his (or his son's) architectural development of the of the temple in Mayilai on the coast (2.3).[7] Simultaneously, about four hundred miles to the south in the Pāṇḍya realm another non-Brahmin poet named Śatakopan ("Nammāḻvār"), who apparently served in the Pāṇḍya provincial administration,[8] composed poems that Śrī Vaiṣṇavas came to believe are vernacular forms of Veda. Among them, two (*Tiruvāymoḻi* 7.6.5 and 8.7.9) draw upon the same esoteric maṇḍala that Pallavamalla had built into his imperial vimāna of three stories.[9]

By at least 800, it appears, Kṛṣṇa worshippers at both ends of Tamil-speaking India shared a common temple and maṇḍala liturgy in which visualization (*dhyāna*) play a significant role.[10] As we shall see, Āṇṭāḷ used that entire geographical span to structure *Nācciyār Tirumoḻi*, and both of her works reveal two ways that Bhāgavatas worshiped at the time in that region: the majority in a congregation united in their shared service of a temple icon, and an elite minority in the solitary quest for enstatic consciousness (*samādhi*).[11]

Judging from her poems, Āṇṭāḷ (Godā, Kotai) and Periyāḻvār (Viṣṇucitta) belonged to the cultural and religious elite. She had received considerable literary training, certainly in classical Tamil and probably in Sanskrit as well, and had developed the ability to use those skills to weave profound and complex poetic tapestries that superficially appear simple. At some period in her life she must have received initiation (*dīkṣā*) into the worship of Nārāyaṇa in the form of Kṛṣṇa, a fact she stated in the first stanza of her first poem (TP 1), when she said that the son of Nanda and Yaśoda, "with black body, red eyes, and a face like the sun and moon, is Nārāyaṇa himself, and he will give us our drum." She used the drum to signify the intended goal of the worship, which was to serve Kṛṣṇa intimately (TP 29). She believed that Kṛṣṇa resided in the temple of Villi's New Town (Śrīvilliputtūr) as the male reclining on the snake in its sanctum; the icon depicts him in the form of Madhusūdana, "slayer of Madhu and Kaitabha," whom her father visualized as Vaṭapatraśāyi, "the baby reclining on the banyan branch in the cosmic flood"—the seer Mārkaṇḍeya had seen him in his own visualization (BP 12.8), and the Kṛṣṇa story (*Kṛṣṇakathā*) says that baby was Yaśoda's own child (BP 10.7.34-37). Viṣṇucitta specialized in visualizing that child, but his daughter focussed her attention on him as an adolescent.

Āṇṭāḷ's Mantra

Āṇṭāḷ's poems suggest that the basis of her system of worship (*sādhanā*) was the fundamental Bhāgavata mantra, the eight-syllable *Om namo nārāyaṇāya*. In the first poem to record her visualizations in her set of fourteen (NT 2.1.) she said, "O man who abides as Nārāyaṇa praised by a thousand names, because our mother's brother's wife received you as her son, surely you will rid us of our pain." She played cleverly with the dual seers Nara-Nārāyaṇa in that statement, because the same sentence may be interpreted to mean that Nara and Nārāyaṇa together had taken birth as Yaśoda's son. The dual seers Nara ("man") and Nārāyaṇa ("the abode of man") suggest that mantra, whose literal meaning is "Om, veneration to the abode of man," and simultaneously represent the relation of the disciple (Nara) to the ācārya (Nārāyaṇa) by means of whom that mantra is transmitted. Moreover, by identifying the envisioned gopīs as children who are Kṛṣṇa's cross-cousins, she invoked the Tamil ideal of such cousins being destined to marry one another, which explains that the pain he will rid them of is longing for him as lover. Right at the beginning, then, she stated her means and her goal, which are the same—Nārāyaṇa.

The mantra appears again in NT 5.11, where she said that "people adept in reciting this verbal garland full of little things are indeed those who say *Namo nārāyaṇāya.*" In the next stanza the envisioned gopī dreamed of her marriage to Kṛṣṇa and expressed the goal of the sādhanā centered on that mantra (NT): "For this life and for seven times seven births, God Nārāyaṇan will take and possess me."

Āṇṭāḷ's initiation had committed her to a liturgical discipline (*sādhanā*) that used maṇḍala, mudrā, mantra, and nyāsa to divinize her body, prāṇāyama to control her breath and purify her mind, and dhyāna to create visions. She and her father followed the Pāñcarātra liturgical school that initiated women, men, non-Brāhmins, and Brāhmins into those esoteric methods of worship, and out of the visions she created in her sādhanā, it appears, she composed her poems. They verbally embody her own experience of Kṛṣṇa, which itself resulted from her personal application of Kṛṣṇa's teaching to Arjuna we noted above: "Those who experience me because of attachment, they are in me and I am in them."

Āṇṭāḷ's Ācārya

Apparently Āṇṭāḷ was not married. She said in NT 1.5 that she would not marry a human, only Kṛṣṇa, and she consistently identified herself with her father Viṣṇucitta and never with a husband or any other patrilineage. Most likely Viṣṇucitta had been her initiating ācārya—tradition assigned him that role in relation to a Pāṇḍya king named Vallabhadeva, and Āṇṭāḷ suggested that he played that role for her, too, in the way she allusively described him in the final signature stanzas of her poems read sequentially.

She first described her father Viṣṇucitta in TP 30 as "master priest of beautiful Putuvai with the cool garland of fresh lotus." The term for priest, *bhaṭṭar,* signifies a Bhāgavata Brāhmin who had received the "consecration of the wheel-and-lotus maṇḍala" (*cakrābja maṇḍala dīkṣā*) that qualified him to serve as a priest for others;[12] and the term for master, *pirā<u>ṉ</u>,* suggests he had special authority, signified perhaps by the lotus garland, which later tradition said he offered daily to the reclining Kṛṣṇa in the New Town temple. In NT 1.10 she described him as "Viṣṇucitta<u>ṉ</u>, chief (*ko<u>ṉ</u>*) of the people of Putuvai," suggesting an authoritative social position in the town. The next three statements describe the sources of his esteemed authority—he belonged to a Brāhmin lineage called Veyar who sang the Veda through rāgas (*paṇ*): "Viṣṇucittaṉ, the leader of Villi's New Town, which prospers those whose work is to sound Veda" (2.10); "master priest, ruler of Putuvai, where people recite the four Vedas through rāgas" (5.11); and "chief of New Town famous for Veyar" (6.11).

Sounding the Veda through music or rāgas probably referred to Viṣṇucitta's own Tamil poems that he composed to meet the needs for vernacular songs to use in temple liturgies. His noted song "Many Years" (*Pallāṇṭu*) is sung in temples to this day, and Āṇṭāḷ mentioned it by that name in TP 26 in a similar liturgical context. The next stanza states that his ability as a composer-performer made him famous, a "master priest whose fame matches beautiful Putuvai" (7.10); and the one following explains that those poems reveal him to be a master at visualizing Kṛṣṇa, "the chief of Putuvai's people, who does not swerve in the enjoyment [of God]" (8.10). As Viṣṇucitta's poems collected in *Periyāḻvār Tirumoḻi* reveal, his enjoyment (*bhogya*) was of Kṛṣṇa whom he perceived through his virtuosity in the discipline of attachment (*bhakti-yoga*).

Two complete stanzas then explain why his skill at visualization was so highly prized. First she said,

> My good friend, God reclining on the cobra bed is a wealthy person, a great person, what can we little people do? Yet if Villi Putuvai's Viṣṇucittar makes his deva come in a powerful way, we see that for sure. (10.10).[13]

Viṣṇucitta's ability to visualize, compose, sing, and probably act out what he sang in mime, somehow enabled his daughter and others to see Kṛṣṇa for themselves. She then explained that he summoned his deva according to the theology of the *Bhagavad-gītā*, where Kṛṣṇa had assured Arjuna that "he desires those who desire him," a succinct summary of 18.64-66, which Bhāgavatas consider the most authoritative statement in that crucial text:

> "The righteous Śrī Raṅgar himself declared the great statement of truth and Viṣṇucitta heard it, 'He desires those who desire [him],' and if he is false to that word, who then will continue a sādhanā?" (11.10)

Her point was that Viṣṇucitta had received that crucial statement as a mantra from his ācārya and acted on it in his worship. She implied that Viṣṇucitta had passed the mantra on to her as her ācārya, and now in her own sādhanā she expected Kṛṣṇa to fulfill his promise. She made that quite clear right at the beginning of the penultimate poem of the set (13.1) where she said, "I repose in a [state] consecrated for the vision of the black deva named Kṛṣṇa." If he did not show himself to her as promised, what would be the point of going on with her sādhanā?

Moreover, when she concluded that poem, she identified herself as "the excellent Godā belonging to Viṣṇucittaṉ, the *nakar nampi* of Villi's Putuvai" (13.10). The word *nakar* can mean both town and temple, and the word *nampi* denotes an elite person greatly esteemed. She used the latter word at least four times in *Nācciyār Tirumoḻi*, but in reference to Nārāyaṇa or to Kṛṣṇa.[14] By using it for Viṣṇucitta here at the end of a poem that begins with her consecrated state, she signaled that he held a position analogous to Nārāyaṇa and his descent as Kṛṣṇa, which is the functional position of the ācārya in sādhanās. Furthermore, she probably intended both meanings of *nakar*: her ācārya was the *nampi* of both the temple and the town.

Āṇṭāḷ's Sādhanā

In her sādhanā, Āṇṭāḷ did not avoid sexual desire in the manner of a radical ascetic, but used it to gain Kṛṣṇa. She addressed her own erotic desire (*kāma*) directly through liturgical action, first invoking it in her body, and then manipulating it to bring her face-to-face with Kṛṣṇa in her inner consciousness where he would take her to himself as the Self (*ātman*) at the center of her being. In the process, she created a poetry rich in the sensual pleasure of him as the only male in her erotic life. In this respect, her rites resembled those of the Buddhist female adept, Sahajayoginīcintā of the 8th century, whose Sanskrit text, "Realization of Reality through Its Bodily Expressions," has recently been analyzed by Miranda Shaw.[15] I doubt, however, that Āṇṭāḷ engaged in sexual rites with a man, although by having brought Vāsudeva into his own heart through mantra, her ācārya would have embodied Vāsudeva Kṛṣṇa for her.[16] In Shaw's analysis, the Buddhist female and her male partner visualized themselves as Buddhas when they employed sexual intercourse in sādhanā; in contrast, Āṇṭāḷ visualized herself as the gopī Piṉṉai longing for that union. Her poetry does not celebrate the joy or bliss of their sexual union, but the "enjoyment" (*bhoga*) of their separation and of her longing for him. Her eventual union with Kṛṣṇa in enstatic consciousness (*samādhi*) she represented by silence and an implied full moon.

According to Āṇṭāḷ, Kṛṣṇa had stimulated desire for him in her heart—the center of consciousness—but had refused to reveal himself to her face to face. Most likely, that initial stimulus had come from the mantra *Om namo nārāyaṇāya* implanted by the ācārya through dīkṣā, a verbal penetration through her right ear into the center of her own soul.[17] She used a sexual metaphor to account for that verbal "seed" of Nārāyaṇa planted inside her own body: "He entered inside and sowed my ruin," her envisioned gopī said in 5.2, using the clandestine sexual union of lovers to describe the mantraic penetration that had committed her to a lover who did not show himself and thus, in the terms of that literary theme, brought her public shame. To restore her honor, he must marry her.

She represented the fulfillment of her longing by two modes of enjoyment (*bhoga*), feasting and sexual union. With other devotees, she sought to feast with Kṛṣṇa at the end of Margali, the goal stated in TP 27 and symbolized by the full moon of Margali. Alone, she sought marital union with him as she stated in NT 1, a solitary experience symbolized by the full moon of Paṅguṉi (*Paṅkuṉi*), a mode of consciousness in which Kṛṣṇa would come to her face-to-face and transport her to enstasy (*samādhi*).

Crucial to her sādhanā was her imaginative identification with a gopī in the Kṛṣṇa story as related in *Bhāgavata Purāṇa* 10, a text that the Kāñchipuram temple reveals had already been put into the basic form in which we now find it by the mid-8th century, prior to Āṇṭāḷ's time.[18] In both sets of poems the envisioned gopī used a member of Kṛṣṇa's family as the means to get to him. In TP 17 she persuaded his cowherd father, mother, and elder brother to let her with her friends go to his bedroom door where he slept with Piṉṉai and awaken him. Piṉṉai was Kṛṣṇa's own cross-cousin who from birth he had been destined to marry, and she appears to have been a form of the goddess Śrī in her mode as Caṇḍika-Durgā.[19]

In Tiruppāvai, Āṇṭāḷ called upon "our Goddess" (*em pāvai*) through a repeated refrain at the end of each stanza, an invocation that suggests the goddess Śrī in her mode as the Power of Delusion or Sleep (*yoga-māyā, yoga-nidrā]*) who becomes Caṇḍika-Durgā.[20] Her presence is implied by the reclining Madhusūdana icon in New Town where Āṇṭāḷ focussed *Tiruppāvai*, and that icon itself alludes to the story of Caṇḍika-Durgā's origins as found in *Devīmāhātmyam* 1.49-78.[21] In turn, the Kṛṣṇa story refers to that story when it relates his birth (BP 10.3.47-4.13) and his theft of the gopīs' clothes while they performed the winter bathing vow that sought him as husband (10.22.1-7). In TP 18-20, the envisioned gopī pleads with Pinnai to awaken Kṛṣṇa so they may address him, and appeals to her explicitly in TP 20 as the goddess Śrī.

In *Nācciyār Tirumoḻi* Āṇṭāḷ shifted the perspective. Although she did not say so explicitly, it is evident that in the envisioned scenes of poems 2-14 she imagined herself to be Pinnai developing from a small girl into the gopī sharing Kṛṣṇa's bed she had addressed in *Tiruppāvai*. Prior to those poems, however, when expressed her ritual intent (*saṅkalpa*) in NT 1.1, she invoked the Bhagavān's formation as "the pre-eminently mighty" passion (*vyūha pradyumna*) impelling her own embodied consciousness and gives rise to the desire (*kāma*) and anger (*krodha*) she feels. In the Kṛṣṇa story, desire and anger took birth as Kṛṣṇa's son by Rukminī named Pradyumna, and as his son by Jambāvatī named Sāmba—rebirths respectively of the devas Kāma and Skanda (BP 10.1.28-30). She invoked those two half-brothers in that first poem in order to get the desire and anger in her own subtle and gross bodies to take her to their paternal source, the Self residing beyond those bodies in the lotus of her own heart. In other words, the passion that impelled her consciousness toward Kṛṣṇa was itself a mode of Kṛṣṇa emanating from her own center. By experiencing the attachment (*bhakti*) created by that passion, she experienced Kṛṣṇa as present in his absence. Yet she passionately longed for his visible sensual presence, and in her poems used two full moons of the calendar to signify what she had in mind.

The Calendar

Those two full moons reveal Āṇṭāḷ's use of the year, the month, and the day-and-night as the frame on which she wove her verbal tapestries. Bhāgavatas commonly organize the year by beginning it with the month that Kṛṣṇa (in BG 10.33) identified as the most auspicious, Mārgaśirṣa. That Sanskrit month is identified with the Tamil month of Mārgaḻi that ends with the winter solstice. Mārgaḻi (Mārgaśirṣa) symbolizes the pre-birth period of the universe, the moment of unmanifest plentitude before space-time emerges from Nārāyaṇa's womb, a "moment" recapitulated by every pre-dawn hour,[22] which is therefore known as "the hour of *brahmā*" (*brahmamuhūrta*)

According to the analogy between a human year and a day in the life of the devas, the month of Mārgaḻi represents the last period of the devas' night, their "hour of *brahmā.*" In Mārgaḻi, the sun prepares to dawn for the divine day, which in the human year occurs at the winter solstice on the first day of the next month. Correspondingly, the month of Tai is the period of about 6-8 a.m. for the devas, the month of Māci is about 8-10 a.m., and the month of Paṅguṉi is about 10-12 m. That period extending from before the winter solstice to the spring equinox represents about 4 a.m. to noon, the most auspicious part of any human day. As the potent sun hidden in darkness begins to rise in Mārgaḻi and matures to its full potential in Paṅguṉi, humans awaken, arise and perform ritual acts (*karma*) intended to feed the devas. Analogously, during those months the devas awaken in Mārgaḻi, and some of them marry later in the morning in Paṅguṉi.[23] To delineate that sequence as a single unit, Āṇṭāḷ began *Tiruppāvai* with the Mārgaḻi full moon and ended *Nācciyār Tirumoḻi* with the Paṅguṉi full moon. To make it even more explicit, she used "Mārgaḻi" as the first word of *Tiruppāvai* and "Tai"—the month following—as the first word of *Nācciyār Tirumoḻi.*

As she stated in NT 1, when she had finished the rites of the bathing vow that thematically structures *Tiruppāvai,* she began the maṇḍala rites that thematically structure *Nācciyār Tirumoḻi:*

> The whole month of Tai I purified the ground and laid out a graceful maṇḍala, and from the first day of Māci I decorated the streets with fine sand and made them beautiful, O god without a body, and wondering "Will I ever live?" I worshiped you and your younger brother—You can direct me to the Lord of Veṅkaṭam whose hand holds the incomparable Wheel that spits hot fire, can't you? (1).

Read one after the other, her two sets of poems embody her experience of herself in relation to Kṛṣṇa as it unfolded over three and one-half months of continuous sādhanā based on the themes of that period. The bathing vow of Mārgaḻi sought good husbands for girls and rain for the country, and on its full moon Āṇṭāḷ sought the communal service of Kṛṣṇa. With the first day of Tai begins the Tamil "marriage season" when alliances may be arranged, and Āṇṭāḷ enlisted Kṛṣṇa's sons to arrange an alliance with their father. Māci's full moon commemorates Śiva's burning of Kāma to ash, and the veneration of that bodiless deva begins on the first day of

Paṅgu<u>n</u>i and culminates fifteen days later when the moon becomes full near the constellation called Paṅgu<u>n</u>i Uttaram (*uttara phalguna*)—it is then that Kāma (erotic desire) joins his wife Rati (erotic pleasure) and the devas marry.

The Full Moon

A full moon functions variously in the Bhāgavata religion based on Veda: as the sign of the ancestral realm of repeated death and birth; as the vessel of soma, the divine drink of insight and wisdom that leads one beyond that realm; and as the fire-sacrifice in which the Bhagavān reveals himself in his complex fullness as a dwarf that swells like the moon to encompass all of space and time. The full moon of the most auspicious month of Mārga<u>l</u>i (Mārgaśirṣa) is especially valued and in *Tiruppāvai* Āṇṭāḷ used it to represent the entire month. Each of its thirty stanzas represents a day in the month, but the action of the poem takes place on the full moon day itself, because its fullness signifies access to the fullness of Nārāyaṇa embodied as Kṛṣṇa. Contrastingly, in the first poem of *Nācciyār Tirumo<u>l</u>i*, Āṇṭāḷ shifted four months later to Paṅgu<u>n</u>i, yet never mentioned its full moon even though that is its goal. Its fourteen poems move day-by-day toward the moon on the fifteenth when devas marry. Consequently, the full moon that symbolizes the longing for a husband is made explicit, while the full moon that symbolizes the fulfillment of that longing remains implicit. Yet the two moons bracket the chronological span that underlies and unites both poetic works.

Lunar Phases, Weather and the Bhagavad-gītā

Let us now turn to Āṇṭāḷ's use of the lunar phases that underlie the *Bhagavad-gītā* and that imply a change in weather. The light-half of the lunar month begins with the moon's appearance on the first day after the new moon, a mere sliver, and extends until it is fully round and brilliant on the fifteenth day. The nights become increasingly light with the moon's soft, cool glow. If we place the first chapter of the *Bhagavad-gītā* on the first day of the waxing moon—probably of Mārgaśirṣa (Mārga<u>l</u>i) as Kṛṣṇa suggested in BG 10.35—and match each chapter to one succeeding day, the fifteenth chapter falls on the day of the full moon. In that chapter (15.20), Kṛṣṇa says that he at last has revealed to Arjuna his most secret or mysterious teaching (*guhyatamam śāstram*), and that whosoever understands it will have his (or her) life's work done. That indeed was Āṇṭāḷ's goal, to have her life's work done on the full moon day of Paṅgun̲i.

As I shall argue below, Āṇṭāḷ used the lunar pattern that underlies the *Bhagavad-gītā* to organize the poems of *Nācciyār Tirumol̲i*, so that there is a direct correlation between her work and Kṛṣṇa's teaching to Arjuna. In other words, *Nācciyār Tirumol̲i* may be read as her experiential commentary on that highly authoritative Bhāgavata scripture.

When the light half of the month falls near the Paṅgun̲i Uttaram, the weather slowly grows hotter. Āṇṭāḷ used the swelling moon of Paṅgun̲i and its increasing heat to express both her growing desire for Kṛṣṇa and the cumulative intensity of the sādhanā she had vowed to observe as reported in the first poem. That paralleled Kṛṣṇa's gradually unfolding revelation to Arjuna culminating in BG 15, but which had unfolded in three distinct phases: chapters 1-6; chapters 7-11; and chapters 12-15. They correspond to lunar phases from the day after the new moon through the full moon marked by first (*eka*), the sixth (*ṣaṣthi*), and the eleventh (*ekadaśi*) days. Āṇṭāḷ matched those phases in the thematic divisions of *Nācciyār Tirumol̲i*. Poem one states her intent for the maṇḍala rites, and her visualizations during those rites produced the poems in three thematic divisions: poems 2-6; poems 7-11; and poems 12-14, with the successful conclusion (*siddhi*) of poem 15 implied. To make that pattern clear, let us consider each phase in the *Bhagavad-gītā* and in *Nācciyār Tirumol̲i* as delineated by the days of the waxing moon.

Days one through six:

The sixth day of the waxing moon concludes a period concerned with conception, childbirth, and family known as the "portion of sexual pleasure" (*rati-kalā*).[24] In the *Bhagavad-gītā*, chapter six similarly brings to a close the theme of Arjuna's family, whose inevitable ruin has led him to give up the fight. Analogously, Āṇṭāḷ's sixth poem celebrates the sexual pleasure that brings family into being, and her envisioned gopī reports a dream of her royal marriage to Kṛṣṇa that anticipates the climax of her sādhanā on the fifteenth day. Moreover, through a verbal echo of poem two that begins *nāmam āyiram* ("a thousand names") and depicts the gopī's prepubescent childhood, poem six begins *vāraṇam āyiram* ("a thousand elephants") and brings to a close her sexual maturation as an adolescent ready for marriage, and in ordinary marriages to progeny—a fact Āṇṭāḷ noted in the signature verse by promising children to those who recite this wedding poem skillfully (which Śrī Vaiṣṇavas today do at weddings).

The sequence of poems two through six bears closer examination. In poems two and three, Āṇṭāḷ developed an older image from classical Tamil literature, that of an idyllic childhood of innocent and immature sexuality when girls make dolls out of sand near a pond and decorate them with flowers, and boys flirt with them and show off by climbing a tree and jumping into the pond.[25] In poem two, the envisioned gopī (Piṉṉai as a child) is a pre-pubsecent girl building sand houses in the street; Kṛṣṇa teases her because she is one of his cowherd kin he is eligible to marry when she matures. In poem three, that same gopī is older and has begun to develop sexually. While bathing with other gopīs in a pond, Kṛṣṇa steals their clothes and teases them erotically: "We won't do *that*," she says, "it's not right—You're a boy and you know these things, don't be in such a hurry" (NT 3.2).

In poem four, the envisioned Piṉṉai has gone through puberty and is ready for sexual union with Kṛṣṇa and longs to marry him. To see if her marriage will actually happen, she plays the "kūṭal," a fortune-telling game based on the joining (*kūṭal*) of lines drawn in the sand. Āṇṭāḷ appears to have followed Vedic timing in this poem. It prescribes sexual union on the even nights from the fourth through the sixteenth after a woman's menstruation.[26] If in this poem she had taken the new moon to represent the envisioned gopī's menstruation—probably her first, which was an auspicious event in Tamil culture—then the "joining" game of the fourth poem, played during daylight on the fourth day after menarche, would anticipate the coming night on which Veda allowed the virgin her first sexual union.

The fifth poem provides evidence for that interpretation, because Kṛṣṇa's pre-marital union with the gopī is now in the past, although he still has not shown his face and she suffers acutely from the shame of her ruined unmarried virginity: "The spotless one holding a sparkling conch in his left hand didn't show me his form when he entered inside and sowed my ruin, and all day as my life pours out he dances about, watching" (5.2; also 10.9). That theme, too, is a classical convention: She had a clandestine sexual union with her lover; he took her bangle, symbol of her chastity, and left promising to return and marry her; waiting, she longs for him desparately, sleepless from frustrated desire, tossed about by the heaving ocean of her own passion. In contrast to that classical version, however, the only boat that can rescue the envisioned gopī is named Vaikuṇṭha, "He who extends everywhere," a name that signifies in Pāñcarātra theology both Nārāyaṇa as Vāsudeva Kṛṣṇa and the realm in which he resides, Kṛṣṇa's "highest home" (*dhāma paramam*) of BG 15.6.

The gopī in that fifth poem recalls all of that as she addresses a *kuyil* bird, another classical theme. She wants the bird to fly to her lover and remind him of his promise to restore both her "bangle (an actual bangle and her sexual purity) and her honor by marrying her.

> Just because I take pleasure in the Lord of Spring, that man the color of black gem who wears a jewel crown, is it right that I lost my bangle?...(1)
> The spotless one holding a sparkling conch in his left hand didn't show me his form when he entered inside and sowed my ruin, and all day as my life pours out he dances about, watching...(2)
> I haven't seen that hero coming anywhere...(3)
> O Kuyil, my bones melt, the lids of my splendid spear-like eyes won't close, and many days now I've been in the sea of sorrow tossing about, for I don't have the boat named Vaikuṇṭha—You, too, know the ache that separation from those you love gives, don't you?...(4)
> I long to see the golden feet of him who dwells in Villi's New Town, and my eyes fight like fish and I can't sleep...(5)
> The Lord of the Senses whom the gods everywhere worship and praise gives me pain, and the beauty of my white pearl-like teeth and my red lips and my breasts has disappeared...(6)
> I long to make love to him who sleeps on the billowing Ocean of Milk, and my breasts swell with pleasure and boil my spirit over and grieve me...(7)
> But that man's broad hand powerfully bends his bow, and he is a gentleman and decent, and we have an agreement between us that only he and I know...(8)
> O Kuyil, I've been caught in a snare the color of a young parrot who's called Śrīdhara...If you want to live in this grove, you'd better tell him with the conch and wheel to come, and you'd better make him bring my golden bangle and give it to me...(9)

> That day he measured the world and I long for him, yet in his slavery he treats me cruelly—I didn't know how I would suffer when the southern breeze and the moon cut me through—so if you want to go on living in this grove, O Kuyil, don't hurt me; go tell Nārāyaṇa to come today, or I'll chase you right out of here...(10)

In the sixth poem, the gopī dreams of her marriage to Kṛṣṇa, and with that the theme of sexual maturation that leads to marriage and family comes to an end, paralleling Kṛṣṇa's analogous conclusion of that theme in BG 6.8-9.

Days seven through ten:

Then, just as Kṛṣṇa in BG 7 shifts Arjuna's attention from attachment to his family to attachment to Kṛṣṇa himself—"Attach your mind to me, son of Pṛthā (BG 7.1)—Āṇṭāḷ in her seventh poem focussed even more intensely on the unseen Kṛṣṇa. The imagined gopī is now fully mature and fully conscious of Kṛṣṇa as her goal: Having given her chastity to an adolescent boy who promised to give it back by marrying her but has done so yet, her attachment to him in their separation (*viraha-bhakti*) is feverish, so she attempts to cool herself by addressing Pāñcajanya; he is the white conch from the cool ocean that Kṛṣṇa held in his left hand when he "ruined" her (5.2), and holds to his lips to blow. She wants to know from Pāñcajanya what Kṛṣṇa's mouth tastes like.

Even though unsatisfied, desiring attachment itself is a mode of Kṛṣṇa's presence to her, because he is present through the absence that causes her entire mind to focus on him, thereby illustrating Kṛṣṇa's instruction, "attach your mind to me" (BG 7.1).[27] Not only is that experience true in ordinary love, but it is more especially so in Pāñcarātra theology, where, as we noted, desire is a form that Vāsudeva Kṛṣṇa takes in his formation (vyūha) as the "pre-eminently mighty" (*pradyumna*) passion (*rāga*) from which both desire (*kāma*) and anger (*krodha*) emerge (BG 3.37). Yet Āṇṭāḷ did not take desire and anger as her enemies, as Kṛṣṇa had taught Arjuna to do when struggling with his attachment to family, for she had already freed herself from family. She took them instead as friendly devas and invoked them both right at the beginning of the work (NT 1.1)—"I worship you and your younger brother." Desire is the main focus of NT 1, and anger will appear in 13.8.

By introducing the conch in poem seven, Āṇṭāḷ signalled at least two themes. One is emancipation from birth and death that comes through attachment to Kṛṣṇa. As the story of Pāñcajanya's origins reveals (BP 10.45.37-50), when Kṛṣṇa blows his conch, it signals his authority over the law of karma and over Yama, ruler of the dead. The conch touching his lips thus anticipates emancipation from death and birth as his promised response to attachment to him. The other theme is water, which continues through poem eleven. The watery conch in Kṛṣṇa's left hand balances the fiery wheel in his right that will appear in poem ten. The water represents the rain that falls in the summer in Tamilnadu, but more especially in the autumnal monsoon that appears in the eighth poem; there the envisioned gopī speaks to dark rain clouds about Kṛṣṇa standing on the distant Veṅkaṭa mountain, Āṇṭāḷ's ultimate goal as she had said in 1.3.

Water and rain clouds signal a change in the weather; the heat of the Paṅgu<u>n</u>i Uttaram increases in the summer with its scattered showers, and then begins to cool with Tamilnadu's crucial monsoon and its association in literature with sexual union.[28] The rains cause flowers and blossoms and restless birds to abound in Viṣṇu's Great Grove (*Māliruñcolai*) north of Madurai. In the ninth and tenth poems, the envisioned gopī tells them about the pain she increasingly feels as she waits for Kṛṣṇa to appear.

Āṇṭāḷ's introduction of shifting weather patterns suggests that she had envisioned the year to be passing, so that beneath the sādhanās focussed on the two full moons that structure her works is the cycle of the year. Accordingly, as the rains give way to the cool and fertile months of "winter," the cycle moves into Mārga<u>l</u>i whose full moon stands at the center of *Tiruppāvai.* Her two poetic works thus form a circle: Paṅgu<u>n</u>i's implicit moon becomes Mārga<u>l</u>i's explicit moon, symbolizing an endless experiential movement from longing to fulfillment back to longing and then again to fulfillment. That, it appears, is the nature of attachment to Kṛṣṇa in separation.

Poem ten contains an important liturgical allusion that we should note in detail, because it reveals the type of liturgy assumed by both the *Bhagavadgītā* and Āṇṭāḷ. The envisioned gopī of NT 10.2 introduces the blazing wheel in Kṛṣṇa's right hand as she addresses flowers in the rain-nourished mountain grove. Mostly likely those flowers that blossomed upward toward the sun were lotuses; their appearance here together with the fiery wheel probably alludes to "the consecration of the wheel-and-lotus maṇḍala" (*cakrābja maṇḍala dīkṣā*), the Pāñcarātra liturgy that we earlier noted had conferred the title of *bhaṭṭar* on Viṣṇucitta. If we turn to a modern description of that dīkṣā, we note that it began on the tenth day of the waxing moon and lasted for three days—a timing that corresponds to this tenth poem and to BG 10.[29]

Āṇṭāḷ's gopī says.:

> O flowers blooming upward, the Light visible beyond the worlds above is the Primordial Person of Veda in whose right hand the Wheel appears, yet without burning like its blazing fire, you can put me among those enlisted there, can't you?

Her faith is that the lotuses are able to *enlist* her into the assembly at Vāsudeva's feet in Vaikuṇṭha, his "highest home." She does not want to be taken there now, which would imply her death, but to be assured of a place there when the time for her death comes, and then to be protected from the burning fire of the wheel; she proably meant protection from the fiery purification of sins, for in *Tiruppāvai* 5, the envisioned gopī had said that when the body, the voice, and the mind focus on Kṛṣṇa in worship, all the sins that have come and those waiting to enter become ash, "like cotton in a fire." Desire for Kṛṣṇa is itself purifying.

The reason she addresses lotuses is explained by the maṇḍala design: Twelve lotuses bloom at the doorways and corners of the square that frames it, and one blooms at the center inside a circle or wheel. Dots placed on that central lotus signify the Bhagavān: eight dots for Nārāyaṇa's eight-syllable mantra, or twelve dots for Vāsudeva's twelve-syllable mantra.[30] By appealing to those maṇḍala lotuses through the voice of her gopī, Āṇṭāḷ invoked that dīkṣā ceremony and appealed to Nārāyaṇa-Vāsudeva as both the goal of her sādhanā and her means to attain it.

That three-day dīkṣā ceremony provides yet another thematic structure for poems ten, eleven, and twelve, which Kṛṣṇa uses in an analogous manner in chapters ten, eleven and twelve of the *Bhagavad-gītā*. In response to Arjuna's confession of faith in him in BG 10.12-18, Kṛṣṇa carefully describes the worlds of spacetime laid out like a maṇḍala in 10.19-42.[31] Let me suggest the way both texts employ that dīkṣā theme by briefly summarizing K. Rangachari's description of the ceremony as it is now practiced.[32]

On the dīkṣā's first day (the tenth day of the waxing moon), the setting of the maṇḍala liturgy is prepared.[33] As noted, that matches Kṛṣṇa's chapter ten and Āṇṭāḷ's poem ten. On the dīkṣā's second day (the eleventh day of the waxing moon), the maṇḍala of the wheel with a lotus at its center is drawn on a platform and the disciple receives consecration. During it, the ācārya repeats on behalf of the disciple a prayer to the Bhagavān that expresses the intent of the envisioned gopī in 10.2:

> We who are bound by family ties completely like so many cows, can hope to be liberated from these bonds only by you; we have no other means except you. For the removal of these bonds your grace is necessary and the only way to secure your grace is by worshipping you. So I pray to you to help this ignorant person depending only upon your mercy on his behalf to get him out of the bonds of Saṁsara. To enable him to do so let him hereafter be permitted by you to worship you.[34]

Analogously in BG 11.36-49, Arjuna appeals to Kṛṣṇa for grace in response to the overwhelming vision of him as burning Time; and in poem eleven, Āṇṭāḷ expressed that same idea through a succinct summary attributed to Kṛṣṇa: "I desire those who desire me" (11.10).

On the dīkṣā's third day (the twelfth day of the waxing moon), the disciple's body is symbolically cremated while her soul is placed at the feet of Vāsudeva who resides in the lotus in the ācārya's heart. Her soul is then reborn into her newly created and purified body and the ācārya serves as her "mother." She receives a new name. The ācārya then utters in her right ear the eight-syllable root mantra and others, and turns her over to the Bhagavān as one who has surrendered herself.[35] Kṛṣṇa in BG 12 implies that such a ritual rebirth has taken place and that Arjuna has surrendered to him, because only then does he give him the most complete and esoteric instruction in the Bhāgavata religion that continues through BG 15. He praises such surrender in 12.11-12: "take refuge in my yoga, perform the renunciation of the fruits of all actions and restrain yourself...[for] unending peace comes from renunciation." Matching that refugee theme in her twlefth poem, Āṇṭāḷ's envisioned gopī asks her friends to take her to the places where Kṛṣṇa may be found, as if seeking refuge.

Keeping that brief excursus into the three-day ceremony of the tenth, eleventh, and twelfth days of the waxing moon in mind, let us turn to the third phase that begins with the eleventh day.

Days eleven through fourteen

The *ekadaśi* day of the waxing moon is for Bhāgavatas an important fast day, a day when the dead and the living communicate.[36] That symbolism emerges in BG 11.21-31, when Arjuna perceives Vāsudeva Kṛṣṇa as Time consuming with his own fiery mouth all the worlds and the dead of the not-yet-fought war. He will later learn that by using the axe of detachment to cut through the worlds of spacetime consumed by Time (BG 15), and by complete attachment to and dependence on Kṛṣṇa (BG 18.57-66), Kṛṣṇa will take him beyond the realms of death and birth into the higher unmanifest body of his own Self.

For Bhāgavatas of the Śrī Vaiṣṇava sect (*sampradāya*), the paradigmatic *ekadaśi* occurs in Mārgaḻi (Mārgaśirṣa: BG 10.35). Its most important celebration in Tamilnadu takes place in the temple of Śrī Raṅgam where thousands gather to step ritually into the presence of Vaikuṇṭha within spacetime, which is on White Island in the Ocean of Milk where the dead live at Vaikuṇṭha's feet.[37] By stepping northwards through a northern gateway at Śrī Raṅgam on that day, devotees symbolically enter the Vaikuṇṭha realm protected from the destruction that Arjuna saw in BG 11 and that Āṇṭāḷ's gopīs desired in NT 10.2.

In her eleventh poem, Āṇṭāḷ placed her envisioned gopī at Śrī Raṅgam on that Mārgaḻi ekadaśi day and focussed her on the reclining Raṅga known as "The Handsome Bridegroom" (*Aḻakiya Maṇavāḷan*). When, in NT 11.1, the gopī describes Śrī Raṅgar reclining on a cobra with mouths of fire, she alludes to the vision of fiery Time that Arjuna had in BG 11. That snake's fire is the fire of Vāsudeva's "plower" formation (*saṁkarṣaṇa*), who first conceives the worlds (BG 14), and then cremates them. Āṇṭāḷ also introduced female companions to the envisioned gopī in this poem and they remain with her to the end of the work; by suggesting the actual devotees in Śrī Raṅgam of her day and those who had passed away to Vaikuntha noted in 10.2, they likewise express the ekadaśi theme.[38]

Interaction between the visualized gopī and her friends shape the remaining poems as she plays the privileged role of Piṉṉai, which now resembles Rādhā in northern traditions. In the twelfth poem, Āṇṭāḷ illustrated Kṛṣṇa's teaching to Arjuna in BG 12.6-7:

> But they who renounce all intentional acts for me and are intent on me, and with a discipline exclusive of others venerate me in visualization, I will lift out of the ocean of repeated death quickly, son of Pṛthā, for their thought belongs to me. (12.6-7)

To illustrate that teaching concretely, Āṇṭāḷ had the gopī in the poem ask her friends to take her to the places where Kṛṣṇa spends time, organized stanza by stanza according to the major outline of the Kṛṣṇakathā of BP 10. Beginning in the capital city of Mathurā where Kṛṣṇa is born a Kṣatriya (1), she moves to the village of Gokula across the Yamunā where he lives in disguise as a cowherd (2), and to Nandagopa's house in that village where he resides (3)—they designate his infancy. Then she moves to the banks of the Yamunā river where he plays (4), to the pool in that river that is purified when he dances the snake Kāliya into submission (5), to the place where he eats sacrificial food (6), to the banyan tree where he fights Pralamba (7), and to the mountain Govardhana that he uses as an umbrella (8)—they designate his childhood and adolescence. She then moves to the kingdom of Dvārakā that he establishes as an island in the western ocean (9)—that designates his Kṣatriya adulthood. In the signature stanza, Āṇṭāḷ promised Vaikuṇṭha (10), his "highest home" beyond the ocean of repeated death.

It appears to me that in that sequence, Āṇṭāḷ used the Kṛṣṇa narrative to outline the process by which the initiate becomes the protected refugee on the third day of the "consecration of the wheel-and-lotus," that is, on the twelfth day of the waxing moon. The clue to this comes from the way the Parameccura-viṉṉagaram (Vaikuṇṭha Perumāḷ Temple) in Kāñchipuram uses the story, as I have discussed elswhere.[39] In sum, Kṛṣṇa's infancy represents the passage of mantras from the initiate's gross body (represented by Mathurā) into her soul (represented by Gokula). His adolescence represents the mantraic "take over" of her subtle body consciousness, culminating in the act of faith in Kṛṣṇa expressed by the story of Indra confessing him as "my God, my Guru, and my Soul" when Kṛṣṇa lifted the mountain Govardhana (BP 10.24-28).[40] (Significantly, BP 10.28 says that Kṛṣṇa showed the cowherds his essential form in the realm of Vaikuṇṭha right after that episode, on the twelfth day of the waxing moon, which corresponds to this poem.) Kṛṣṇa's Kṣatriya stage of life at Dvārakā represents his continuing protection of the refugee during her lifetime, and his realm of Vaikuṇṭha represents her destination at death.

Āṇṭāḷ's thirteenth poem likewise parallels BG 13. There Kṛṣṇa teaches Arjuna about the distinction between the material body (*śarīra*) as the "field" and the conscious Self as the "knower of the field" (13.1), and about himself as that "knower of the field" in every "field" (13.2): The Self (*ātman*) in every material body is Kṛṣṇa. When he concludes that brief instruction, he says that the person attached to him who knows that teaching is fit to exist in Kṛṣṇa's own mode of being (12.18).

In her poem, Āṇṭāḷ played with the theme of the "body" and of existing in Kṛṣṇa's "own mode of being."[41] Her envisioned gopī first states that she has received the dīkṣā that will allow her to see Kṛṣṇa: "I repose, consecrated for the vision of the black deva named Kṛṣṇa" (13.1), suggesting that Āṇṭāḷ brought herself into the picture, sitting, we may imagine, reposed at her maṇḍala in the rites of the sādhanā. Then—as if to bring Kṛṣṇa's body to her and blend it with hers so that she will exist in Kṛṣṇa's own mode of being—the envisioned gopī urges her companions to bring parts of Kṛṣṇa's attire for her to wear: his yellow silk waistcloth as her fan (1), his soft, cool, beautiful basil for her hair (2), his wild flower garland for her breast (3), the saliva from his mouth (4) and from his flute (5) to sprinkle and to smear on her face, the dust from the paths he has trod for her body (6), and his shoulders for her breasts (7). Suddenly, her anger interrupts in the eighth stanza:

> If I see Govardhanan̲, I'll grab my fruitless breast by the root, rip it out, and throw it on his chest, and *then* I'll be free of my burning."

Nevertheless, it quickly subsides, and in the ninth stanza she desires only to be held to his chest, even if briefly. And in the signature stanza Āṇṭāḷ echoed Kṛṣṇa's promise in BG 12.6-7—"I will lift out of the ocean of repeated death quickly"—when she said that those adept in praising these words of desire and intense longing "will be free from the ocean of sorrow."

The fourteenth poem that concludes the set also parallels BG 14. There Kṛṣṇa tells Arjuna the "supreme knowledge of omniscient knowledge" (14.1), which leads those who know it to his own nature (14.2) beyond the death and birth of spacetime. His nature is to be both the Father and the Mother of all forms:

> My womb is great *brahmā*, and I plant the embryo in it; the arising of all existing beings comes from that, son of Bharata. In all wombs, son of Kuntī, whatever forms come into being, great *brahmā* is their womb and I the father who gives the seed. (14.3-4)

The metaphor of the father uniting with the mother to conceive the child explains the conception of spacetime and all its inhabitants by the single Nārāyaṇa, for as Vāsudeva he is the Father, and as the Śakti Śrī Lakṣmī, the Mother.

Āṇṭāḷ used that same paradigm to govern her final poem. The envisioned gopī, now approaching "Vrindā's Forest" (*Vrindāvana*), questions her companions over and over if they have seen Kṛṣṇa, and they say they have, there in Vrindāvana, and they describe to her the deeds of the cowherd hero who is to become her lover. Unstated yet implied is the coming union by which she will function as his womb and receive his seed to hold within her and be truly herself. Then she will be like the Goddess Śrī Lakṣmī of BG 14.3-4 through whom Vāsudeva gives rise to all the worlds, which Kṛṣṇa describes in BG 15.1-3 with the metaphor of the aśvattha tree growing from the "seed" he planted in the great *brahmā* womb. Yet Āṇṭāḷ did not compose a poem matching BG 15's revelation of that most secret of teachings (*guhyatamam śāstram*) (BG 15.20). She left it implied by the Paṅguṉi full moon and depicted by the anticipating wedding dream of poem six.

Breasts and bangles

Of all the symbols Āṇṭāḷ used to portray her enjoyment of Kṛṣṇa in these poems, her breasts and bangles are perhaps the most striking, for in shape they remind us of the full Paṅguṉi moon, which itself measures the increasing heat of her passionate burning (*tapas*). As she told us in poem one, her breasts portray the erotic desire of her physical body: "Since I was young my full breasts have been craving constantly and have swelled up and I have resolved that they are only for the Lord of Dvārakā." In poem two, where she began to envision herself as the pre-pubescent bride-to-be of Kṛṣṇa, she imagined that they had not yet begun to mature and she is impatient with Kṛṣṇa's teasing erotic play. By poem five, however, the breasts of the imagined gopī swell with pleasure and give her grief. From poem seven they desire Kṛṣṇa intensely. And in poem twelve, repeating Āṇṭāḷ's resolve of 1.4-5, she insists, "They will go into no other mouth than Govinda's" (12.4).[42]

Yet because he still has not appeared, her frustrated desire leads her in poem thirteen to threaten to rip one off and throw it on his chest. That allusion to the Kaṇṇaki story of Madurai's burning,[43] however, she immediately mitigates by evoking *Tiruppāvai* 19 where Piṉṉai lies with her breasts on Kṛṣṇa's chest, her burning passion cooled by union with him—it is that Piṉṉai she wants to be:

> If in this birth I can't perform an intimate service for Govinda that will end the pain in my round breasts, what's the use of doing tapas in another? If only he would take me to his superb and auspicious chest, then if one day he looked me in the face and told me in truth to leave, it would still be wonderful.(13.9)

While female breasts manifest hot desire in the poems, bangles signify female sexual chastity (*kaṟpu*), which is not the absence of sexual activity, but the restriction of it and of thoughts about it to one's spouse.[44] As an immature child in poem two, the envisioned gopī wears bangles on her arms, but in poem five she has already lost a golden one to her clandestine lover. They agreed that he would return and through marriage restore her chastity, yet in poem eight he has still not brought the bangle back. And by poem eleven he has not only taken all her bangles, but also her whole body, and still he has not revealed himself face to face, even though, as she says in poem thirteen, she has been initiated into the vision of him.

Temples and Icons

Let us conclude by considering Āṇṭāḷ's use of temples and icons to structure these poems. We noted that in *Tiruppāvai* she focussed on the reclining Madhusūdana icon in the inner shrine of the temple in New Town. In the poems of *Nācciyār Tirumoli,* however, she conducts her rites at a maṇḍala outside the sanctum and uses a pilgrimage route extending from New Town to Veṅkaṭam as a theme to achieve their goal, namely, to compel her desire for Kṛṣṇa (itself a mode of Kṛṣṇa) to "shoot" her into him standing on Veṅkaṭam (NT 1.2).

In her daily visualization (*dhyāna*) at that sacred maṇḍala, Āṇṭāḷ used specific temples to construct her visions. Probably she had visited these temples in pilgrimage, but now she visited them only through disciplined thought impelled by desire. "Because I long to see the golden feet of him dwelling in Villi's New Town," her envisioned gopī says, "my eyes fight like fish and I can't sleep" (NT 5.5). As that statement shows, the vision she longed for was not the one she had when she walked to the door of New Town's sanctum. Nor, it seems, was it one she could create through the discipline of *dhyāna.* What she wanted was the vision given directly by Kṛṣṇa himself, a vision qualitatively different from all others, because seeing it would be merging with it as lovers merge in sexual union and experience the pleasure of being "not-two while remaining different" (an approxmimate rendering of *viśiṣṭa-advaita*, the Vedānta theology developed three centuries later by the ācārya Rāmānuja at Śrī Raṅgam, who was especially attached to Āṇṭāḷ's *Tiruppāvai*).

In the inner sanctum (*garbhagṛha*) of Vaiṣṇava temples in Tamilnadu, the immovable and fundamental icon is sculpted in one of three different postures: sitting, reclining, or standing. Each posture has a specific meaning in its context. As noted earlier, between c.775 and 866, temples with a sanctum on each floor of a three-story house had been placed throughout the length of Tamilnadu, beginning apparently with the Parameccura-viṉṉagaram of Kāñchipuram (c.770). An icon portraying a specific posture of the Bhagavān was placed in each sanctum so that a devotee could climb stairs from one floor to the other and sequentially venerate him in the fullness of his threefold manifestation, each stage represented by a specific bodily posture. One of those temples stands in Madurai today, known popularly as the Kūṭal Aḻagar Temple. Poems by Āṇṭāḷ and Periyāḻvār suggest that it stood there already in their lifetimes, recently built, perhaps, under the influence of the Bhāgavata emperors in Kāñchipuram.

The Kūṭal Aḻagar Temple houses Kūṭal Aḻagar, "The Beautiful Lord of *Kūṭal*," an ancient name for Madurai that means "the joining." It can refer to the joining of roads, or of landscapes, or of people, or of a male and female in sexual union. Āṇṭāḷ used *kūṭal* in poem four for the game that forecasted the gopī's joining Kṛṣṇa in marriage. Kūṭal Aḻagar may mean the Beautiful Lord of all of those joinings, including the joining of all three of his postures in a single vertical *vimāna*. But as Āṇṭāḷ used the word, it referred to the gopī's joining with "our beautiful Lord" of Kūṭal (4.10).[45]

In contrast to the temples in the Pāṇḍya and Pallava capitals, those in New Town, Śrī Raṅgam, and Kumbhakonam (Kuṭantai) have only one floor, and in each the central icon is reclining. Those in Viṣṇu's Great Grove (Māliruñcolai), Uraiyūr, Kaṇṇapuram, and Veṅkaṭam also have only one floor, and in each the central icon is standing. Āṇṭāḷ used those varied postures in specific ways when she thematically journeyed from New Town to Veṅkaṭam as allusions in the poems suggest.

From New Town's reclining icon (2-3), she moved north to Madurai's three icons (4-7) with special attention to the standing one, as her reference to the icon standing in Kaṇṇapuram suggests (4.2). From there she moved north to Viṣṇu's Great Grove and its standing icon (8-10).

Moving further north to the Kaveri river and to Śrī Raṅgam's reclining icon (11), she turned east to Uraiyur's standing icon (12), and then along the river to Kutantai's reclining icon (13) in the delta. From there she moved directly north to Kāñchipuram and to its temple's standing, reclining, and sitting icon's (14). From there she would go north to Veṅkaṭam. Āṇṭāḷ used those three postures with specific Bhāgavata meanings in mind:

The standing icon represents Kṛṣṇa as the heroic lover within the limitations of spacetime. As Dwarf he measured out that realm and as bridegroom he walks to the gopī in poems six and fourteen. Dwarf also appears to represent Kṛṣṇa as embodied in the ācārya through mantra, who, like the stone icon, operates on the sādhaka's physical senses to attach them to Kṛṣṇa.

The reclining icon represents the bridegroom with whom she will unite on the marriage bed in the enstatic consciousness of *samādhi*. It signifies the unmanifest destroyer and begetter of spacetime who reclines in the sādhaka's own heart even as he encompasses spacetime in an unmanifest body.

The sitting icon, present in Madurai and Kāñchipuram, represents Āṇṭāḷ's ultimate goal, beyond the transcendent consciousness of *samādhi*. It signifies Vāsudeva Kṛṣṇa as the highest unmanifest Light, the consciousness and being of Vaikuṇṭha that penetrates everywhere. He is the origin and sustainer of the reclining form, and he embodies himself as the standing form and the ācārya. The sitting Bhagavān represents the all-encompassing higher unmaifest realm that Kṛṣṇa identified in BG 15.6 as his "highest home" (*dhāma paramam*) and "the Light visible beyond the worlds above" that Āṇṭāḷ longed for in 10.2.

Given those meanings, it is significant that in the first poem, where Āṇṭāḷ described her sādhanā, she directed her attention to the standing Veṅkaṭam about four hundred miles to the north on the northernmost border of the ancient Tamil realm. There Kṛṣṇa stands as the goal of her sādhanā and the means to attain it, as the gateway through which she will step "northward" into the reclining mode of his being, and "northward" from there to his feet in the sitting mode.[46]

Let us briefly consider how she used those temples and iconic postures to unfold her poems. In poems two and three that visualize the prepurbertal gopī, Āṇṭāḷ alluded frequently to the reclining icon of New Town as sleeping on the cosmic ocean or on the banyan leaf or on the snake. Kṛṣṇa there is himself young but nevertheless sexually alert.

When the gopī has matured sexually in poems four through seven, her attention turns to the temple in Madurai with its three floors for icons, which represents Mathurā in the north. In stanza four, when she plays the *kūṭal* game to see if she will marry her lover, the "joining" she has in mind is with Kṛṣṇa, "the master of Mathurā" (4.6). In her signature verse of poem five, Āṇṭāḷ appears to have referred to the three icons aligned vertically in the Madurai temple. She began with the standing icon, "the one who took three strides," Dwarf as Thrice-strider (Vāmana Trivikrama) whom she desired. Then she named the reclining icon, "my Lord the color of the sea with eyes closed," whom the envisioned gopī had asked the kuyil bird to address. Then, near the end of the stanza, she promised that those adept in reciting this poem would be reciting the mantra "Veneration to Nārāyaṇa," which is what those who dwell in Vaikuṇṭha ceaselessly do at the feet of the enthroned Lord. She then noted that the highest unmanifest Vāsudeva sitting in Vaikuṇṭha once stood on earth as Kṛṣṇa by beginning the next poem with the description of her dreamed marriage (6.1), where Nārāyaṇa, surrounded by a thousand elephants, walks to their wedding as Kṛṣṇa, "king of Mathurā's people" (6.5).

Articulating the theme of Madurai/Mathurā even more clearly in this sixth poem, the envisioned gopī dreams in 6.3 that Antari, "The Goddess in the Sky," plays the role of the bridegroom's sister, and dresses her in the wedding sari and garlands her with flowers. That is a very specific allusion to Madurai tradition: Antari is "the goddess with the eyes of a carp (*Aṅkayaṛkaṇṇi*), known also as Mīnākṣī, who is Caṇḍika-Durgā, the younger sister of Kṛṣṇa (Viṣṇu) residing in Madurai as Śiva's queen. When Aṅkayaṛkaṇṇi married Śiva, Kṛṣṇa (Viṣṇu) performed the rite of giving her to the bridegroom, and now at her brother's marriage, Aṅkayaṛkaṇṇi performs the ritual of dressing her future sister-in-law.[47]

The last of the Madurai poems is seven, where the gopī addresses Kṛṣṇa's conch. Twice she refers to Kṛṣṇa by the name Vāsudevan, a name with an intended double meaning. Interpreted as "son of Vasudeva," it means Kṛṣṇa whose father was Vasudeva and mother was Devakī, who was born in Mathurā, and who eventually rescued Mathurā from Kaṁsa's oppressive rule. Interpreted as "God (*deva*) who dwells (*vasu*) in all things, and in whom all things dwell," it means Kṛṣṇa as the highest unmanifest mode of Nārāyaṇa in Pāñcarātra theology. That Para Vāsudeva sits on the throne in Vaikuṇṭha, Kṛṣṇa's "highest home," and in his left hand holds the conch that is the focus of her sensual longing.

Moving north of Madurai, Āṇṭāḷ used poems eight, nine, and ten to focus on Kṛṣṇa on the mountain of Viṣṇu's Great Grove (*Maliruncolai*, known today as the Alagar Temple). She linked that temple explicitly to the icon standing in the mountain temple of Veṅkaṭam, for the envisioned gopī mourns that the heroic and beautiful lord (*Sundaraṉ*, A̲lakar, Ala̲kapirāṉ) standing on those two hills cheated her of her chastity.[48] The specific details she gives of Viṣṇu's Great Grove, including the promise of rich food offerings to him standing there, suggest that Āṇṭāḷ knew the temple well.

She reached Śrī Raṅgam and its reclining icon of Raṅganātha, the Handsome Bridegroom, in poem eleven.[49] In 11.1-3, she identified him as the bridegroom reclining on the snake who stole the envisioned gopī's bangle. In the remaining verses, she developed the meaning of the reclining icon as mediator between our world of spacetime and Kṛṣṇa's transcendent Vaikuṇṭha. When the Bhagavān reclines and sleeps, theology says, he dreams or recalls the various forms he takes when he descends into spacetime as avatār and the envisioned gopī mentions some of them in 11.4-8: Dwarf (4), Thrice-strider (5), Inner Dweller (6), Raghava Rāma (7), Boar (8), and Kṛṣṇa as Kṣatriya who took Rukminī from Śisupala to be his chief queen (9). Āṇṭāḷ concluded with Kṛṣṇa's promise in BG 18.65-66 to take to himself anyone who takes refuge in him—an ironic point, because Kṛṣṇa had not yet fulfilled that promise in the case of the gopī, and remaining poems develop the irony further.

The gopī's anxiety about Kṛṣṇa's appearance reaches its climax in poem fourteen. She asks her companions if they have seen him yet, and, as we see in stanzas two and three, they answer "Yes, and he is on his way":

> Govardhanaṉ the young bull has left me to suffer while he plunders Gokula, eating everything, reeking of rancid milk, have you seen him?—Yes, we've seen Vrindāvana where he plays with others, his garland of wild flowers flashing like lightning mixed with clouds. (2)
>
> The beloved lord born as Desire, the bridegroom who creates desire and tells all kinds of lies, have you seen him coming here?—Yes, we've seen Vrindāvana where he comes under the wings of Vinatā's son Garuḍa, who keeps them stretched out to protect him from the spreading heat above. (3)

The latter stanza portrays Garuḍa accompanying the bridegroom to his wedding like a canopy shielding him from the heat, and the "spreading heat above" suggests, of course, both the hot weather that the Paṅguṉi Uttaram marks and the heat of passion and ascetic tapas.[50] The bridegroom is Desire (*māl*) himself, the lover who stimulates desire (*māl*) in others and tells the sorts of lies lovers tell. Āṇṭāḷ has apparently alluded to the fourteenth day of the moon known as "Kāma's fourteenth," a fast day in preparation for the Paṅguṉi Uttaram full moon on the fifteenth when sensual desire (*kāma*) and sensual pleasure (*rati*) will come together.

Āṇṭāḷ explicitly stated here what we noted earlier about her own passionate desire for Kṛṣṇa as a mode of Kṛṣṇa. Through the gopī she said that her own passionate longing had all along been a mode of Kṛṣṇa's presence within her, simultaneously the desire's source and its only satisfaction.

This final poem's last three stanzas reveal that the gopī's union with Kṛṣṇa in his transcendent and enthroned fullness is immanent. Once more Āṇṭāḷ alluded to the three iconic posturesand this time she probably meant the imperial Viṣṇu-house in Kāñchipuram, because it would have been the last stop before the mountain of Veṅkaṭam. Moving from its top stanctum down, the gopi describes Kṛṣṇa first as standing, then as reclining, and finally as sitting; and her companions may represent pilgrims that Āṇṭāḷ had once met there returning from forested Veṅkaṭam, which in this poem they speak of as Vrindāvana:

> The gracious and auspicious Tirumāl holds a white conch, wears a golden garment, and has a wheel, have you seen him?—Yes, we've seen Vrindāvana where he plays, standing with clusters of fragrant flowers rolling around his broad shoulders like a swarm of drunken bees. (8)
>
> "Create the universe" said the Lord who is purity itself, and in play gave Brahmā and the others the cool and large flower of his navel and made it into a home, have you seen him?—Yes, we've seen Vrindāvana where he entered the wilderness to hunt down Dhenuka and the elephant and the bird and slay them quickly, and he will come. (9)
>
> Viṣṇucitta's Godā spoke of the sight of the Supreme Being, who was gracious to the elephant of stout legs, on earth there in Vrindāvana, and those who take her words as medicine and live with them constantly in mind, will exist forever at the feet

of the master with stout legs, never to leave. (10)

That final signature stanza implies that Āṇṭāḷ, too, will see Kṛṣṇa in the Veṅkaṭa forest, for the friends of the envisioned gopī in the previous stanza have seen Kṛṣṇa there and tell her he will come when he has completed his tasks, leaving us to anticipate the fifteenth poem, which does not exist.

That final stanza also records details about Āṇṭāḷ through her use of the story of Gajendra, "The Indra of Elephants." Gajendra, the emblem of egoistic ignorance immersed in the pleasurable pool of family life, while on an island in the Ocean of Milk had been grabbed by a "grasper" in a pond, the emblem of desire based on ignorance (BP 8.2-4). About to drown, he took refuge in the Bhagavān, asking not for salvation from death but from ignorance. Instantly the Bhagavān appeared on Garuḍa, slew the grasper, and transformed Gajendra into an attendant in Vaikuṇṭha; and like all the residents there, his form resembled his master's in whose mode of being he now existed.

That story alludes to the Pāṇḍyas of Madurai, which was Āṇṭāḷ's political context, because Gajendra had been a Pāṇḍya king in his previous birth, and that Pāṇḍyan now served at the feet of the Bhagavān enthroned in Vaikuṇṭha, the realm represented by the icon seated in the bottom floor sanctum. The story also alludes to Āṇṭāḷ herself and to the reciter of her poems she referred to in the stanza. Like Gajendra's prayer, her poems will evoke Vāsudeva Kṛṣṇa's gracious love (*aruḷ*). Not only will he come to her in *samādhi* at the full moon, he also will enlist her and the reciter of her poems among those in his Vaikuṇṭha realm.[51] Yet if we believe that Āṇṭāḷ will get what she wanted, their positions there will differ. Like Gajendra, the reciter will reside with others at Vāsudeva's feet, while Āṇṭāḷ will reside at his side, transformed into a mode of the Goddess Śrī Lakṣmī herself—as the Goddess Earth into whom he will plant his seed to bring forth the universal aśvattha tree of BG 15.[52] But that is where Āṇṭāḷ as poet and virtuoso devotee disappears into the Āṇṭāḷ of theology and hagiography, and where this study ends.

ENDNOTES

1. Using *Tiruppāvai,* with the explanations of Periyavāccāṉ Piḷḷai and Aḻakiyamaṇavāḷapperumāḷ Nāyaṉār, published by P. B. Annaṅkarācāriyar (Kanchipuram, 1970); and *Nācciyār Tirumoḻi,* with the explanation (*vyākyāṉam*) of Periyavāccāṉ

Piḷḷai, published by S. Kiruṣṇasvāmi Ayyaṅkār (Tirucirappalli, 1953 ?).

For a discussion of Āṇṭāḷ's works, see Dehejia and also Friedhelm Hardy, *Viraha-Bhakti: The early history of Kṛṣṇa devotion in South India* (Delhi, Oxford, New York, 1983), pp.414-429.

2. For a discussion of Āṇṭāḷ as a paradigm of devotion, see Dennis Hudson, "Bathing in Krishna: A Study in Vaiṣṇava Hindu Theology," *Harvard Theological Review* 73 (1980):539-566. For a contrasting discussion of Āṇṭāḷ and her poems, one that considers them in the context of literature rather than liturgy, see Friedhelm Hardy, *Viraha-Bhakti*, pp.414-429.

3. *Śrīmad Bhāgavata: The Holy Book of God*, tr. by Swami Tapasyananda in 4 volumes (Sanskrit text with English translation) (Madras, 1980-1982).

4. For a discussion of Periyāḻvār's works, see Hardy, *Viraha-Bhakti*, pp.402-413.

5. Following the thought of K. V. Raman, Professor of Archaeology and Ancient History, University of Madras, in oral conversation. For a different chronology, see Hardy, *Viraha-Bhakti*, pp. 261-269. For reasons to be discussed elsewhere, I think Raman is correct.

6. *Maṅgalanāṭāḻvāṉ* in Tamil, *Maṅgalarāshtra-bhārtṛi* in Sanskrit. At his repeated petitions, the emperor gave land to sixteen Brahmans in that ancient Chola region to form a village in what is now the Nāgapattinam Taluk of Tanjore District. For the grant, see *Epigraphia Indica* 18 (1925-26), pp. 115-124; see also C. Minakshi, *Administration and Social Life Under the Pallavas*, rev. 2nd edition, ed. by K. K. Pillay (Madras, 1977), pp. 85-86, 142, and 207).

7. Around the Tiruvallikkeni Temple in Mayalai (now in Madras city), "the king of the southern ruler [the Pāṇḍyan] and of the Toṇḍai people [in the Pallava domain]" built a "permanent cool park, tank, wall, storied house [probably a vimāna], and hall" (2.3.10). I discussed those poems briefly in "Tirumaṅgai's Poems About the Emperor Nandivarman II Pallavamalla (732-796)" presented to the Eighth International Conference Seminar on Tamil Studies, Tañjāvūr, Tamilnadu, January 5, 1995.

8. See Friedhelm Hardy, *Viraha-Bhakti*, pp.254-255.

9. A. K. Ramanujan translated them in *Hymns for the Drowning* (Princeton, 1982), pp. 29 and 67; and I discussed them in "Kṛṣṇa in Theology and Architecture," pp.159-164.

10. I discussed the early diffusion of the Bhāgavata religion (Bhāgavata dharma) in the Tamil south in "Vraja Among the Tamils: A Study of Bhāgavatas in Early South India," *Journal of Vaiṣṇava Studies* 3.1 (Winter 1994), pp.113-140.

11. The distinction in tāntric sādhanās between the communal and the solitary is discuseed by Teun Goudriaan and Sanjukta Gupta, *Hindu Tāntric and Śākta Literature* (Wiesbaden, 1981), pp.1-9. For a concise discussion of fundamental elements in tāntric Hindu traditions, see Sanjukta Gupta and Richard Gombrich, "Kings, Power and the Goddess," *South Asia Research* 6 (1986), pp.123-138. Michael Strickmann offered a definition that fits this study: "Such rites are "Tantric" if we

accept as a minimal definition of this imprecise but useful term that they center upon the visualization by the officiant of the deity to whom the rite is addressed, with whom the officiant then proceeds to identify himself or otherwise unite." Michel Strickmann, "Homa in East Asia," *Agni: The Vedic Ritual of the Fire Altar*, vol. 2, ed. Frits Staal, (Berkeley, 1983), p.418.

12. Described by K. Rangachari, *The Śrīvaiṣṇava Brāhmans*, Bulletin of the Madras Government Museum, New Series—General Section, Vol. II, Pt.2 (Madras, 1931), pp.101-114. He noted on p.113 that Brahmins who underwent the dīkṣā received the title *bhaṭṭar*.

13. This is a slightly revised form of the translation in "Āṇṭāḷ Alvar: A Developing Biography."

14. In 6.6 and 6.8; in 10.10; and in 12.1.

15. Miranda Shaw, *Passionate Enlightenment* (Princeton, 1994), pp.179-194.

16. There is a suggestion, however, of the ācārya touching her body during the rites of her dīkṣā. Through its use of the *Bhāgavata Purāṇa*, the Vaikuṇṭha Perumāḷ Temple reveals that Dwarf the Thrice-strider represents the ācārya in rites of refuge and protection. Accordingly, Āṇṭāḷ suggested that the ācārya touched her body in his role as the Bhagavān when she described her sādhanā in TP 1.7 and said:

> I cook green paddy with sugarcane and I cook *aval* from fresh rice with brown sugar, and I worship you with the mantras of Brahmins with good voice, O Manmatha—So you will give me the greatest glory in this world, the experience of Trivikrama, who long ago measured out the land, touching me with his auspicious hands on my lustrous belly and soft full breasts, won't you?

Such touching corresponds to rites in the "consecration of the wheel-and-lotus mandala" (*cakrābjamaṇḍala dīkṣā*) to be discussed later. While the ācārya embodies Vāsudeva in his heart-lotus, the initiate's body is ritually burned and his or her soul is believed to reside in the ācārya's heart at Vāsudeva's feet; after the body is purified, the soul passes into it from Vāsudeva in the ācārya's heart as a ritual rebirth; while lying beside the ācārya with blindfolded eyes (like a newborn, with the ācārya as the mother), the ācārya touches the purified body in six places; after further rites he then touches the initiate's body four times: from the feet to the knee, from the knee to the navel, from the navel to the heart, and from the heart to the head. Āṇṭāḷ's reference to her belly and breasts correspond to the navel and the heart. See Rangachari, *The Śrīvaiṣṇava Brahmans*, p. 113.

17. The soul (*jīva*) is the "causal subtle body" (*kāraṇa-sūkṣma-śarīra*), which consists of three sheaths of matter within the subtle body (*sūkṣma-śarīra*) composed of breath (*prāna*); they consist of mind (*manas*), subject-object perception (*vijñāna*), and joy (*ānanda*)—the last immediately enveloping the Self (*ātman*) that consists of omniscient knowledge (*jñāna*). The subtle body of breath is itself encased by the

gross physical body (*sthūla-śarīra*) made of food (*annam*). The fundamental eight-syllable mantra accordingly passes from the gross physical body through the right ear into the causal subtle body or soul and stays there permanently, thereby turning the initiate into a "walking temple" that serves as a "house" for the Bhagavān in his mantraic "body."

18. I discussed that in "The Śrīmad Bhāgavata Purāṇa in Stone: The Text as an Eighth-Century Temple an its Implications," *Journal of Vaiṣṇava Studies* 3.3 (Summer 1995), pp 137-182.

19. I discussed her more fully in "Pin̲n̲ai, Kṛṣṇa's Cowherd Wife," *The Divine Consort*, eds. by J.S. Hawley and Donna Wulff (Berkeley, 1982), pp. 238-261.

20. Commentators on the poem, however, universally regard *pavai* in that refrain to refer to the vow (*vrata*) of bathing in honor of the goddess.

21. Translated by Thomas B. Coburn in *Encountering the Goddess: A Translation of the Devī-Māhātmya and a Study of Its Interpretation* (Albany, 1991), pp.29-86.

22. J.C. Irwin observed that the month following Mārgaśirṣa is Māgha (the Tamil month Tai), the occasion every twelve years of the "Festival of the Bowl" (*Kumbhamela*) at the confluence of the Gaṅgā and Yamunā rivers, which celebrates the birth of the universe. That implies that Mārgaśirṣa is the period of fertile expectation just before the birth. See "The Prayāga Bull-Pillar: Another Pre-Aśokan Monument," *South Asian Archaeology* 1979, ed. Herbert Hartel (Berlin, 1981), pp.313-340, esp.p.318. The considerable complexities of the calendar were discussed admirably by Karen L. Merrey in "The Hindu Festival Calendar," *Religious Festivals in South India and Śrī Lanka*, eds. Guy R. Welbon and Glenn E. Yocum (New Delhi, 1982), pp.1-26. In the same volume, H. Daniel Smith discussed "Festivals in Pāñcarātra Literature," pp. 27-50.

23. The Paṅguni Uttaram festival was present among Tamils during Saṅgam times and associated with the Chola capital of Urantai near Śrī Raṅgam. It may have been connected then with marriage, for the standing icon at Uraiyūr (Urantai) is known today as "The Handsome Bridegroom" (*A̲lakiya maṇavāḷa̲n̲*). See George L. Hart III, *The Poems of Ancient Tamil: Their Milieu and Their Sanskrit Counterparts* (Berkeley, 1975), pp.45-46; and L.V. Gopalan, "Woraiyur," *Sri Vaishnava Divya Desams (108 Tiruppathis Sung by Azhwars* (Madras, 1972), p.4

Fred W. Clothey noted that the *uttaram nakṣatra* is the constellation in which all gods are said to marry and described the Paṅguni Uttaram marriage of Murugan in *Rhythm and Intent (Ritual Studies from South India* (Madras, 1983), pp.121; 129-130. Not all deities today marry in Paṅguni, but many do. For example, a Tamil *pañcāngam* (almanac) for 1968-69 listed the wedding of Āṇṭāḷ and Viṣṇu in Śrīvilluputtūr, of Viṣṇu on Maliruncolai, and of Viṣṇu in Tirumukūrkkovil, all on the Paṅguni Uttaram (Panguni 19/ April 1). At Tirupparankun̲r̲am near Madurai, the Lord married three days later and in Tirucculikkovil two days earlier. In 1982, Viṣṇu at Maturāntakam was married on Paṅguni Uttaram (Paṅguni 25/April 7) as was Varadarāja̲n̲ at Kāñchipuram; and in Kumbhakonam he was married two days later and in

Kāṭayakkuṭi seven days earlier. See Pañcāngam, *Rāmanāthapuram Setusamasthāṉam... Kilaka Varuṣa Vākkiya Pañcāngam* (Madurai, 1968), pp.9-13; and *Tunmati-Varuṣattiya Pañcāngam* (Puttukoṭṭai, 1981), pp.70-80.

24. Saṣṭhi, the goddess who is the sixth day (*ṣaṣṭhi*) of the lunar month has jurisdiction over the matters of life and death in the family, especially of chidren. Among Tamils today the paradigmatic *ṣaṣṭhī* is the *Skanda ṣaṣṭhī* of the Tamil month of Aypaci (October-November). It celebrates family life in the themes of the conception, birth, maturation, and marriage of Skanda who was born from Śiva to defeat a demon. He does this on the sixth day after the new moon. His wife is Ṣaṣṭhī, also known as "Army of the Gods" (*Devasenā*). The story also implies the story of Śiva burning Kāma, for only Kāma could arouse Śiva from his ascetic withdrawal to beget Skanda and he was burned to ashes in the process.

Stories connected with two vows directed to the goddess Ṣaṣṭhī were described by B. A. Gupte in *Hindu Holidays and Ceremonials: With Dissertations on Origin, Folklore and Symbols*, 2nd ed. rev. (Calcutta, 1919), pp. 211-213. Fred W. Clothey discussed the *Skanda ṣaṣṭhī* in *The Many Faces of Murukan: The History and Meaning of a South Indian God* (The Hague, 1978), p. 135; in *Rhythm and Intent: Ritual Studies from South India* (Madras, 1983), pp. 95-96; and in "Skanda-Ṣaṣṭhī: A Festival in Tamil India," *History of Religions* 8 (1969):236-259. Akos Oster reported that *ṣaṣṭhī* in Bengal is connected with the domestic group and the life cycle in *Play of the Gods: Locality, Ideology, Structure, and Time in the Festivals of a Bengali Town* (Chicago and London, 1980), pp.34-35 and 95.

25. *Puṟanāṉūṟu* 243 portrays this imagery as translated by Geroge L. Hart III, *Poets of the Tamil Anthologies: Ancient Poems of Love and War* (Princeton, 1979), p. 192. Āṇṭāḷ followed a long tradition of Tamil love poetry. For example, Kapilar in *Kalittokai* 54 wrote a poem that has themes important to her poems: the woman's hair-knot with its flower garland, her painted breasts which the lover fondles, his strokes over her body, their sexual union, and her dream of marriage. For a translation, see A. K. Ramanujan, *Poems of Love and War: From the Eight Anthologies and the Ten Long Poems of Classical Tamil* (New York, 1985), pp. 199-200. There is also the famous story of Murugan's premarital union with Valli: See David Dean Shulman, *Tamil Temple Myths: Sacrifice and Divine Marriage in the South Indian Śaiva Traditions* (Princeton, 1980), pp.275-281; and Kamil V. Zvelebil, *The Smile of Murugan: On Tamil Literature of South India* (Leiden, 1973), pp. 91-93.

26. Jan Gonda, *Vedic Ritual: Non-Solemn Rites* (Leiden and Koln, 1980), p. 246; and P. V. Kane, *History of Dharmaśāstra*, vol.2, part 1, 2nd ed. (Poona, 1974), pp. 204-205.

27. The centrality of Kāma in Āṇṭāḷ's poetry illustrates what Sudhir Kakar and John Mundar Ross said about poems depicting the love of Rādhā and Kṛṣṇa: "Separateness and union are not different categories of love, as the convention of Indian poetics would have it, but are merely different phases of the cycle of love, both intimately connected through the workings of desire. The lover's and the

poet's dwelling on apartness represents his or her renouncing a possession that would deflate desire...Below the surface sadness lies the lover's *need* to create impediments to the enjoyment of their love, to *deliciously* postpone delight, to suspend ecstasy in time, make it all last forever." *Tales of Love, Sex and Danger* (New York, 1987), p. 91.

28. Unlike the monsoon of most of India that falls between June and September, Tamilnadu receives its crucial monsoon in September and October. Since Mārgaḻi, the beginning of a new ritual calendar, begins in December, the rains anticipate that cycle. Moreover, if one considers the precession of the equinoxes, Mārgaḻi in the ninth century would have been closer to the rains by about twenty-three days (assuming, of course, that the weather patterns remained stable as the equinoxes precessed). See P. V. Kane, *History of Dharmaśāstra*, 5.ii, p.222.

29. Described by Rangachari, *The Śrīvaiṣṇava Brahmans* pp.101-114.

30. Rangachari, *Śrī Vaiṣṇava Brahmans*, pp.108 and 110.

31. He may also have included the square sacrificial hall (*yāgamaṇḍapa*) in which it stands as described by Rangachari, *Śrī Vaiṣṇava Brahmans*, pp.101-112, and plate XI. I have analyzed 10.19-42 as based on such a mandala pattern in an unpublished study, "Kṛṣṇa's Maṇḍala."

32. Rangachari, *Śrī Vaiṣṇava Brahmans*, pp.101-114.

33. It includes establishing the hall for the fire scrifice (*yāgamaṇḍapa*), the *aṅkurārpaṇam* ceremony of planting seeds in mud, choosing the ācārya, arranging the pots, invoking deities into the pots and the maṇḍapa structure according to their directional positions, performing a homa with the root mantra and others, and filling pots with nine kinds of grains (Rangachari, *Sri Vaisnava Brahmans*, pp. 101-107).

34. Rangachari, *Śrī Vaiṣṇava Brahmans*, pp.111-112.

35. Rangachari, *Śrī Vaiṣṇava Brahmans*, pp.112-114.

36. See Census of India, P. K. Nambiar and K. C. Nārāyaṇa Kurup, *Fairs and Festivals*, Census of India 1961, vol. IX: Madras, Part VII-B (Madras, 1968), p.18.

37. Paul Younger described "Vaikuṇṭha Ekadaśi" as recently celebrated in Śrī Raṅgam in "Singing the Tamil Hymnbook in the Tradition of Rāmānuja: the *Adyāyanotsava* Festival in Śrīraṅkam." *History of Religions* 21 (1982):272-293, esp. pp.273 and 278. See also Census of India, *Fairs and Festivals*, pp.18-21; amd P. V. Jagadisa Ayyar, *South Indian Shrines* (New Delhi, 1982), p.447. For *ekadaśi* in general, see Kane, *History of Dharmaśāstra* 5.1:95-121.

The eleventh day as associated with the dead is suggested by the vedic ritual of collecting the bones of the cremated body on the tenth day after cremation and offering the first *śrāddha* for the deceased on the eleventh. The eleventh day as associated with new life is suggested by the injunction in the *gṛhya-sūtras* that the mother is to arise after ten days of pollution from childbirth and an oblation is to be made to the lunar birthday (*tithi*) of the child. The oblation, presumably, takes place on the eleventh day after the birth and it is to be repeated every month for the first year, just as the *śrāddha* is for the dead. For death, see *Saṅkhāyana-gṛhya-sūtra* 1.24-25, in

Gṛhya-sūtras, *The Gṛhya-sūtras: Rules of the Vedic Domestic Ceremonies,* Part 1, tr. Hermann Oldenberg (Oxford: Clarendon Press, 1886), pp.49-52.

38. Āṇṭāḷ also suggested the sequence of days from the eleventh through the fourteenth with other calendrical allusions: In the twelfth poem she identified Kṛṣṇa as Vāmana-Trivikrama twice (12.2 and 9), a specific reference to "Vāmana's Twelfth" (*Vāmana dvadaśī*), which occurs just before "Kāma's Thirteenth" (*Madana triyodaśī*) and "Kāma's Fourteenth" (*Madana caturdaśī*). That pattern indicates that the twelfth could be designated "Kāma's Twelfth" (*Madana dvadaśī*).

39. Most fully in my unpublished study, "The Body of God," and partially in "The Śrīmad Bhāgavata Purāṇa in Stone."

40. Quoting N. Raghunathan's translation, *Śrīmad Bhāgavatam,* vol. 2 (Madras, 1976), p. 263.

41. She may have used a specific symbolism of the thirteenth day in this thirteenth poem. Vasudha Narayanan noted that Śrī Vaiṣṇavas believe themselves to be in a state of pollution until the thirteenth day after a death. On that day, the ceremonies of "adoption of auspiciousness" are celebrated. In the case of a married woman (*sumaṅgalī*) who dies, her body is anointed with oil, turmeric powder, flowers, etc., and auspicious gifts are distributed to other married women. Moreover, the dead *sumaṅgalī* (believed now to be with the Bhagavan in Vaikuṇṭha) may be requested by other married women to bestow auspiciousness through the ceremony of the *sumaṅgalī prārthana.* The auspiciousness of the bride about to become a *sumaṅgalī* is also used as an analogy for the auspiciousness of the devotee (the *prapanna*) whom the ācārya offers to the Bhagavān, for that devotee is about to become his "bride." See Vasudha Nārāyaṇan, "The Two Levels of Auspiciousness in Śrīvaiṣṇava Ritual and Literature," *Journal of Developing Societies* I (1985): pp.55-64.

42. The word *vāy* can mean "mouth" or "door." Śrī Vaiṣṇava ācāryas read it to mean "door" and interpreted Āṇṭāḷ to mean that her breasts will go only into Kṛṣṇa's door. That interpretation preserves the erotic meaning that Hardy avoided by interpreting her breasts as intended for the mouth of baby Kṛṣṇa (*Viraha-Bhakti,* p.424). I think Āṇṭāḷ's envisioned sexual maturation and erotic focus on the Paṅguni Uttaram eliminates the theme of nursing the baby Kṛṣṇa. Her intent here is to give the sexually mature Kṛṣṇa the pleasure of kissing her breasts and enjoying her whole body.

43. Kaṇṇaki burned down the city of Madurai when she tore off her left breast and threw it on the ground. Her "heat" was generated by her own faithfulness to her husband Kovalaṉ. The act was prompted by Kovalaṉ having been unrighteously executed by order of the Pāṇḍya king Neṭuñceliyaṉ.

Āṇṭāḷ's use of that story illustrates her subtlety. Perhaps she alluded to a popular version of the story in which Kaṇṇaki's breast struck the Pāṇḍya king's chest and killed him. Obeyesekere recorded such a version in Śrī Laṅkā: "You pulled out your right breast out of sorrow and rage, and threw it like a flaming torch to burn the city...The king ran through seven doors and the breast followed him and killed him by striking his chest" (Gananath Obeyesekere, *The Cult of the Goddess Pattini* (Chicago and London, 1984), p.586, verses 68-69).

That version indicates that she thought of Kṛṣṇa as the king of Madurai (Mathurā). The female breast as the locus of burning heat also brings in the story of Maturai's ruling goddess, Aṅkayarkaṇṇi (Mīnākṣī). She had a conquering third breast until she met Śiva. The desireous breast of Āṇṭāḷ's envisioned gopī, Kaṇṇaki's burning breast, and Aṅkayarkaṇṇi's conquering breast are all suggested by this allusion. All three stories, moreover, end with marriage: Kaṇṇaki joins Kovalan in heaven where she is the goddess of faithful wives, Pattini; the bodiless Kāma is restored to Rati in a form only she can see; and Śiva and Aṅkayarkaṇṇi marry and rule Maturai. The angry desire to burn up Kṛṣṇa is thus an angry expression of her desire to marry him.

44. The ācārya Parāśara Bhaṭṭar, in his comment on the name *Kṛtalakṣaṇaḥ* in the *Śrīviṣṇu-sahasranāma-bhāṣyam,* observed that just as the bracelet and other ornaments indicate the chastity of a woman, so the wearing of the discus brand indicates the connection of the person to Viṣṇu. (Reference from Vasudha Narayanan, *Bhakti and Prapatti in the Śrīvaiṣṇava Tradition,* MS (1988), p.231. See also Hardy, *Viraha-Bhaki,* p.176, n.191; and p.179, note 202.

45. I have also discussed *Kūṭal* in "Madurai: The City as Goddess," *Urban Form and Meaning in South Asia: The Shaping of Cities from Prehistoric to Precolonial Times,* eds. Howard Spodek and Doris Meth Śrinivasan (Washington, D.C., 1993), pp. 125-142.

46. Singaravelu Mudaliar in *Abhithana Chintamani: The Encyclopedia of Tamil Literature* [in Tamil] (New Delhi, 1982 [reprint of 1899], pp.1558-1564, listed the sacred places praised by the Āḻvārs and organized them in the traditional fashion that suggests the role of Veṅkaṭam as "gateway" to the north. It is analogous to the northern gateway through which devotees in Śrī Raṅgam step into Vaikuṇṭha on "Vaikuṇṭha Ekadaśi."

That order begins from the most distant realm: Vaikuṇṭha is the absolutely transcendent realm; the Ocean of Milk is the first place within the "north country." It is followed by regions on our Jambu continent from the Himalayas south: Śālagrama, Bādri Ashrama, Ayodhyā, the banks of the Ganges River, the Naimica Forest, Gokula, Mathurā, Govardhana, Ahobila, Dvārakā and Veṅkaṭam. Then follow the sacred places in Toṇḍai country, Chola country, Pāṇḍya country, etc. Veṅkaṭam links the "far north" and the Tamil region proper. For the iconic postures of these northern realms, see L. V. Gopalan, compiler, *Śrī Vaishnava Divya Desams (108 Tiruppatis)* (Madras, 1972), pp.77-140.

47. For the marriage of Śiva and Aṅkayaṛkaṇṇi (Mīnākṣī), see Hudson, "Two Citrā Festivals in Madurai" and "Madurai, the City as Goddesss."

48. The standing icons in Nāgapaṭṭiṇam and in Uraiyūr may also be implied, four-armed figures of great beauty that Tirumaṅgai linked with Kūṭal Alagar in Madurai (*Periya Tirumoḻi* 9.2.5). The context of the poem indicates that the stand-

ing icon in Madurai is described. That may mean that Tirumaṅgai referred to the standing icon of the Kūṭal Alagar vimāna, or to a standing icon that existed in Madurai before that three-floored vimāna was built, probably in the early 9th century. Given that we know that Tirumaṅgai was alive in the last decade of the 8th century, either is possible.

49. The icon in Śrī Raṅgam is of a mature male reclining without the lotus of Brahmā. It thus portrays the Bhagavān *after* he has eaten and swallowed spacetime (*brahmāṇḍa*) and *before* he gives birth to it again. Once he had eaten spacetime, he lay down on the banyan leaf in the form of an infant (Vaṭapatraśāyi), the form identified with the reclining icon in New Town. Being an infant, that form of Viṣṇu is prepubertal and non-sexual. The Lord of Raṅga is that infant grown into a mature male whose sexuality is the key to the future of the universe. With the eaten universe now in the womb in his belly, he holds destruction and death together with future regeneration, a coalescence of death and erotic love that Āṇṭāḷ sought to transcend by her union with him. For the reclining icon at Śrī Raṅgam, see T.A. Gopinatha Rao, *Elements of Hindu Iconography*, vol. I. pt. 1 (Madras, 1914), p. 269.

50. Āṇṭāḷ's use of Garuḍa in this verse may also be an allusion to her use of the *Garuḍa mantra* in her tantric rituals at the maṇḍala. Though commonly associated with the cure of snake bites, it is a mantra useful for attaining all manner of worldly desires. Whether the *Kāśyapa-saṁhitā* is a genuine Pāñcarātra text, however, is not certain. See H. Daniel Smith, *A Descriptive Bibliography of the Printed Texts of the Pāñcarātrāgama.*, vol.I, Gaekwad's Oriental Series, no. 158 (Baroda, 1975), pp. 107-112.

51. Nammāḻvār made the same connection between union with Kṛṣṇa and the story of Gajendra in *Tiruvāymoḻi* 8.7.2. See John Carman and Vasudha Narayanan, *The Tamil Veda: Piḷḷān's Interpretation of the Tiruvāymoḻi* (Chicago and London, 1989), p.104.

52. That point was suggested in *Parama-saṁhitā* 24.33-38 in a discussion of *dhyāna*. The discussion ends with a description of the seated Vaikuṇṭha, known there as *Śrī Kāma Parameṣṭi,* and with the statement that whoever worships that form attains rather soon the unchanging Śrī (*Śriyam prāpnoti susthiram*). See *Paramasaṁhitā (of the Pāñcarātra)*, ed. and tr. S. Krishnaswami Aiyangar, Gaekwad's Oriental Series No. 86 (Baroda: Oriental Institute, 1940).

THE "OTHER" ĀṆṬĀḶ: PORTRAIT OF A 12TH CENTURY ŚRĪVAIṢṆAVA WOMAN

Nancy Ann Nayar

The life and activities of every Hindu who lives within society are governed by a traditional, textually sanctified socio-religious code called the *dharma* (duty). For women, there exists a separate *dharma*—which is called *strīdharma* (the religious duties of women)—the heart of which is *pativratya* (loyalty and fidelity to the husband, expressed in his service). The women subjects of the hagiographical texts of the Hindu bhakti traditions have been remembered most often for a devotion that they expressed in vivid and compelling poetic compositions. According to the flow chart presenting the lives of these women-saints composed by A.K. Ramanujan, almost all in one way or another defied societal norms regarding the ideal or acceptable behavior for Hindu women (*strīdharma*).[1] Undermining the traditional ideals of Hindu womanhood represented by such popular heroines as Sītā and Savitrī, some avoided marriage altogether while others, such as Mīrābāī, deserted husbands and in-laws who interfered with their devotional practices. Indeed, of the more than a hundred women-saints studied by Ramanujan, only two endured marriage, and they were bad marriages at that![2]

A comprehensive historical understanding of the religiosity of Vaiṣṇava women in general, and Śrīvaiṣṇava[3] women in particular, must take into account the less well-documented lives of "ordinary" women who practiced devotion to God within the state of marriage, living within the confines of their community's prescriptions. Some authors have come dangerously close to generalizing about the entire community of female Vaiṣnavas/Śrīvaiṣṇavas regarding marriage and women's devotion. For example, it has been repeatedly suggested that—even though theoretically there was no contradiction in the pursuit of devotion and the life of a householder—for women, the dichotomy and tension between marriage and devotion to a personal god persisted and was never successfully resolved.

The poetess-saint Āṇṭāḷ ("she who rules") is the most famous female devotee in the world of Tamilian Vaiṣṇava bhakti. Infused with passionate longing for union with God, her poetry is representative of the highly emotional devotion which originated in Tamilian South India. She is also especially remembered for her defiance of Hindu norms for women's behavior in her refusal to marry a human husband, because she considered herself married to God.

Yet, the Śrīvaiṣṇava tradition, which recognizes her poems as part of the Tamil Veda equal in revelational status to the Sanskrit Veda, is first and foremost a tradition of householders. What about the vast majority of devotee-women who did *not* defy society by refusing marriage, but lived as wives and mothers? In order for a balanced understanding of Śrīvaiṣṇava religiosity, the lives of these women, who lived in conformity with the rules of *strīdharma* as understood by their community, should also be taken into account wherever records (admittedly few and far between) are available.[4]

Episodes from the life of "another" Āṇṭāḷ, who lived a life of *strīdharma* during the twelfth century, have been recorded in several important Śrīvaiṣṇava texts. This "other" Āṇṭāḷ was the wife Kūreśa, (Tamil, Kurattāḻvāṉ) a prominent Ācārya, Sanskrit poet, and disciple of the Viśiṣṭādvaita philosopher-theologian Rāmānuja. She was also the mother of Parāśara Bhaṭṭar, a prolific author and one of Rāmānuja's successors in an Ācārya-lineage that extends up to the present day. Although we do not possess any of Āṇṭāḷ's own reflections on her life-experiences, and although she is wholly unknown outside her own tradition and much less famous even within it than Āṇṭāḷ the poetess, the fact that this "other" Āṇṭāḷ has been remembered at all in a wholly male-dominated hagiographical literature is itself testimony to the strength of her character. A study of the episodes in which she is mentioned affords us a brief glimpse into the life of a woman who, by virtue of the men around her, was actively involved in the Śrīvaiṣṇava community of Śrīraṅgam during the twelfth century. Because there is so little information on *strīdharma* as lived by Tamilian Vaiṣṇavas, the portrait of Āṇṭāḷ that appears in the major Śrīvaiṣṇava hagiographical texts (brief as it is) is of no little significance.

We have been reminded that "one must gain access to the past primarily through available scriptural and literary sources, even though the absence of autobiographies and texts composed by women themselves makes reconstruction of the religious dimensions of women's lives tenuous at best".[5] Keeping this in mind, let us look at the recorded episodes from the life of this "other" Āṇṭāḷ, one of the few women who inhabits the historical memory of the Śrīvaiṣṇava community, albeit as a minor figure.

I. A Composite Portrait of Āṇṭāḷ[6]: Episodes in the Life of a 12th Century Śrīvaiṣṇava Woman

Āṇṭāḷ resided with her learned, well-to-do, and generous husband Kūreśa in the Brahmin village (agrahāra) of Kūram, located approximately twenty miles west of the important intellectual and cultural center of Kāñcīpuram, in what is now Tamil Nadu. Kūreśa ("lord of Kūram") is remembered for the compassion he displayed in his affectionate provision of food for the blind, lame and destitute, and for the five *stotras* that he composed in praise of the Lord and His consort. The couple must have worshipped at Kūram's Keśava Perumāḷ Temple, which had been constructed during the eighth century by the Pallava King Nandivarman II.[7]

Āṇṭāḷ Follows Kūreśa as He Renounces the World

According to an episode recorded in *Prapanna Amṛtam*, the goddess Śrī-Lakṣmī wanted to meet Kūreśa, so her consort Lord Varadarāja, the main icon in the Varadarāja Swāmi Temple in Kāñcīpuram, ordered His devotee Kāñcīpūrṇa[8] to fetch him. Moved by the kindliness and compassion of Lord Varadarāja and his consort, Kūreśa immediately renounced all of his worldly possessions and set out for Śrīraṅgam, the center of the Śrīvaiṣṇava sampradāya.

Unlike other women who returned to their parental homes when their husbands renounced the world, Āṇṭāḷ followed her husband's lead, keeping only a golden cup which she hid in the end piece of her sari. As the couple entered a path leading into the forest on their way to Śrīraṅgam, Āṇṭāḷ became fearful. Reassuring her that only the rich need be afraid, Kūreśa told her to give to him any wealth that she might have kept. Surprised, she then confessed to him about the golden cup which she had brought for his drinking water, saying: "Since you have given everything in charity (*dāna*), I took only this [cup]." Kūreśa took the "priceless gem-studded cup," threw it into the bush and said to Āṇṭāḷ: "Now there is nothing to fear. Come happily with me." Freed from fear, she continued following him. When they reached Śrīraṅgam, they worshipped Śrīraṅgarāja, the main icon at the Śrīraṅgam Temple in the city now known as Tirucciráp-paḷḷi. On hearing of the arrival of Kūreśa, the "author of the [*Śrī*] *Bhāṣya*" (Rāmānuja) was thrilled and through his disciples had Kūreśa brought to his *maṭha*.[9]

The text refers to Āṇṭāḷ as a *sādhvī* ("pious woman," "female renunciate"), a *svadharmānurodhinīm* ("one who follows her own *dharma*") and as a *sad-harmacaraṇīm* ("one who follows the same *dharma* [as her husband]" or simply "a virtuous wife").[10] Parallels to the *Rāmāyaṇa* reinforce *Prapanna Amṛtam*'s portrayal of Āṇṭāḷ's *strīdharma:* a married couple gives away all its wealth to the poor (as did Rāma and Sītā), and a wife willingly follows her husband into the forest (as Sītā followed after Rāma).

Āṇṭāḷ Becomes a Mother: The Conception and Birth of Parāśara Bhaṭṭar and Śrīrāma Piḷḷai

Having moved from the stage of the householder proper to a life of renunciation, Āṇṭāḷ and Kūreśa were living the Śrīvaiṣṇava equivalent of the third stage of life called *vanaprastha.*[11] As its name suggests, in pan-Indian Hinduism this stage of life involves retiring to the forest, but for the Śrīvaiṣṇava it most often involves living a life of renunciation in one of the Lord's terrestrial abodes (in this case, Śrīraṅgam). Kūreśa continued to live with his wife, but all of the major hagiographical texts convey the idea that he had renounced ordinary married relations with her. Indeed, the *Guru Paramparā Prabhāvam* describes Kūreśa as being "detached from everything including the prescribed or permitted activities."[12] This life-style also appears to have involved begging for food, and Kūreśa and his wife received alms in the way of food everyday "from the houses of learned people."

One day during the rainy season an ongoing downpour prevented Kūreśa from his usual task of begging for alms, and so he went to bed hungry.[13] A horn is blown at the time Lord Raṅga's nightly feeding, which takes place just before He is put to bed. On hearing the horn, Āṇṭāḷ mentally addressed Lord Raṅga thus: "Your devotee has gone to sleep hungry, while you are enjoying [Your] food." Upon hearing this, Lord Raṅga is said to have immediately appeared in a dream to a temple servant named

Uttama Nampi and requested him to honor Kūreśa by presenting him with all of the temple paraphernalia, including food. In obedience to the Lord's command, Nampi arrived at the home of Kūreśa and Āṇṭāḷ. Displeased by his wife's concern that the Lord had taken food while her husband went to bed hungry, Kūreśa reprimanded her. Then both of them partook of the *prasāda*[14] from the temple. The *Guru Paramparā Prabhāvam* states that the *prasāda* was the cause (*hetu*) of the conception of Bhattar and Śrīrāma Piḷḷai, the twin sons born to Āṇṭāḷ and Kūreśa.[15] Prof. K.K.A. Venkatachari has suggested that the depiction of the couple in the texts suggests that their life of renunciation included the renunciation of marital relations. Nevertheless, he regards Kūreśa's and Āṇṭāḷ's eating of the *prasāda* previous to the conception of their sons as analogous to the *Rāmāyaṇa* story of Daśaratha, who took *pāyasam* (rice pudding) at the conclusion of his fast (*vrata*) for a son. According to Hindu custom, when such a fast is concluded, the couple is expected to sleep together. In other words, the *prasāda* consumed by Kūreśa and Āṇṭāḷ functions as a symbol of the Lord's grace in giving them a child, and the actual physical conception of the sons was in the normal way.[16]

Āṇṭāḷ as Wife and Mother

In several incidents from the period of Bhaṭṭar's early life we can observe Āṇṭāḷ involved in the quite ordinary worries that go with raising a family. The stories, however, reveal little of her character. What is significant about the stories from this time period is their depiction of the underlying harmony that pervaded the household of Āṇṭāḷ and Kūreśa. The major episodes connected with Bhaṭṭar's childhood are those in which the family members fear for him because of his superior intelligence. His intellectual acumen was revealed in his debate with a man called Sarvajña Bhaṭṭar, a well-known scholar who entered the town of Śrīraṅgam with great pomp and show. The child engaged in such intelligent questioning of the scholar that the family feared for Bhattar's very safety. We are told that his mother Āṇṭāḷ sprinkled holy water (*śrī-pāta-tīirttattai*) over him in order to protect him from harm.[17] Because of his precocity in Vedic studies, Bhaṭṭar one day left the classroom in the middle of the lessons and started playing in the street. Informed of this, his parents questioned him only to discover that their son's memory was so acute that he could perfectly recite for them the lesson of the previous day. Seeing this, Kūreśa and Āṇṭāḷ were again full of fear and said: "We shouldn't allow him to go out for a long time."[18]

The story of the arrangements for Bhaṭṭar's marriage reveals the cohesiveness of the close-knit Śrīvaiṣṇava community. Āṇṭāḷ and Kūreśa, the Ācārya Rāmānuja, and Lord Raṅga Himself all worked in close cooperation. When Bhaṭṭar reached marriageable age, his father was faced with a dilemma as to how to celebrate his son's marriage, given that his relatives were worldly people. He went to his Ācārya Rāmānuja, who suggested an alliance with the relatives of Periya Nampi, for then Bhaṭṭar's own *sūtra* and *śākhā*, Brahmin and Śrīvaiṣṇava status would not be compromised. Kūreśa accepted his Ācārya's suggestion and, after discussing it with Āṇṭāḷ, asked for the girl through Rāmānuja. However, Periya Nampi hesitated to accept the arrangement. Although he knew about Bhaṭṭar's "birth in a noble family," he hesitated because the marriage would result in an alliance with a new family. As time passed, Āṇṭāḷ became concerned and suggested to her husband that they should perform their duty by arranging their sons' marriages at once. Faced with a dilemma, Kūreśa went to the great Lord [at Śrīraṅgam], worshipped Him and asked Him what should be done. The Lord told Kūreśa that He would appropriately arrange the marriage Himself. That night He appeared in a dream to the girl's parents and suggested the marriage. The next day some members of Periya Nampi's family came to Kūreśa to tell him that they would give their daughter Akkacci to Bhaṭṭar. The wedding was then conducted "with great celebration."[19]

Sometime after Bhaṭṭar's marriage, Kūreśa was blinded by an evil Coḻa king because of his refusal to acknowledge that Śiva is greater than Lord Viṣṇu-Nārāyaṇa. Due to the enmity between Rāmānuja and a "king" known in the Śrīvaiṣṇava texts as Kṛmikanṭha ("the worm-necked one"), when Kūreśa returned to Śrīraṅgam the temple servants and gatekeepers would not permit him to enter the temple because he was the disciple of Rāmānuja. Someone in the crowd called Kūreśa a "holy man"/ "religious ascetic" (*sādhu*), and the gatekeepers were about to let him enter in spite of their animosity towards his Ācārya. However, Kūreśa chose to affirm his relationship with Rāmānuja over service to Lord Raṅga, and so he started off to Tirumāliruñcolai with his sons, daughters-in-law and wife.[20] Unfortunately, Āṇṭāḷ's reaction to the trying circumstances of that difficult time has not been recorded, but she bore the adversities in unity with her family.

Āṇṭāḷ As Widow: Woman of Faith and Moral Authority

When the situation in Śrīraṅgam returned to normal, Kūreśa, his family and Rāmānuja returned to Śrīraṅgam and resumed their usual lives. Sometime after their return, Kūreśa was granted the boon of his choice by Lord Raṅga. Kūreśa chose to go at once to Paramapada, Lord Viṣṇu's Supreme Heaven. Kūreśa and Rāmānuja had an emotional last meeting, but when Kūreśa began following him to his *maṭha,* Rāmānuja asked him to go no further. Rejoining his wife Āṇṭāḷ, Kūreśa called their sons to his side and handed them over to the Lord and His consort: "Lord Raṅga and Śrī are here, so [even without me] there will be nothing lacking for you." Having entrusted them to Rāmānuja, at whose feet, he said, they should take refuge, he commanded them always to obey their mother Āṇṭāḷ. We see here the wife of an eminent Śrīvaiṣṇava Ācārya as one member of the "larger," close-knit community of the Ācārya-disciple lineage. Kūreśa died (lit.: "went to Paramapada") meditating on the feet of Rāmānuja, with his head in the lap of his disciple Piḷḷai Piḷḷai Āḻvāṉ, and his feet in the lap of Āṇṭāḷ.[21]

Prapanna Amṛtam contains a more compelling picture of Āṇṭāḷ's and Rāmānuja's response to Kūreśa's choice of the boon of Paramapada. Distressed at the coming separation from his beloved disciple, Rāmānuja slowly returned to his *maṭha* with his eyes full of tears. In contrast, Āṇṭāḷ responded to the news of her impending widowhood with a surprising equanimity: "[On being told by Kūreśa of his choice of Paramapada as a boon, she] declared herself in agreement with his idea, and bowing down to her husband's feet, stood near him with her hands in the position of supplication, without any kind of [inner] disturbance."[22]

Bhaṭṭar continued to honor his mother after attaining a position of prominence in the Śrīvaiṣṇava community. On the instruction of Rāmānuja, Bhaṭṭar decided that he would attempt to bring a Vedāntin residing in the "western country" (of Melkote) "into our philosophical school" (*nammuṭaiya tarśanattile*) so that he might eventually become "the chief administrator of our *darśana*" (*tarśana pravarttaka*). On Bhaṭṭar's return to Śrīraṅgam from a ten-day debate in which he defeated the well-known Vedic scholar, he was received with great pomp and circumstance by his disciples and the temple servants. Yet, immediately after praising Lord Raṅga in the Inner Sanctum of the temple and receiving all temple honors—and before beginning to instruct all of this devotees in the meaning of the *darśana*—he returned home and prostrated before his mother Āṇṭāḷ.[23]

It is noteworthy that in the episodes cited above Āṇṭāḷ for the most part remained in the background, even though she is important enough to be mentioned by name in these almost entirely male-dominated texts. However, several character-revealing incidents occurred when she was a widow which show her to have been a woman of great faith and moral authority. These incidents further reveal a woman who, while practicing *strīdharma* and with her family as her central concern, is surprisingly detached from the usual self-centered, worldly concerns regarding the family members.

One Vīrasundarabrahma Rāya came into conflict with Āṇṭāḷ's son Parāśara Bhaṭṭar, who had objected to Vīrasundara's proposal to demolish the house of Kūreśa's disciple Piḷḷai Piḷḷai Āḻvāṉ during the construction of a rampart wall around the Śrīraṅgam Temple. Vīrasundara must have made a lot of trouble for the leader of the Śrīvaiṣṇava community, for Bhaṭṭar and Nañjīyar (the Vedāntin converted by Bhaṭṭar who moved to Śrīraṅgam and became his disciple) were unable to continue residing in Śrīraṅgam and were forced to move to Tīrukottiyur. At Vīrasundara's death, some Śrīvaiṣṇavas went to convey the news to Āṇṭāḷ and told her that "Bhaṭṭar's enemy" had passed away. The Śrīvaiṣṇavas began joyously throwing their upper cloths into the air for, after all, Bhaṭṭar would now be able to return to Śrīraṅgam. In contrast, Āṇṭāḷ entered her house, bolted the doors, and holding her stomach with great suffering, started crying loudly. The fact that Virasundara had died unrepentant after committing a great sin against her son Bhaṭṭar disturbed Āṇṭāḷ tremendously.[24]

Another episode related in *Guru Paramparā Prabhāvam* concerns Āṇṭāḷ's insistence on drinking the water in which her son Bhaṭṭar's feet had been ritually washed (*śrī-pāta-tīrtta*). Knowing that Bhaṭṭar himself would object to this act of humility on the part of his mother, she had his feet washed through someone else. A member of the community who questioned her action suggested to her that her behavior was inappropriate. Āṇṭāḷ confidently replied: "Do you think that we have to take only the *tīrtha* which comes from the images installed by others? Are we not allowed to take *tīrtha* from the images made by ourselves?". When the Śrīvaiṣṇava proved unable to comprehend her reply, she explained herself by quoting a stanza by Tirumaṅkai Āḻvār to the effect that if a small boy worships God, is he still to be considered a small boy? The understanding given by the *Guru Paramparā Prabhāvam*'s author is that even if one is a disciple or son, because of his great wisdom we have to follow him as a devotee.[25]

Yet, observe Āṇṭāḷ's reaction to the death of the very son whose śrī-pātatīrtta she insisted on drinking. When Bhaṭṭar was a mere twenty-eight years old, Lord Raṅga, pleased with his preaching, presented him with all the temple honors. Overcome with joy, the Lord granted Paramapada to Bhaṭṭar. Bhaṭṭar joyfully accepted this gift from the Lord, and the community honored him by carrying him on a plank to his home, where he was blessed by his mother Āṇṭāḷ. He explicated several Śrīvaiṣṇava sectarian texts, and while expounding on a phrase from *Periyāḻvār Tirumoḻi* 5.4.2, "his entire body shook, and smiling and with his hands folded in supplication (*añjali*)...his skull broke open and...he went to Paramapada."[26]

Informed of the event, Āṇṭāḷ came quickly, and embraced her son "without agitation in her body, suffering in her heart, change of face, or flowing of tears." She said:

> The Lord has taken [my son] just like...bees take the honey from the flower by smelling it. In that same way, knowing fully well Bhaṭṭar's tenderness, the Bee of Heaven (that is, the Lord) has taken him. Here the great loss is for Raṅganātha and Śrī, whereas the great gain is for the Lord of Paramapada and those who reside there.

In contrast to Āṇṭāḷ, who demonstrated strength and fortitude, Bhaṭṭar's disciple and successor as chief Ācārya of the *darśana*, Nañjīyar, was "fallen on the ground like an uprooted tree, crying and repeating the name of Bhaṭṭar."[27]

Later when Āṇṭāḷ and some of Bhaṭṭar's disciples entered into the house, they found Bhaṭṭar's twin brother Śrīrāma Piḷḷai singing stanza 3.8.1 from *Periyāḻvār Tirumoḻi*: "As the morning dew drops on the day's new flower, blossoming in the lovely lotus pond, the pollen and inner petals fall away: its beauty fades, Alas!"[28] Śrīrāma Piḷḷai, too, then fell onto the ground and cried loudly. [Once again] Āṇṭāḷ proved to be the strongest of the lot, saying to Bhaṭṭar's disciples who were present in the house: "He [Śrīrāma Piḷḷai] is not fit to be Kūreśa's son". Then turning towards him, she said: "Oh son, I think you have 'cousin-jealousy,' and are not able to tolerate [your brother's] great fortune." Śrīrāma Piḷḷai then gave up his sorrow, rose from his seat, fell at the feet of his mother Āṇṭāḷ and begged her forgiveness.

In the section of the Śrīraṅgam temple chronicle *Koyil Oḻuku* called "The Glory of Kūranārāyaṇa Jīyar,"[29] an episode involving Āṇṭāḷ is mentioned that appears to be unique to that text. Its inclusion in this important work substantiates the fact that Āṇṭāḷ was well-known in the community and indeed, from time to time (although being a woman and therefore having no official position in the temple), did not hesitate to use her authority in certain aspects of temple affairs even after becoming a widow:

> During the time that [Bhaṭṭar's successor] Nañjīyar was managing the *darśana,* one of the Viṇṇappañ-ceyvārs[30] became unfit to serve in the Lord's shrine. Out of compassion for him, [Kuratt] Āḻvāṉ's respected wife Āṇṭāḷ (*āḻvāṉuṭaiya tevikaḷ āṇṭāḷ*) called Kūranārāyaṇa Jīyar, who had taken refuge in the auspicious feet of Alvan while that great person was present in Tirumāliruñcolai. An elderly man well-versed in the profession of his Ācāryas and a great specialist in mantras, [Kūranārāyaṇa Jīyar] had become a *sannyāsi* and was living in Śrīraṅgam. [Āṇṭāḷ] said to him: "You promised to use your mantras in the service [of the Lord] (*kainkaryattile*). Now make this Viṇṇappañ-cevyār fit for the Lord's service (*perumāḷ kainkaryattukku yokyarām*). Thus, Kūranārāyaṇa Jīyar produced [the *stotra* called] *"The Hundred [Stanzas in Praise] of Sudarśana [Lord Nārāyaṇa's Discus]" (Sudarśana Śaṭakam).* [The recitation of this *stotra*] freed the Viṇṇappañ-ceyvār from his illness, and made him fit [to participate] in the worship service [of the Lord].[31]

II. Issues Raised by the Life of Āṇṭāḷ

As shown by the episodes from her life and the terminology used to refer to her in *Prapanna Amṛtam* (*sādhvī, sadharmacariṇīm, svadharmānurodhinīm*), Āṇṭāḷ lived her life in conformity with *strīdharma* as understood by the Śrīvaiṣṇava community. This brief but precious glimpse into the household of Āṇṭāḷ and her husband Kūreśa afforded by the hagiographical texts raises several pertinent questions regarding the Śrīvaiṣṇava community in general and the community of Śrīvaiṣṇava women in particular.

Life of the Householder vs. Sannyāsa

In the Śrīvaiṣṇava community, the householder life is normative. The universalization of salvation by surrender to God (*prapatti*) eliminates the difference between male and female, low caste and high, and householder and sannyasi. Indeed, Śrīvaiṣṇavas are positively discouraged from the taking of *sannyāsa*, because salvation by means of simple but total surrender to the Lord (*prapatti*) is as easily available to householders as it is to world-renunciates. Nowadays a recurrent theme has been articulated by a variety of authors: that while males may easily fulfill the roles of householder and devotee simultaneously, there is an irreconcilable conflict between the householder life and the life of devotion to God for women. This view is usually based on the fact that almost all of the female devotional poetesses protest marriage to a mortal man in one way or another. Contemporary feminist literature has made much of this.[32]

It has, indeed, been suggested that *pativratya* (devotedness to the husband) comes into active conflict with devotion to God when the devotee is female. This conflict, it is maintained, makes the simultaneity of marriage and a life of devotion, which is possible for male devotees, impossible for women.[33] On the basis of the documentation on the lives of women poetesses, this notion is certainly well-founded. Other evidence, however, points to the fact that—in the Śrīvaiṣṇava community, at least—it was more often than not the men who found the roles of householder and devotee imcompatible.

Three major Śrīvaiṣṇava Ācāryas during the first few centuries of the tradition—Rāmānuja, Bhaṭṭar's successor Nañjīyar, and Manavāḷamāmuni—took *sannyāsa* because of the problems caused by the insistence of their wives or other family members on too many of the requirements of Brahmin orthodoxy. All three figures are said to have found the demands of married life an obstacle to their devotion. Katherine Young has observed that the radical theology of the Śrīvaiṣṇavas was often compromised by the Brahmin women themselves, "in the sense that their norm was Brahmanical orthodoxy, not Tamil liberalism."[34] However, there appears to have been mutual understanding and a unity of purpose in the lives of Āṇṭāḷ and Kūreśa. That unity of purpose was manifest at the time of Kūreśa's leaving for Śrīraṅgam. Alaka Hejib has expressed the Hindu wife's dilemma at the possibility of her husband taking *sannyāsa* thus:

> The crowning amgibuity [that the Hindu wife] confronts is this: She loses her 'God' and the opportunity to fulfill her *pativratya* (devotedness to her husband) if she permits his *saṁnyāsa*. On the other hand, she becomes destructive toward him if she restrains his *saṁnyāsa* for the purpose of her *pativratya*. The

> question here is: how should she resolve this dilemma and the ambiguity of her wifely duties and emerge as a 'good wife'?[35]

Did Kūreśa originally intend to renounce all social obligations (that is, take *sannyāsa*), or did he all along expect Āṇṭāḷ to accompany him in the intermediate stage of renunciation called *vanaprastha*?[36] The texts are not clear on this point. It is important to note, however, that Kūreśa's motivation was not the desire for salvation itself (*sannyāsa* is not a necessary requirement for that). Rather, his decision was an expression of his deep personal response to the compassion shown to him by Lord Varadarāja and Śrī. Āṇṭāḷ appears successfully to have "resolved" her supposed "dilemma" by supporting her husband in his decision and renouncing the world along with him. On the basis of the available textual evidence, we can view her action either as a sincere expression of unity with her husband in his response to the Lord, or simply as an expression of her *strīdharma,* that is, following her husband solely in order to serve him as her 'god'.

Strīdharma and Devotion

For the Śrīvaiṣṇava married woman following the socially accepted path of *strīdharma,* the one-pointedness of devotion to the Lord—in which mind, emotions and action converge—must be directed to a human husband as well. This idea is founded on the words of *Rāmāyaṇa* (a key text in the development of Śrīvaiṣṇava theology) thus: *strīṇām bhartā hi daivatam* ("Indeed, the husband constitutes divinity for a woman").[37] It has been argued that the worship of the god (*pati*) in the home shrine, which is analogous to the devotion expressed to the husband as *pati* (the term means both "husband" and "lord"), may from the point of view of the religious psychology of the Hindu wife, approximate the state of polyandry: one woman with two "husbands" for which she cooks, serves and to whom she is devoted.[38] And indeed, as we have seen, marriage to a human husband has been problematic for almost all of the women bhakti-poets. Among the most famous of them, only one, the Maharastrian Bahīnabāī, remained married while pursuing her life as God's devotee. Even she expressed the great difficulties of marriage (her husband was a Śākta and opposed her devotional pursuits), and even had suicidal impulses partly because of the tension her marriage produced.[39]

Yet as we observe the Śrīvaiṣṇava household of Āṇṭāḷ and Kūreśa, we see two very interesting phenomena which may in part explain why Āṇṭāḷ was able to combine devotion to the Lord and the service of her husband. Firstly, for Śrīvaiṣṇavas a woman's service of and devotedness to her husband (*pativratya*) is analogous to a man's service of and devotedness to the Ācārya.

Remember how, upon his return to Śrīraṅgam during troubled times, Kūreśa was faced with the decision of whether to enter the temple to serve Lord Raṅga or remain faithful to his Ācārya Rāmānuja who had fallen out of favor with the temple servants. Kūreśa chose loyalty to his Ācārya over the direct service of Lord Raṅga. Similarly, for a Śrīvaiṣṇava woman devotion to the husband and to the Lord are not in as direct a conflict as it may appear; rather, devotion to the husband is an expression of devotion to the Lord.

Secondly, Kūreśa was the primary object of Āṇṭāḷ's devotion and service, yet he objected to being the recipient of Āṇṭāḷ's service when she went too far in her performance of duties based on the notion of *strīdharma*. For example, at the time of their renunciation of the world when they had begun walking through the woods on the way to Śrīraṅgam, Kūreśa threw into the bush the golden cup that Āṇṭāḷ had saved for his drinking water. Again, Kūreśa expressed displeasure when Āṇṭāḷ complained to Lord Raṅga about His being well-fed while her husband went to bed hungry. In other words, Kūreśa was not a man who demanded the service of his wife, or in any way took advantage of her willingness to serve.

Emotional *Bhakti* and *Prapatti*

A highly emotional type of religious devotion originated in the Tamil lands during the sixth to tenth century, of which the Āḻvār poems are the first expression. Emotional religiosity is highly respected among Śrīvaiṣṇavas and one can witness it even today in the tears and ecstatic symptoms brought on in some individuals at recitations of the poems of the Tamil Veda.

Unfortunately, the brief portrait that we have of Āṇṭāḷ does not reveal to us the extent to which she was or was not involved in an emotional form of bhakti. Yet, the portrait that we have of her reminds us that emotionalism is not a necessary constituent of Śrīvaiṣṇava religiosity; and in this sense, it cannot be the only model for Śrīvaiṣṇava spirituality. In and of itself, emotionalism is not salvific, and is important only to the extent that the experiences of deep longing for union with the Lord, and the painfulness of the experience of separation from Him, may serve to drive the desperate devotee to total surrender. The goal of all Śrīvaiṣṇavas—the eternal servitude of Lord Viṣṇu and his consort Śrī in the Supreme Heaven (Paramapada)—arises from the devotees' total surrender to God (*prapatti*), Who is both the means and the goal. The importance of this radical new idea (Śrīvaiṣṇavas are sure of their salvation and are in no danger of losing *mokṣa* at the end of their lives) is attested to in many passages of *Guru Paramparā Prabhāvam* which are concerned with the death of the Ācāryas. Indeed, for Śrīvaiṣṇavas death is the certain culmination of and final escape from the rounds of births and deaths. The emotionalism of some of the Āḻvārs represents the extremity of passionate longing for God and an inability to bear separation from Him. But for the Śrīvaiṣṇava, this desire is symbolically expressed in the hagiographical literature in the "choosing" of the boon of Paramapada, as well. The deaths of Kūreśa and Bhaṭṭar (lit: their "going to Paramapada") and Āṇṭāḷ's response to their choice of that boon reveals her own deep belief in the efficacy of *prapatti* and a typically Śrīvaiṣṇava attitude concerning the certainty of salvation. However, for Āṇṭāḷ herself, there is no particular difference between life lived close to the Lord's iconic presence in Śrīraṅgam or life in Paramapada. When commenting on Bhaṭṭar's death, she says: "Here the great loss is for Raṅganātha and Śrī, whereas the great gain is for the Lord of Paramapada and those who reside there." The relationship of intimacy with God which is so powerfully and passionately expressed in the poetry of the ninth century Āṇṭāḷ is present in a more subdued way in the stories of our "other" Āṇṭāḷ.

The Moral Authority of Āṇṭāḷ

In the episodes which mention Āṇṭāḷ, we often see her caring for the members of her family. We observe her on her way to Śrīraṅgam, protecting her son, showing concern for her family. Yet, she invests the conventional roles of wife, mother, and widow with a strong moral authority. While her family is clearly the center of her life, in every major incident related in the texts she is shown to be gifted with a surprising lack of familial possessiveness or self-centeredness, as she views each family member within the context of a strong personal faith. This is especially noticeable in her response to the deaths of her husband and son, where she outshines even such Śrīvaiṣṇava leaders as Rāmānuja and Nañjīyar. Āṇṭāḷ's moral authority creates an immediate response in those associated with her (for example, Śrīrāma Piḷḷai).

Conclusions

What has been called the "silent history" of women is most silent regarding women devotees who lived a life of *strīdharma*. In the episodes related in *Guru Paramparā Prabhāvam* and *Prapanna Amṛtam* we have a brief but rare glimpse into the life of a woman who did not defy the rules of society by refusing marriage or leaving her husband, but fulfilled the traditional roles of wife, mother, and widow.

There are two models of feminine behavior in the bhakti traditions: the women-saint who defies societal norms and the ordinary woman who follows her *strīdharma*. They have been compared to the two basic types of Hindu goddesses: the solitary goddess of the folk traditions and the goddess-consort of the classical tradition. The feminine behavior of the women-saints such as Mīrābāī resembles that of the solitary goddesses of the folk tradition, who are defiant, dramatic and full of fury and restlessness. Practitioners of *strīdharma* may be compared to the goddesses of the classical tradition, such as Śrī-Lakṣmī (or her incarnation Sītā), who live lives of domesticity.[40]

The relationship between Āṇṭāḷ and Kūreśa is infused with one particular quality that is not found in any of the depictions of married life contained in the writings by and about the women-saints. To be sure, Āṇṭāḷ serves her husband and looks out for his welfare. But Kūreśa never exploits his position as husband and, indeed, shows deep respect for his wife (as, for example, in their mutual renunciation of the world and his inviting her to walk "happily" with him to Śrīraṅgam). In this, their relationship mirrors that of the Supreme Couple. An especially important and distinguishing feature of the relationship between Lord Viṣṇu-Nārāyaṇa and His consort Śrī-Lakṣmī is the way in which they act in co-operation with one another. The inherent harmony of the Supreme Couple is an important feature of the Śrīvaiṣṇava understanding of Śrī as Īśvarī, the mistress and creator of the universe. In many *stotra* stanzas composed by Āṇṭāḷ's husband Kūreśa and her son Bhaṭṭar, the goddess' creatorship of the worlds is praised. A common theme with both of these poets is that all attainable power or wealth in this world are dependent on Śrī's benevolent glance. On the other hand, many of their stanzas point to the more traditional Vaiṣṇava teaching on the creatorship of Lord Viṣṇu. The passages depicting the creative power of Śrī's glance and those extolling Lord Viṣṇu's creatorship are reconcilable only when the harmony of the Divine Couple is taken into account. Śrī has a central cosmological role according to the teachings of Śrīvaiṣṇavism, but it is neither instead of Viṣṇu's nor in competition with His. Celebrated in stanzas of praise, the two apparently divergent views of creation become reconciled only in the light of the single will and the mutual enjoyment of the Divine Couple.[41]

Everywhere in the texts under consideration here, we see the close cooperation of Kūreśa and Āṇṭāḷ: in his acceptance of her as a companion to him in his renunciation of the world, in the eating of the *prasāda* from the temple which resulted in the birth of twin boys, in the arrangements for Bhaṭṭar's marriage, and in Āṇṭāḷ's response to Kūreśa's choice of the boon of Paramapada.

Āṇṭāḷ and Kūreśa's singleness of purpose (the service of Lord Viṣṇu whether directly or through the service of the husband and/or Ācārya) and their mutual respect for one another's person and vocation are critical factors that enabled Āṇṭāḷ to live a life of devotion to God within the context of *strīdharma*.

Appendix: Sources on the Life-Episodes of Āṇṭāḷ

This composite portrait of Āṇṭāḷ is based on several Śrīvaiṣṇava hagiographical texts, including (1) Pi<u>n</u>pa<u>l</u>akiya Perumāḷ Jīyar's *Ā<u>r</u>āyirappaṭi Kuruparamparāprapāvam* [hereafter, *Guru Paramparā Prabhāvam* or GPP], (2) *Prapanna Amṛtam* [hereafter PA], and (3) *Koyil O<u>l</u>uku* [hereafter KO].

Guru Paramparā Prabhāvam (The Splendor of the Lineage of Gurus): The majority of the episodes mentioning Āṇṭāḷ are contained in the earliest and most important Śrīvaiṣṇava hagiography, the GPP. GPP is a Maṇipravāḷa text which relates the activities of the Ā<u>l</u>vārs and Ācāryas, and all but two of the episodes on the life of Āṇṭāḷ reviewed above are based on that source. GPP was reputedly composed by Pi<u>n</u>pa<u>l</u>akiya Perumāḷ Jīyar approximately one hundred and fifty years after the period of Rāmānuja and his disciples. That GPP is based on pre-existing oral tradition is confirmed in text itself. Concerning the section on Parāśara Bhaṭṭar, its author says:

> Bhattar's glory cannot be comprehended. We have told it according to our understanding, just as we have heard it.[42]

Among the four works of sacred biography, it has a special place within the Śrīvaiṣṇava tradition in that it is the only hagiographical text on which public discourses are given and before which prostration is performed. B.V. Ramanujam has attested to its importance within the tradition: "[GPP is] a work which every traditional scholar is said to master sitting at the feet of his Ācārya."[43] B.V. Ramanujam and K.K.A. Venkatachari are in agreement that the accounts of the Ācāryas related in the text have a fair degree of historical accuracy. Dr. Venkatachari's argument is based on the fact that "the oral traditions about the lives the teachings of the Ācāryas could be preserved, handed down, and eventually recorded", and he regards the stories as "probably true unless obviously mythical...[due to the] direct succession of teachers during this period."[44] But as is the case with most oral traditions, chronology has frequently become blurred, two or more stories may be combined into a single tale, or a story may become "embellished" over time as each story teller adds his own particular details.

Prapanna Amṛtam (The Ambrosia of Those Surrendered [to the Lord]: PA is a Sanskrit *kāvya* written in Purāṇic style. The actual date of the work is disputed, but for certain it was composed within the period of the mid-sixteenth to the late seventeenth century. Large portions of PA are direct translations from GPP, although it does contain a few episodes which are most likely derived from a separate oral tradition (for example, the story of Āṇṭāḷ's following of her husband when he renounced the world and set out for Śrīraṅgam). While the germ of the new episodes is most probably historical (for example, Kūreśa's wealth, prestige and generosity to the poor in his village of Kūram), the text does contain exaggerations and embellishments that go beyond GPP. Even so, B.V. Ramanujam regards it as one of the more historically reliable Śrīvaiṣṇava hagiographies, because even though it is literary rather than historical in style, "it [PA] has strictly followed the *Ārāyirappaṭi* [GPP] almost as a literal translation of that work."[45]

Koyil Oḻuku (The Chronicle of the Śrīraṅgam Temple): *Koyil Oḻuku* (*koyil* means "temple" in general or "the Śrīraṅgam Temple" in particular; *oḻuku* means "record" or "register") is the chronicle of the Śrīraṅgam Temple, the center of the Śrīvaiṣṇava community. Its main purpose is to record benefactions made to the temple by princes and chieftains of different ages. Compiled over a long period of time, it also includes detailed references to the Śrīvaiṣṇava Ācāryas and their connections with the temple.[46] The chronology contained in the text is, at times, quite confused. V.N. Hari Rao suggests that the jumbled sequence may be due to the constant revisions of the original, the shortcomings of the scribes, or interpolations made by scribes.[47] At any rate, the fact that Āṇṭāḷ, who had no official position in the temple, is mentioned at all is a tribute to the impact that her strong personality made on the Śrīvaiṣṇava community of her time.

NOTES

I am grateful to the Shastri Indo-Canadian Institute for financing the research on which this article is based.

[1]A.K. Ramanujan, "Talking to God in the Mother Tongue." *Manushi.* Nos. 50, 51, 52 (1989), pp. 9-14 at p. 12.

[2]Rāmānujan, "Talking to God," p. 14.

[3]Śrīvaiṣṇavas are worshippers of Lord Viṣṇu Who is eternally accompanied by his consort Sri-Laksmi. Centered in the Tamil-speaking area of South India, Śrīvaiṣṇavas call their tradition the Ubhaya Vedānta ("both Vedāntas"), because they accord equal revelational status to the Sanskrit Veda, as interpreted by Rāmānuja, and the Tamil Veda comprised of four thousand stanzas of Tamil poetry composed by twelve Vaiṣṇava devotees dating from the sixth century to the tenth century C.E., ten of whom are called "Āḻvārs" or "those immersed in God."

[4]There may well be a parallel here with the Christian faith. This same dichotomy—between saints who are "married to God" and revered for their visions and ecstatic experiences, and the ordinary Christian—was present in the popular thinking of Catholics during much of the Church's history. In the nineteenth century, St. Therese of Lisieux's "little way" recovered the value of the quite ordinary lives of the faithful, who express their love for God in the ordinary experiences of life, in dryness and in dark faith.

[5]Katherine K. Young, "Hinduism." In *Women in World Religions,* ed. by Arvind Sharma (Albany: State University of New York Press, 1987), pp.59-103 at p. 60.

[6]For a discussion of the relative historical reliability of the sources on Āṇṭāḷ's life, see Appendix.

[7]On the basis of inscriptional evidence cited in N. Subrahmanian, *History of Tamilnad* (Madurai: Ennes Publications, 1968), pp. 117-18. The Pallava King Nandivarman II (A.D. 731-798), who must have been a devout Vaisnava, had constructed both the Vaikuṇṭha Perumāḷ temple in Kāñcipuram and the Keśava

Perumāḷ Temple at Kūram.

[8]According to the *Periya Tirumuṭi Aṭaivu*, Kāñcipūrṇa was born "in the fourth caste" (*caturtla varṇattil*), was the disciple of Periya Nampi, the confidante of Lord Varadarāja of Kāñci, the author of *Devarājaṣṭakam* and "well-wisher of author of *Śrī Bhāṣya*" (Rāmānuja). In Piṉpaḻakiya Perumāḷ Jīyar, *Ārāyirappaṭi Kuruparamparāprapāvam*, ed. by S. Kirusnasvāmi Ayyaṅkār [hereafter *Guru Paramparā Prabhāvam*] (Tirucci: 1975), pp. 553-611 at p. 571.

[9]*Prapanna Amṛtam* 37:22-39

[10]*Prapanna Amṛtam* 14:1-36. Note that the *Guru Paramparā Prabhāvam* does not mention Āṇṭāḷ at all in its depiction of Kūreśa's departure for Śrīraṅgam. According to that text, one of Yāmuna's disciples went to Kāñcipuram to fetch Rāmānuja and take him to Śrīraṅgam, ostensibly to become Yāmuna's successor in the Ācarya-lineage. Kūreśa served Rāmānuja by fetching his icon and belongings from the *maṭha*, and then joined him as he was led away to Śrīraṅgam. GPP, pp. 179-80.

[11]According to pan-Indian Hinduism, there are four stages of life (*āśrama*): that of the celibate student (*brahmacarya*), that of the householder (*gṛhasthya*), that of the forest-dwelling renunciate, who may live with his wife although practicing chastity (*vanaprastha*), and that of the world-renouncer, who is no longer bound by social obligations (*sannyāsa*).

[12]*Guru Paramparā Prabhāvam*, p. 229. I am indebted to Dr. K.K.A. Venkatachari for assistance in the translation of this difficult text.

[13]*Guru Paramparā Prabhāvam*, p. 220

[14]*Prasāda (prasāttai)* is food presented to the Lord's iconic incarnation in the temple, the remnants of which are offered to the devotee as the Lord's gratuitous blessing.

[15]*Guru Paramparā Prabhāvam*, pp. 230-31.

The later text *Prapanna Amṛtam* tells a similar tale: Kūreśa "took the *prasāda* [brought to him from the temple] and joyously gave it to his wife. Only because of that (*tenaiva hetunā*), did the virtuous wife (*sādhvī*) conceive the partial-incarnation of Parāśara and Vyāsa (*parāśarasya vyāsasya bhāgena*)...By the grace of the Lord at [Śrī]raṅgam (*raṅgeśānugrahāt*) two very splendorous sons were born...from Kūreśa (kūreśat)...(38. 13-22).

Koyil Oḻuku tells a similar story. See, *Koil Oḻugu: The Chronicle of the Śrīraṅgam Temple with Historical Notes*, ed. and translated by V.N. Hari Rao (Madras: Rochouse and Sons Publishers Litd., 1961) [hereafter, KO, English], p. 103-104, and *Koyil Oḻuku*, ed. by Pandits (Madras: Ananta Muttiraksar Cala, 1090) [hereafter, KO, Tamil], pp. 100-101.

[16]From an interview in Bombay, December 1986

[17]*Guru Paramparā Prabhāvam*, pp. 233-34

[18]*Guru Paramparā Prabhāvam*, p. 234

[19]*Guru Paramparā Prabhāvam*, pp. 235-36.

According to the episode as related in *Prapanna Amṛtam* it is not Periya Nampi (Mahāpūrṇa), but Āṇṭāḷ, who has a doubt about the appropriateness of the marriage because the family of the girl was from a lineage of Brahmins settled in the Śrīraṅgam area, rather than in their own area of Kāñcīpuram. Kūreśa suggested to her that this lineage was in no way inferior to theirs. Āṇṭāḷ apparently accepted his judgement, because the marriage ceremony was performed after Kūreśa went to Lord Raṅga who then appeared in a dream to Periya Nampi. Nampi's cousin then "under the guidance of Lord Raṅga," gave the daughter in marriage to [Lord] Raṅga's son (*raṅga-putrāya*) (39:33-49).

[20]The general outline of this story is confirmed by Kūreśa's *Sundarabāhu Stava*, vs. 129-131 (Lord Sundarabāhu is the main icon of the temple in Tirumāliruñcolai).

[21]*Guru Paramparā Prabhāvam*, p. 276

[22]*Prapanna Amṛtam* 58:1-6

[23]*Guru Paramparā Prabhāvam*, pp. 344-45

[24]*Guru Paramparā Prabhāvam*, p. 352

[25]*Guru Paramparā Prabhāvam*, p. 356

[26]*Guru Paramparā Prabhāvam*, pp. 359-360

[27]*Guru Paramparā Prabhāvam*, p. 361

[28]Translation by Lynn Marie Ate, "Periyāḻvār's 'Tirumoḻi'—A Bāla Kṛṣṇa Text From the Devotional Period in Tamil Literature" (Madison, Wisconsin: Ph.D. Dissertation, 1978).

[29]*Koyil Oḻuku* gives long recital of the achievements and work of Kūranārāyaṇa Jīyar, interspersed with hair-raising episodes of his occult powers. He was a *sannyāsī* who had no official connection with the temple administration, but because he was popular he was given some important rights in the temple at the request of some of the temple servants. He became the founder and first occupant of the throne of the Śrīraṅganārāyaṇa Jīyar at Śrīraṅgam. See, KO (English), pp. xiii and 115-16n.

[30]Some of the duties of the group of temple servants called the Viṇṇappañceyvār are: playing on the musical instrument called the *viṇā* at dawn, reciting the names of God at the beginning of the daily worship service, singing during the bathing of Lord Raṅga or when the moveable icon is taken in procession during festivals, enacting the deeds of Lord Visnu's incarnations and illustrating them with gestures during the *Tirumoḻi* and *Tiruvāymoḻi* festivals, and so forth. See KO (English), pp. 78-79.

[31]KO (Tamil), pp. 108-09

[32]A few examples will suffice: "We have no equivalent among the bhaktins of the normal male bhakta, of someone like Tiruvalluvar, for example, who was a great devotee and a good householder at the same time. Thus, all bhaktins protest marriage to a mortal man..." Uma Chakravarty, "The World of the Bhaktin in South Indian Traditions—The Body and Beyond." *Manushi.* Nos. 50, 51, 52 (1989), pp. 18-29 at 23-24.

And again: "While male bhaktas could follow their chosen path while remaining householders, this was near impossible for women. The vast majority of women bhakta poets in one way or another opted out of married and domestic life, and remained childless. A Tukaram could deal with a noncooperative wife by ignoring her, for she could only object to his way of life; she could not actively obstruct it. But for a Mirabai or a Bahinabai, the impediments created by husband or in-laws took the form of violence that could easily have proved fatal. Thus, most women bhakta poets could proceed on their chosen path only by discarding the marital tie altogether. Some refused marriage, others walked out of oppressive marriages." Madhu Kishwar, "Introduction," *Manushi.* Nos. 50, 51, 52 (1989), pp. 3-8 at p. 5.

[33]Madhu Kishwar and Ruth Vanita, "Poison to Nectar: the Life and Work of Mirabai." *Manushi.* Nos. 50, 51, 52 (1989), p. 92.

[34]Katherine Young, "Śrīvaiṣṇava Feminism: Intent or Effect?" *Studies in Religion/ Sciences Religieuses* 12:2 (1983), pp. 183-190 at p. 190.

Rāmānuja was prompted to renounce the world ("take *sannyāsa*") because of his wife's Brahminical orthodoxy. Periya Nampi (a member of the community of "forelock" Brahmins who were considered socially inferior to the Vaṭama Brahmins who lived in the Kāñcīpuram area), along with his wife, were residing in Rāmānuja's home while Nampi was instructing Rāmānuja in Śrīvaiṣṇava doctrine. The story has it that some drops of water fell from a vessel carried by Periya Nampi's wife into a vessel being carried by Rāmānuja's wife, who complained that her water pot was now polluted and furthermore, taunted her husband's teacher's wife about her lower caste status. Periya Nampi saw the quarrel, reprimanded his wife, and immediately left with her for Śrīraṅgam. When Rāmānuja returned home he was shocked at the news, became furious with his wife, sent her back to her parents and shortly thereafter became a *sannyāsi.* An episode contained in *Guru Paramparā Prabhāvam,* cited in John Braisted Carman, *The Theology of Rāmānuja: An Essay in Interreligious Understanding* (New Haven: Yale University Press, 1974), pp. 31-32.

While Kūreśa's sons, Parāśara Bhaṭṭar and Śrīrāma Piḷḷai, remained householders, Bhaṭṭar's disciple and successor in the Ācārya-lineage, Nañjīyar, took *sannyāsa.* Nañjīyar was the great Vedāntin scholar who was defeated in a ten day long debate by Bhaṭṭar. Accepting Bhaṭṭar as his Ācārya, he wanted to follow him to Śrīraṅgam, but Bhaṭṭar told him to remain where he was and continue feeding Brahmins everyday. The great Vedāntin now frequently provided hospitality to Śrīvaiṣṇavas. One day when two Śrīvaiṣṇavas, tired from their journey, came to his house, his two wives treated them disrespectfully, ignored them and refused to serve them themselves. On learning of this incident, the Vedāntin (Nañjīyar) decided to take *sannyāsa* because his two wives did not understand the importance of extending hospitality to newcomers. So he divided his huge wealth into three parts, giving one part to each of his wives and saving the remainder for his Ācārya Bhaṭṭar. He went to Śrīraṅgam and prostrated before Bhaṭṭar who was pleased, embraced him, and said: "Our *jiyar* has come (*namuṭaiya ciyar vantār)*...From that day he was known by the name "Nañjīyar" ("our *jīyar*"). *Guru Paramparā Prabhāvam*, pp. 344-346.

A later episode from the life of Nañjīyar is important, because it dramatically reveals the Śrīvaiṣṇava attitude towards the renunciation of the world. One day Nañjīyar wanted to carry Bhaṭṭar's palenquin, and was shouldering the stick. When Bhaṭṭar told him that this was inappropriate for a *sannyāsi*, Nañjīyar responded:

> I have taken the form [of a *sannyāsi*] because [I believed that it was] appropriate for your service. If this form is an obstruction to your service, then I prefer to have my former old white cloth back. *Guru Paramparā Prabhāvam*, p. 347.

[White cloths are worn by householders, while *sannyāsis* wear saffron cloths.]

Later, in the late fourteenth or early fifteenth century, the great Ācārya Maṇavāḷa Māmuni undertook an intensive study of Rāmānuja's *Śrī Bhāṣya* in Kāñcīpuram. Upon his return to his home in Śrīraṅgam, he renounced his householder status and became a *sannyāsi* because he believed that the observation of pollution conventions due to his family ties was interfering with his worship of the Lord at Śrīraṅgam. *Yatīndrapravana Prabhāvam* of Piḷḷai Lokāṉ Jīyar, ed. by U.V. Satakopa Ramanujacharya (Tamil text), pp. 41-42, cited in Patricia Y. Mumme, *The Śrīvaiṣṇava Theological Dispute: Maṇavāḷamāmuni and Vedānta Deśika.* (Madras: New Era Publications, 1988), pp. 15-16.

[35] Alaka Hejib, "Wife or Widow? The Ambiguity of the Problems Regarding the Marital Status of the Renounced Wife of a Saṁnyāsī (1982, p. 82 and 7), cited in Young, "Hinduism," p. 86.

[36] KO (English), p. 105 and KO (Tamil), p. 102-103

[37] *Rāmāyaṇa*, Ayodhyākāṇḍa 39:29 and 30, cited in Young, "Hinduism," p. 79.

[38] Young, "Hinduism," p. 76

[39] Ruth Vanita, "Three Women Sants of Maharashtra: Muktabai, Janabai, Bahinabai." *Manushi.* Nos. 50, 51, 52 (1989), pp 45-61 at p. 58

[40] A.K. Rāmānujan, "Talking to God," p. 14

[41] For a detailed study of the Śrīvaiṣṇava view of Śrī, especially as Īśvarī, see my

Poetry As Theology: The Śrīvaiṣṇava Stotra in the Age of Rāmānuja (Wiesbaden: Otto Harrassowitz, 1992), pp. 221-256. See especially pp.232-242.

[42]*Guru Paramparā Prabhāvam*, p. 364 (emphasis added)

[43]Ramanujam, *History of Vaishnavism in South India up to Rāmānuja* (Annamalainagar: Annamalai University, 1973), p. 48

[44]K.K.A. Venkatachari, *The Maṇipravāḷa Literature of the Śrīvaiṣṇava Ācāryas* (Bombay: Ananthacharya Research Institute, 1978), p. 12 and B.V. Rāmānujan, *History of Vaishnavism in South India*, p. 59

[45]B.V. Rāmānujam, *History of Vaishnavism in South India*, p. 73. For arguments justifying the late 17th century as the date for PA, see p. 66.

[46]KO (English), p. vii

[47]KO (English), p. xii

THEOLOGY DOES HELP WOMEN'S LIBERATION: ŚRĪVAIṢṆAVISM, A HINDU CASE STUDY[1]

Katherine K. Young

Introduction

Conservative[2] roles for brahmanical women developed between the 6th century B.C.E. and the 3rd century C.E., a period of upheaval in northern India because of a changing economy, urbanization, challenges to the Vedic world view by the increasingly popular heterodox religions (Buddhism and Jainism), the elaboration and specialization of Vedic knowledge, and foreign invasions/migrations. These upheavals are related to a decline of status for women: the age for marriage gradually decreased (*Gobhila Gṛhyasūtra* 3:4.6; *Vasiṣṭadharmasūtra* 17.70), prepubertal marriage becoming the guarantee of female loyalty and chastity. Whereas once women were copartners with their husbands in the performance of ritual (*Āpastambadharmasūtra* 2:5.11.12), they gradually became marginal and silent participants. Whereas at least some women had had access to Vedic education, by the time of the Dharmaśāstras, this was increasingly challenged (culminating in the brahmanical feminine reality of the absence of formal education or Vedic knowledge). They also could not abandon a husband (*Manu* 9:46; 9:101) with a few exceptions and were not to remarry if their husband died before them (*Manu* 5:161–165). This decline in status is represented by a number of misogynistic statements about women's ignorance, impurity and infidelity (*Mahābhārata*, anuśāsana parva 19:6; 38:12; 38:29; 19:93; *Rāmāyaṇa*, Āraṇyakāṇḍa 45:29–30; etc.).

This decline in the status of women may also be related to the incorporation of the behavioural codes of various warrior groups (some of them outside the Aryan culture of the Gangetic plain), which introduced modalities of femininity from heroic circles into the *Mahābhārata* and *Rāmāyaṇa*. A woman's loyalty, devotion and service to her husband to the point of death was parallel, for example, to a male warrior's loyalty, devotion, and service to his leader to the point of death. At the same time that the female heroic code was being integrated in the Hindu epics and beginning to define more general norms of feminine behaviour (*strīdharma*), it is likely that brahmin men were projecting their anxiety onto women. This occurred because of the reasons mentioned previously, especially the threats to their livelihood related to Buddhist and Jain criticism of their sacrificial system and the importance they attributed to Vedic knowledge. Accordingly, women came to be viewed as threatening the social order through miscegenation (*Bhagavadgītā* 1:41) and creating the problems of the Kaliyuga (a time of degeneration). In their frustration at not being able to control their world, brahmin men may have attempted, as a substitute, to control their women, and no doubt found the ideals embodied in the heroic code of female behaviour useful in this regard.

The concept of *pativrata* epitomizes these developments. *Pativrata* means either a vow (*vrata*) to obtain a husband (*pati*) or a vow to protect a husband's health and life (and by extension the well-being of the patrilineal family). Central to this vow is the woman's loyalty, devotion, and service to her husband who is her god (*Rāmāyaṇa*, ayodhyākāṇḍa 24:26–27; *Mahābhārata*, anuśāsana parva 146.55, etc.). Her identity is primarily that of wife and mother (*Śatapatha Brāhmaṇa* 4:1.5.9; *Manu* 5:154) and her character is to be defined by virtues such as self-sacrifice, chastity, and dependence (*Manu* 5:146–148; 9:29–30; *Mahābhārata* anuśāsana parva 123; 146:4–6). In conservative, brahmanical circles, women were often denied the higher and critical stages of *sādhanā* (religious discipline such as asceticism and renunciation) and *sādhya* (goal, i.e., salvation). Occasionally they became maritally insecure on account of the threat of a husband's *saṁnyāsa* (renunciation). If their husbands died before them, they had the "official" choices of widowhood, a highly restrictive and disciplined existence, minimalizing their needs (Kane 1:545; 1:583–585) or *sati* (self-immolation on the funeral pyre of their husband), a practice no doubt originating in the heroic circles mentioned previously, being the female equivalent of the husband's death in battle or his self-willed death to avoid being tortured and killed by the enemy (Young 1989).

This brahmanical norm, which had already absorbed kṣatriya norms, was in turn generalized to become the norm ostensibly for all women though in fact the lifestyles of many other castes and tribal women remained much more free, unless their group was upwardly mobile and encouraged women to imitate elite norms.[3] But because of this brahmanical norm for women embodied in the concept of *strīdharma,* women were equated to śūdras (lowest caste) (*Manu* 5:139; *Yājñavalkya* 1:21; *Baudhāyanadharmasūtra* 2:1. 11–12, etc.) or *mlecchas* (foreigners, barbarians, non-aryans) in a number of texts because all these groups were without Vedic education. Women, especially brahmin women, thus lost out by and large on ritual and educational status for a variety of reasons, which contributed to a dramatic decline in their general status.

With the rise of the Gupta dynasty (4th–5th century C.E.) and the spread of Vaiṣṇavism and Śaivism, however, the position of śūdras began to improve.[4] Because of women's association with the śūdras, this may have been a turning point for the improvement of women's status as well, though this is more difficult to demonstrate aside from *Bhagavadgītā* 9:32, which says that "*even* (*api*) women, vaiśyas, and śūdras shall attain the supreme goal." An orientation of inclusivity, universality, and equality is found in some Purāṇas of the period. In some bhakti circles, women were viewed as capable of salvation. *Vratas* (fasting), *japa* (chanting the name of God), and *bhajans* (singing praises of the deity) were all religious activities available to them to pursue salvation. In other orthodox circles there was a deliberate ambiguity regarding women's destiny, leading to a "swing" between rebirth and liberation, depending on the context or women's own appropriation of it.

One bhakti tradition that illustrates this improvement in the position of women is the sect called Śrīvaiṣṇavism, a Vaiṣṇava sect in Tamil Nadu that recognizes the devotional poetry of the Āḻvārs (7th–9th century C.E.) as the Tamil Veda and the theological and philosophical writings of a series of Ācāryas from the 11th century C.E. to the present. Whereas according to many brahmanical texts women were consigned to rebirth, Śrīvaiṣṇava women, according to the traditional texts of this sect, were not to entertain the possibility of rebirth. Rather, they were to be absolutely certain that surrender to God (Nārāyaṇa-Viṣṇu-Kṛṣṇa) assured them of *mokṣa* (liberation) at the time of death. Moreover, unlike the concessive mood of *Bhagavadgītā* 9:32, Śrīvaiṣṇava texts often praise women as exemplary devotees.

After describing the position of women in Śrīvaiṣṇavism (based on the hymns of the Āḻvārs and writings of the Ācāryas), I shall discuss why a theology of liberation supportive of women's liberation developed. More specifically, I wish to know (1) whether there was a motive on the part of Śrīvaiṣṇava male thinkers to be supportive of women by advocating for women the same salvific orientation granted twice-born (*dvija*) men in order to provide a Hindu counter-challenge to the heterodox religions of Buddhism and Jainism that had championed the cause of women, (2) whether their motive was to reform brahmanical religion, (3) whether their motive was to preempt a revolt by women themselves from the restrictive brahmanical norms of *strīdharma,* (4) whether their motive was to provide continuity with images of independent maidens in caṅkam poems and thereby connect the bhakti movement with an archaic touchstone of Tamil identity, or (5) whether their motive was a recognition of the strength of Tamil women, thanks to a tradition of cross-cousin marriage and women's ownership of property. My answer will be sought mainly in South Indian Śrīvaiṣṇava literature (written in Tamil, Sanskrit, and Maṇipravāḷa) from the 7th to the 20th century C.E., though on occasion I shall examine views of women in the earliest Tamil poetry (*caṅkam*) of the 1st century B.C.E. to 3rd century C.E. and in the transitional texts of the 3rd century to the 6th century C.E.

Śrīvaiṣṇava Views on Women

An orientation of inclusivity, universality, and equality is found in the hymns of the Āḻvārs (e.g. Nammāḻvār's *Tiruvāymoḻi* 3.7.1; 3.7.8–9). The Śrīvaiṣṇava Ācāryas—brahmin male teachers who have intellectually guided Tamil Vaiṣṇavism by writing commentaries and treatises—have been proud of their Tamil bhakti heritage.[5] They have promoted the idea that the Tamil hymns of the Āḻvārs (the Vaiṣṇava poet-saints who lived between 600 and 900 C.E.) are equal, if not superior to, the Sanskrit Veda (Carman and Narayanan 1989). God, they have argued, prefers Tamil because of its sweet sound and its easy accessibility to devotees. Because they have considered one of the Āḻvārs an outcaste (*pāṇaṉ*)[6] and one a low caste (śūdra)—Tiruppāṇ and Nammāḻvār respectively—and one poet–saint is a woman (Āṇṭāḷ), the Ācāryas' theological reflections have stressed the universality of means (*upāya*) and goal (*upeya*) for all devotees of Nārāyaṇa-Viṣṇu-Kṛṣṇa. In this way they have sanctioned Tamil Vaiṣṇavism, which has not endorsed ideas of rigid caste hierarchy (despite some sectarian variation regarding how caste is to be understood and practiced) but rather has promoted the idea of everyone being the servant/slave (*aṭiyaṉ*) not only of God but also of other devotees.

Simultaneously, they have denied that aspect of brahmanism which has maintained exclusive accessibility to *mokṣa* on the criterion of being twice-born (*dvija*), that is, having undergone the ritual of initiation to Vedic learning (*upanayana*) which leads to study of the Vedas and Vedic ritual expertise.[7] Unlike many women who have not had access to Vedic expertise and so can not fulfil the prerequisite for *mokṣa* (in those circles that deem it essential), Śrīvaiṣṇava women have had access to *śruti*, because of the claim that the hymns of the Āḻvārs are the Tamil Veda. They thereby fulfil this prerequisite (i.e., knowledge of *śruti* or Veda) for liberation. This can account for the liberation orientation of women in the Śrīvaiṣṇava texts in contrast to the rebirth orientation prescribed for women in many Dharmaśāstric passages.

By the 17th-18th centuries, two sects emerged in Śrīvaiṣṇavism: the Teṉkalai and the Vaṭakalai. Drawing from the writings of various Ācāryas over the centuries—especially Piḷḷailokācārya and Vedāntadeśika respectively—they developed somewhat different doctrinal views and then superimposed their "reading" of their teachings onto the history of Śrīvaiṣṇavism as a whole. The following discussion is based on the sectarian interpretations of the theology of the two emergent sects; accordingly, it is a synchronic and sectarian analysis of the Ācāryas' views, an approach necessitated by the large time span covered in this article; nevertheless, the arguments of particular Ācāryas will be noted and some reflections of an historical nature will be provided.

Women in the Śrīvaiṣṇava tradition have had access to a path to salvation; the nature of this path has differed, however, according to the sect. For the Teṉkalai branch of Śrīvaiṣṇavism, spontaneous surrender (exemplified by the Āḻvārs) or the *pañcasaṁskāra* ritual[8] (especially hearing the mantras) performed by the Ācāryas or the Jīyars (brahmin ascetics) is viewed as the universal path to salvation.[9] Because the path is universal, equality is stressed. Equality is to be expressed by serving the devotees of the Lord. To think of a devotee in terms of caste (*varṇa*) is said to be a heinous act, comparable to examining the genitals of one's own mother; such a devotee becomes an outcaste (*cāṇḍāla*) (Piḷḷailokācārya, *Śrīvacanabhūṣanam* 196-200). As extra insurance that the path is truly universal (and God will not ignore the devotee), Maṇavāḷamāmuni describes how Rāmānuja's surrender was an act done on behalf of everyone (the concept of *ācāryābhimāna*) in his commentary on *Śrīvacanabhūṣanam* (408–409; 411; 425; 429; 447-448; 463); in his *Yatirājaviṁśati* (the final verse), and in his *Ārtiprabandam* (4; 22).[10] Finally, various religious acts that involve no special expertise such as chanting the name of God, offering flowers to him, or serving him (*seśatva*) are said to be a means (*upāya*) to salvation.

Although there is the act of surrender (whether spontaneous, a ritual, or the intercessory act by Rāmānuja on behalf of all), Teṉkalais ultimately place emphasis on the fact that it is God alone who saves out of his grace, and salvation does not depend on any action, method, or path. This view is called collectively *prapatti* and distinguished from bhaktiyoga.[11] Bhaktiyoga is characterized by the performance of the duties of caste and stage of life (*varṇāśramadharma*), Vedic rituals in the tradition of *pūrvamīmāṁsā*, the perspective of *naiśkāmyakarmayoga* (the yoga of performing actions without desire for their results) of the *Bhagavadgītā* (as elaborated by Rāmānuja in his commentary), and yogic meditation in the tradition of *uttaramīmāṁsā* as articulated in the *Brahmasūtras*. Because God alone saves (implying that human methods are ultimately futile) and because surrender can be done by anyone at any time, bhaktiyoga is not mandatory. For the Teṉkalais, therefore, *prapatti* takes precedence over bhaktiyoga; nevertheless, brahmin men usually have knowledge of the Vedas and perform Vedic rituals, for these are pan-Indian definitions of brahmanical status not easily renounced.

Vedāntadeśika, whose thinking is central to the Vaṭakalai sect, accepts the idea of service to the Lord and his devotees and is against offending the latter, warning that pride, be it by birth as a brahmin or status as a devotee, is bad (*Rahasyatrayasāra* 15). Nevertheless, he insists (following Rāmānuja's commentary on *Bhagavadgītā* 18:66) that the rules of *varṇāśramadharma* be maintained by everyone, even within the community of practicing devotees. Moreover, the ritual of *pañcasaṁskāra* must be followed by another ceremony of *prapatti*, which is no mere ritual, for there must be rigorous preparation.

Despite their differences, Śrīvaiṣṇavas claim that eligibility for salvation is universal. Therefore, *any* woman can surrender to God and thereby achieve liberation at the time of death. Teṉkalai Śrīvaiṣṇavas are fond of remembering the incident of Draupadī in the epic *Mahābhārata* when they think of *prapatti*. Piḷḷailokācārya, in his *Mumukṣuppaḍi* tirumantram 16, states that Draupadī, when she was being disrobed by a Kaurava prince (Duśśāsana) who claimed that he had won her clothes in a gambling match, remembered the Lord's instruction to call on him in moments of danger. And so she cried out "Govinda," thereby taking refuge in him. She was provided endless material by the Lord to cover herself until the prince admitted defeat.

Piḷḷailokācārya also discusses this incident in his *Śrīvacanabhūṣaṇam*, stating that there is no restriction of time and place for *prapatti* (sūtra 26) and that this can be seen by everyone (sūtra 28). In his next sūtra (29) he observes that Draupadī performed *prapatti* without taking a sacred bath or *snāna* (part of most rituals). Maṇavāḷamāmuni elaborates on this point as follows: "Draupadī did her *prapatti* without *snāna* (bath) means: when she came into the *sabhā* dragged by Duśśāsana she said 'neither am I willing to come to the *sabhā* nor are you allowed to take me into the *sabhā* in the presence of my gurus (teachers) because I have my period (*rājasvalā*) wearing only one sari...[the *Mahābhārata* is then cited and Maṇavāḷamāmuni comments] In this way one who is impure without taking a bath performed *prapatti*. By this [example] people who practise *prapatti* need not make any special effort. Thus freedom from the restriction [of impurity] has been shown." In other words, even though Draupadī was menstruating (usually a time of impurity), God accepted her total surrender to him and saved her from the situation. Hence, *prapatti* is for *everyone at any time.*[12] Because women's menstruation had been a symbol of impurity in orthodox brahmanical circles, brahmin women had been required to segregate themselves from the family for three days (Kane 3:80 3ff). In Śrīvaiṣṇavism, by contrast, the removal of the stigma associated with the impurity of menstruation in the theological context of liberation is a dramatic gesture towards women's equality with men (though, to my knowledge, brahmin women of both sects up to this century observed segregation during their menses). The concept of the universalization of eligibility therefore supercedes the distinction of male and female.[13]

Moreover, because *prapatti* is "easily available," Śrīvaiṣṇava women (and śūdras) have confidence that they will attain liberation. In fact, they are not to contemplate the alternative of rebirth, for such a thought detracts from their single-minded attention (*ekāgratā*) on God, which is to characterize surrender. It also leads to insecurity, lack of confidence in God's grace, and confusion. Death signifies only a change of locus for the relationship. Consequently, death is to be viewed as a joyous occasion for the soul. Entertaining the possibility of rebirth precludes the relinquishing of one's self to God. Śrīvaiṣṇava theology is categorical on this point. The question of destination at the time of death engenders ambiguity in the individual's mind: temporary heaven (*svarga*), temporary hell (*naraka*), or rebirth as a brahmin, a man, a woman, etc. If people are thinking about fulfilling desires on the ordinary level (*vyavahāra*), they cannot selflessly and steadily direct their mind toward God.

Thus, in Śrīvaiṣṇavism at the time of death a person is to focus his or her thoughts on God and view death as a joyous moment that initiates the journey from life on earth to Vaikuṇṭha, the supreme Heaven. Śrīvaiṣṇavas refer, for example, to the death of a devotee as "gone to the auspicious land" (*tirunāṭukku eḻuntaruḷiṉar*) or "reached Paramapadam" (*paramapadam aṭaintar*). Unlike the Vedic death rituals in which Vedic mantras refer to the deceased as a polluting corpse (*preta*) and view death itself as an inauspicious event, the Śrīvaiṣṇava *śrīcūrṇaparipālam* ceremony (at least in Teṉkalai circles) at the time of death views the dead body as categorically auspicious. Significantly, the one hundred stanzas of Nammāḻvār's *Tiruviruttam*—in which the Āḻvār as a female lover expresses her eagerness to unite with her beloved who is the Lord himself—is chanted (Young 1983, 392). For the Śrīvaiṣṇava, desire for, even mere thought of, rebirth is not an option. It is a sin. Consequently, all Śrīvaiṣṇavas, *women and men*, are to avoid the orientation of rebirth. This point distinguishes Śrīvaiṣṇava texts from conservative brahmanical ones that suggest or imply that women are to be rebirth-oriented because they do not have knowledge of the Vedas and the auxiliary branches of learning (*vedāṅga*), often a preliminary step to salvation.

Therefore, women's confidence in salvation is engendered because women have access both to scripture and to the means (*upāya*) to salvation—i.e., the Tamil Veda and *prapatti* (surrender)—without need for any special kind of competency (*adhikāra*), like knowledge of the Vedas (the requirement or preference of brahmin men according to the Vaṭakalais and Teṉkalais respectively). Because the means is said to be non-different from the goal, in the sense that surrender to God is most likely to be reciprocated by God's grace as salvation, liberation is virtually guaranteed.[14] In fact, Śrīvaiṣṇavas who have surrendered are to live in this world as if liberated.

Teṉkalais allow women to repeat Vedic mantras. Piḷḷailokācārya, in his *Parantapaṭi*, says, for example, that just as the word mother (*ammā*) comes spontaneously to an individual when in trouble, in the same way AUM comes spontaneously.[15] Therefore, everyone is eligible to repeat this mantra.

Vedāntadeśika is, however, more conservative and upholds the view that women and śūdras are not to repeat the sacred syllable AUM. In his discussion in the *Rahasyatrayasāra*, for instance, Vedāntadeśika offers a number of proof texts to support his position that AUM is not to be repeated by women and śūdras. He quotes from the *Mahābhārata* (verse unknown) that a śūdra should not utter the names of the Lord with the *praṇava* (the sacred syllable). And he quotes from the *Nāradīyakalpa* (source unknown) that the chanting (*japa*) of the *aṣṭākṣara* (that is, the *tirumantra*) has been prescribed for women and śūdras and is to be performed without the dative suffix (e.g. *namo nārāyaṇa*). Women and śūdras are to perform the chanting without the *svara*, without the *praṇava* (AUM), and without touching the limbs (*aṅganyāsa*). To support his position, he quotes a number of passages from the *Varāhapurāṇa* (source unknown) to the effect that (1) a low caste person sings the praise of Bhagavān and utters the mantra *namo nārāyaṇa*; (2) that if one goes to Vaikuṇṭha uttering the *mūlamantra* (i.e. *namo nārāyaṇa*), one will never return; (3) that if one is to utter the name of Bhagavān, one should say *namo nārāyaṇa*; and (4) that the middle of the *aṣṭākṣara* is appropriate for everyone if the first and the last syllables (i.e. AUM and the dative suffix) are removed just as the sugar-cane with eight joints becomes suitable for all, if the root and the top are cut off.

Vedāntadeśika concludes that even though the ritual of *prapatti* is perfect albeit a momentary event (and hence one does not need to do anything more to achieve salvation[16]), there is delight in chanting the mantra as a fruit of *prapatti*. For those who practice bhaktiyoga, *prapatti* is to be viewed an accessory of the path. Vedāntadeśika notes that the Āḻvārs also refer to the mantra as *namo nārāyaṇa* and cites *Periyatirumoḻi* 6:10:1 and *Mutaltiruvāntai* 57 and 95 to this effect. Finally, he classifies the mantras without the AUM or *praṇava* as *tantrika* and those with the AUM as *vaidika* (Rajagopala Ayyangar, trans. *Rahasyatrayasāra* 1956, 296–297).[17]

In sum, Piḷḷailokācārya, who allows the mantra AUM for anyone, appears more liberal when compared Vedāntadeśika. In the final analysis, however, this distinction of who can pronounce AUM amounts to a nonissue for Śrīvaiṣṇavas, for the mantra is not necessary for salvation, though it may be chanted out of enjoyment or as an accessory. The Vaṭakalai use of a distinct form according to gender or caste is also virtually a non-issue, except to maintain a semblance of orthodox form to help preserve the brahmanical tradition at a time when universal religion threatened to make it obsolete.

Prapatti, besides bypassing the need for Sanskrit and Vedic expertise, bypasses another barrier to liberation for Śrīvaiṣṇava women: *saṁnyāsa* (renunciation of family life and asceticism). According to the *Ācāryahṛdayam*, the Ācāryas "live with their wives and children and enjoy God experience also" (Damodaran 1976, 77). Although some of the Ācāryas have been ascetics, i.e. *jīyars* (Narayanan 1990, 161–190), their renunciation is not the ideal to be emulated by all. The religious path of *saṁnyāsa* has remained an alternative, which has not been officially encouraged at the expense of the householder orientation. The corollary of universal eligibility for salvation, therefore, is conceptual transcendence of the distinction of the yogī and the non-yogī. According to the Teṉkalais, because yogīs do not have higher status than *prapannas* or bhaktas, women who have surrendered to the Lord have the same status as yogīs. By contrast, the Vaṭakalais think that because a yogī or *saṁnyāsī* leads a more rigorous and pure life than a householder and accepts his meals only from orthodox Śrīvaiṣṇava brahmins, he should not prostrate to a householder, unless the householder is his own Ācārya. It is striking that among the Teṉkalais even a guru is to prostrate to a woman. Vaṭakalais prostrate, however, only to their mothers, elder sisters, and the wives of the Ācāryas (Rangachari 1931, 47). A Teṉkalai *saṁnyāsī*, who does not have to beg his food, not only receives obeisance from a householder but also pays obeisance to one (Rangachari 1931, 46).[18] Despite such sectarian distinctions on minor points, Śrīvaiṣṇavas agree that being a householder and a spiritual seeker need not be mutually exclusive orientations. The Ācāryas, after all, have viewed them as normatively simultaneous and mutually enhancing activities. Consequently, a woman's mundane and supramundane goals are parallel to a man's goals and not in conflict with them. Men prostrating to some women no doubt has lessened the scope for misogyny.

For these reasons, the position of women in Śrīvaiṣṇavism (inclusive of Śrīvaiṣṇava brahmin women) has been different from the position of women described in the Dharmaśāstras, which have been influential in conservative brahmin circles since the time of Manu. On closer inspection the difference appears more radical than initially surmised, especially in the Teṉkalai sect. It is not just that a woman has equal opportunities for salvation in Śrīvaiṣṇavism. It is that her relationship with God is paradigmatic for male devotees. Salvation, according to Śrīvaiṣṇava theology, is defined as the love between God and the devotee. Because Śrīvaiṣṇavas worship the god Nārāyaṇa-Viṣṇu-Kṛṣṇa who is male, they must be female in this marital relationship.[19] The male Āḻvārs often sing from the perspective of a woman with whom they have totally identified, as in the following Tamil hymn by Tirumaṅkaiyāḻvār: "Even the memory pains my sinful heart. The Lord encircled my tresses with fragrant buds and gave such love I thought separation would kill me" (*Periyatirumoḻi* 9:3:5). Such love, however, is natural to a woman. Therefore, she is exemplary for the tradition as evidenced by the high regard given to Āṇṭāḷ, who came to be considered a goddess.

Piṉpaḻakiyaperumāḷjīyar in his *Guruparamparāprabhāvam 6000* argues, for instance, that Āṇṭāḷ's love is more natural than that of the other Āḻvārs, because it is the love of a woman for a man. A man has *to assume* the role of a woman-in-love; he must imaginatively participate in feminine psychology in order to relate to God as Beloved.[20] In the *Ācāryahṛdayam* by Aḻakiyamaṇavāḻap-perumāḷnāyaṉār, it is asked why Nammāḻvār should imitate the state of a lady in love. The answer is that he does not really try to imitate a lady but as soon as he sees the beauty, valour and good nature of God, these qualities make him feel like a lady in love. Because the essential quality of the soul (*ātman*) is dependence on God (*paratāntrya*), he attains the status of a lady before the Lord. Moreover, it is said that while the Āḻvār is in the state of knowledge he speaks in his natural form and while he is in a state of overpowering, intoxicating love, he speaks as a woman but even the speech of a lady is natural (Damodaran 1976, 60–61).

According to the Āḻvārs, love of God expressed as surrender and taking refuge is salvific. Sometimes this love is portrayed as a woman's surrender to her husband in marriage. Āṇṭāḷ, for instance, dreams of her marriage to the Lord, "O Kuṭal, join up[21] that I may caress the feet of the bridegroom reclining at Māliruñcolai, that generous Lord worshipped by the wise (*Nācciyārtirumoḻi* 4:1)" or "O Toḻi, I dreamt that the King of the citizens of Maturai entered [the marriage hall] with such firm steps that [the earth] vibrated in all directions. Beautiful young women carrying lamps radiating light along with pots ceremoniously welcomed [him]" (*Nācciyārtirumoḻi* 6:5). The *Guruparamparāprabhāvam 6000* elaborates on Āṇṭāḷ's dream and tells the story of how she married Kṛṣṇa as Lord Raṅganātha at Śrīraṅgam and "merged" with him there.

The love relationship or marriage between the devotee as the feminine lover and God as the masculine Beloved is paradigmatic for the tradition. Although the bhakti saints sing of love and marriage in a manner similar to the earlier caṅkam poets—whose poetry reflects the ancient Tamil view of secret, erotic love (*kaḷavu*) between the lover and beloved as akin to marriage (*kaṟpu*)[22]—the Ācāryas often portray the relationship between the devotee and God as arranged marriage and take a more metaphorical view of the lover-beloved stanzas. "These people of yours are given away [to you] by the Ācāryas who praise you, and they are being married by you [as their] husband. They assume servitude (*kiṁkaratva*) as the *maṅgalasūtra* for the accomplishment of great, unique pleasure (*bhogaviśeṣa*) in the world" (Vedāntadeśika, *Śaraṇāgatidīpikā* 30). In this verse, the Ācārya is the one who arranges the marriage. Just as a married woman is to serve her husband faithfully, so the devotee is to serve God eternally as symbolized by wearing the sacred thread of marriage (*maṅgalasūtra*).[23]

Aḻakiyamaṇavāḷap-perumāḷnāyaṉār, probably following a work by Nañjīyar (*Ātmavivāha*),[24] creates an extended metaphor of the marriage between the soul and God.[25] Just as a woman marries her husband for support and joy, so the soul marries God, who is beautiful and the protector of the worlds, for support and joy. Just as the sacred thread is the symbol of marriage worn by a woman, so the *tirumantra* is the symbol of the soul's relation to the Lord. Just as for four days after marriage the bride and bridegroom cannot have intercourse, though the bride knows that she is married and only the husband has the right to enjoy her, so the soul knows that even though it is separated from God they are married and only God has the right of union. Just as the bride leaves her native home and all her relatives, so the soul through initiation by the Ācārya, leaves its birth place on earth and goes to its husband's home in Heaven. Just as the bridegroom leads the bride and people come to pay their respects, so God leads the soul through the path of light (*arcirādimārga*) and the celestial beings come to pay their respects. Just as the bride reaches the outskirts of her husband's village and takes a bath, so the soul bathes in the sacred river Virajā. Just as after bathing, the husband's relatives will decorate the bride, so heavenly women will come with garlands, *tulasī*, silks, and ornaments and decorate the soul like a bride to make it fit for the Lord's enjoyment. Just as the bride enters into the house of her husband, so the soul will enter into the home of the Lord. And just as the bride embraces her husband and enjoys everything with him, so the soul embraces the Lord, enjoying henceforth everything with him.

The lover–beloved relationship is popular in the Śrīvaiṣṇava tradition, but other relationships are also explored. Here again, feminine psychology may be involved. The devotee, for example, may identify with the role of mother in order to relate to God as child. Identifying with and fully enjoying the feminine modality is a central *modus vivendi* of spirituality. It would seem that the effect can be none other than positive and deep appreciation of femininity.[26] Indeed, this appreciation of women characterizes the commentarial tradition as well as the Tamil scripture itself (the hymns of the Āḻvārs).

Although fully conversant with technical exegesis of Sanskrit scripture, the Ācāryas consider the essential criterion of good commentary to be communicability of insight to all devotees. Maṇavāḷamāmuni, in his introduction to Piḷḷailokācārya's *Mumukṣuppaṭi,* says, for example, that although Piḷḷailokācārya has written three works already—one short, one long, and one just the right size—these were too Sanskritic. Because they were not easily understood by women and the innocent, he made this one without such defect. The Ācāryas make their teachings accessible by using popular language, especially metaphors and similes drawn from everyday experiences (as with the simile of marriage cited above), to make abstruse points of theological doctrine understood *and enjoyed.* They draw from a woman's experience with ease. Periyavāccāṉpiḷḷai, in his commentary on Nammāḻvār's *Tiruvāymoḻi* 4:10:2, remarks, for example, "if one asks how the Lord, enjoying all comforts in his heavenly abode, can choose such a comfortless place to dwell in [i.e. here on earth], it may be replied that it is because God is like the mother, who, though provided with a very comfortable [bed]..., chooses to lie at the feet of her offspring to caress and comfort them. So too God chooses to come down to earth and dwell in this temple in order to be near his devotees" (Venkatachari trans. 1978, 48).

Similarly, Piḷḷailokācārya uses a number of metaphors and similes that refer to women. In his *Śrīvacanabhūṣaṇam* 372 he compares the good that comes from God's grace to the mother's milk that has been given spontaneously by her to the child. In his *Mumukṣuppaṭi,* in the context of discussing the *tirumantra* (*aum namo nārāyaṇāya*), he states: "like a mother who refuses to leave either her husband's bed or her child's crib, her nature is to remain without leaving either the first or last letters" [and Maṇavāḷamāmuni comments on this *sūtra* as follows]...As befitting her...nature [to serve], in order to give him pleasure, a wife does not leave her husband's bed. As appropriate to her protective nature, in order to watch over him, a mother stays by her child's crib. In the same way, Śrī [the Goddess] also clings to her delighting and protecting roles as appropriate to her relationship with her husband and children. Thus she remains without leaving either the letter *a*—the first letter which refers to the Lord, her husband, or the letter *m*—the last letter which refers to the *cetanas* who are her children" (Mumme trans. 1987, 59–60). The point of this passage is to show how the Goddess Śrī—and by extension every married woman—is the paradigmatic model for the devotee, because her nature is to serve, just as it is the nature of the devotee to do so. Periyavāccā<u>n</u>piḷḷai, in the introduction to his commentary on Āṇṭāḷ's *Tiruppāvai,* says that although it is unnatural for a man to look at another man and have affection towards him, it is natural (*paḷḷamatai*: literally a channel carrying water to lands in a low level, hence that which happens with natural ease) for a woman looking at a man to have such affection.[27]

It is implied in such Śrīvaiṣṇava texts that a married woman has an advantage in her surrender to and service to God not only because she does these things in every day life, but also because she is an embodiment of the Goddess. Just as Śrī serves her husband, protects her children, and mediates between them, so does the human wife. Piḷḷailokācārya in *Mumukṣuppaṭi sūtra* 112 states: "As it is said 'Being close to him for all time, without any break, [may we render flawless service],' this service is to be carried out in all places, at all times, and under all conditions [and Maṇavāḷamāmuni comments]...when a wife wears the *maṅgalasūtra* it shows that she belongs to none other than her husband. In the same way, bearing the *tirumantra* shows that the *cetana* belongs to none other than the Lord. To explain this idea he describes this [*tirumantra*] as a kind of *maṅgalasūtra*" (Mumme trans. 1987, 90). In the next *sūtra* (113), Piḷḷailokācārya observes that the *tirumantra* is "like a *maṅgalasūtra* which has eight threads [woven into] three strands [and Maṇavāḷamāmuni comments that]...unlike the ordinary *maṅgalasūtra* which has sixteen threads and two strands, the *tirumantra*—which has eight holy syllables and three words—is like a *maṅgalasūtra* with eight threads and three strands" (Mumme trans. 1987, 91). The Ācārya concludes in *sūtra* 114 that "this means that the Lord will protect the soul as a husband (*pati*) [and Maṇavāḷamāmuni comments that]...calling this [*tirumantra*] a *maṅgalasūtra* [means] that the Lord will be a husband [or master, lord, protector—*pati*] for the soul embellished with it and will protect him" (Mumme, trans. 1987, 90–91).

In these passages, the *maṅgalasūtra,* the auspicious thread (*sūtra*) worn by married women in Tamil Nadu to symbolize their marital state, is compared to the *tirumantra,* an auspicious short sentence (*sūtra*). The word *sūtra* from the word *siv,* to sew, refers to a string; the sacred thread or cord (*yajñapavīta*) worn by the twice–born (*dvija*); and that "which like a thread runs through or holds together everything, rule, direction; a short sentence or aphoristic rule, and any work or manual consisting of strings of such rules hanging together like threads" (Monier-Williams ([1889] 1970, 1241). According to Manu (2:67), marriage is the *upanayana* for women. By analogy, the *maṅgalasūtra* functions as the *yajñapavīta*. In the *upanayana*, the teacher traditionally begins the period of Vedic learning by instructing the student in the chanting of AUM. In the same manner, the Śrīvaiṣṇava Ācārya instructs the initiate in the *tirumantra*, which begins with AUM. Just as wearing the *maṅgalasūtra* symbolizes that a woman is married and belongs only to her husband, so hearing the *tirumantra* symbolizes that the soul is initiated into Śrīvaiṣṇava learning, is now married to God, and belongs only to him.[28]

Piḷḷailokācārya uses another simile with feminine symbolism in *sūtra* 147 of *Mumukṣuppaṭi*: "The feet of the *śeṣī* is the place of refuge (*turai*) where the *śeṣas* settles down, just as a child places his mouth on the breast [and Maṇavāḷamāmuni comments that]...the holy feet are the place of refuge with their master (*śeṣī*) in accord with their true nature [as *śeṣas*]. This is just like when a nursing child, ignoring all other parts of his mother's body, puts his mouth on the breast which is designated just for him (Mumme, trans. 1987, 125). This simile goes to the core of a woman's identity as mother. In such ways the commentators relate theology to life. Nothing is too sacrosanct or too pedestrian for this activity.

Śrīvaiṣṇavism (especially the Teṉkalai branch) is overtly supportive of women when compared to other Hindu *darśanas* that accept knowledge of the Veda and the auxiliary branches of learning (*vedāṅga*) as prerequisite to, and *saṁnyāsa* as penultimate to, liberation. Rāmānuja in his commentary on *Bhagavadgītā* 9:29 says that God stays among the devotees as if they are superior to him (*madutkṛṣṇesiva*). These devotees include women as well as men. In fact, the Tamil bhakti appreciation of women goes well beyond the bhakti agenda to proselytize the religion, thanks to the Śrīvaiṣṇava motifs of enjoyment and variety. For Śrīvaiṣṇavas, the term *anubhāva* (experience) means the fullness of experience occasioned by the variety of emotional relations with Nārāyaṇa-Viṣṇu-Kṛṣṇa. The acknowledgement of diversity on the philosophical level and the appreciation of variety on the emotional and aesthetic levels, form the basis of Viśiṣṭādvaita (literally, the nonduality of that which is differentiated), the Śrīvaiṣṇava system of philosophy. Therefore, it is conceivable that *anubhāva* may be extended to the idea of God's enjoyment of the variety of emotional relations created by the difference of sex (male and female) and gender roles.

In sum, there are many differences between the conservative brahmanical view of women and the Śrīvaiṣṇava perspective when one compares accessibility to scripture (Sanskrit Veda or Tamil Veda), restriction of the means to and goal of liberation (*dvija* male or *prapanna*), death (polluting or auspicious), destiny (rebirth or supreme Heaven), mode of life (asceticism or householder), status (woman as inferior or woman as equal/preferred), and experience as a source for analogies (male or female) respectively.

Why this Difference between Conservative Brahmanism and Śrīvaiṣṇavism?

One wonders whether this positive regard for women found in the Śrīvaiṣṇava texts, both scripture and commentary, has been a conscious intent on the part of the Āḻvārs and Ācāryas to be supportive of women, and if so what have been their motives.

1. Was their motive to answer the challenge of Buddhism and Jainism?

It may be argued that Śrīvaiṣṇavas promoted a view of women as capable of salvation to counter the challenge of the Buddhists and Jainas who had founded monastic Orders for women and had made the soteriological goal practically as well as theoretically available for them. Now, this is certainly an argument from silence, for there are no texts that explicitly attribute such motives to the Śrīvaiṣṇava Āḻvārs and Ācāryas, though some of the former certainly criticized the heterodox religions in their poems and some of the latter attempted to refute Buddhism and Jainism through philosophical arguments.[29] There may be some truth, however, in the proposition that brahmin leaders a number of centuries earlier had had such a concern, which remained implicit in the later bhakti tradition. According to Arvind Sharma (1979, 66–67), citing the *Vinaya Piṭaka*, the formal establishment of an order of monks was so popular among the elite classes that it was perceived by brahmins as threatening the institution of marriage and the economic basis of society.

As noted previously, by the time of the *Bhagavadgītā*, salvation had been extended to women, although *Bhagavadgītā* 9:32 was more a concession than a call for reform. And by the 3rd to 5th century C.E., some brahmins were integrating the popular worship of Viṣṇu and Śiva into the brahmanical world view, and this was represented by some passages in the *Mahābhārata*.[30] In this context, they took up the challenge of attracting women to a brahmanized bhakti as part of their missionary endeavour to meet the challenge of Buddhism and Jainism with a revived religion sensitive to both universal and brahmanical concerns. This new brahmanized bhakti Hinduism promoted an easy path to salvation within the family itself rather than necessitating a radical break from it (i.e. the requirement to live an ascetic life in a monastery). This helped to create a popular brahmanical challenge to the heterodox religions.

Accordingly, we find in the Tamil bhakti hymns of the Āḻvārs and Nāyaṉmārs a message addressed to women and an attempt to image the religion as inclusive of women and interested in women's concerns—such as vows (*vratas*) for attaining a husband and for the welfare of the family. Maṇikkavācakar's *Tiruvempāvai* is a case in point from Tamil Śaivism, for in verse 9 there is a triple conflation among: (1) the idea of being the slave/servant of God and serving him, (2) the idea of being a slave to other devotees, worshipping their feet, and serving them, and (3) the idea of a woman being the 'slave' or servant of her husband, doing his bidding, and serving him, which is the traditional role of a Hindu woman according to the brahmanical norms of *strīdharma*.[31] Because service to husband is one of the key requirements of the good wife, the language of service reflects a woman's traditional orientation and concept of appropriate feminine behaviour. The statement that they will marry only the Lord's devotees as their husbands gives us a clue to the religious competition of the period and the attempt to make the sect endogamous. Maidens often performed vows to obtain husbands. The bhakti poets say that if the Lord will give them the blessing of marrying his servants, they will lack nothing in their lives.

Āṇṭāḷ, an Āḻvār, makes fertility and prosperity the more general results of performing the Mārkaḻi vow. In her *Tiruppāvai,* she speaks through the voice of young girls who are performing the Mārkaḻi vow, associates the vow with bhakti, and transforms the vow into a woman's way to proselytize the greatness of Kṛṣṇa (singing in verse 1 that they'll bathe so that everyone will sing of his fame). In this manner, she makes women active participants in the great missionary enterprise. She also promotes the idea of salvation for women who now, doing penance and rejoicing, can think of that path that will free them from *saṁsāra,* enabling them to enter Heaven (verses 2 and 10). It comes as no surprise, then, to find that when a brahmanized bhakti Hinduism developed in Tamil Nadu, it not only promoted universal salvation within the context of the family (*kula*) of devotees (which implied within the individual family context as well), but it also directed special attention to women.

Even though Vedic religion in its new form as a brahmanized bhakti movement mounted an offensive against the heterodox religions, which from their inception had criticized the brahmanical tradition, this certainly did not cause the immediate decline of Buddhism and Jainism. After all, Mahāyāna Buddhism had also made the claim that the householder can attain the supreme goal. Both Buddhism and Jainism, moreover, had provided róles for lay women such as offering gifts (*dāna*) and worship, and Jains had extended monastic traditions such as fasting and fasting to death (*sallekhanā*) to the laity.

In Tamil Nadu, Buddhists and Jains may have been actively appealing to women as well. Feminine heroines and deities are featured, for instance, in Tamil epics such as the Buddhist inspired *Manimekaḷai* and the Jain inspired *Cilappatikāram* (5th century C.E.?). Although the Tamil Jain appeal to women drew on some earlier Jain traditions, there seem to have been some unique Tamil developments. Orr (forthcoming) concludes the following from her examination of the inscriptional evidence: (1) Jain religious women had property (unlike the Jain monastics in other parts of India); (2) they were called *kuratti* (from Skt. guru) and had female disciples (*manaikkiyar*), which suggests lineages of women; (3) there was no specific link of these women to monastic organizations proper; (4) at least one had the status of being a wife; and consequently, Jainism had probably developed an indigenous Tamil form, which possibly included a new category of Jain women with a status between that of a nun and a lay person.

Cross-fertilization between Jainism and Hinduism in Tamil Nadu arising out of competition cannot be ruled out. According to Orr (1995b and forthcoming), inscriptions of the 8th-9th centuries in the southernmost districts of Tamil Nadu (Maturai, Tirunelveli, and Kanyakumari) indicate that Jainism had developed shrines, located within the monastic sites (*paḷḷis*); these shrines had images that were worshipped with food offerings as were the images in the Vaiṣṇava and Śaiva temples. She notes that there is an association of the *paḷḷis* with local authorities in the countryside (the *sabhaiyar, ūrar, nāḷḷavar*), just as Hindu temples had such associations. Of interest to the present discussion is the fact that the Jains seem to have developed independent shrines to the Yakṣīs as goddesses perhaps by the 8th-9th centuries, prior to development of separate goddess shrines in the Tamil Hindu tradition, which can be traced only from about the 10th century (Orr 1995b). This suggests that the latter may have been in imitation of the independent Jain goddess figures.

Orr is quick to point out, however, that there remained important differences between Jain and Hindu women. (1) The model of the Jain religious woman does not seem, for instance, to have been the model that inspired the Hindu "temple women" (i.e. women identified by certain terms such as *tevaraṭiyar* and other characteristics),[32] because they were localized phenomena in different parts of Tamil Nadu (not connected by networks and institutions) or of different times (about four centuries separating the Jain religious women and the Hindu "temple women" at Kalugumalai, a site in Tiruvelveli). (2) The model of the Jain religious woman also did not inspire any quasi-ascetic status for Hindu women.[33] (3) The model of the Jain religious woman as *kuratti* (guru) certainly did not become the model for any Hindu woman. I would add to the latter point that this did not happen because of the exclusion by Manu, Bhāskara and others of women from Vedic education and the fact that in Śrīvaiṣṇavism brahmin male Ācāryas made sure that they alone were the teachers, though they were happy to accept women as their students.

In short, the relation of Jainism and bhakti Hinduism between the 7th and 13th centuries is complex. Nevertheless, Jainism (and Buddhism) decline by the 13th century C.E. and bhakti Hinduism emerges as the foremost religion in Tamil Nadu. I would argue that this occurred in part because the Āḻvārs and Ācāryas inherited but also contributed to a bhakti agenda that not only directly promoted universal salvation and appealed to women but also indirectly or directly countered the heterodox religions as a way to achieve ascendency in the subcontinent. A case can be made that their motive for extending religious education and salvation to women may have been to cause the decline of Buddhism and Jainism. At the same time it must be recognized that there is only indirect evidence for this in the texts.

2. *Was their motive a desire to reform the brahmanical tradition?*

One of the interesting case studies here is that of *sati* and widowhood.

There are many examples of *sati* in Tamil Nadu in the caṅkam period (Arunachalam 1978), and there are stones commemorating such acts as late as the 7th century C.E. in parts of the South. It is striking, however, that no images or eulogies of *sati* appear in the hymns of the Āḻvārs, and there are no discussions of *sati* in the works of the early Ācāryas. This may be due to a general Vaiṣṇava abhorrence of religious violence (which was associated with some radical Śaivite sects).

In the *Śrīvaiṣṇava Samayācāra Niṣkarṣa* (the Essence of Śrīvaiṣṇava Normative Behaviour) by Piḷḷailokamjīyar (which may have been written between the end of the 16th and the 18th centuries),[34] there is, however, an extensive discussion of *sati* and widowhood from the Śrīvaiṣṇava perspective. It may make explicit what had been an implicit understanding in the tradition. Perhaps this discussion was provoked because of growing Hindu debate over *sati* in the wake of Muslim and Christian criticisms.

Piḷḷailokamjīyar gives the "general" law of *sati* by quoting a text (source unknown) to the effect that a husband who kills a brahmin or forgets the help rendered by a friend will be purified when his wife throws herself into his funeral pyre. A woman who does not burn herself along with her husband's body will not obtain release from her female body (that is, she will always have rebirth as a woman). Moreover, a woman who follows her husband at death will purify her maternal and paternal families as well as her in-laws of three generations. These commandments of *anumaraṇa* (following the husband in death, i.e. *sati*) pertain, he notes, to an *amumukṣustrī*, that is, a woman who does not desire liberation (*mokṣa*). Furthermore, even if a Śrīvaiṣṇava does not understand this classification and accepts *sati*, *sati* is against *śruti* and *smṛti*. (As will become clear in the following discussion, a Śrīvaiṣṇava who performs *sati* will become a śūdra and is not really a Vaiṣṇava.)

The question is then raised: but how are these commandments to perform *anumaraṇa* against *śruti*, etc. for a Śrīvaiṣṇava woman? The answer is this. The author refers to a discussion of *anumaraṇa* in the *Vijñāneśvara* which states that Śaṅkha and Aṅgiras say that a woman who follows her husband in *anumaraṇa* will remain together with him in *svarga* for three and one half million years. After commenting on how the inseparability of husband and wife is demonstrated by the act of *sati*, it is said that this is a common dharma for women inclusive of the outcaste (*cāṇḍāla*) whether one is pregnant, a young girl, or has no progeny, because *anumaraṇa* is a general rule for everyone. Then too it is said that the injunctions (*vidhis*) prohibit *anugamana* (i.e. *anumaraṇa*) for brahmin women by the command of Brahmā. A woman belonging to the brahmin community who follows her husband in *anumaraṇa* by killing herself (*ātmaghāta*) neither reaches *svarga* (heaven) nor makes her husband reach *svarga*. The author then asks whether Vaiṣṇava women can have *anumaraṇa* or not and concludes that the general rule is that brahmin women are not allowed to practice *anumaraṇa* and therefore Śrīvaiṣṇava brahmin women are not allowed to practice it.

The author seems to endorse, however, a general notion of self-willed death for everyone (including women, children, youth, and old people). If they do it intentionally and because of performance of *śrīkārya* (i.e. service for Viṣṇu), they will reach Vaikuṇṭha and become liberated. Another stanza is quoted to the effect that if they have any dispute over wealth, food grains, garments, and garlands (presumably at the temple), at that time a Vaiṣṇava can intentionally kill himself (or herself?) by a weapon or other means and will definitely reach Vaiṣṇava *loka* from whence there is no rebirth. Finally, the *Vāmana Purāṇa* is cited: if a man gives up his body for the work of Lord Raṅgeśa (i.e. Nārāyaṇa-Viṣṇu-Kṛṣṇa), all the dead in his family will reach Paramapaḍa. This discussion draws from another medieval concept of self-willed death, that of the servant who is loyal to his master onto death (Settar and Kaliburgi, 1982, 30-31; 36). I know of little evidence for such a practice within Śrīvaiṣṇavism (for one of the few existing examples see *Journal of Vaiṣṇava Studies*, 3.3, p. 95); this discussion, therefore, could be but a theoretical one on the part of this author.

Next, the author Piḷḷailokamjīyar notes that there are some śāstras in which it is said that a wife who embraces her Śrīvaiṣṇava husband at the time of cremation and is burnt in the fire, also reaches Vaiṣṇava Pada (i.e. supreme Heaven). The issue of dying with the husband (*sahagamana*) is more problematic than *anumaraṇa*, for *sahagamana* is a legitimate act for brahmin women according to a number of *smṛtis* (and Śrīvaiṣṇavism is a very brahmanized bhakti tradition). To circumvent the legitimacy of *sahagamana*, Piḷḷailokamjīyar points out that this *śloka* is not for the Śrīvaiṣṇava who desires liberation (*mumukṣu*). Rather, it is applicable only to the first six kinds of Śrīvaiṣṇavas (who are not considered real Śrīvaiṣṇavas according to him) belonging to the ten-fold classification. This discussion concludes with the comment that if a Śrīvaiṣṇava woman desires to do *sahagamana*, she should be known as a non-Vaiṣṇava (*avaiṣṇava*). Thus, the author, by introducing various kinds of Śrīvaiṣṇavas and a new criterion—that is, being desirous of liberation (*mumukṣu*)—eliminates the problem of *sahagamana* for brahmin women, because every real Śrīvaiṣṇava is to be desirous of liberation and not entertain the thought of rebirth. All real Śrīvaiṣṇava women, whether brahmin or non–brahmin, are *prapannas* and therefore desirous of salvation and consequently are not to practice *sati* of any form. Such is the rather convoluted logic. Although the author is against *anumaraṇa* as a way for women to follow their husband in death, he accepts, on the authority of some Purāṇic statements, other types of self-willed death. Once again, I managed to find only a few examples of the practice of self-willed death in the Śrīvaiṣṇava tradition, and so the present discussion seems to be more theoretical than anything else.

The position of widowhood also seems to be considerably more liberal among some Śrīvaiṣṇavas than the prevailing brahmanical norms. Teṉkalai women, for example, do not shave their heads. This has been a common practice for brahmin widows until recently, for Vaṭakalai, Smārta and Mādhva brahmin widows have all followed this custom. More importantly, the Teṉkalai widow is considered auspicious, for it is believed that her husband has gone to supreme Heaven (i.e. Vaikuṇṭha). This contrasts with the categorical inauspiciousness of the Hindu widow who has been viewed (perhaps after the 10th century until recently) as an ogress or a witch who caused her husband's untimely death (Hejib and Young 1988, 73–85).

Such evidence suggests that at least one of the brahmin Ācāryas took a stand against *sati* and the customs associated with widowhood (though the Vaṭakalais were more conservative, maintaining some brahmanical norms). This has the appearance of being a late reform when considered in the light of pan-Indian brahmanical practices. If the Śrīvaiṣṇavas had never endorsed *sati,* however, this would be less a question of reform (unless the practice had nevertheless entered the tradition, perhaps with the growing conservatism after the 13th century as discussed later in this article). But the question is also whether the motive of the Śrīvaiṣṇava Ācāryas was reform per se or whether it was, in part, the corollary of their own theology. That is, because it is a sin to think of rebirth, how can a woman be a *sati* desiring to join her husband in the next life, for seven lives to come, or for a temporary visit to lower heaven (*svarga*)? Then too how can a woman be an *inauspicious* widow, when she is to rejoice that her husband's death means that he has been saved? On the contrary, theological logic dictates that the moment of death is auspicious and if the moment is auspicious, then a widow will share that auspiciousness. Accordingly, I conclude that it is difficult to determine whether the Ācāryas had a conscious motive to reform the tradition. If they did, it was likely based on a general and early Vaiṣṇava brahmanical abhorrence of violence. If reform was not a conscious motive, the positions on *sati* and widowhood were but the logical outcomes of certain theological positions. It is also possible that there was an early Vaiṣṇava negative reaction to practices such as *sati.* This was later made more explicit when Hindus began to reply to foreign criticisms against the practise.

3. Was their motive to preempt a revolt by the women themselves from the restrictive brahmanical norms of strīdharma?

Elsewhere I have suggested that Āṇṭāḷ may have "revolted" against her parents because she did not want an arranged marriage but desired instead to marry only the Lord (Young 1985). Given Āṇṭāḷ's radical interpretation of devotion to the Lord and her eventual status as a goddess who was incarnated on earth, it is possible that later Śrīvaiṣṇava women would have emulated her or demanded an institutional basis for Hindu female asceticism. But the male Ācāryas of the next period, true to brahmanical insistence on marriage for a woman, sought a new solution to the incipient polarization of women's acceptance of marriage as the norm and their denial of human marriage to love God alone. By the concept of *prapatti* and by asserting the idea that any householder, male or female, can attain salvation, they managed to circumvent further feminine deviation from the norms of *strīdharma* (i.e. denial of marriage). Accordingly, Āṇṭāḷ is cherished as unique. No one can rival her single-minded concentration on the Lord. Because of her uniqueness, Āṇṭāḷ becomes the intercessor for all (similar to the role attributed to Rāmānuja). With Āṇṭāḷ as mediatrix and *prapatti* as the virtual guarantee of salvation, later Śrīvaiṣṇavas can enjoy the world "as if" liberated and await peacefully the moment of death when they will join their "husband" in Heaven.

Even today Śrīvaiṣṇavas reenact annually the marriage of Āṇṭāḷ and the Lord at temples throughout Tamil Nadu and at such places as Vṛndāvaṇa and Mathurā in the North. For they believe that Āṇṭāḷ's marriage to God is none other than their own. In their appropriation of her poetry, which is sung on this occasion, they sense the deep integration of southern and northern motifs so central to their identity as Śrīvaiṣṇavas. But although they may be inspired by Āṇṭāḷ, they do not try to emulate her extraordinary behavior, thanks to the Ācāryas' solution to the opposition of dharma and *mokṣa* by suggesting that salvation can be achieved as a householder. An example of how the Ācāryas may have tried to preempt a revolt by women following the example of Āṇṭāḷ is the fact that although there are allusions in her poetry that Āṇṭāḷ herself rejected marriage to a human man because she wanted to marry only God, Pinpalakiyaperumāḷjīyar says that she is a manifestion of the Goddess Earth (Bhūdevi). She is also linked to Sītā who was born from a furrow. Thus, the hagiography makes her into the example of the ideal married wife, symbol of feminine chastity and loyalty, by viewing her as an incarnation of the Goddess who married God or Sītā who married Rāma! Be that as it may, Āṇṭāḷ's revolt was not a revolt to constitute a new theology. Āṇṭāḷ's theology, was, in fact, found in the bhakti poems of earlier male Āḻvārs such as Nammāḻvār, though it took a young girl to internalize it and interpret the injunction to love God alone as an injunction for a woman to deny marriage. It was also not emulated by other women after her.

Moreover, there is no evidence that the theology of the Ācāryas was derived from an original pro-woman theology written by women intellectuals who were rebelling against brahmanical norms. Besides Āṇṭāḷ, there was only one other woman in Śrīvaiṣṇavism who contributed to the tradition through her writings. This was Koṉeridāsyai, who wrote a commentary on Nammāḻvār's *Tiruvāymoḻi* called the *Tiruvāymoḻi Vācakamālai* or *Vivaraṇa Caṭakam.*[35] The uniqueness of her commentary is that she connects the entire *Tiruvāymoḻi* with the very first verse, which she defines as the essence of the whole work. Once again, Koṉeridāsyai was hardly the originator of the theology, though she was a skilled interpreter. Āṇṭāḷ (here Kūrattāḻvāṉ's wife, not Āṇṭāḷ the bhakti poet-saint), was also a female intellectual. According to the *Guruparamparāprabhāvam 6000*, she was considered very scholarly; men consulted her to clarify their doubts, but unlike Koṉeridāsyai she did not write anything. Despite these examples, it must be admitted that the positive imaging of women in Śrīvaiṣṇavism cannot be traced, by and large, to women themselves (poets or commentators) and their revolt from restrictive brahmanical norms; it is largely a product of brahmin male thinking.

4. Was their motive a way to provide continuity with the earliest Tamil poetry (caṅkam)?

In the Tamil caṅkam literature of the 2nd century B.C.E. to third century C.E., the *akam* genre, which portrays the secular love relationship between hero and heroine, usually has the persona of a woman-in-love.

Here a maiden is the complement of the man on the model of equal but different. The poetry is characterized by a vigorous realism regarding the complexities of human psychology: joy, annoyance, charm, innocence, haughtiness, and fear. Here there is no inhibiting ideal psychology for a maiden such as the brahmanical ideal of preseving the sexual innocence of maidens. Rather, there is realization of a maiden's personality and sexuality through full interaction with the hero. A maiden of the *akam* poems is bold in pursuit. She is no shadow of a man, no ethereal virgin, no romantic creation of the poets' hyperbole divorced from life, and no daughter secluded and passively awaiting an arranged marriage.

The *akam* poetry reflects, no doubt, the cultural language of love in the megalithic society of Tamil Nadu, a heroic warrior society experimenting with individualism and sexual freedoms in courtship (as did other heroic societies around the world according to Sagan 1985, 204-225; 275-276; 375-376). This megalithic society, which existed prior to the first written records, may have continued in the hinterlands, such as in the *kuriñci* or hill areas, in the caṅkam period, hence the innuendos of physical embrace in the *kuriñci* poems. It may be surmised that with the development of female chastity and arranged marriage in the urban areas, the megalithic practices of romantic love were being marginalized (the wife associated with the *marutam* region or cities on the rich agricultural plains, for example, is associated with the house and is imaged more as the *pativrātya* ideal based on chastity and loyalty if not seclusion). Just as this was happening, however, the memory of romantic love was being preserved in folk songs, bardic verses, and court poetry about the hero and heroine.

This folk and literary embodiment of romantic and individualistic love underwent a second transformation between the 3rd and 5th centuries C.E.[36] with the gradual development of a religious (bhakti) poetry, incorporating the caṅkam motifs of the lover and beloved. The psychology of the heroic Tamil maiden was preserved in the new bhakti genre as the ideal devotee. In general, such incorporation of the ancient Tamil tradition of poetic love themes gave a powerful impetus to the bhakti movement. In particular, it may have contributed to a Tamil tradition of strong women.

The Āḻvārs were the heirs of the *akam* genre. Because the hymns of the Āḻvārs were the subject of a huge commentarial literature and because they were constantly chanted in the Śrīvaiṣṇava temples and homes in the later centuries, the ancient model of Tamil maidenhood continued, albeit in its bhakti transformation, and was constantly remembered and reinforced on the religious plane in the community of devotees. It may be concluded that Śrīvaiṣṇavism as a whole contributed to the maintenance of some central features of archaic Tamil identity, despite the fact that individual Āḻvārs and Ācāryas may not have been conscious about the motive of the early leaders of the Tamil bhakti movement to provide a touchstone for Tamil identity at a moment when Tamilians could have reacted negatively to massive social change produced by the integration of northern religious motifs and practices, not to mention immigrants from the North.

5. Was their motive a recognition of the fact that Tamil women had comparatively more autonomy and had property that could be given to the temple?

The sense of self–possession on the part of Tamil women (inclusive of brahmin women) may have been enhanced by the practice of cross-cousin marriage in Tamil Nadu (which allowed the wife to maintain strong ties with her natal family and to inherit property). Thomas R. Trautman (1981) has demonstrated that there was a proto-Dravidian system of cross-cousin marriage (that is, the children of a brother and sister are cross-cousins), derivatives of this system being found today not only in South India but also in the Deccan and other pockets of Dravidian culture as well. Gloria Lalonde (1985), in her statistical study of the changing status of women in modern India, notes that women in the southern states (including Tamil Nadu) have a higher status than in those of North India and argues, based on a study of regional data on sex ratios, life expectancy, infant mortality rates, literacy, employment, and physical quality of life index that this is based mainly on their differences in kinship and marriage systems, not differences in religion, money spent on development, etc.

Unlike in the North, where a woman leaves her natal family, marries into a family of a distant village, and has a low status in her husband's home in her early years as wife, in the South, a woman remains in close contact with her natal family. Following Dyson and Moore's definition of autonomy as the capacity to manipulate one's environment, Lalonde finds that it is higher in the southern states where women have greater freedom of "movement and association of adolescent and adult females; post–marital residence patterns and behavioral norms that do not rupture or severely constrain social intercourse between the bride and her natal kin; the ability of females to inherit or otherwise acquire, retain, and dispose of property; and some independent control by females of their own sexuality—for example, in the form of choice of marriage partners (Lalonde 1985, 55 quoting from Dyson and Moore 1983, 45). Lalonde notes that women today are active in the labour force in the south; this may be related to the type of farming, the North having male-dominated plough agriculture, the South wet rice cultivation. The fact that bride price rather than dowries was given in the South may have benefited women as well.

Neither Trautman nor Lalonde look at the issue of women and property in Dravidian cross-cultural marriage systems historically. But the fact that there seems to be a number of references to women donating their property in the inscriptions of Tamil Nadu may allude to a system of inheritance or income that favours women when compared to that of the North. These are intriguing questions and need further exploration. For the time-being, it is enough to suggest that if southern women have comparatively greater autonomy today, thanks to the benefits of cross-cousin marriage, they no doubt enjoyed such benefits in the past as well. Therefore, there may be some truth to the assertion that the Āḻvārs and Ācāryas recognized the comparatively greater autonomy of Tamil women and their ownership of property.

***

To conclude, there may be some truth to all of the Ācāryas' motives analyzed, even though some may have been embedded in the ongoing tradition and not consciously discussed. I think that there may have been an implicit attempt to counter the Buddhists and Jainas by making the religion more attractive to women. There may have been a desire to reassert abhorrence of *sati* in the wake of foreign criticisms of this practice (alternatively, to reform the practice if had entered the tradition). Because at least one women, Āṇṭāḷ, revolted against male authority and was idealized as a goddess, there may have been a desire to prevent other such revolts especially by female intellectuals by honouring women as wives who are the preeminent devotees. And there may have been a desire to create a link with images of independent young women in caṅkam poetry in order to situate the bhakti tradition in archaic Tamil identity and culture. And there may have been a desire to acknowledge women, because women had a position of some strength in the Tamil tradition, thanks to their role in the early heroic society, to cross-cousin marriage, and to the related fact that they often had property at their disposal. Hence, there is some truth to all of my initial propositions regarding why Śrīvaiṣṇavism has been supportive of women if one takes a long view of the history of bhakti and entertains the possibility of both conscious and semi-conscious motives.

In general, though, I suggest that the Ācāryas' position on women was primarily an outcome of bhakti theology. Early leaders may have initially desired to incorporate women for the sake of proselytism but once they came to view liberation as universally attainable in this life and possible to pursue as a householder, they had a set of theological premises that could not be bypassed or destroyed without destroying the Śrīvaiṣṇava tradition itself. Because doctrine is more stable than ritual in some sectarian contexts, it may have been maintained despite ritual and social changes. The theology, accordingly, was largely responsible for exploration of a positive view of women in the Śrīvaiṣṇava texts and its continuity over the centuries. And yet, it is only fair to say that although the bhakti tradition certainly improved the lives of some Tamil Vaiṣṇava women, it managed to do so without making change a *cause celèbre* and drawing attention to this fact, which may have created unnecessary tension with the conservative brahmins, if not a lowering of the status of Śrīvaiṣṇava brahmins in their eyes.

I must add some qualifications to this discussion of the liberal nature of Śrīvaiṣṇavism, however. There still remained some negative views of women in Śrīvaiṣṇava circles. A case in point is that of looking on women as temptresses. If the male Āḻvārs addressed their poems to everyone, encouraged women to love the Lord and sing his praise, and themselves worshipped the Lord through impersonating a woman in love, they still sometimes viewed women as a snare or temptress. This was a pan-Indian convention. The Vaiṣṇava Āḻvārs Toṇṭaraṭippoṭi and Tirumaṅkai speak, for example, of committing a number of sins such as falling in love with women (see *Tirumālai* 5; 16; 33 and *Periyatirumoḻi* 1:6:1-2; 1:6:4; 1:9:2; 3:6:5; 6:2:4-5). So did the Ācāryas. The Ācāryas, according to the author of *Ācāryahṛdayam*, avoid falling "in the trap of ladies' eyes and will be caught [instead] in the net of the lotus eyes of God" (Damodaram 1976, 79). In this context the tension is not between being a householder and a yogī but between enjoyment of worldly pleasure and turning to God and his "family of devotees" as refuge. Woman as prostitute is viewed by men as the symbol of worldly desire; such attraction must be surmounted for a man to seek refuge. Occasionally, a wife, children or the biological family as a whole is viewed negatively as a snare. In the later period, with the growth of Śrīvaiṣṇava ascetic orders, the interpretation of women being a snare to worldly ways and preventing a man's reorientation to God was likely reinterpreted in a traditional ascetic manner as women's prevention of men from becoming ascetics or their subsequent temptation of the ascetic away from his vows of renunciation.

Another case in point of a lack of sensitivity to women despite the theology is the brahmanical tendency to Sanskritize the tradition, which may have had the effect of alienating if not excluding some women from dimensions of the religion (because many did not know Sanskrit). Although the Ācāryas were Tamils in that they lived in Tamil Nadu, they were also brahmins who helped to preserve and integrate northern or Sanskritic culture. Their exegetical task was not only to comment on the Tamil hymns of the Āḻvārs but also on Sanskritic works, especially those that refer to Nārāyaṇa-Viṣṇu-Kṛṣṇa. Their acknowledgment of *ubhayavedānta* (the two "*vedāntas*" understood, for instance, as the *śruti* or revealed texts and the hymns of the Āḻvārs) contained an inevitable tension between two distinct though interrelated orientations: the Sanskritic and the Tamil. Periyavāccāṉpiḷḷai captures this tension in his reference to the following episode: "Once Vaṅkīpurattunampi had been to pray to the Lord (Viṣṇu). While paying obeisance to the Lord, he stood close to some women of the cowherd community who were also praying. Mutaliyāṇṭāṉ, seeing this, accosted Vaṅkīpurattunampi and said: 'Why do you go and stand amidst these (illiterate) cowherd women while praying to the Lord, when you could very well stand amidst the Vaiṣṇava bhaktas?' To this Vaṅkīpurattunampi said: 'It is true that we have a little learning. These people may be illiterate but the Lord's grace is on them like water which flows from a higher to a lower level.' Then Mutaliyāṇṭāṉ asked 'What did they pray? And what did your grace pray?' Vaṅkīpurattunampi replied: 'They prayed to the Lord (in pure Tamil): 'Please drink and eat these fruits. Please wear this golden sacred thread. Live a hundred years. Wear this silk upper-cloth.' My prayer was in [Sanskrit]:...'Be victorious, be victorious.' Then Mutaliyāṇṭāṉ said: 'So you could not forget your rough sounding [Sanskrit]...even at this place. It seems that we will continue to be the same wherever we are. Please come over here'" (Venkatachari trans. 1978, 43-44). Although for Śrīvaiṣṇava women and non-brahmins,[37] knowledge of Sanskrit, Veda, and *vedāṅga* (the auxiliary branches of learning) was not a prerequisite for liberation, it still had high status in the community. The Sanskrit texts had to be related to the Tamil scriptures and their meaning interpreted for the members of the community without knowledge of Sanskrit. Because women and non-brahmins generally did not know Sanskrit, they could not be Ācāryas in a formal sense. Being an Ācārya was a prerogative of brahmin men, though Koṉeridāsyai and Āṇṭāḷ were female intellectuals.

One last caveat should be made. Although the theology is supportive of women, this support does not seem to translate into visibility, at least in the inscriptions from Śrīraṅgam. Orr (1995a) points out that there are references to only 50 women out of 2047 inscriptions located at this most important Śrīvaiṣṇavism temple. Of these 50 women, moreover, 20 are royal women and most of these are women of the Hoysala royal family in the 13th century.

Some Reflections of an Historical Nature

I wish to argue in this section that once a positive view of women is embedded in the theology of a tradition, it may serve to safeguard women's interests when the society is under stress and fundamental values begin to erode. With this hypothesis in mind, I will revisit the 13th-15th centuries, and take a look at the 19th-20th centuries, both periods of social upheaval.

The pioneering inscriptional work by Orr is useful once again to sort out social changes. She notes (1994a) the following when surveying the inscriptional record of the 8th-13th centuries C.E. (1) Queens, place women, queens of minor chiefdoms, and Jain religious women, who had all been active, as donors and involved in land transactions early in the period, no longer performed such activities and there seems to be a loss in their autonomy by the 13th century. (2) Whereas early in the period brahmin women were commonly identified by their hometowns, this is less the case late in the period, perhaps indicating less willingness by those who issue the inscriptions to recognize their independent status. Moreover, whereas early in the period they were referred to by Tamil terms for wife, late in the period the Tamilized form (*pāryai*) of the Sanskrit *bhāryā* became common, perhaps indicating a process of Sanskritization. (There was a concomitant decline in their status to that of wife only rather than donor—half of the references to women in the early medieval inscriptions refer to them as donors, but only 17% do after 1300: Orr 1995d.) Although brahmin women (following a trend of land consolidation by brahmin men) gained more access to land for some time, there was a decline in women's property by inheritance or marriage gifts very late in the period. (3) In general, whereas early in the period a woman was the independent actor or central figure in a property transaction or had the inscriptional records made in her own name, by the end of the period this was far less common, an official male (*mutukaṉ*) frequently acting as intermediary. This decreasing independence occurred for "temple women" as well, even though their numbers increased at the end of the period and even though they developed greater group identification, matrilineal status, and more institutional rights (ritual functions such as singing and dancing, waving the fly-whisk, etc.) at this time. Although there was not a uniform decline, for brahmin women gained more property for some time and "temple women" gained an institutional foothold, nevertheless there are indicators that women's position was declining. (4) With the loss of women's independence, there was a growth of symbolism of the divine couple or of goddesses.

There were other changes occurring. Orr (1995c) observes from comparing the early and late medieval inscriptions at Śrīraṅgam that in the latter (unlike the former) the following have become predominant if not new: (1) the works of the Āḻvārs and Ācāryas are increasingly incorporated into temple liturgy,[38] (2) temple worship has become more elaborate and a system of temple honours expressed through proportional distribution of offerings and special rituals for individuals has developed, (3) temple administration has become more formalized and hierarchical, (4) there is now more hereditary succession from the Ācārya, (5) asceticism has become popular, (6) there is the formation of *matas/maṭhas* headed by a figure called the *jīyar,* and (7) there is more royal patronage and interference in the temple, especially by the Vijayanagara kings who helped to restore Śrīraṅgam traditions after the Muslim invasion.

The question arises: why were these conservative tendencies developing by the end of the 13th century?

> (1) Orr suggests that "as the threat of competition from Jainism and Buddhism receded in Tamil Nadu and as Hindu institutions came to be increasingly well-established, it may have seemed feasible and desirable to adopt measures that exclude women but would enhance the prestige of temple priests and teachers, as religious authorities" (1994b, 124). To this I would add the observation that men have been more willing to work for women's "liberation" when there is external pressure. This occurred, for instance, during the colonial period. Faced with foreign criticism of their

treatment of women, Indian male leaders took up the challenge of reform for women and provided important leadership. After Independence, however, women leaders of the women's movement have noted a tendency for them to return to male domination (Young 1993a and 1993b).

(2) There may have been pressure to incorporate conservative Āgamic texts. The legitimation of the Pāñcarātra by Yāmuna in his *Āgama Prāmānya* in the 11th century, the development of the concept of *ubhayavedānta* (the inclusion of both Tamil and Sanskritic traditions), and the increasing influence of Pāñcarātra texts (for temple ritual and architecture) in the temple circles of Tamil Nadu may have encouraged the incorporation of the Sanskrit Āgamas by the Śrīvaiṣṇava Ācāryas. Orr (1994b, 122; 139) points out that the early Āgamas such as the *Pauṣkara Saṁhitā* are comparatively inclusive and tolerant of the ritual roles[39] of family women whereas the later *Śrīpraśna Saṁhitā*, at least some of which was composed in Tamil Nadu in the Chola period, consigns most women's ritual roles to a special class of courtesans; women are not eligible to receive the higher teachings of the Āgamas; the temples sponsored by them are not considered *sattvic*; other forms of religious giving by women go unacknowledged; and there are more warnings to avoid menstruating, pregnant, or immoral women. But Orr (1994b, 112-113) also points out that even in the most liberal Āgamas, women, who may have the initial rite of initiation and perform some ritual activities, may not have higher forms of initiation. Therefore they are not eligible for spiritual practices, teaching, or temple priesthood. Nor are they eligible for salvation, although this is never stated explicitly in the Āgamas. This, she suggests, may reflect an attempt to make the Āgamas appeal to the orthodox by incorporating the conservative images of *strīdharma* found in the Dharmaśāstras.

(3) It is likely that in this period orthodox brahmins moved south to escape the Muslim domination of the North and brought with them a more conservative brahmanism. These new migrants, though they moved into the temple milieu, may have been reluctant to embrace the universal spirit of the Āḻvārs (and Nāyaṉmārs), especially where women were concerned, either because of a long-standing ambivalent view of women based on Manu, Bhāskara, and others or because the turbulent times had caused them to project their fears onto women (Tulsīdās's portrayal of Sītā, the heroine of the great Hindu epic *Rāmāyaṇa* as weak and passive being a case in point). Orr (1995a) notes that in the early 14th century the term *bhaṭṭar* seems to refer to brahmins associated with reciting Veda and Purāṇa, performing *yajña*, and practicing medicine who have begun

to dominate the Śrīraṅgam temple and to have large landholdings around it. I would add that it is conceivable that these *bhaṭṭar* represent a migration of "northern" brahmins to Śrīraṅgam.

(4) The Muslim invasions into Tamil Nadu in the 14th century may also have contributed to a more conservative mood that was projected onto women, even though they did not succeed in maintaining their hegemony over the area for a long period of time. The Vijayanagara kings who had become patrons of the Śrīraṅgam and Tirupati temples, for example, introduced more conservative forms of dress modeled on that of Muslim rulers. In addition, knowledge of the dominance of Islam in North India may have proved sufficiently threatening to Hindu consciousness to cause southern Tamil brahmins to retrench in orthodoxy or at least project orthodoxy onto women.

(5) As the bhakti movement became mainstream, ascetic orders became attached to temples as *maṭas*. This integration of asceticism may have introduced a more masculine-oriented if not misogynistic element into the bhakti tradition, which had been hitherto largely a householder tradition.

(6) Temple women themselves may have preferred the security of a fixed ranking acknowledged by the temple than status based on entrepreneurial skills, even though this contributed to loss of agency in the long run. In any case, they may not have had much choice in the matter because caste identity and hierarchy had become much more important in the temple milieu.

These various factors may have contributed to a growing conservatism, and this conservatism in turn may have been the impetus for the development of a dialectic in the Śrīvaiṣṇava tradition over several generations of Ācāryas (13th-15th centuries). First, the writings of Piḷḷailokācārya and Aḻakiyamaṇavāḷap-perumāḷnāyaṉār may represent a reassertion, or at least a desire for a greater ritual linkage with the Āḻvār tradition when faced with this growing conservatism. Second, their imaging of the Āḻvārs and Ācāryas as greater than life, indeed, as incarnations of the deity, may have been inspired by sectarian rivalry (incarnation as a manifestation of that which is already divine has a higher status than liberation which has to be achieved through spiritual discipline as, for example, in the Advaitin concept of the *jīvanmukta*). Third, the writings of Vedāntadeśika may represent both the growing conservatism in its own right as well as his reaction to Piḷḷailokācārya and Aḻakiyamaṇavāḷap-perumāḷnāyaṉār's liberal reaction to it. His conservatism may have been influenced by the influence of the Vijayanagara rulers, who had absorbed some Muslim influence even as they rallied Hindus against it. Fourth, Maṇavāḷamāmuni's reassertion of Piḷḷailokācārya's position may have been a reaction both to Vedāntadeśika's more conservative stance and to other social forces of his day.

With the changes in the inscriptional record and the dialectic reflected in the texts in mind, let us consider Orr's proposal (1995c) that some sectarian texts of the period, such as the *Koyil Oḻuku*, are retrospective in nature, seeking legitimation of their own positions by projecting their fears, views, or new organizational structures onto the Śrīvaiṣṇavism of an earlier period, especially onto the figure of Rāmānuja. The idea of Rāmānuja's establishing the 74 families for a hereditary lineage would be a case in point, for the inscripitions of Rāmānuja's period do not attest to such a hereditary definition of Ācārya status, nor, for that matter, do internal references in the writings of the Ācāryas themselves. If the debate was fierce enough with the future direction of Śrīvaiavism at stake, it is even possible that the story of Rāmānuja's life was reworked to legitimate certain ideas. With these ideas in mind, let us examine a few key incidents recorded in the *Guruparamparāprabhāvam 6000* by Piṉpalakiyaperumāḷjīyar. Controversy surrounds the dating of this text. Many scholars today accept the date as 13th century, though Friedhelm Hardy, dates it much later.[40] A later date (15th century?) makes sense in the context of the present discussion, although the issue of dating demands a thorough investigation using both inscriptional and textual sources.

This text, which contains the often mythicized stories of the lives of the Āḻvārs and Nāyaṉmārs, tells how Rāmānuja became an ascetic. Piṉpalakiyaperumāḷjīyar describes how Rāmānuja decided to take *saṁnyāsa* because of his wife's refusal to ignore the rules of brahmanical dharma, which constituted the basis for brahmanical purity. When Rāmānuja's wife and the wife of his guru (Kāñcipūrṇa) met at the village well, they began to argue over the respective purity of their pots. This led Kāñcipūrṇa, who had observed the incident, to leave Kāñci and go to Śrīraṅgam. When Rāmānuja could not find his teacher, he came to learn about the quarrel between the wives over purity and his guru's sudden departure to avoid future trouble. The story recounts Rāmānuja's anger toward his wife because she had treated his teacher's leaf (plate) as polluting, because she had not only denied hungry men food but had also lied about it, and finally because she had quarreled with his guru. Calling her worldly and selfish, he sent her back to the home of her parents and became an ascetic. This incident is held responsible for Rāmānuja's *saṁnyāsa.* The author implies that Rāmānuja knew that the solidarity of the Śrīvaiṣṇava community of devotees, inclusive of brahmins and non-brahmins, could only be achieved if such brahmanical rules were renounced. He then describes how, after Rāmānuja became an ascetic, he established his own *maṭa* near a temple in Kāñci. One of his disciples is said to have been the Advaitin Yādavaprakāśa, who took the name Govindaperumāḷ/Govindajīyar and wrote the *Yatidharmasamuccaya,* a book of rules for Śrīvaiṣṇava ascetics.

This story can be read in three ways. One is that Rāmānuja's wife was conservative and tried to uphold her brahmanical *strīdharma* and family custom in the face of his liberalism, and that this led to an irreconcilable conflict and his *saṁnyāsa* or renunciation (this is the traditional interpretation within the community). Another is that the story reflects a more general struggle between liberals (stressing the "family" of all devotees) and conservatives (stressing the hierarchy of caste, with brahmanical superiority openly acknowledged) in the Śrīvaiṣṇava community. A third possibility is that the story was created to legitimate ascetic orders in Śrīvaiṣṇavism by viewing Rāmānuja as an ascetic and attributing to him a disciple, Yādavaprakāśa, who is described as not only the author of the *Yatidharmasamuccaya* but also originally an Advaitin (Advaita is a tradition known for its ascetic orders). It may be no coincidence that Pi<u>n</u>palakiyaperumāḷjīyar, the author of the *Guruparamparāprabhāvam 6000* in which these stories about Rāmānuja are found, was an ascetic as his name indicates.[41] Because asceticism had often been legitimated by anti-women views in the Hindu tradition (as true of other religions), it should not surprise us to find such a case here as well, although Pi<u>n</u>palakiyaperumāḷjīyar himself generally wants to counter conservatism. This story also serves to underscore the Śrīvaiṣṇava (Viśiṣṭādvaita) superiority to Advaita, hence the conversion of Yādavaprakāśa, an indication of the sectarian rivalry of the day). It is possible that Śrīvaiṣṇavism was instituting orders of ascetics to compete with those of the Advaitins and the Śaiva Siddhāntins.

Another story found in the *Guruparamparāprabhāvam 6000* is about how Tirukoṭṭiyūr Nambi revealed the secret meaning of the eight-syllable *tirumantra* (*aum namo nārāyaṇa*) to Rāmānuja and how Rāmānuja went up to the second-floor balcony of the temple tower at Tirukoṭṭiyūr, and breaking the vow of secrecy, shouted the meaning out from the temple tower for a group of Śrīvaiṣṇavas gathered below to hear. It is noteworthy in this account that it is the interpretation of the meaning of the mantra and not its utterance per se, which is the subject of conflict. There had been a long-standing tradition by the Ācāryas (Bhaṭṭar, Nañjīyar, Periyavāccaṉpiḷḷai, Vatakkuttiruvītip-piḷḷai) to compose stanzas or commentaries called *rahasyas* to explicate the mantras to all Śrīvaiṣṇavas and in the course of doing this to expound on a range of Śrīvaiṣṇava doctrines. I have already noted how women such as Koṉeridāsyai and Āṇṭāḷ were female intellectuals, and how the Ācāryas had made a special effort to include women in their teachings. It is possible in the wake of the growing conservatism of the 14th-15th centuries, that the universal accessibility of the Ācāryas' teachings in the form of the *rahasyas* was under threat. To bolster the legitimacy of women's (and non-brahmin's) accessibility to them at a time of growing brahmanical orthodoxy and ascetic influence, Piṉpalakiyaperumāḷjīyar (whom I am tentatively dating in the 15th century) told a story about how Rāmānuja (acknowledged as the chief Ācārya of the tradition) broke a vow of secrecy. In other words secrecy of teaching may have been coming into vogue in Piṉpalakiyaperumāḷjīyar's time in orthodox or ascetic Śrīvaiṣṇava circles and this ascetic felt it was important to hold to the more traditional liberal position of the Ācāryas' openness to teach all Śrīvaiṣṇavas.

Stories in the *Koyil Oḻuku* about how some temple priests attempted to poison Rāmānuja and how the high priest opposed Rāmānuja's changes to the organization of temple servants (from a fivefold to tenfold schema) also suggests a more complex and hierarchical organization, a development that reflects a period of time considerably after Rāmānuja's period according to the inscriptional evidence discussed previously. The fact that the *Koyil Oḻuku* also refers to two incidents about how Rāmānuja was going to replace, or was requested to replace, non-brahmins with brahmins in the temple adminstration but decided not to, suggests to me that the period of the 15th-16th century was one of brahmanical ascendency, thanks to the migrations of northern brahmins and the growing conservatism, and that this led to an attempt to marginalize or displace non-brahmins who had long-enjoyed a central role in the Śrīvaiṣṇava temple. The struggle over status and ranking seems to have been extremely acrimonious (some of the stories speak of attempts by some figures to poison others), threatening the very foundations of the tradition, which were then shored up by invoking the authority of Rāmānuja.

In sum, the tension between liberal and conservative strands of the brahmanical tradition, existing from Gupta times, may have resurfaced with the social changes in Tamil Nadu in the 13th-14th century, which began to polarize the Śrīvaiṣṇava tradition. This created a doctrinal dialectic, the eventual outcome several centuries later being the formation of two sects. Despite this dialectic, women's status did not decline significantly, thanks to the conservative nature of scripture (here the hymns of the Ā̱lvārs) and theology (conservative, that is, with reference to maintaining the status quo, not the theology itself, which was liberal).

If the many social changes of the 13th-14th centuries had caused one crisis for Śrīvaiṣṇava women, those of the 19th-20th centuries, a period of Western colonial domination, caused another. During this period, the British contributed to brahmanical conservatism by codifying personal/family law for all women on the basis of conservative brahmanical customs of *strīdharma.* What happened to Śrīvaiṣṇavism in such a milieu? Did it become more conservative? It is clear that at the end of the nineteenth century, Śrīvaiṣṇava leaders still viewed women as capable of liberation. The *Śrīvaiṣṇavadharmaratnākara* by Gopāladāsa, which was written around the end of the nineteenth century, says:

> *na jātibhedaṁ na kulaṁ na liṅgaṁ na guṇakriyāḥ|*
> *na deśakālau nāvasthāṁ yogo hyayamapekṣate||(18:4)*
>
> This yoga does not take into account distinctions of caste, family, sex, qualities, actions, time, place, and state (i.e. age).
>
> *brahmakaṣetraviśaḥ śūdrūḥ striyaṁścātarajāstathā|*
> *sarva eva prapadyeran sarvadhātāramacyutam||(18:5)*
>
> Brahmins, kṣatriyas, vaiśyas, śūdras, women and marginal figures all may seek refuge (*prapadyeran*) in the Imperishable One who is the supporter of all.

An increase of conservative brahmanical norms in Śrīvaiṣṇavism, even in the Teṉkalai sect, may be evident, however, in an early twentieth century text, the *Śrīvaiṣṇava Tīpikai (Dīpikā)* by A̱lakiyamaṇavāḷa-rāmānuja-ekānki-svāmikaḷ. The author seems to be a Teṉkalai, for a number of works by Piḷḷailokācārya, a key Ācārya for that sect, are mentioned. In order to understand this growth in conservatism and to analyze a full description of Śrīvaiṣṇava norms for women at this time, I shall first translate the portion of the text relevant to women (226–237) and then discuss it.

> Before sunrise a woman should rise from the bed, prostrate to her husband as well as to the Lord, and chant the *guruparamparā* and *dvayam mantra*. After attending the call of nature, she should brush her teeth, gargle, and purify the home by spreading cowdung mixed with water on the ground. Then, having washed all other places for the domestic tasks [such as the grinding stone], she should go to a tank, well, or pond for her bath.
>
> A married woman should have a sacred bath in the following manner. She should apply tumeric all over her body and sprinkle tumeric water on her head. If she had sex the previous night, if it is Friday, or if it is a special day such as a time to start a vow, a new moon, an eclipse, etc. she must also wash her hair and have an oil bath, not using soap or talcum powder. After her bath a woman is not to have contact with a dog, cat, cock, crow or a woman who has not performed *pañcasaṁskāra* (i.e. is not initiated as a Śrīvaiṣṇava). She is not to touch any potsherds,[42] nor any cloth that has not been washed and dried separately, nor any bones. Widows should bathe completely each day.
>
> Then she is to perform *ācamanam* (sipping of water) and chant [non-Vedic] mantras such as *keśavāya namaḥ; nārāyaṇāya namaḥ;* and *mādhavāya namaḥ*. Putting on her sari which has not been touched, she applies the Tiruman (an auspicious white clay mark between the eyebrows in a U shape and over that a *tilaka* which must be in a straight line, like a modified *ūrdhva puṇḍra*). Folding her palms together (*añjalimudrā*), she chants the *guruparamparā*, the *tirumantram*, *dvayam*, and *carama ślokas*, and the *ācārya taṉṉiyaṉ*.
>
> Afterwards, she drinks sacred water (*śrīpadatīrtha*) taken from the *tīrtha-vaṭi* and prostrates to the Lord (Bhagavān) and the devotees (bhāgavatas). She then cleans the vessels used for cooking with clay from under the tulasī plant and tamarind. She fetches the water for cooking, drinking and washing in separate vessels. She must cover everything in the kitchen with a lid, clean the rice, dal, vegetables etc., prepare them, and then cook

them while chanting Āṇṭāḷ's *Tiruppāvai* [and other hymns].

When the food is prepared, it is offered to God, husband and other devotees (Bhāgavatas). She then eats from what remains. After taking food, she may wear flowers, sandal paste, and chew betalnut (these, however, are denied to widows).

She is to share with men the qualities of a Bhāgavata. Bhāgavatas are those who have unquestionable knowledge, devotion, and freedom from all worldly desires, who follow the śāstras, who control their inner consciousness and outer sense organs, and who have qualities such as compassion, forbearance, and selflessness. They are free from desire for wealth and desire. They have the discriminative ability to distinguish command from prohibition. They have good faith in their Ācārya and have clarity because of having memorized the *Divyaprapandham* (the 4000 hymns of the Āḻvārs) and the *rahasyagranthas* (literally, the secret works, a classification of Śrīvaiṣṇava treatises). They have neither likes nor dislikes; they know no other god; they do not lie; they do not have jealousy, anger, or vengance. Free from such defects, they have knowledge of *Arthapañcakam, Rahasyatrayasāram, Tattvatrayam, Śrīvacanabhūṣaṇam,* etc. With control over their diet with reference to restraint of time, place, and ingredients, with friendliness and good social relationships, they who possess such qualities are Bhāgavatas, following the good people. They are not Bhāgavatas who have only a good appearance but no compassion in their heart, who are full of deceit, and who extract money from others.

In the evening a Śrīvaiṣṇava woman is to light the lamps in the *pūjā* room, hall, kitchen and other places such as the front courtyard. Then she is to prepare food according to procedure, offer it to God, serve her husband and others, and then take the remaining herself. Thinking of Hari, the Lord, she goes to bed.

During menstruation, the Śrīvaiṣṇava woman is to stay in the hidden place and on the fourth day at noon, she has her bath (*snāna*) including her "head bath" in the river, tank, well, etc. She is to prepare food for herself but is not to feed anyone else.

She is not to do the following things:

1. She is not to sleep to sunrise without attending to the call of nature, washing, and doing other domestic work.

2. After sunrise, she is not to clean the home and brush her teeth while standing or waste time by gossiping, especially in the morning; she must take a bath in the morning and not delay it.

3. She is not to place a *tilaka* (dot on the forehead), cook, nor offer food to God, nor serve food to the husband before taking a bath.

4. She is not to delay marking her forehead with the *ūrdhva puṇḍra* (Vaiṣṇava sectarian mark) after her bath.

5. She is not to have a bath and prepare the food etc. without having an *ūrdhva*.

6. After her bath she is to have not only the śrīcūrṇam (red line) but also the *tiruman* (which distinguishes a woman as a Śrīvaiṣṇava).

7. She is not to wear the same sari after her bath.

8. She is not to take a bath without tumeric powder.

9. After bathing, she is not to wash the sari that was worn during the bath.

10. If she happens to wash later, it is as if she enters the home without a bath.

11. The garment must be pure, i.e., untouched and if worn to receive guests, etc. who arrive suddenly before the bath, she must wear a pure sari after the bath.

12. She must not sleep during the daytime. If she happens to have a nap, then it is prohibited to prepare food, etc, unless she has a new bath.

13. If she sheds tears, attending any other work is prohibited without a bath.

14. She must not prepare food during the time of worship (*pūjā*) or pollute food being served by sneezing or talk loudly so that saliva may fall.

15. She is not to add lime made of shell (animal content) with betalnut.

16. She is not to use any imported hair oil.

17. She is not to use any foreign perfume.

18. She is not to use any imported cloth.

19. She is not to accept and wear *vibhūti* from other religious groups nor is she to tie any *rakṣā* beads as talisman [since they are associated with the god Śiva].

20. She is not to allow great anger, uncontrollable anger, jealously, back biting, self-praising or harsh words.

21. She is not to read any novel composed by the imagination, which disturbs the purity of her mind.

22. She is not to talk intimately with another man, laugh with him, move in front of him, move close to him, touch him, look at him or think of him.

23. She is to sit in front of her husband on a lower level and is not to stretch out her legs or lie there. She is not to walk noisily, talk loudly, talk against her husband, act against his desire or wish, or go to another man's place.

24. Widow should not wear ornaments and coloured saris (they must be white or brownish), chew betal leaf, decorate their hair, move with men, talk unnecessarily, and eat excessively.

25. The following defects are to be removed by both married women and widows: smoking, snuffing, chewing tobacco, taking modern medicines that are not Āyurvedic, drinking soda, coffee, and brandy. A woman is not to pass urine while standing up. And she is not to give up the Vaiṣṇava tradition and chastity toward God.

This section of the *Śrīvaiṣṇava Tīpikai* is similar in some respects to other codes of brahmanical conduct for women such as the *Strīdharmapaddhati* of

Tryambakayajvan, a Maharastrian who migrated to Tamil Nadu and ruled over Tanjavur in the 17th century, a time of Muslim domination in many parts of India (Leslie 1989). Just as Tryambakayajvan prescribes proper behaviour for different times of the day—before dawn, at dawn, during the day and evening—so does the author of the *Śrīvaiṣṇava Tīpikai*. The former, however, represents an orthodox brahmanical tradition based on the daily household *yajñas*, especially the *saṁdhyā*, going back to the traditions of the *gṛhyasūtras*, whereas our text represents a sectarian bhakti tradition. Despite these differences, it is obvious the Śrīvaiṣṇava daily household routine is based directly on the orthodox brahmanical one: in both the wife should rise before her husband, prostrate to him, meditate on a chosen deity (*devatādhyanam*), perform *ācamanam* (ritualistically sipping water), answer the call of nature, brush the teeth, gargle, bathe, prostrate to respected individuals, offer food to them, eat from what remains, etc. but the discussions, at least in the *Strīdharmapaddhati*, are much more elaborate than in the Śrīvaiṣṇava text. Despite the similarities there are also differences, mostly of a sectarian kind. Accordingly, the Śrīvaiṣṇava woman should prostrate to God and Bhāgavatas, meditate on Viṣṇu as her chosen deity, and (not just her husband), put on the sectarian emblem, the *tiruman*, (inclusive of the red tilaka rather than the common tilaka, a dot, which symbolizes an auspicious marital state).

In such texts there seem to be some aspects of behaviour that are emphasized or reserved for women. An example of the former is the emphasis on purity. Traditional brahmanical life, as is well known, is structured on the polarity of pure (*śauca*) and impure (*aśauca*). *Snāna*, the sacred bath done daily and on special occasions, is an expression of such purity; its non-performance, an expression of impurity. But in this code of behaviour, purity for women and the reasons for bathing also seem to be a patriarchal way to control women. It is important to note, first of all, that bathing in the past was generally a public phenomenon; it was done in the river, temple tank, or sea. Because it was traditionally done at sunrise, a bath at any other time of day attracted attention. Thus, not only was it a great inconvenience if a woman had to bathe because she took a nap or cried, but also it may have shamed her publicly, for the disturbance of a routine made others take notice. Then too other patriarchal indicators borrowed from the conservative brahmanical tradition are apparent in this text such as eating food only after the husband and others have been served,[43] sitting lower than the husband, obeying him, fulfilling his desires, and being restricted to housework in the private sphere. Our author is also conservative regarding widows. If death is auspicious in Śrīvaiṣṇavism, then it is curious that the brahmanical norms for widows are being prescribed: they are not to wear flowers or sandal paste, they are not to wear coloured saris, they are not to eat betalnut, and they are to eat a minimum amount of food.

Given all the restrictions to protect women against foreign influence such as not using foreign hair oil, perfume, cloth, soda, coffee, and brandy, it is possible that once again the increasing conservatism was a reaction to British domination. It is also possible that men were changing through Western contact and wanted their women to remain traditional or the women themselves wanted to maintain a conservatism in the face of change. This may have caused even Śrīvaiṣṇava Teṉkalai brahmins to resemble other conservative brahmin communities despite the pro-woman theology of their past. Indeed, Rangachari observed in the early 20th century that the Śrīvaiṣṇava brahmins are an exclusive group with certain sectarian customs but in general following the same rituals as other brahmins (Rangachari 1931, 1).

Despite insistence on many conservative brahmanical customs, it is striking, nevertheless, that according to this text, women are to share the Śrīvaiṣṇava realm of sectarian learning along with men. They are to know the *guruparamparā* (the lineage of teachers), various mantras, the ācārya taṉiyaṉ, the four thousand hymns of the Āḻvārs, including Āṇṭāḷ's *Tiruppāvai*, various philosophical/theological works of the Ācāryas such as Piḷḷailokācārya's *Arthapañcakam*, *Rahasyatrayasāram*, *Tattvatrayam*, and *Śrīvacanabhūṣaṇam*. Moreover, like men they are to maintain their sectarian identities through the wearing of the sectarian emblem, the *ūrdhvapuṇḍra* and by avoiding Śaiva influence. And like Śrīvaiṣṇava men, women are to cultivate various qualities such as knowledge, devotion, indifference to worldly objects, control, compassion, forbearance, and being without ego, wealth, and desire.

Similarly, a positive appreciation of women is captured in the late text *Śrī-śaṇḍilya-viśiṣṭa-parama-dharma-śāstra*, which has been influential in modern Śrīvaiṣṇava circles.[44]

putrānbhṛtyānkalatraṁ ca bhaktamāśritameva ca|
nitya kuryādupāyena bhagavadbhaktibhāvitān|| 163

He should always endeavor by various means to make sons, servants, wife, the one devoted to him, and the one dependent on him [alternatively, the wife who is devoted to him and dependent on him] devoted to God.

aputrā vā saputrā vā bhaktā dakṣā ca karmasu|
yā strī tām varjayedbhartā na kadācidapi priyām||164

A woman who is devoted to God and skilled in karma (rituals) [alternatively, who is devoted to her husband and skilled in domestic duties], whether she is without a son or with a son, that dear woman a husband should never abandon.

putrārthaṁ nodvahedanyāṁ karmaputrā hi yoginaḥ|
aputropi paraṁ yāti karmī nānyo'pi satsutaḥ||165

For the sake of a son he many not marry another woman. For the yogīs have karma as their son. A person who performs karma though without a son reaches the Supreme and another [who is not a karmī does not], even though having an excellent son.

na strījito bhavedbhartā na cāśakyeṣu yojayet|
guṇānna kathayetstrīṇāmasaktassaktavadvaset||166

A husband should not be hen-pecked by a woman (literally conquered by a woman: *strī-jitaḥ*) nor should he make her do impossible tasks [i.e. beyond her energy or strength]; he should not extol the virtues of [other] women; he should live as if attached but be detached.

nirbhayāssuhṛdo loke yathā syussarvajantavaḥ|
snigdhaṁ jitaṁ yathā ca'syātsvakudumvaṁ tathācaret||167

He should act in such a manner that his own family feels deeply affectionate to him and won over and in such a manner that all beings in the world may be fearless and friendly.

yathaśāstramupādānagācaredbhoganisspṛhaḥ|
bhāgavaddharmalabhena tṛpto yassa sukhī bhavet||168

Unattached to enjoyment, he should perform *upādāna* (withdrawing the sense organs from the external world) in accor-

> dance with the śāstras. Satisfied with the acquisition of dharma for the Lord (*bhāgavat-dharma-labhena*), he indeed becomes happy.

These verses show that marriage and family life are to be situated within the larger framework of devotion to God. A husband's responsibility is to turn his whole household toward the supreme Lord (rather than to demand or assume that a woman must treat her husband as god according to the conservative brahmanical code of *strīdharma*). The orientation of such a husband is to be focused on religion as the goal of a householder, not on *artha* (wealth) and *kāma* (desire), as dictated by the concept of *gṛhastha* according to the traditional definition of *varṇāśramadharma*.

Moreover, the worth of a woman is to be recognized by her religious behaviour, not by her fertility as was common in orthodox brahmanical circles at the time. If the prevailing normative texts for women declare that her *raison d'etre* is to bear sons, because a son is viewed as necessary for the performance of her husband's death rituals (*śrāddha*) and passage to heaven, here, by contrast, the *raison d'etre* of a woman is to be devoted to God (though this does not exclude having children). If she does not bear a son, the text declares, she cannot be abandoned (authors of the Dharmaśāstras had declared that there was no divorce, though a man was allowed to abandon his wife or take another wife in cases of infertility or bearing only daughters (Kane 2:552; 620). Such a prescription rescues a woman's status from reduction to nature and elevates it not only to culture but also to the supreme spiritual goal.

The text also warns the husband to appreciate his wife's intrinsic worth by not comparing her to other women (thereby causing insecurity and jealousy as a means of wielding male power). It notes that just as yogīs attain salvation without sons because they perform karma (actions that characterize the life of a yogī; alternatively the maintenance of ritual actions),[45] so does a husband because he does his karma (i.e. dharma or duty as a husband or ritual actions). The author then describes the ideal complementarity between husband and wife, which avoids the extremes of conquering the other or demanding the impossible. In other words, he advocates a balance between the extremes of female and male power. Like the one of *sthitaprajña* (steady insight) of *Bhagavadgītā* 2:55–72, a husband should live as if attached but be ever above attachment. Such detachment is, however, not ordinary indifference, for one fulfils one's dharma only when there is spontaneous and deep affection by all members of the household. Herein lies the challenge: to give and receive the greatest love, to direct everyone and everything to God, and to be content, firm in judgment, and wise. In this way a man comes to be honoured not qua maleness nor power but by worthiness as judged by wife and God!

Conclusion

Despite many changes, Tamil Śrīvaiṣṇavism must be remembered when the topic is traditional Indian women. For its theology concurs with a "liberation theology." From today's perspective of women's liberation, it may have been in need of greater implementation, given the invisibility of women in the inscriptions at Śrīraṅgam (likely indicative of other temples and the tradition at large), or as Ācāryas and priests. And its language of service, while fully in the religious idiom, may have been experienced more negatively by women than men, the rhetoric of the naturalness and superiority of women's service not withstanding. Again, this comment may be anachronistic and ethnocentric, for it comes from a society in which women have come to question the feminine ideal of service to others especially if it is thought to define their essential nature or confine them to the private sphere. Be that as it may, it is only fair to say that Śrīvaiṣṇavism integrated a domestic and spiritual life for women, and this was a major accomplishment in brahmanical circles. With today's new mood, this time on the part of women themselves for greater freedom from the restriction of patriarchal and brahmanical norms, it will be interesting to see if Śrīvaiṣṇava women, especially Teṉkalai women, return to their own liberal theological heritage and rediscover it as a springboard to a true universal theology sensitive to the concerns of contemporary women but also to the rich heritage of the past.

NOTES

[1] I would like to thank Dr. K.K.A. Venkatachari, Director, Akshardham, Gandhinagar, Gujarat, India, for help in locating the relevant passages and the many helpful discussions that made this article possible. I would also like to thank Dr. Leslie Orr of Concordia University for providing her forthcoming articles on the Chola inscriptions and for critically reading several versions of the manuscript. Finally, I would like to thank S. Khan for her special effort on

the computer that made it possible to meet my deadlines. This article is an extention and substantial rewriting of my 1983 article entitled "Śrīvaiṣṇava Feminism: Intent or Effect?," published in *Studies in Religion* (*Sciences Relijeuses*, vol. 23, no. 1:61-68).

[2]I am using the terms conservative and liberal in this article not with any specific modern political connotations but in the more general sense of "tending to favor the preservation of the existing order and to regard proposals for change with distrust...traditional in manner" and "having, expressing, or following social or political views or policies that favor non-revolutionary progress and reform" respectively (Morris, ed. 1970).

[3]Orr 1994a.

[4]See smṛtis such as Yājñavalkya, Nārada, Kātyāyana; the didactic portions of the epics (*Mahābhārata*, śānti and anuśāsana parvas), and *Viṣṇu, Mārkaṇḍeya*, and *Bhaviśya Purāṇas*. Passages in such texts declare that śūdras are not to be slaves, they are to be paid improved and regular wages with reduced taxes, they can bear arms, they may perform *saṁskāras*, and they may be reborn as a brahmin through good conduct.

[5]A historical presentation of the development of doctrine would take into consideration the references in the works of Yāmuna, Rāmānuja, Piḷḷa<u>n</u>, Kureśa, Parāśarabhaṭṭar, etc. See Narayanan (1987)., Carman (1974), Carman and Narayanan (1989), Nayar (1992), and Mumme (1988).

[6]See Katherine K. Young and Leslie Orr (1988), "The Symbol of the Bard (*pāṇa<u>n</u>*) in Tamil Hagiographies" for a discussion of the fact that there is no internal reference to the *pāṇa<u>n</u>* in the stanzas by Tiruppā<u>n</u> Ā<u>l</u>vār and the history of this identification.

[7]Because Nammā<u>l</u>vār, a śūdra, was considered foremost among the Ā<u>l</u>vārs for his philosophically refined devotion and Āṇṭāḷ, a woman, was the esteemed example of a lover in the lover-Beloved relationship (see the ensuing discussion), the theology had to uphold their spiritual eminence. In my discussion of *Bhagavadgītā* 9:32 (Young 1986) I argue how Rāmānuja struggled to promote a theology of universal salvation at the same time that he sought to maintain brahmanical orthodoxy and hegemony by insisting on performance of prescribed duties. In the later hagiographic literature, the Ā<u>l</u>vārs were considered divine, and Āṇṭāḷ was viewed as a goddess; thus, they symbolized the concept of universal salvation.

[8]The initiation into Vaiṣṇavism is called the *pañcasaṁskāra* ceremony or five rites, because it consists of *tāpa; puṇḍra; nāma; mantras*; and *yajana* (that is, branding, wearing sectarians marks; taking a new name; chanting the *mūla* (*tirumantra*) and *dvaya* mantras; and worshipping God respectively).

[9]Mumme notes, however, that today "though Pañcasaṁskāra is mandatory for Śrīvaiṣṇava Brahmins and Cāttatas, very few members of any non-Brahmin Vaiṣṇava

caste (perhaps one or two per extended family) seek out an ācārya or jīyar and undergo the initiation ritual which formally affiliates them with the Śrīvaiṣṇava sect. The strict ritual and dietary rules to be observed after Pañcasaṁskāra are a deterrent" (1993, 124).

[10]Vedāntadeśika in his *Rahasyatrayasāra* (chapter 11) also made the point that Rāmānuja's disciples were saved because of their connection to him.

[11]For a history of the development of these doctrines see Narayanan 1987.

[12]The incident of Draupadī is often used by the Ācāryas to suggest that *prapatti* can be performed at any time and any place, but today this is not the case because the Ācāryas refuse to perform the ritual during the three days of menstrual impurity. This information was provided by Dr. K.K.A. Venkatachari, Director, Akshardham, Gandhinagar, Gujarat.

[13]Rāmānuja establishes this point in his commentary on *Bhagavadgītā* 4:11: "*...kimatra bahuna, sarve manuṣyāḥ madanuvartanaikamanorathā mama vartma matsvabhāvaṁ sarvam yogināṁ vāṅmanasāgocarampai svakīyaiścakṣurādi-karaṇais-sarvaśassvāpekṣitais-sarvaprakārairanubhūyānuvartane*" (See Narasimhacarya ed., 1910–1911, 279–80).

[14]Vaṭakalais, following Vedāntadeśika, admit, however, that it may be delayed if one commits many sins, if a twice-born man does not observe the duties of caste and stage of life, or if one does not follow the practices of a Śrīvaiṣṇava.

[15]See *Parantapaṭi* in *Aṣṭadasarahasyam* of Piḷḷailokācārya 1911, 52.

[16]As mentioned previously, a person will still continue to perform *varṇāśrama-dharma* out of the enjoyment of the rules of the game of life.

[17]Mumme (1993, 129) points out that today when non-brahmin Bhāgavatas were asked to explain why most of them were Teṉkalai, they observed that Vaṭakalai Ācāryas, when giving the *tirumantra* during the *pañcasaṁskāra* ritual, do not give the mantra AUM to women or non-*dvijas*.

[18]Mumme (1993, 128) notes, however, that today Śrīvaiṣṇavas despite the rhetoric of liberal prostration, rarely do a full prostration except when there is equal status or before the Ācārya or Jīyar: "It is highly unlikely that a Brahmin would ever fully prostrate to a non-Brahmin...I found no consistent difference between Vaṭakalai and Teṉkalai regarding who prostrates to whom."

[19]Because Viṣṇu is male, there is a theological constraint; everyone must "be married to" a male god. That the antecedent Tamil *akam* poems, depicting the love relationship between the hero and heroine, often utilized the persona of the woman-in-love encourages this identification of the devotee as a woman.

[20]Though the male Āḻvārs *assume* the stance of a woman-in-love, it appears that they so identify with the role that the emotions invoked are actually experienced. The devotee becomes, as it were, the Beloved: various aspects of love on the

human level, in all their concreteness and power, become directed to God. Thus, feminine psychology must be explored and appreciated on the mundane level to become the *modus vivendi* for the encounter with the divine. Although it is certainly true that the relationship of lover and Beloved is a poetic convention taken from the caṅkam poetry, it also seems that the genre inspires and, in turn, is infused with the Āḻvārs' own spirituality and psychology.

[21] *Kuḷal* is a game dated to caṅkam times that is played by young girls. They make a wish and then, with eyes closed, try to draw a circle on the ground. If they succeed so that the lines "join up," they think that their wish will come true.

[22] *Kaḷavu*, however, is secret and *kaṟpu* is public. Once there is a secret relationship involving the meeting of hearts, marriage is implied according to the code of honour.

[23] Though this may reflect a social shift toward arranged marriage, it is more likely that arranged marriage was practiced increasingly by Tamil brahmins and by some Tamil non-brahmin elite from the caṅkam period.

[24] This was suggested to me by Dr. K.K.A. Venkatacari.

[25] The following is paraphrased from Damodaran 1976, 61–63.

[26] In a similar way role-playing and encounter groups are techniques developed by modern psychotherapy to develop awareness of an alternative psychology.

[27] *puruṣaṉ puruṣaṉnaikkaṇṭu snehippatiluṅkāṭṭil strī puruṣaṉaikkaṇṭu snehikkai paḷḷamaṭai yākaiyāle...*

[28] See also *Ācāryahṛdayam* where the Ācāryas are said to be like Sītā. Just as Sītā exists only for the Lord and serves as the intermediary between God and his devotees, so do the Ācāryas (Damodaran 1976, 76).

[29] The argument from silence need not cast a serious doubt regarding lack of intention in Hinduism. The cultural agenda of promoting tolerance—given the potentially divisive plurality based on different races, languages, and religions—created an ethic based on an etiquette of not speaking negatively of another group not to mention directly harming it. When one looks at the numerous religious texts produced in ancient and classical India and when one understands that there was real and serious religious rivalry, one is struck by how few negative remarks are, in fact, made about other religions. Rather, silence may be viewed not as the absence of rivalry but rather as a function of the ethos of tolerance. There are exceptions, of course, as in the case of Tirumaṅkaiyāḻvār and Maṇikkavācakar who overtly criticized Jains and Buddhists.

[30] *Mahābhārata*, 24 aśvamedha parva 14; variant reading of the critical edition, app. 4, 3373.

[31] See Katherine K. Young, "The Pāvai Poems: A Study of Gender and Hinduism" [forthcoming].

[32]According to Orr, they may also be identified with a place or temple, sometimes being provided with support from the temple or assigned particular functions in the temple.

[33]It is possible that Āṇṭāḷ, who rejected human marriage, is a case in point (Young 1986)

[34]This tentative dating was provided by Dr. K.K.A. Venkatachari in a personal communication in 1983. When it was published in the early 20th century, the editors noted that they collated the manuscripts.

[35]In the manuscript of this text, the first 13, the 15th, and the 16th leaves are missing. The colophon of the work says that it is written in the Āṅkirasa year in the month of Mārkaḻi. It is an explanatory commentary (*vivaraṇa-caṭaka*) of the first stanza and is a garland of words offered to the feet of the Lord of Kumpakoṉam temple by Koṉeridāsyai who does service (*aṭimai*) to him. The text has been edited by Navalpakam Sri Devanathachariar and published by S. Gopalan. This information was furnished by Dr. K.K.A. Venkatachari.

[36]Although the extant Āḻvār poetry has been dated from the 7th century and the Nāyaṉmār from the 5th or 6th, these dates are tentative. I suggest that the development of the Āḻvār poetry likely occurred over several centuries before it assumed the conventionalized format that we find with the extent bhakti poems. The earlier date for the period as suggested here not only posits enough time to account for this development, it also allows for contributions to the emergent mythos and temple worship from regions to the north of Tamil Nadu, which can be traced from the fourth century C.E.

[37]Because of a different social structure in Tamil Nadu that did not fit the Sanskritic depiction of the four castes (*varṇa*) and because the bhakti traditions emphasized the *family* of devotees to avoid caste discrimination, the term non-brahmin came to represent everyone who was not a brahmin, though the term śūdra was used on occasion for ideological reasons.

[38]There is some evidence that images of the Āḻvārs and Ācāryas had been incorporated into the architecture of the temple. For instance, Bhattar, "salutes the icons of a variety of divine beings, Āḻvārs, and Ācāryas in the shrines surrounding, for instance, the Inner Sanctum of the Śrīraṅgam Temple" (Nayar 1992, 96). Also there is an inscription from 1191 C.E. in the Varadarajaswami temple at Kañci that refers to Rāmānuja's image (inscription 641) and an inscription from 1256 C.E. in the Melkote that refers to donation to maintain a shrine for Rāmānuja identified as *bhāṣyakāra sannidhi* (inscription no. 23) (Nayar 1992, 103 quoting Raman and Gopal).

[39]These include singing and dancing; participating in festival processions; lighting, placing or removing auspicious lamps; preparing *pavitras* (purifying threads); and preparing of ritual ingredients such as tumeric.

[40]Hardy 1983, 243 argues that most of the hagiographies such as the *Guruparamparāprabhāvam 6000* are based on the *Divyasūricaritam*. This point was originally argued by T.A. Gopinatha Rao in his *History of Sri Vaisnavas* (see B.V. Ramanujam 1973, 14 note 4); he noted that the author must have been a contemporary of Rāmānuja's for the text does not mention Rāmānuja's life. Ramanujam (1973, 13–118) examines the whole problem of the chronology of the hagiographies, concluding that the author of the *Divyasūricaritam* was not a contemporary of Rāmānuja's. Observing that the author describes a *paramparā* and adds his name at the end, suggests to Ramanujam, and with good reason, that the author is later in time and is attempting to legitimate a lineage by connecting it to Rāmānuja while he is still living (27). If *Divyasūricaritam* is indeed later, this does not rule out the possibility that it was earlier than the *Guruparamparāprabhāvam 6000* or that both of these texts had a common source. As noted previously, the interest in explicit hierarchy and lineage seems from the inscriptional evidence to be a product of the late medieval period, that is, after the 13th century.

In the *Guruparamparāprabhāvam 6000* by Pi<u>n</u>palakiyaperumāḷjīyar, there is a quote from the *Ācāryahṛdayam* of A<u>l</u>akiyamaṇavālap-perumāḷnāya<u>n</u>ār (13th century), one from the *Saṅkalpasūryodayam* of Vedāntadeśika (14th century), and one from *Lakṣmī Kavya* (15th century). Ramanujam dismisses these as interpolations, but given other evidence that suggests a date after Vedāntadeśika's time, these references may be an important clue for the dating of the *Guruparamparāprabhāvam 6000* (see Ramanujam 1973, 49-50). The *Periyatirumuṭi-aṭaivu*, which is assigned to the 15th century, mentions the *Guruparamparāprabhāvam* of Pi<u>n</u>palakiyaperumāḷjīyar. From the information presented here it is conceivable that the *Guruparamparāprabhāvam* is also a work of the 15th century. It may have drawn from other no longer extant works on the lives of the Ā<u>l</u>vārs and Ācāryas but discussed them in terms of the theology of the 15th century. For example, it was A<u>l</u>akiyamaṇavālap-perumāḷnāya<u>n</u>ār and Maṇavālamāmuni who elaborated on the idea of *ācāryābhimāna;* the author of the *Guruparamparāprabhāvam* refers to this and to the Ā<u>l</u>vārs and Ācāryas as divine beings. This evidence also tends toward a 15th century date for the *Guruparamparāprabhāvam* in my estimation. (For further discussion of the development of the concept of Acarya, see Nayar 1992, 92-1000.

[41]There is evidence from another source to support this line of reasoning that *maṭas* are being legitimated through association with Rāmānuja: the inscriptions. According to Orr (1995a and personal communication), no references to jīyars are not found in inscriptions at the time of Rāmānuja. From 1225 to 1325 there are references to jīyars, but there are no references to jīyars as heads of groups of ascetics, nor are their names suggestive of pontifical status (instead, they contain the term *dāsa,* i.e., servant/slave), nor are there referenc-

es to jīyars as connected to *maṭas* at Śrīraṅgam. Rather, the term *maṭa* seems to refer to a feeding house. In fact, of the other four references to *maṭas*, notes Orr, three refer to feeding Śrīvaiṣṇavas and one to a *maṭa* connected with the *paṭṭar* (*bhaṭṭar*). Orr points out that there are four inscriptions referring to ascetics at Śrīraṅgam; they use the terms *aṭikaḷ* or *saṁnyāsī*, not *jīyar*. There is one inscription from the late 13th or early 14th century, she observes, that links *tridaṇḍi-saṁnyāsīs* to a *maṭa* named after a Pandya king, though there is no reference to jīyar. In fact, in one instance when the term jīyar is used, it refers to a priest. She observes that there are several 15th century inscriptions that refer to the Śrīraṅga-nārāyaṇa-jīyar. She further notes that it is only in the 16th century that references to jīyars become common in the inscriptions and are directly associated with *maṭas* (which continue to be feeding houses, now feeding the disciples of the jīyars). In light of this inscriptional evidence, it is curious that according to the *Koyil Oluku* and the lineage (*paramparā*) of the Śrīraṅga-nārāyaṇa-jīyar that the *maṭa* of this lineage was established in 1126 C.E. with Kura Nārāyaṇa Jīyar as its first pontiff (Orr following Jagadeesan 1977, 164-65). The traditional date of Rāmānuja's death is 1137 and a scholarly date is 1157 (Carman 1974, 27).

The preceding inscriptional evidence strongly suggests that because the first references to the Śrīraṅga-nārāyaṇa-jīyar occurred in the 15th century and the association of jīyars and *maṭas* became common only in the 16th century that the attribution of the establishment of the lineage to the 12th century and during the lifetime of Rāmānuja is an anachronism, likely to give status to the lineage by its implied association with Rāmānuja who is considered an ascetic. Orr notes that, according to the tradition of the Yatirāja Maṭha at Melkote, this *maṭha* was founded by Rāmānuja at about the same time.

This discussion raises the question of whether Rāmānuja himself was an ascetic. It is striking that there is no reference internal to Rāmānuja's own works to substantiate this claim, and he himself emphasizes the maintenance of *varṇāśramadharma* (the duties of caste and stage of life) in *Bhagavadgītā* 18:66. Moreover, to my knowledge there are no such references internal to the works of his immediate disciples such as Kureśa, Bhaṭṭar, and Piḷḷan, though they refer to Rāmānuja on many occasions. The first reference internal to the Śrīvaiṣṇva Ācāryas occurs in a work by Vedāntadeśika. Another work referring to the life of Rāmānuja is *Iramanuca-nuṟṟantāti* attributed to Tiruvarankattu Amutanar and commented on by Maṇavālamāmuni (but not mentioned by Vedāntadeśika). Because in v. 43 it alludes to *Ācāryabhimāna*—uttering the name of Rāmānuja will remove the Kali (yuga)—and the text also says that Rāmānuja will defeat the six false religions (v. 49), it is possible that it is late, but in this case it should be remembered that the verse is similar to that of one of Rāmānuja's immediate disciples, Bhaṭṭar, who speaks of the sage Rāmānuja driving way the demon in the form of Kali Yuga (in this case, however, it is by bhakti, not by intellect)

(*Śrīraṅgarāja stava* 1:3) (Nayar 1992, 99). This work, however, does not focus on Rāmānuja as an ascetic. In any case it was written before the 15th century, because of Maṇavālamāmuni's commentary.

Vedāntadeśika in his *Yatirājasaptati*, eulogizes Rāmānuja and refers to him by a number of names suggestive of his renunciation (Narayanan 1990, 170). Now, in light of the other evidence, should we assume that Vedāntadeśika thinks that Rāmānuja really was an ascetic, a *yati*? Or is there another possible explanation for Vedāntadeśika's calling him such? It is possible, given Vedāntadeśika's poetic imagination, that he is using the term *yati* as a play on words. As Narayanan (1990) points out, the name Rāmānuja literally means "the younger brother of Lord Rāma," thus Lakṣmaṇa. Narayanan suggests that because Lakṣmaṇa gave up his own family life to follow Rāma, so Rāmānuja gives up his family life as well, i.e. he became an ascetic. But another interpretation is possible. Lakṣmaṇa is famous for serving Rāma. In the same way Rāmānuja (like his namesake) is famous for renouncing worldly life (but not necessarily his family) and serving the Lord. It may be that Vedāntadeśika, a master at innuendo, plays on the word renouncer (*yati*) and gives it a new twist to fit the life of Rāmānuja. And perhaps it was after this literary work, that a later ascetic of the 15th century interpreted the references to Rāmānuja as *yati* literally in the sense of *saṁnyāsī*, for he saw an opportunity to link the new *maṭas* of jīyars to Rāmānuja as their spiritual head and founder, by viewing him as an ascetic.

I have found a similar scenario in Śaiva Siddhānta. There are no internal references to Maṇikkavācakar as an ascetic in his *Tiruvācakam*, though he was initiated by a guru (whom I identify not as a human guru but as Śiva Dakṣinamūrti at Peruntuṟai). I argue that it was in the 14th and 15th centuries that an Ācārya of Śaiva Siddhānta wanted to connect the ascetic tradition with a Nāyaṉmār and looked to Maṇikkavācakar and his surrender to the "guru," now understood as a human guru, to do this (Young 1993).

According to the *Yatīndrapravāṇa Prabhavam*, Maṇavāḷamāmuni himself became a jīyar (after he had married and had a son) and took over Rāmānuja's old *maṭa*. The text also describes how he and his followers were competing with Vedānta Deśika's supporters for temple control throughout South India; Mumme comments that "this is surely an anachronism" (1988, 19) and more reflective of the 17th-18th century when this hagiography and the Vaṭakalai account were written. Nonetheless, it is possible that Maṇavāḷamāmuni, who was born at Nammāḻvār's birthplace, educated in the vicinity, and no doubt most likely a strong supporter of the Āḻvār tradition could have been instrumental in trying to maintain a liberal tradition at Śrīraṅgam, especially when instituting temple reforms. This could have contributed to subsequent strife between different factions, a strife projected into the hagiographical stories about Rāmānuja.

Besides the *Guruparamparāprabhāvam 6000*, one finds reference to Rāmānuja as a *yati* (ascetic) in the *Yatirājavaibhavam* by Āndhrapūrṇa. This is also a hagiographical account, subject to the same possibility of a late date, or a least one some time after the life of Rāmānuja. From his name, this author was from Andhra. According to a story told in the *Guruparamparāprabhāvam 6000*, Rāmānuja wanted him to worship a festival image being taken in procession, and he refused (Narayanan 1987, note 5, 223). This is indeed curious in light of the Śrīvaiṣṇava tradition of image worship. The story possibly hints at some conflict between the author who may have an interest in asceticism (demonstrated by the title of his story of Rāmānuja's life and his disinterest in image worship) and the Tamil Śrīvaiṣṇava temple community. It is not impossible that he was an ascetic (originally of Advaitin leanings?) during the Vijayanagara period, who was originally from Andhra, but had joined a new *maṭa* in Tamil Nadu, and then composed this story (perhaps drawing on other traditional accounts that had preserved memories of Rāmānuja) to associate Rāmānuja with asceticism as a way to legitimate the latter. Be that as it may, the other reference to Āndhrapūrṇa besides in the *Yatirājavaibhavam*, is in the *Guruparamparāprabhāvam*, itself where he is called a disciple of Yāmuna.

In short, there is certainly no clear internal references in Rāmānuja's own works that he was an ascetic, nor are there any such references in the works of his disciples. The dates of the hagiographies are subject to debate, many of them definitely late. The inscriptional evidence points to the fact that the *maṭas* became popular only in the 15th and 16th century, and there was an institutionalization of Śrīvaiṣṇava asceticism only at that time. This whole subject needs careful investigation. In the meantime the *Guruparamparāprabhāvam 6000* and other texts cannot be accepted uncritically for their chronology.

[42]After a clay pot is used, it is polluted and so is broken. To touch any of these sherds transmits the pollution of the pot.

[43]Eating after men is a common rule in many horticultural societies and early states that are concerned to buttress gender hierarchy. See Sagan 1985, 91.

[44]This information was provided by Dr. K.K.A. Venkatachari.

[45]The *Yatidharmasamuccaya*, a Śrīvaiṣṇava manual for ascetics, gives many rules to govern the life of an ascetic; it also states, that an ascetic should do occasional rituals and penances if he has broken the rules (Olivelle 1995).

BIBLIOGRAPHY

Primary Sources

Aḻakiya Maṇavāḷa Rāmānuja Ekāṇki Svāmikaḷ, 1968, *Śrīvaiṣṇava Tīpikai*, 2 Parts, Madras: K. Nārāyaṇa Reṭṭiyār.

Āṇṭāḷ, 1923, *Nācciyār Tirumoḻi* with commentary of Periyavāccāṉ Piḷḷai, Madras: Śrī Vaiṣṇavakranta Mutrāpaka Sapaiyārāl.

Āṇṭāḷ, [n.d.], *Tiruppāvai* with commentary by Periyavāccāṉ Piḷḷai, ed. by Ce. Krsnamacarya, Madras: Commercial Press.

Ārāyirappaṭi Guruparamparāprapāvam of Pinpaḷakiyaperumāḷjīyar,.1975, (reprint), ed. by S. Kṛṣṇasvāmī Ayyakar, Tirucci.

Caturvedi, Shivasahayaji, 1926, *Satidāha*, Hindi translation of the Bengali, Allahabad: Chand Karyalaya.

Jīyar, Śrīraṅganārāyaṇa and Ayodhyā Rāmānujajīyar, 1911, *Aṣṭādasararahasyam of Piḷḷailokācārya*, Madras: Ānanta Press.

Monier-Williams, Sir Monier, [1899] 1970, *A Sanskrit–English Dictionary*, Oxford: Clarendon Press.

Mumukṣuppaṭi by Piḷḷailokācārya, 1970, ed. by Śrī Kṛṣṇasvāmi Ayyaṇkār, Tiruccirāppaḷḷi.

Nālāyira Tivviyap Pirapantam, 1981, Cennai: Tiruvenkaṭattāṉ Tirumaṉṟam.

Olivelle, P., 1976–77, *Vāsudevāśama Yatidharmaprakāśa: A Treatise on World Renunciation*, 2 parts, Vienna.

Piḷḷailokamijīyar, *Śrīvaiṣṇava Samayācāra Niṣkarṣa*, Details unavailable.

Śrīmadbhagavadgītā, 1910–1911, Sanskrit text, with commentaries by Rāmānuja, Vedānta Deśika, Śaṅkara, Ānanda Tīrtha, Jayatīrtha, 3 volumes, ed. by A.V. Narasiṁhācārya, Madras: Ānandāśrama Press.

Śrī Parāśara Viśiṣṭa Paramadharma Śāstra, 1929, with Hindi Commentary, Kāñcī: Śrīprativādibhayaṅkara Matha.

Śrīśaṇdilya-viśiṣṭa-parama-dharma-śāstra, 1930, with Hindi commentary, Śrī Prativādibhayaṅkara Matha.

Śrīvacanapūṣaṇam by Śrī Piḷḷailokācārya, 1936, with Maṇavḷamāmuni's commentary, ed. by P. Raghava Ramanuja Swami, Madras: R. Rajagopala Naidu, Celvarangan Press.

Śrīvaiṣṇavadharmaratnākara by Gopāladāsa, 1972, (Bhāṣāṭīkā), ed. by Gaṅgaviṣṇu Śrīkṛṣṇadāsa, Kāñcī: Śrī Prativādibhayaṅkara.

Stotramālā, 1969, Kāncipuram: Granthamālākāryālayaḥ.

Sukthankar, V.S. and S.K. Velvalkar, eds., 1961, *The Mahābhārata*, vols. 6 & 13, Poona: Bhandarkar Oriental Research Institute.

Tamil Lexicon (University of Madras: MTL), 1982, (reprint), 6 vols., Madras: University of Madras.

Tirukkoneṟitāyai, *Tiruvāymoḻi Vācakamālai* (*Vivaraṇa caṭakam*), ed. & Notes by Navalpakam Sri Devanathachariar, Devakottai: Published by S. Gopalan.

Vedāntadeśika, 1940, "Śaraṇagatidīpikā." In *Stotrāvalīvibhāgaḥ*, ed. by Aṇṇaṇgarācārya, Kāñci.

Venkatachari, K.K.A. ed., 1978, *Divyasūri Caritam*, Bombay: Ananthacharya Indological Research Institute.

Viucittar, 1969, (reprint), *Periyāḻvār Tirumoḻi Vyākkiyāṉam*, (Tamil Script), ed. by P.B. Aṇṇaṇgarācharya, Kancheepuram.

Secondary Sources

Altekar, A.S., 1962, *The Position of Women in Hindu Civilization*, Delhi: Motilal Banarsidass.

Altekar, A.S., 1965, *Education in Ancient India*, Varanasi: Nand Kishore & Bros.

Arunachalam, M., 1978, "The Sati Cult in Tamil Nadu," in *Bulletin of the Institute of Traditional Cultures*, Madras.

Ate, Lynn Marie, 1988, *Periyāḻvār's "Tirumoḻi"—A Bāla Kṛṣṇa Text from the Devotional Period in Tamil Literature*, UMI Dissertation Information Service.

Balasubramanian, C., 1976, *The Status of Women in Tamilnadu During the Sangam Age*, Madras: University of Madras.

Basu, Jogiraj, 1969, *India in the Age of the Brahmanas*, Calcutta: Sanskrit Pustak Bhandar.

Buhler, Georg, tr., 1988, "The Sacred Laws of the Āryas: as Taught in the Schools of Āpastamba, Gautama, Vasishta, and Baudhāyana," Part II, Vāsishta and Baudhāyana, Oxford: Clarendon Press.

———. tr. [1886] 1907, *The Laws of Manu* translated with Extracts from Seven Commentaries, Delhi: Motilal Banarsidass.

Carman, John B., 1974, *The Theology of Rāmānuja. An Essay in Interreligious Understanding*, New Haven and London, Yale University Press.

Carman, John and Vasudha Narayanan, 1989, *The Tamil Veda: Piḷḷan's Interpretation of the Tiruvāymoḻi*, Chicago: University of Chicago Press.

Cutler, Norman, 1979, *Consider Our Vow*, Madurai: Muttu Patippakam.

———. [forthcoming] "The Making of the Pāvai Poems," Manuscript.

Damodaran, Guruswamy, 1976, *Ācārya Hṛdayam: A Critical Study*, Tirupati: Triumala Tirupati Devasthanam.

Dubois, Abbe J.A., [1906] 1959, *Hindu Manners, Customs and Ceremonies*, tr. and ed. by Henry K. Beauchamp, Oxford: Clarendon Press.

Falk, N.A., 1980, "The Case of the vanishing nun: the fruits of ambivalence in Indian Buddhism," in *Unspoken Worlds: Women's Religious Lives in Non-Western Cultures*, ed. by N.A. Falk and R.M. Gross, San Francisco: Harper & Row.

Folkert, Kendall W., 1989, "Jain Life at Ancient Mathura. The heritage of late Victorian Interpretation," in *Mathura: the Cultural Heritage*, ed. Doris Meth Srinivasan, New Dehli: American Institute Of Indian Studies.

Jagadeesan, N. 1977. *History of Sri Vaishnavism in the Tamil Country* (Post-Ramanuja) (Madurai: Koodal Publishers).

Hart, George L., III, 1975, *The Poems of Ancient Tamil: Their Milieu and Their Sanskrit Counterparts*, Berkeley: University of California Press.

Hardy, Friedhelm, 1979, "The Tamil Veda of a Sudra Saint: Nammalvar" in Gopal Krishna, ed. *Contributions to South Asian Studies*, vol.1, Delhi:

Oxford University Press, 28-87.

———. 1983, *Viraha-Bhakti: The early history of Kṛṣṇa devotion in South India,* Delhi: Oxford University Press.

Hari Rao, V.N. 1961, ed and trans. *Koil Olugu: The Chronicle of the Srirangam Temple with Historical Notes.* Madras: Rochouse Sons.

Hejib, Alaka and Katherine K. Young, 1988, "Sati, Widowhood and Yoga," in *Sati: Historical and Phenomenological Essays,* Arvind Sharma with Ajit Ray, Alaka Hejib and Katherine K. Young, Delhi: Motilal Banarsidass.

Jacobson, Doranne and Susan S. Wadley, 1977, *Women in India: Two Perspectives,* New Delhi: Manohar Book Service.

Jaini, Padmanabh S., 1979, *The Jaina Path of Purification,* Berkeley: University of California Press.

Jha, Mohamahopadhyaya Pandi Ganganath, tr. [1916] 1974, *The Pūrva Mīmāṁsā Sūtras of Jaimini,* 2 vols., New York: AMS Press.

Kaliyanam, G., 1971, *Guide and History of Sri Andal Temple, Srivilliputtur,* Srivilliputtur, Tamilnadu [India]: Sri Nachiar Devasthanam.

Kane, P.V., *History of the Dharmaśāstra,* 1973–1977 (reprint), 5 vols., Poona: Bhandarkar Oriental Research Institute.

Lalonde, Gloria, 1985, "National Development and the Changing Status of Women in India: A State-by-State Analysis," M.A. Thesis, McGill University.

Leslie, I.J., 1986, "Strīsvabhāva: The Inherenent Nature of Women," in *Oxford University Papers on India,* vol. 1, Pt. 1, Delhi: Oxford University Press.

———. 1989, *The Perfect Wife: The Orthodox Hindu Woman according to the Stridharmapaddhati of Tryambakayajvan,* Dehli: Oxford University Press.

Majumdar, R.C., ed., 1953, *The Age of Imperial Unity,* Bombay: Bharatiya Vidya Bhavan,

Morris, William, ed., *The American Heritage Dictionary of theEnglish Language* (Boston, American Heritage Publishing Co., 1970.

Mumme, Patricia Y., 1987, *The Mumukṣuppaḍi of Piḷḷai Lokācārya with Maṇavāḷamāmuni's Commentary,* Bombay: Ananthacharya Indological Research Institute.

———. 1988, *The Śrivaiṣṇava Theological Dispute: Maṇavāḷamāmuni and Vedānta Deśika,* Madras: New Era Publications.

———. 1993, "Rules and Rhetoric: Caste Observance in Śrīvaiṣṇava Doctrine and Practice," in *Journal of Vaiṣṇava Studies* 2/1, 113–139.

Narasimhiengar, M.T., trans., 1910, *The Upadeśa-ratna-mālā or Necklace of Precepts,* Madras, R. Venkateshwar & Co.

Narayanan, Vasudha, 1987, *The Way and the Goal: Expressions of Devotion in the Early Śrīvaiṣṇava Tradition,* Washington, DC: Institute for Vaishnava Studies.

———. 1990, "'Renunciation' in Saffron and White Robes," in *Monastic Life in the Christian and Hindu Traditions: A Comparative Study*, Studies in Comparative Religion, vol. 3, Mellen Press.

Nayar, Nancy Anne, 1992, "The Śrīvaiṣṇava Stotra: Synthesizing the Tamil and Sanskrit Vedas," in *Journal of Vaiṣṇava Studies* 2/1, 55–79.

Ojha, Catherine, 1981, "Feminine Asceticism in Hinduism: Its Tradition and Present Condition," *Man in India* 61/3, 254–283.

Olivelle, P., 1974, "The notion of āśrama in the Dharmaśāstras?," in *Wiener Zeitschrift für die Kunde Sudasiens*, vol. XVIII.

———. 1978, "The integration of renunciation by orthodox Hinduism," in *Journal of the Oriental Institute* 28/1, 27–36.

———. 1984, "Renouncer and renunciation in the *Dharmaśāstras*," in *Studies in the Dharmaśāstras*, ed. by R.W. Lariviere, Calcutta.

———. 1995, *Yatidharmasamuccaya: Rules and Regulations of Brahmanical Asceticism*, Albany: State University of New York Press.

Orr, Leslie C., 1994a, "Wife, Patron or Devotee: Diversity and Change in Women's Identities in Medieval Tamil Nadu," paper presented at the 23rd Annual Conference on South Asia, Madison, Wisconsin.

———. 1994b, "Women of Medieval South India in Hindu Temple Ritual: Text and Practice," *Annual Review of Women in World Religions*, 3:107–141.

———. 1995a, "The Vaiṣṇava Community at Śrīraṅgam in the Early Medieval Period," in *Journal of Vaiṣṇava Studies* 3/3, 109–36.

———. 1995b, "Jain Worship in Medieval Tamil Nadu," paper presented at the International Conference on Approaches to Jaina Studies, University of Toronto.

———. 1995c, "Retrospective Realities: Community and Leadership in a Medieval Hindu Temple," paper presented at the Canadian Society for the Study of Religion, Montreal.

———. 1995d, "Shifting Feminine Ground: The 'Meaning' of the Devadāsī from Medieval to Modern Times," paper presented at the Annual Meeting of the South Asia Council of the Canadian Asian Studies Association, Montreal.

———. [forthcoming] "Jain and Hindu 'Religious Women' in early medieval Tamilnadu," in John E. Cort, ed. *Open Boundaries: Jains in Indian History and Culture.*

Radhakrishnan, S. trans., 1960, *The Brahma Sūtra: The Philosophy of Spiritual Life*, London: George Allen & Unwin.

Rajagopala Ayyangar, M.R., 1956, *Śrimad Rahasyatrayasāra of Śri Vedāntadeśika*, Kombakonam, Agnihothram Ramanuja Thatachariar.

Ramanujan, A.K., 1982, "On Women Saints," in *The Divine Consort*, ed. by J. Stratton Hawley and Donna Marie Wulff, Berkeley: Religious Studies Series.

Ramanujam, B.V., 1973, *History of Vaiṣṇavism in South India up to Rāmānuja*, Annamalainagar Tamilnadu: Annamalainagar University Press.

Rangachari, K., 1931, *The Sri Vaishnava Brahmans,* Bulletin of the Madras Government Museum, Madras: Printed by the Superintendent Press.

Reynolds, Holly Baker. [n.d.], "Women's Performance of the Mārkaḻi Vow," Manuscript.

Sagan, Eli, 1985, *At the Dawn of Tyranny: the Origins of Individualism, Political Oppression and the State,* New York: Alfred A. Knopf.

Sampatkumaran, M.R., trans., 1969, *The Gītābhāṣhya of Rāmānuja,* Madras: Prof. M. Rangacharya Memorial Trust.

Settar S. and Kaliburgi K.K., 1982, "The Hero Cult," in *Memorial Stones in South India,* Settar and Sontheimer, eds., Dehli: Manipal Power Press.

Sharma, Arvind, 1979, *Thresholds in Hindu-Buddhist Studies,* Calcutta: Minerva Sociates (Publications).

———. 1986, *The Hindu Gītā: Ancient and Classical Interpretations of the Bhagavadgītā,* London: Gerald Duckworth & Co.

Shastri, Shakuntala Rao, 1969, *Women in the Vedic Age,* Bombay: Bharatiya Vidya Bhavan.

Stein, Burton. 1968, "Social Mobility and Medieval South Indian Hindu Sects." In James Silverberg, ed. *Social Mobility in the Caste System in India,* the Hague: Mouton.

Sundaram, P.S., 1987, *Andal: Tiruppavai, Nachiyar Tirumozhi,* Bombay: Ananthacharya Indological Research Institute.

Thibaut, George, [1890 & 1896] 1962, *The Vedānta Sūtras of Bādarāyaṇa,* with the commentary by Śaṅkara, 2 vols., New York: Dover Publications.

Trautmann, Thomas R., 1981, *Dravidian Kinship,* Cambridge: Cambridge University Press.

Upadhyaya, Bhagwat Saran, 1974, *Women in Ṛgveda,* New Delhi: S. Chand & Co.

Venkatachari, K.K.A., 1978, *Śrīvaiṣṇava Maṇipravāḷa,* Bombay: Ananthacharya Indological Research Institute.

Vidyārṇava, Sniśa Chandra, 1974, *Yajñavalkya Smriti,* in *The Sacred Books of the Hindus,* vol. 21, ed. B.D. Basu, New York: AMS Press Inc.

Wilson, H.H., 1870, *The Vishnu Purana: A System of Hindu Mythology and Tradition,* vol. 5, London: Trūbner & Co.

Yamunacharya, M., 1970, *Rāmānuja's Teachings in His Own Words,* Bombay: Bharatiya Vidya Bhavan.

Yang, Anand, Sept.-Dec. 1987, "The Many Faces of Sati in the Early Nineteenth Century," in *Manushi: A Journal About Women and Society,* no. 42-43, 26-40.

Young, Katherine K., 1978, "Beloved Places (*ukantaruḷiñanilaṅkaḷ*): The Correlation of Topography and Theology in the Śrīvaiṣṇava Tradition of South India," Ph.D. dissertation, Montreal: McGill University.

———. 1981, "Why are Hindu Women Traditionally Oriented to Rebirth Rather than Liberation (*mokṣa*)?," in *Third International Symposium on Asian Studies,* Hong Kong: Asian Research Service.

———. 1983a, "Śrīvaiṣṇava Feminism: Intent or Effect?," *Studies in Religion (Sciences Religieuses)* (Vol. 12, No. 2), pp. 183–190.

———. 1983b, "Dying for *bhukti* and *mukti:* The Śrīvaiṣṇava Theology of Liberation as a Triumph Over Death," *Sciences Religieuses/Studies in Religion,* vol. 12/no. 4, Fall.

———. 1983c, "Tīrtha and the Metaphor of Crossing Over," in *Studies in Religion/Sciences Religieuses,* vol. 23, no. 1: 61–68.

———. 1986, "On the Model of Jaina Sallekhanā: Āṇṭāḷ's Fast to Death," paper delivered at American Academy of Religion, Atlanta.

———. 1987a, "Introduction," in *Women in World Religions,* ed. by Arvind Sharma, Albany: SUNY Press, 1–36.

———. 1987b, "Hinduism," in *Women in World Religions,* ed. by Arvind Sharma, Albany: SUNY Press, 59–103.

———. 1993a, "Introduction," in *Today's Woman in World Religions,* ed. by Arvind Sharma, Albany: SUNY Press, 1–37.

———. 1993b, "Women in Hinduism," in *Today's Woman in World Religions,* ed. by Arvind Sharma, Albany: SUNY Press, pp. 75–135.

———. 1993c, "Introduction," *Religion and Women,* ed. by Arvind Sharma, Albany: SUNY Press. pp. 1–38.

———. 1993d, "The Pāvai Poems: A Study of Gender and Hinduism," paper delivered at American Academy of Religion, Washington, DC.

Young, Katherine K. and Leslie C. Orr, 1988, "The Symbolism of the Bard (*panan*) in Tamil Hagiographies," paper delivered at Research Triangle, Conference on Religion in South India, North Carolina.

Younger, Paul. 1993, "Srirangam," in George Michell, ed. *Temple Towns of Tamil Nadu.*

ABOUT THE CONTRIBUTORS

Nancy M. Martin has recently completed her Ph.D. in the History of Religions at Graduate Theological Union in California (July 31, 1995). Her dissertation focuses on Mīrābāī: "Dyed in the Color of Her Lord: Multiple Representations in the Mīrābāī Tradition." She is now Assistant Professor in the Religion Department at Chapman University in Orange, California.

Andrew Schelling teaches at The Naropa Institute in Boulder, Colorado, where he is Chair of The Jack Kerouac School of Disembodied Poetics. A poet, translator, editor and essayist, he has traveled widely through South Asia, Europe, and North America. Books include *For Love of the Dark One: Songs of Mirabai* (Shambhala, 1993), *The India Book: Essays and Translations from Indian Asia* (O Books, 1993), and *Dropping the Bow: Poems from Ancient India* (Broken Moon, 1991), which won the Academy of American Poets prize for translation in 1992.

Jan Brzezinski has a Ph.D. in Sanskrit Literature from the School of Oriental and African Studies at the University of London. He is presently teaching a course on World Religions as well as Sanskrit and Hindi at the University of Manitoba, Canada.

Kim Knott is a Senior Lecturer in Religious Studies at the University of Leeds, England. She is author of two books (including *My Sweet Lord: The Hare Krishna Movement*) and a number of articles on contemporary Hindu movements in diaspora, and directs the Community Religions Project at Leeds which publishes and encourages research on minority religions in Britain. In recent years her research and writing has focused on women in religions, and she is currently preparing a cross-cultural study on women and destiny for publication.

Steven J. Rosen is the author of twelve books on Vaiṣṇavism and related subjects, including the edited volume *Vaiṣṇavism: Contemporary Scholars Discuss the Gauḍīya Tradition* (Delhi: Motilal Banarsidass, 1994) and the hagiographical works, *India's Spiritual Renaissance: The Life and Times of Lord Chaitanya*; *The Six Goswamis of Vrindavan*; and *Lives of the Vaishnava Saints: Shrinivas, Narottam, and Shyamananda*. He is currently the editor and publisher of the *Journal of Vaiṣṇava Studies*.

Mary McGee is Associate Professor of Classical Hinduism in the Department of Religion at Columbia University where she is also Director of the Dharam Hinduja Indic Research Center. She has contributed articles on aspects of domestic Hinduism, with particular attention to the religious lives of Hindu women, to edited volumes, encyclopedias, and journals. Most of her field work has been conducted in Maharashtra, Bahiṇābāī's home region. She is currently completing her book, *Duty and Desire*, on the vrata tradition in India.

D. Dennis Hudson is Professor of Religion at Smith College. A specialist on religion in Tamil Nadu, Hindu-Christian relations in nineteenth-century India, and on various south Indian temples, he has recently focused on the Mīnākṣī temple in Madurai. He is a frequent contributor to JVS and other scholarly journals.

Nancy Ann Nayar is quickly becoming well-known for her research on the Śrīvaiṣṇava tradition of South India. She has published a breakthrough work, *Poetry as Theology: The Śrīvaiṣṇava Stotra in the Age of Rāmānuja* and she is currently working on Periyavāccāṉ Piḷḷai's commentary on Yāmuna's *Stotra Ratna* and *Catuḥ Ślokī*. Her latest book is *Praise-Poems to Viṣṇu and Śrī: The Stotras of Rāmānuja's Immediate Disciples*.

Katherine K. Young's areas of specialization include Tamil Vaiṣṇavism, gender and religion, and ethics, and she is a frequent contributor to academic journals. She also has several edited volumes to her credit and often contributes to scholarly encyclopedias. A renowned expert on the Śrīvaiṣṇava tradition of South India, she currently holds the position of Associate Professor on the Faculty of Religious Studies at McGill University, Canada.

SELECTED KEY WORD INDEX